ALSO BY THESE AUTHORS

Warp Speed: America in the Age of Mixed Media

Blur: How to Know What's True in the Age of Information Overload

THE
ELEMENTS
OF
JOURNALISM

THE
ELEMENTS
OF
JOURNALISM

REVISED AND UPDATED 4TH EDITION

What Newspeople Should Know
and the Public Should Expect

BILL KOVACH & TOM ROSENSTIEL

CROWN

NEW YORK

A Crown Trade Paperback Original

Published in the United States by Crown,
an imprint of Random House, a division of
Penguin Random House LLC, New York.

CROWN and the Crown colophon are registered trademarks
of Penguin Random House LLC.

Grateful acknowledgment is made to Cable News Network, Inc. (CNN)
for permission to reprint a text excerpt from the show *Crossfire* (October 15, 2004).
Reprinted by permission of Cable News Network, Inc. (CNN).

Originally published in hardcover in the United States by Crown Publishers,
an imprint of the Crown Publishing Group, a division of Penguin Random House LLC,
New York, in 2001 and subsequently revised and published in paperback by
Three Rivers Press, an imprint of the Crown Publishing Group, a division
of Penguin Random House LLC, New York, in 2007 and 2014.

LIBRARY OF CONGRESS CATALOGING-IN-PUBLICATION DATA
Names: Kovach, Bill, author. | Rosenstiel, Tom, author.
Title: The elements of journalism / Bill Kovach & Tom Rosenstiel.
Description: Revised and updated 4th edition. | New York: Crown, [2021] |
Includes bibliographical references and index.
Identifiers: LCCN 2021012286 (print) | LCCN 2021012287 (ebook) |
ISBN 9780593239353 (trade paperback) | ISBN 9780593239360 (ebook)
Subjects: LCSH: Journalistic ethics. | Journalism—United States.
Classification: LCC PN4756 .K67 2021 (print) | LCC PN4756 (ebook) |
DDC 174.9097—dc23
LC record available at https://lccn.loc.gov/2021012286
LC ebook record available at https://lccn.loc.gov/2021012287

Printed in the United States of America on acid-free paper

crownpublishing.com

3rd Printing

Book design by Alexis Capitini

For Lynne
and for Beth and Karina

PREFACE TO
THE FOURTH EDITION

B ill Kovach often says that every generation creates its own journalism.

That change doesn't happen gradually. It occurs in fits and starts, as momentous events or dramatic cultural shifts force newsrooms to reexamine themselves.

Look back at the twentieth century and you can see these moments. The notion of applying a more scientific or objective method to gathering news, for instance, came in response to World War I and the Russian Revolution, as thoughtful journalists tried to reckon with failures of their profession at a time when democracy around the world was in doubt. The Hutchins Commission, which developed modern notions of press responsibility, came about after World War II, with the rise of electronic media and attempts by fascist regimes to make an evil science of propaganda. The first edition of this book, twenty years ago, was in response to the fragmentation of media caused by the emerging new technologies of cable and the internet and a new wave of sensationalism that resulted in the face of the financial pressures those technologies created.

Today, in 2021, a new reexamination of journalism is under way. That reckoning is the result of the convergence of disparate but powerful forces. Journalism is threatened by the collapse of its advertising model. It is threatened by a culture at the all-powerful platform companies such as Facebook, Twitter, and YouTube, which is built around what separates people—so they can be targeted for advertising—rather than what unites them. It is threatened by the rise of despotic leaders around the world who want to denigrate a free press and the fact-based approach to civic life that it represents. And it is driven by a reckoning in newsrooms over the failure of usually white- and male-dominated staffs to understand, care about, and cover people of color and the systemic racial injustice in the country. At the same time, those same newsrooms have managed to almost entirely alienate people in the United States who call themselves conservative.

The first step for a field in crisis is to recall the fundamentals that informed the field in the first place. It is critical, next, to be able to distinguish which fundamentals are enduring from the everyday routines or practices employed to put those principles into practice. For example, the need to verify accounts to get to a more accurate understanding of civic life is a fundamental principle. The tools we use to do that verification change with new technology, with algorithms that can match pictures to place and history, check identification, even search for quotes. Yet it is astonishing how wedded professions become to their habits and how easy it is to mistake cherished routines for something more fundamental.

The second step for a field in crisis, then, is to identify and abandon worn-out practices, to rethink how best to fulfill its fundamental principles, and to recognize new ways to perform the services that society requires of it.

The elements of journalism that we describe in this book are nothing more than a description of what society requires of those who produce the news—whether they do so in a large professional setting or for a one-person newsletter they produce in their spare time and distribute on a platform designed for sole producers like Substack.

When we produced the first edition of this book in 2001, we set out to identify the fundamental principles society required of a free press. Those principles were not as widely understood or shared among those in the news as most people thought. We were being asked in effect: *What makes journalism different from all the other forms of publishing we call media?*

When we produced the second and third editions of this book in 2006 and 2014, we were increasingly asked a different question: *To what extent do the principles that guided journalism in the nineteenth and twentieth centuries still apply? Indeed, are there any principles at all?*

Our answer then was that the aspirations of journalism had not changed. For example, people still needed journalism to be as accurate as possible. Journalism is still essentially a discipline of verification. But the methods we use to make the news accurate, the disciplines by which we verify accounts, have changed substantially with the advent of supercomputing at our fingertips, with live tweeting and video cameras in every cellphone—and that is the case whether someone is a professional journalist working in a large newsroom or an accidental eyewitness who video-records a shooting.

Today for this fourth edition we are asked a different question. People are not asking if the elements are still relevant. They seem to be asking if we can articulate them again, updated for newer times, because we are in a moment of change, which always calls for a reminder of first principles.

The question, in turn, is not whether technology has rendered the old principles obsolete. It is whether it is still possible for a common public square to exist; whether people who disagree are capable of finding consensus on basic facts; and whether a journalism of open-minded passionate inquiry is still possible, or whether people in newsrooms will abandon inquiry in favor of argument, because facts seem not to matter.

Journalism is facing a crisis of survival. And lack of clarity about the purpose of journalism lies at the center of that crisis. If those who practice journalism and those who consume it do not understand journalism's purpose in society and cannot differentiate journalism from political advocacy and propaganda, or opinion mongering from reporting, if they do not understand the discipline of verification or the requirements of passionate, open-minded inquiry, it is not journalism that is threatened. It is democracy. For a decade, democracy has been in retreat around the globe. It is not an accident that journalism has been hobbled—financially and by its own mistakes—at the same time. Democracy and the press, as Joseph Pulitzer warned a century ago, really do rise and fall together.

Journalism has no claim on the public's attention other than in the name of democracy. It grew out of the Enlightenment in the early seventeenth century to make information about civic life once held by the few—usually in royal courts or in secret parliaments—available to the many, to create that public square. Today our public square is breaking apart. The pool of common facts is shrinking. That is a failure of journalism practice, a reflection of technology, and a threat to democracy everywhere.

At the same time journalism is often stronger than ever before. Rulers who believe that they can lie and alter perception by repeating their lies have questioned the integrity of journalists by demonizing the press with epithets like "enemy of the people" and "fake news." Journalists in response have raised the level of proof in their reporting. They have become more transparent. They have involved the public more in their reporting. Journalism has been hobbled, but it isn't dying. It is becoming more of a collaboration. And journalists are not being replaced. Their role has become more complex and more critical.

As the contours of the digital revolution have grown clearer, we have become even more confident that not only do the elements of journalism endure—but in an age when anyone may produce and distribute news, they matter more.

What has been transformed—profoundly—is how those who produce news fulfill those principles.

Whether a news report is produced by a public eyewitness, funded by a grant from an advocacy nonprofit, or delivered by a conventional news source, we still need it to be truthful. But in an age when false rumors may be tweeted in real time, how someone reporting the news fulfills the principle of truthfulness has changed substantially. A reporter cannot ignore what is already public or has been reported elsewhere. He or she must note the false rumor's presence, track its impact, and show why it should be disbelieved or what would need to be established for it to be proved true.

Saying that the principles of journalism endure should not be mistaken for an argument in favor of nostalgia and resistance to innovation. To the contrary, it is a call for a deeper and broader application of journalism's purpose—adapted to the new ways that news is gathered and delivered, and suited for a new time.

Readers familiar with this book's previous editions will find changes throughout the new one. Many of the examples illustrating the ideas we are conveying have been replaced. In some cases, newer developments have been added to the existing illustration because they build on one another and together tell a more complex story. The new edition deals with the rise of authoritarianism around the world and the demonization of the press and fact-based reporting by leaders like Donald J. Trump. It also touches on the role and culture of the platform companies and their culpability, naïveté, arrogance, and ineptitude in dealing with bad actors foreign and domestic who have exploited their platforms and algorithms to sow political chaos in the United States and elsewhere. It also wrestles more with the question of whether citizens (by which we mean all people consuming information in a civic context, not citizenship as a legal status) even want factual information or are more motivated by political affirmation, and what consequences the answer might have for the notions of an informed public.

In the first edition, we argued that the real meaning of objectivity had more to do with transparency than the absence of bias—an argument that was challenging and controversial when we introduced it then. Today, the notion of objectivity is being questioned again, largely because it is misunderstood. Meanwhile, new terms that may be even more problematic, such as *moral clarity,* have come into use. We argued two decades ago that a transparent method of verification was the most important tool for professional journalists trying to answer doubts the public had about their work. Now it is also a way to invite the public into the production of the news, to create a collaborative journalism that is better than either journalists or citizens could produce alone.

In the chapter on journalism as a public forum, the nature of that forum has expanded dramatically with innovations in social media. In the second edition, we talked about how what linguist Deborah Tannen dubbed the "Argument Culture," in which media staged polarizing debates in order to attract an audience, was giving way to something new: media that offered affirmation and reassurance rather than pyro-technic debate. We called this a new Journalism of Affirmation because it built an audience around partisan reassurance, and this neopartisan journalism has grown in popularity since 2007. The Argument Culture of the early years of cable news, in effect, has been replaced by the An-swer Culture of propaganda, reassurance, and reaffirmation. This new culture is even more polarizing than the one it replaced. In this fourth edition, the question of whether journalism as a public forum can pro-vide healing to divided societies is the issue that dominates thinking in newsrooms.

In chapter 4, on verification, we address directly the new reckon-ing over objectivity, terms like *moral clarity,* and the search for a better description of the journalistic goal of trying to make the world of civic events comprehensible in nearly real time to audiences who disagree. Then in chapter 5, on independence, we go deeper than before over the failure of the industry to wrestle with diversity, equity, and inclusion and the implications of identity and journalistic independence.

No part of this book has been untouched by the galvanic forces of technology, fragmentation, economic chaos, and the rise of antidemo-cratic movements around the world. The platform companies such as Facebook and Google are now the most important media forces shap-ing our information lives, and their algorithms, which are designed to distinguish us from one another to help them sell targeted advertising, have helped bad actors know what can separate us politically, creating rich opportunities for authoritarians to exploit. Despots, in turn, will always call the press the enemy of the people for the simple reason that journalism is a force for democracy.

What fundamental principles guide that force, what threatens those principles from within and without, and how the profession can survive are what this book is about.

Bill Kovach & Tom Rosenstiel, January 2021

CONTENTS

INTRODUCTION

When anthropologists began to compare notes on the nature of communication in the world's few remaining primitive cultures, they discovered something unexpected. From the most isolated tribal societies in Africa to the most distant islands in the Pacific, people offered strikingly similar definitions of news. They shared gossip. They talked about their leaders. They even looked for the same qualities in the messengers they picked to gather and deliver their news: people who could run swiftly, gather accurate information, and retell it in an engaging way. While tastes have ebbed and flowed and news has been at times more or less serious, historians have discovered that the basic news values have remained relatively constant throughout time. "Humans have exchanged a similar mix of news . . . throughout history and across cultures," historian Mitchell Stephens has written.[1]

How do we explain this continuity and consistency? The answer, historians and sociologists have concluded, is that news satisfies a basic human impulse. People have an intrinsic need—an instinct—to know what is occurring beyond their own experience, the events over the next hill.[2] Being aware of events we cannot see for ourselves engenders a sense of security, control, and confidence. Understanding others is how we understand ourselves. One writer has called it "a hunger for awareness."[3]

One of the first things people do when meeting a friend or acquaintance is to share information. "Have you heard about . . . ?" We want to know if they've heard what we have, and if they heard it the same way. There is a thrill in a shared sense of discovery. We form relationships, choose friends, and make character judgments partly on the basis of whether someone reacts to information the same way as we do.

When the flow of news is obstructed, "a darkness falls" and anxiety grows.[4] The world, in effect, becomes too quiet. We feel alone. The late John McCain, former US senator from Arizona and presidential candidate, wrote that in his five and a half years as a prisoner of war in Hanoi, what he missed most was not comfort, food, freedom, or even his family and friends. "The thing I missed most was information—free uncensored, undistorted, abundant information."[5] In classes on news at SUNY Stony Brook, students were put through news blackouts, cut off from all media. They began to wear clothes not suited to the weather, carry umbrellas unnecessarily, and became anxious.[6]

Call it the Awareness Instinct.

News is how we learn about the world beyond our direct experience. It is how we discover what has occurred and what might happen next with friends, family, neighbors, and people around the country and the world. We need news to live our lives, protect ourselves, bond with each other, and identify friends and enemies. What we came to call journalism is simply the system societies generate to supply this information about what is and what's to come. News also helps us make sense of the world by adding more context and helping us answer new questions as we gather more information. That is why we care about the character of the news and journalism we get: News influences the quality of our lives, our thoughts, and our culture. News from its beginning created what technologists today call the "social flow" of information. Writer Thomas Cahill, the author of several popular books on the history of religion, has put it this way: You can tell "the worldview of a people . . . the invisible fears and desires . . . in a culture's stories."[7]

At a moment of revolution in communications, two decades of war in the Middle East, rising global populism, and raging pandemics, what do the stories we tell ourselves say about our worldview—our fears, desires, and values?

On the eve of the digital revolution, twenty-five journalists gathered at the Harvard Faculty Club on a rainy Saturday in June 1997. Around the long table sat editors of several of the nation's most important newspapers, as well as some of the most influential names in television and radio, several of the top journalism educators, and some of the country's most prominent authors. We were among those gathered. The digital age was only beginning, but the journalists gathered that day already thought something was seriously wrong with their profession. They barely recognized what they considered journalism in much of their colleagues' work. Instead of serving a larger public interest, they feared, their profession was damaging it.

The public, in turn, had already started to distrust journalists, even hate them—and this was before the birth of the internet as a meaningful force in the life of the public. (Indeed, fully half of the decline in trust in media occurred before the advent of the Web as a consumer platform.) And it would only get worse. In 1999, less than half of Americans (45 percent) believed the press protected democracy, nearly ten points lower than in 1985, Pew found.[8] By 2020, the number had fallen further—to just 30 percent; more people felt the press hurt democracy, 36 percent, with nearly as many, 33 percent, unsure.[9]

The problem was not just public perception. By the late 1990s, many journalists were beginning to share the public's growing skepticism about the press. "In the newsroom we no longer talk about journalism," said Maxwell King, the editor then of *The Philadelphia Inquirer*, that day in Cambridge. Another editor agreed: "We are consumed with business pressure and the bottom line." The concern wasn't that the values of news had deteriorated. It was that news companies had begun to operate in a way that suggested they no longer believed in those values.

News was becoming entertainment, and entertainment news. Journalists' bonuses were increasingly tied to profit margins, not to the quality of their work. As the discussion drew to a close, Columbia University professor James Carey offered what many recalled as a summation: "The problem is that you see journalism disappearing inside the larger world of communications. What you yearn to do is recover journalism from that larger world."

And a more profound disruption was coming. Digital technology had not yet eroded the advertising revenue model that financed journalism. Newspaper revenue, for instance, would continue to grow for seven more years, peaking in 2005. News companies, which focused energy on gathering and verifying the news, still dominated the flow of public information. They had not yet ceded power to technology companies, the so-called platforms, whose values were steeped in massing huge audiences by resisting editing, review, verification, or a focus on what people had in common. The platforms would build their businesses on what separated people—isolating people by their interests, demographics, and political beliefs, even their prejudices and hate, so they could target advertising. At the millennium, what worried some of the leaders of America's journalistic and educational institutions was commercialization—the sense that the leaders of the news industry had become more concerned with growing profits to please investors and had lost confidence that investing in better, more innovative journalism could help them engage new audiences.

Before their business had begun to collapse, in other words, many of the country's most influential journalists were already worried about an important existential question threatening the news industry and potentially undermining democracy. If journalism—the system by which the public gets news—was being subsumed by commercialization, what would replace it? Advertising? Entertainment? E-commerce? Propaganda? Ideological news? Fragmentation? And what would the consequence be? The idea of user-generated content, news in which everyone participated—including state-sponsored agents using disinformation—was not yet a topic of serious discussion beyond a few digital pioneers.

Most of the people in that room had seen the industry undergo enormous changes throughout their careers. For a century prior to the internet, disruptive technologies and new formats emerged roughly every fifteen to twenty years. Radio had come in the 1920s, followed by television in the 1950s (delayed by World War II), cable television, and then the deregulation of electronic media in the 1980s that helped give way to the new era of partisanship on radio and TV. With each new technology, new forms of entertainment emerged to compete for people's attention. The incumbent media would change, lose some hold on the audience, and then adapt as a smaller entity.

At its best, journalism has survived because it provides something unique to a culture: independent, reliable, accurate, and comprehensive information that citizens require in order to make sense of the world around them. A journalism that provides something other than that subverts democratic culture. This is what happens when governments control the news, as happened in Nazi Germany and the Soviet Union. We see this today in places like Singapore and China, where news is controlled to encourage capitalism but discourage participation in public life. (When you see the term *citizen* used in this book, it is not meant to refer to anyone's legal or immigration status. We use it here, as we have in all four editions, to describe any and all members of a community as civic actors in the community, not simply consumers or customers operating in a commercial dimension.)

Is the public's growing discontent with journalism, which began in the 1980s, a rejection of journalism's values? The rise of partisan outlets transmitting mis- and disinformation makes that question more pressing. But the data continue to show that declining trust has more to do with the perception that journalists have failed to live up to those values. The data on trust, for instance, continue to suggest that even today the public has not given up its expectation that the news will be independent and reliable, or that news will be produced by people who are operating in the public interest. Data from the Pew Research Center more than a decade ago showed that a clear majority—64 percent—of the public preferred getting news from sources that had no political point of view—and those numbers have barely budged since.[10] In 2020, the Reuters Institute came up with roughly the same number, 60 percent. The public largely also still expects the news to be produced by skilled professionals; what disappoints them is that the news has not lived up to those promises. By 2019, for instance, 74 percent of Americans considered inaccurate information online a major problem, 70 percent considered pressure from ownership to slant the news a major problem, and 66 percent cited "too much bias in stories that were supposed to be objective."[11]

On one level, the credibility crisis is ironic. Many news companies had tried to adapt to a changing marketplace by delivering what they thought the public wanted, trying to make the news more like entertainment. Television news in particular had leaned toward celebrity scandal and true crime to lure viewers back—and had done so unsuccessfully. The number one topic on nightly news in the 1990s was crime, and this during a decade when crime was dropping. While stories such as the O. J. Simpson trial and the murder of a child named JonBenét Ramsey would buoy ratings briefly, audiences began to sense they were being exploited. Research found that the public decried media sensationalism—a fact some in the news business dismissed as public hypocrisy. In the years that followed, a fascination with page views in the era of clickbait became a new metric increasing the pressure against public interest journalism values. Newsrooms watched real-time page view data and turned to listicles, slideshows, and other techniques in the hope of maximizing digital advertising revenue—not fully grasping that the page view was a flawed metric that measured the attention-grabbing but ultimately alienating story equally with one that built loyalty, was shared, and might turn someone into a subscriber.

Distracted by their shortsighted effort to keep audiences interested in old platforms and managing costs to protect profits, news companies missed something essential: People were not abandoning news. They simply were abandoning traditional formats in favor of newer, more convenient ones. First, twenty-four-hour cable news was a more immediate way to check out headlines than waiting for the evening newscast at 6:30, even if the later evening newscast might be a better product. Soon enough, the Web would prove to be far more convenient, deeper, and, eventually, more portable.

Journalists were culpable, too, for the growing discontent and migration of the public. They staked too much faith in traditional definitions of quality news and failed to study the changing news audience. They had followed a business logic of elite demographics, which encouraged neglecting communities of color because their markets were less attractive to advertisers, alienating key potential audiences and adding to the problem of structural racism. They saw the internet as a threat to what they knew and failed to recognize it as an opportunity to reach new audiences in new ways with new forms of content. The gathering in Cambridge in 1997 was a signal that, even before the digital disruption, many of the country's best journalists sensed their industry had lost its way by losing focus on the public and on a journalism that served its needs.

In short, the collective failure of the news industry to adapt to the digital revolution was rooted in a crisis of confidence about news that had been sounding alarms a decade earlier, and failures of the press to reach all of its communities that went back even further.

In the years since then, one group of oligarchies has been replaced by another. Media companies that produced news and subsidized its creation largely by selling advertising have been replaced by an even smaller number of near-monopoly technology companies that effectively control access to the internet by curating other people's content, selling personal data, making devices, producing operating systems, selling apps, organizing content, and selling products online. Brands such as *Newsweek* and *U.S. News & World Report* are gone. Google and Facebook have a share of the public's attention that those old media empires could never have imagined.

And as those technology companies rose to a level of power far exceeding that ever possessed by the news companies they shoved aside, trust in the news dropped again by half—to the point that political leaders all over the world could denounce inconvenient facts surfaced by journalists as "fake news," decry major journalism institutions as "failing" enterprises on the wrong side of history, and lie with a new level of brazenness.

In both moments of crisis, at the dawn of the internet age and two decades later, the same question pertains: As citizens, do we have access to independent, accurate information that makes it possible for us to govern ourselves?

The group of journalists in Cambridge that day in 1997 decided on a plan: engage journalists and the public in a careful examination of what journalism was supposed to be. As a group, we set out to answer two questions: If newspeople thought journalism was somehow different from other forms of communication, how was it different? And if they thought journalism needed to change but some core principles couldn't be sacrificed, what were those enduring principles?

Over the next two years, the group, calling itself the Committee of Concerned Journalists, organized the most comprehensive and systematic examination ever conducted by journalists of news gathering and its responsibilities. We held twenty-one public forums, which were attended by three thousand people and involved testimony from more than three hundred journalists. We partnered with a team of university researchers who conducted more than one hundred three-and-a-half-hour interviews with journalists about their values. We produced two surveys of journalists about their principles. We held a summit of First Amendment and journalism scholars. With the Project for Excellence in Journalism, which was run by one of the authors, we produced nearly a dozen content studies of news reporting. We studied the history of the journalists who came before us, and we conducted training in newsrooms nationwide.

The ideas in this book began as the fruit of that examination, and they have deepened and expanded with years of study since. What you read here is not an argument about what journalism should be. Rather, it is a distillation of how those engaged in creating journalism interpret what the public thinks journalism is for and how, in turn, journalists should deliver it. It is predicated on the belief that the history and values by which journalism evolved should inform the journalism of the new century and any moment of reckoning about journalism in a new moment of unrest. There is no reason for the new journalism to be a repudiation of the best of the old, for journalism has always been a living thing. Every generation, building on what came before, has created it anew.

Consequently, we offer here a set of principles for anyone who might produce news in the twenty-first century, whether a professional in a newsroom, a public eyewitness posting pictures, or a live-streaming service trying to distill the reports, falsehoods, and conversation from social media and turn them into news. It also offers a guide to what values consumers should look for in the news they encounter.

The first edition, published in 2001, was a description of the theory and culture of journalism at the end of the twentieth century. The second edition, from 2007, began to account for the arrival of the digital age in a more sustained way. The third edition, from 2014, explored the relevance of journalism's core values in the face of the collapsed economic model that had shrunk most organized newsrooms, and the rise of social media that had transformed news into a broader and more pluralistic process. This new fourth edition examines the relevance of journalism's core mission in a new phase of democracy's history, when the promise of the technology platforms has dimmed and the weaknesses of the new ecosystem of news have been exposed.

Some of the language we use has taken on a different connotation since earlier editions of this book. While once, as we said in the preface to this edition, the word *journalist* described a member of an organized profession working in what C. W. Anderson, Clay Shirky, and Emily Bell have called Industrial Journalism—now it describes anyone who might find him- or herself producing news and who aspires to do it ethically and responsibly.[12] Yet while these new content producers might be considered "citizen journalists" trying to understand their community, today they might also be paid government agents publishing disinformation with the clear goal of disrupting the internal politics of another country.

This is an important change, but in many ways a less fundamental one than some imagine. We have always argued here that the question has never been who is or isn't a journalist. It is whether the work produced lives up to the character of what we would call journalism. That is still true.

Even before the epochal changes brought by the digital age, the roots of what has occurred were firmly planted. While most journalists could not easily articulate a theory of journalism (or even agree if they were engaged in a profession with shared principles in the first place or just a craft with a set of routines), most people in society expected journalists to operate according to professional theory.

To add to the confusion, our educational system expects students to graduate high school and college fluent in concepts of algebra, geometry, foreign language, and literature. Yet there is little serious demand or coherent effort to teach young citizens to comprehend what we think should be considered as the literature of civic life—the news.

This lack of clarity about journalism—for both the public and newspeople—has weakened journalism and democracy. If one accepts the tenet that democracy and journalism rise and fall together, journalism's failures have acted as an accelerant to the polarization of American politics, the rise of despotic instincts and hate speech, and the failure of the country to address the pandemic, with a consequent economic crisis. A lack of clarity about what journalism should be and how to intelligently consume the news has also left both journalists and the public less equipped to cope with the effects of the digital transformation. As the platform companies, in a toxic mix of arrogance, naïveté, and greed, adopted policies that helped fuel polarization and manipulation by actors trying to intervene in our democracy, a fawning press was partly but not entirely caught unawares—as were the platforms themselves. In short, the Web and the changes it has brought demand more, not less, clarity of purpose and responsibility from those who produce the news (as well as those who distribute it), and greater awareness from those who consume it.

Unless we can grasp and reclaim the theory and practice of a free press, we risk allowing our first constitutional right to disappear. The quality of the journalism we consume now is far more a matter of what the public demands than simply what publishers want or can afford to provide. And a free press is distinct from free speech. The acts of reporting and commenting on the day's events relate to each other, but they are not synonymous. The quality of our democratic life depends, in short, on the public having the facts and being able to make sense of them. And that, even in a networked age, requires journalists. Whether we have them will increasingly depend on whether citizens can recognize the difference between propaganda and news—and whether they care.

For all the changes, there remain clear principles we require of our journalism. They are principles the public has a right to expect. Support for these principles has ebbed and flowed over time, but they have survived because they ensure that the news the public gets will be useful and reliable, even in an ever more complex world. Journalists who have adapted most successfully to the demands of this new world have done so because they innovated while being guided by these values. They are the elements of journalism.

The first among them is that the purpose of journalism is to provide people with the information they need to be free and self-governing.

To fulfill this task:

1. Journalism's first obligation is to the truth.
2. Its first loyalty is to citizens.
3. Its essence is a discipline of verification.
4. Its practitioners must maintain an independence from those they cover.
5. It must serve as a monitor of power.
6. It must provide a forum for public criticism and compromise.
7. It must strive to make the significant interesting and relevant.
8. It must present the news in a way that is comprehensive and proportional.
9. Its practitioners have an obligation to exercise their personal conscience.
10. Citizens have rights and responsibilities when it comes to the news as well—even more so as they become producers and editors themselves.

Why these ten? Some readers may think items are missing here. Where is fairness? Where is balance? Where, some might ask these days, is moral clarity? As we researched journalism's past and looked toward its future, it became clear that a number of familiar and even useful ideas associated with news were too vague to rise to the level of essential principles of journalism. Fairness, for instance, was so subjective a concept that it offered little guidance on how to operate. Balance, on the other hand, was an operational method that was so limited it often distorted the truth.

Many ideas about the elements of journalism are wrapped in myth and misconception. That journalists should be protected by a wall separating business and news is one myth. It was a convenient but often self-defeating idea, which ultimately allowed business practices to swamp newsrooms and became a significant impediment to the news industry's adapting to meet the challenges of the digital age. It is even less helpful now when journalism must expand to survive and the future will depend heavily on creating news that consumers are willing to pay for directly.

Another myth was that independence required journalists to be neutral. This confusion arose when the concept of objectivity became so mangled it began to be used to describe the very problem it was conceived to correct. If our work here does nothing else—and it was never more important than in this fourth edition—we want to recapture the original meaning of objectivity intended when the concept migrated from social science to journalism early in the twentieth century. Objectivity was not meant to suggest that journalists were without bias. To the contrary, precisely because journalists could never be objective, their methods had to be. In the recognition that everyone is biased, in other words, the news, like science, should flow from a process for reporting that is defensible, rigorous, and transparent. Thus, when we use the term *objectivity* in this book, we mean it as objectivity of method—its original meaning—not objectivity of consciousness, the idea that objectivity means neutrality, a blank slate, or some impossible denial of the subjective self. This notion of objectivity as a method or process is even more critical in a networked age when propaganda, disinformation, and rumor can travel more easily, and when populists, fabulists, and those who would denigrate factualism are gaining influence worldwide.

In the new open ecosystem of news and information, the role of professional journalists is smaller, and the role of citizens is larger. But not all voices are equal. Those with the means to prevail in an open marketplace—money, organized strategies for dissemination, and carefully designed networks to magnify a message's reach—have an advantage. If the "industrial" or professional press of the twentieth century constituted a fourth estate, and the new open system of citizens as producers and witnesses now constitutes a fifth estate, it is important to recognize that this new group also includes the institutions and actors journalists once called newsmakers—as well as state-run ministries of misinformation—all of whom want to influence the public for commercial and political purposes. Yet it is an oversimplification to imagine that more sources of information mean more truth. In a crowded news landscape, the power of a single government leader is amplified all the more because his or her voice echoes over a crowded din. It is harder, not easier, for truth to survive. It is easier to create doubt. For all of the utopian enthusiasm, if we lose sight of the principles that make news trustworthy, the contributions of a smaller fourth estate and the new contributions of a fifth together will add up to something less than what society needs. And if the press, in response, abandons for commercial or political reasons the principles of independent open-minded inquiry that the public requires, we will lose the press as an independent institution, free to systematically monitor the other powerful forces and institutions in society.

In the new century, one of the most profound questions for a democratic society is whether news can survive as a source of independent and trustworthy information or whether it will give way to a system of self-interested propaganda, of citizens consuming information in narrow channels or "filter bubbles," where disinformation and false claims we want to believe are more likely to flourish. For twenty years we have been raising the question in this book of whether journalism as an independent source of verified information can survive, and our sense of alarm during that time has only risen. The answer is still uncertain. It will depend not just on the availability of reliable news but also on whether citizens learn to recognize which news is reliable; on what we demand of the news and those who produce it; on whether we have the clarity and conviction to articulate what an independent press means; and on whether, as citizens, we care.

Some may ask whether there is a specific program laid out here to do that, to "fix" journalism's problems. Our answer to that comes in two parts.

The first is that the yearning for a formulaic solution, a single defining moment, or a bold action does not reflect how change occurs.

The second part of the answer—the reason one will not find here a five- or ten-point program to solve the problems of journalism's role in society—is that our collective experience of more than eighty years in this business suggests a clearer lesson on how to find that solution.

The answer will be found when those who produce the news master the principles of journalism and rigorously apply them to the way they work and think every day. And it will be found in citizens recognizing good work, creating their own, and thereby generating more demand for it. The solution will be found the same way that athletes perfect performance: in the repetition of doing, until these elements become second nature. This is what will breed clarity of purpose, confidence of execution, and public respect.

The key to this, first, is to distinguish between the principles that guide journalism's purpose and not to confuse them with the more ephemeral techniques that one generation develops in a specific medium to fulfill those principles. Only by recognizing the primacy of principles, and not confusing them with practices, can journalism evolve in a new century in a way that enables it to ethically fulfill the same democratic purpose it has fulfilled in the past and to create a new journalism that a wired citizenry will trust as reliable.

THE
ELEMENTS
OF
JOURNALISM

1
WHAT IS JOURNALISM FOR?

On a gray December morning in 1981, Anna Semborska woke up and flipped on the radio to hear her favorite program, *Sixty Minutes per Hour (60MPH)*. Semborska, who was seventeen, loved the way the comedy revue pushed the boundaries of what people in Poland could say out loud under communist rule. Although it had been on the air for some years, *60MPH* had become much bolder with the rise of the labor union Solidarity. Sketches like one about a dim-witted communist doctor looking vainly to find a cure for extremism were an inspiration to Anna and her teenage friends in Warsaw. The program showed her that other people felt about the world the way she did but had never dared express. "We felt that if things like these can be said on the radio then we are free," she would remember nearly twenty years later.[1]

But when Anna ran to the radio to tune in the show on December 13, 1981, she heard only static. She tried another station, then another. Nothing. She tried to call a friend and found no dial tone. Her mother called her to the window. Tanks were rolling by. The Polish military government had declared martial law, outlawed Solidarity, and put the clamps back on the media and on speech. The Polish experiment with liberalization was over.

Within hours, Anna and her friends began to hear stories that suggested something about this crackdown was different. One story involved the dogwalkers in a little town called Świdnik, in eastern Poland. Every night at seven-thirty, when the state-run television news came on, nearly everyone in Świdnik went out and walked his or her dog in a little park in the center of town. It became a daily silent act of protest and solidarity. We refuse to watch, the people were saying in deed if not word. We reject your version of truth.

In Gdansk, there were the black TV screens. People there began moving their television sets to the windows—with the screens pointed out to the street. They were sending a sign to one another, and to the government. We, too, refuse to watch. We also reject your version of truth.

An underground press began to grow, on ancient hand-crank equipment. People began carrying video cameras and making private documentaries, which they showed secretly in church basements. Soon, Poland's leaders acknowledged that they were facing a new phenomenon, something they had to go west to name: the rise of Polish public opinion. In 1983, the government created the first of several institutes to study public opinion. Similar institutes would soon sprout up throughout eastern Europe. But public opinion was something that totalitarian officials could not dictate. At best, they could try to understand it and then manipulate it, not unlike Western democratic politicians. But they would not succeed.

After the Soviet bloc collapsed, leaders of the movement toward freedom would look back and think that the end of communism owed a good deal to the coming of the new information technology and the effect it had on human souls. In the winter of 1989, Lech Walesa, the man who shortly would be elected Poland's new president, visited journalists in Washington. "Is it possible for a new Stalin to appear today who could murder people?" Walesa asked rhetorically. No, he said, answering his own question. In the age of computers, satellites, faxes, VCRs, "it's impossible." Technology now made information available to too many people, too quickly. And information created democracy.[2]

In retrospect, if we look at the evolution of democracy in Russia or China, at threats to it in parts of Europe, or at genocidal regimes in Africa, it is impossible not to think Walesa was caught up in the euphoria of the moment. But his sentiment was less a reflection of naïveté than a burst of optimism coming from a part of the world that was just discovering technology and its power to do good and inspire people to fight for their freedom. And in six years, the internet would be fully converted from a scientific and governmental system to a commercial one, available for everyday use.

What is journalism for? For the Poles and others in the emerging democracies of eastern Europe, the question was answered with action. Journalism was for building a sense of community that the government could not control. Journalism was for citizenship. Journalism was for democracy. And as Czech president Václav Havel told a group of journalists gathered in Prague in 1991, journalism was for taking back the language from a government that had subverted it with propaganda that undermined freedom of thought itself. Millions of people, empowered by a free flow of information, became directly involved in creating a new government and new rules for the political, social, and economic life of their country. Is that always journalism's purpose? Or was that true for one moment, in one place?

Today, the question "What is journalism for?" is the implicit subject of much of the discourse found online about technology and news, in the rise of misinformation and staunchly activist outlets presenting themselves as news and in a seemingly endless series of conversations about how to find a sustainable path for journalism to survive. While that discourse often has the political and the moral zeal of a revolutionary movement, it is far healthier than the lack of reflection about journalism's purpose that tended to dominate the twentieth century.

In the United States, during much of the last century, journalism was something of a tautology. If you owned a printing press or a broadcasting license, journalism was whatever you said it was. When we began our journey some twenty years ago to identify the core principles that underlie reliable news, Maxwell King, then editor of *The Philadelphia Inquirer*, summarized this lack of reflection by offering the answer journalists of the time were likely to provide: "We let our work speak for itself." What that too often meant, however, was that journalists confused their good intentions with good practice. They aspired to be fair, therefore they must be. And they took it as a given that because newsrooms were insulated from commercial concerns, they were working in the public interest.[3]

These simplistic answers were more harmful than journalists recognized. They invited skepticism from the public. And as the public's ability to comment openly in a worldwide interactive space grew, that skepticism became more focused and impassioned. If those who produced the news could not explain themselves, it was not illogical to think that maybe journalists' motives weren't that virtuous in the first place. By their silence, newspeople led colleagues on the business side to believe their newsrooms were filled with smug, moralistic idealists. Journalists failed to think critically about why they did what they did, because they imagined their motives were so plainly virtuous it went without saying.

In a marketplace that's become more open and competitive, the simplistic refrain that "journalism is a public service that speaks for itself" has been exposed for its vacuity. Now that anyone with a computer can claim to be "doing journalism" (and the one doing it might actually be a state-controlled bot rather than a real person), technology has created a new economic organization of journalism in which the norms of the profession are being pulled and redefined, and sometimes abandoned altogether. Sometimes these norms are being abandoned by traditional news institutions themselves. Spend any time with cable news today and you will see major commercial news outlets that have descended into partisan audience gathering for ratings. These outlets create a damaging model in the public mind of journalism as advocacy, which reinforces the criticism of the press as part of a political faction.

Perhaps, some suggest, the definition of journalism has been expanded by technology so that now anything can be seen as journalism. On closer examination, as the people of Poland and other nations that have escaped government control have demonstrated, the purpose of journalism is defined not by technology, or by journalists or the techniques they employ, but by something more basic: the function news plays in the lives of people.

For all that has changed about journalism, its purpose has remained remarkably constant, if not always well served, since the notion of "a press" first evolved more than three hundred years ago. And for all that the speed, techniques, and character of news delivery have changed, and are likely to continue to change ever more rapidly, a clear philosophy of journalism flows from the function of news and has remained consistent and enduring.

The primary purpose of journalism is to provide citizens with the information they need to be free and self-governing.

As we have listened to citizens and journalists and watched the impact of technological disruption, it has become clear that the news function encompasses several elements. The news helps us define our communities. It helps us create a common language and common knowledge rooted in reality. And it helps identify a community's goals, heroes, and villains. "We proceed best as a society if we have a common base of information," former NBC anchorman Tom Brokaw told the team of academic research partners who helped us identify the principles of journalism.[4] The news media serve as a watchdog, push people beyond complacency, and help amplify the voices of the forgotten and less powerful. "I want to give voices to people who need the voice . . . people who are powerless," said Yuen-Ying Chan, a former reporter for the New York *Daily News* who created a journalism training program in Hong Kong.[5] The late James Carey, one of the most innovative thinkers about news the country has ever produced, put it this way decades ago: "Perhaps in the end journalism simply means carrying on and amplifying the conversation of people themselves."[6] The rise of the internet, blogs, social media, and mobile devices provides space for citizens to create their own journalism and obviously make this vision more relevant and contemporary than ever.

This definition has held so consistent through history, and proven so deeply ingrained in the thinking of those who produce news through the ages, that it constitutes a foundation for imagining journalism in the future. It is difficult, looking back, to separate the concept of journalism from the concept of creating community and later democracy. Journalism is so fundamental to that purpose that, as we will see, societies that want to suppress freedom must first suppress the press. They do not, interestingly, need to suppress capitalism. At its best, as we will also show, journalism helps us understand how citizens behave.

This definition of journalism as social connection and information flow also opens up a wider and more innovative picture of journalism moving forward. It reveals that journalism has always been more of a service—a means for providing social connection and knowledge—than a fixed product—an outlet's stories or advertising.

Today, ironically, the long-standing theory and purpose of journalism are being challenged as if they were at odds with the conversation of people. We think that is both ahistorical and self-destructive.

Among some in the digital space, there is a tendency to dismiss journalistic values as if they were self-serving for journalists and disconnected from the public. At the same time, platforms are being created on the Web that provide social connection (restaurant reviews, entertainment updates, information about local goods and services) but create no journalism and have little or no connection to the civic good that journalism provides. Some of these companies offer gathering places where journalism is present, but it is simply another commodity flowing through them, to which no particular special value is assigned. And in their euphoria, and greed, this commodification of news inside the platforms has led to another problem those companies themselves never foresaw. Because their economic model was built on globalized targeted advertising—by identifying what separated people from one another demographically, politically, and by interest—they created a perfect petri dish for foreign governments and bad-faith domestic actors to sow political disruption and antipathy and disrupt faith in democratic elections. The platforms have failed to understand or reckon with the weaknesses of the ecosystems they built. It is not in their short-term economic interests to reform them, and now, as legacy companies themselves, they cannot adequately imagine a different future. Just as the journalistic institutions they replaced failed to innovate to meet changing audience needs, the technology companies are now failing to innovate to meet the public's need.

There has also been a shift in journalists' relationship with government in this transition. The threat from government is no longer simply censorship—withholding information that is in the public interest. Using new technology, government has more and more tools to subvert the press by trying to supplant it with its own content while also censoring. That list of tools includes creating pseudojournalism in the form of faux news websites, video news releases, subsidies to "media personalities" willing to accept money to promote policy, and more. Government officeholders, from the president to members of the local city council, now maintain their own direct channels to engage with the public, including offering the video feeds that generate the impression many official events don't need to be "covered" by the press because they are already "public." The Obama administration used technology to cast a wide net to try to identify, prosecute, and intimidate government employees who might talk to the press. The Trump administration went further—and inspired other antidemocratic populist leaders to follow suit. Not only did it more aggressively try to sideline the press by relying on technology to speak directly to voters, it lied and invented and defended its falsehoods by suggesting that facts raised by journalists were "fake," or that journalists who criticized the administration were "the enemy of the people." It also amplified the conspiracy theories of fringe groups as a way of further dividing the country. The goal of all this was not to make people believe the fake claims that it had invented. It was to get them to doubt everything—including news that was real—and in frustration place their faith instead in the word of a leader.

Matched with the economic collapse in the advertising model that has financed news for 120 years, these forces amount to a growing threat to journalism as an independent source in society for monitoring power, spotting abuse, alerting the public to problems, and creating social connection. Those social goods could well be washed away in the flood of communication from commercial, political, and government sources. Perhaps for the first time in history, the real meaning of the First Amendment—protecting a free press as an independent institution—is threatened by the government's not acting primarily as censor but instead offering a competing view of reality.

Some will listen to this discussion and contend that it's dangerous, or even antiquated, to attempt to define journalism. To define journalism, they will argue, is to limit it. Maybe doing so violates the spirit of the First Amendment: "Congress shall make no law . . . abridging the freedom of speech or of the press." This is why journalists have avoided licensing in the manner of doctors and lawyers. They also worry that defining journalism will only make it resistant to changing with the times, which probably will run it out of business. This supposedly forward-looking view has dominated thinking at the platform companies. It frees them of responsibility, feeds their revenue, and lays implied claim to constitutional responsibility.

In truth, the resistance to a definition of journalism is not a deeply held principle but a relatively recent and largely commercial impulse. At a more innovative point in journalism's history, publishers at the beginning of the twentieth century routinely championed their news values in front-page editorials, opinion pages, and company slogans, and just as often publicly assailed the journalistic values of their rivals. This was marketing. Citizens chose which publications to read on the basis of their styles and their approaches to news. It was only as the press began to assume a more corporate, more homogeneous and monopolistic form that it became more reticent. Lawyers advised news companies against codifying their principles in writing for fear that they would be used against them in court. Avoiding definition was thus a commercial strategy, not a principle born of First Amendment freedoms.

On the other side, some will argue that not only should journalism's purpose be unchanging—its form should be constant as well. They see changes in the way journalism looks from when they were young, and they fear that, in the memorable phrase of Neil Postman, we are "amusing ourselves to death." These critics miss a different fact. Every generation creates its own journalism largely in reaction to the limits of the previous generation, the social movements of the current era, and technological advances that allow production and/or distribution of content more effectively. But the purpose and the underlying elements of journalism, we have found, have proven remarkably constant, just as we have discovered since we first wrote this book that there are strong consistencies in the essential values of journalists across countries, cultures, and political systems, despite many superficial differences.

Although professional journalists historically have been uncomfortable defining what they do, they have fundamentally agreed on their purpose. When we set out to chart the common ground of news-people, this was the first answer we heard: "The central purpose of journalism is to tell the truth so that people will have the information that they need to be sovereign." It came from Jack Fuller, an author, novelist, lawyer, and then president of the Tribune Publishing Company, which produced the *Chicago Tribune*.[7]

Just as intriguing, when new entrants begin to produce news and information—even those who would initially never call themselves journalists—they often adhere to the same concepts of purpose that Fuller described. Omar Wasow, founder of a website called New York Online and one of the earliest of the self-described "garage entrepreneurs," wanted to help create citizens who were "consumers, devourers and debunkers of media . . . an audience who have engaged with the product and can respond carefully."[8] Almost a decade later, in 2006, Shawn Williams created *Dallas South Blog* to focus on issues of concern to African Americans in South Dallas and the rest of the country. By 2013, the blog was called *Dallas South News* and described itself as "a non-profit news organization utilizing technology, social media and journalistic principles to empower and inform underserved communities."

Almost two decades later, new entrants are still coming in to address unmet needs that traditional journalism has ignored. In 2011, a local city planner and land use consultant started a Facebook page entitled Jersey Shore Hurricane News in the days before Hurricane Irene struck the mid-Atlantic. He provided information and community around the storm and corrected falsehoods. It grew into an example of a two-way news organization that inspired others.[9] Five years later Jersey Shore Hurricane News was covering a range of topics, had 250,000 likes and a partnership with Listening Post, and was engaging the community in person, too.[10]

We wanted to make sure the ideas we heard from the leading voices about journalism's core principles weren't just the random views of a few people, so in collaboration with the Pew Research Center for the People & the Press, we asked journalists at the millennium what they considered the distinguishing feature of journalism.[11] Those working in news volunteered this democratic function by nearly two to one over any other answer.[12] We also collaborated with developmental psychologists at Stanford, Harvard, and the University of Chicago, whose open-ended, in-depth interviews with a hundred more journalists revealed the same conclusion. "News professionals at every level . . . express an adamant allegiance to a set of core standards that are striking in their commonality and in their linkage to the public information mission," they wrote.[13]

Ethics codes and journalism mission statements bear the same witness. The goal is "to serve the general welfare by informing the people," says the code of the American Society of News Editors, now called the News Leaders Association.[14] "Give light and the people will find their own way," read the masthead of the Scripps Company. It is no less true of outlets formed in the twenty-first century. "To expose abuses of power and betrayals of the public trust by government, business, and other institutions, using the moral force of investigative journalism to spur reform through the sustained spotlighting of wrongdoing," declares ProPublica's mission statement.[15] "To provide journalism and civic engagement opportunities, enabling citizens and institutions to build a better city to live, work, and play," reads the mission statement of the *San Antonio Report,* a digital start-up in that city.[16]

Those outside news, too, have understood that journalism has broader social and moral obligations. Listen to Pope Francis in 2018: "If responsibility is the answer to the spread of fake news, then a weighty responsibility rests on the shoulders of those whose job is to provide information, namely, journalists, the protectors of news. In today's world, theirs is, in every sense, not just a job; it is a mission."[17]

This democratic mission is not just a modern idea. The concept of creating sovereignty has run through every major statement and argument about the press for centuries, not only from journalists but also from the revolutionaries who fought for democratic principles, both in America and in virtually every developing democracy since. And as a new generation of journalists inspire a new reckoning in newsrooms, one responding to the rise of despotic antimedia sentiments and to outrage over racial injustice and racism, the sense of democratic mission is if anything stronger.

THE AWARENESS INSTINCT

When historian Mitchell Stephens studied how news has functioned in people's lives throughout history, he discovered a remarkable consistency. "The basic topics with which . . . news accounts have been concerned, and the basic standards by which they evaluate newsworthiness, seem to have varied very little," he wrote. "Humans have exchanged a similar mix of news with a consistency throughout history and cultures that makes interest in this news seem inevitable, if not innate."[18] Various scholars have identified the reason for this. People crave news out of basic instinct—what we call the Awareness Instinct. They need to be aware of events beyond their direct experience. Knowledge of the unknown gives them security; it allows them to plan and negotiate their lives. Exchanging this information becomes the basis for creating community and making human connections. This is equally true of people who get information from polarized news sources, such as Fox or MSNBC. Their desire for information is the same, even if their definition of which information seems true is different.

News is that part of communication that keeps us informed of the changing events, issues, and characters in the world outside. In former times, historians have suggested, rulers used news to hold their societies together. It provided a sense of unity and shared purpose. It even helped tyrannical rulers control their people by binding them together around a common threat.

History reveals one other important trend. The more democratic the society, the more news and information it tends to have. As societies first became more democratic, they tended toward a kind of prejournalism. The earliest democracy, ancient Greece, relied on an oral journalism in the Athens marketplace in which "nearly everything important about the public's business was in the open," journalism educator John Hohenberg wrote.[19] The Romans developed a daily account of the Roman Senate and political and social life, called the *acta diurna*, transcribed on papyrus and posted in public places.[20] As European societies became more authoritarian and violent in the Middle Ages, communication waned and written news essentially disappeared. It is no accident that the rise of despotism in the early twenty-first century coincides with a weakened journalistic ecosystem and the rise of social media platforms so susceptible to manipulation by extremists, conspiracy theorists, and foreign state–controlled agents.

THE BIRTH OF JOURNALISM

As the Middle Ages ended, news came in the form of song and story, in news ballads sung by wandering minstrels.

What we might consider modern journalism began to emerge, in the early seventeenth century, literally out of conversation, especially in public places. In England, the first newspapers grew out of coffeehouses—numerous enough for some to be known for specializing in certain kinds of information. They became so popular that scholars complained that "nothing but news and the affairs of Christendom is discussed."

Later, in America, journalism grew out of pubs, or publick houses. Here, the bar owners, called publicans, hosted spirited conversations about information from travelers, who often recorded what they had seen and heard in logbooks kept at the end of the bar. The first newspapers evolved out of these coffeehouses when enterprising printers began to collect the shipping news, tales from abroad and more gossip, and political arguments from the coffeehouses and to print them on paper.

With the evolution of the first newspapers, English politicians began to talk about a new phenomenon, which they called public opinion. By the beginning of the eighteenth century, journalists/printers had begun to formulate a theory of free speech and a free press. In 1720, two London newspapermen, writing under the pen name "Cato," introduced the idea that truth should be a defense against libel. At the time, English common law had ruled the reverse: not only that any criticism of government was a crime but that "the greater the truth, the greater the libel," since truth did more harm.[21]

Cato's argument had a profound influence in the American colonies, where discontent against the English Crown was growing. A rising young printer named Benjamin Franklin was among those who republished Cato's writings. When a fellow printer named John Peter

Zenger went on trial in 1735 for criticizing the royal governor of New York, Cato's ideas became the basis for his defense. People had "a right . . . both of exposing and opposing arbitrary power . . . by speaking and writing the truth," argued Zenger's lawyer, who was paid by Franklin, among others. The jury acquitted Zenger, shocking the colonial legal community, and the meaning of a free press in America began to take formal shape.

The concept became rooted in the thinking of the founders, finding its way into the Virginia Declaration of Rights (written in part by James Madison and George Mason), the Massachusetts Constitution (written by John Adams), and most of the new colonial statements of rights. "No government ought to be without censors & where the press is free, no one ever will," Thomas Jefferson would tell George Washington.[22] "The freedom of the Press is one of the greatest bulwarks of liberty," read the Virginia Declaration of Rights, "and can never be restrained but by despotic governments."[23]

Neither Franklin nor Madison thought such language was necessary in the federal Constitution, but two delegates, Mason of Virginia and Elbridge Gerry of Massachusetts, walked out of the convention, and with men like Thomas Paine and Samuel Adams they agitated the public to demand a written bill of rights as a condition of approving the Constitution. A free press thus became the people's first claim on their government.

Over the next two hundred years the notion of the press as a bulwark of liberty became embedded in American legal doctrine. In 1971 the Supreme Court ruled, in upholding *The New York Times*'s right to publish the secret government documents called the Pentagon Papers, that "in the First Amendment, the Founding Fathers gave the free press the protection it must have to fulfill its essential role in our democracy. The press was to serve the governed, not the governors."[24] The idea affirmed over and over by the courts is a simple one, First Amendment scholar Lee Bollinger, then president of the University of Michigan, told us at one of our gatherings for this book: Out of a diversity of voices the people are more likely to know the truth and thus be able to self-govern.[25]

Even when journalism was dominated by the yellow press at the eve of the twentieth century, or the tabloid sheets of the 1920s, building community and promoting democracy remained a core value. At their worst moments, Joseph Pulitzer and William Randolph Hearst appealed to both the sensational tastes and the patriotic impulses of their audiences. Pulitzer used his front page to lure his readers in, but he used his editorial pages to teach them how to be American citizens. On election nights he and Hearst would vie to outdo each other, one renting Madison Square Garden for a free party, the other illuminating campaign results on the side of his newspaper's skyscraper.

Whether one looks back over three hundred years or three thousand years, it is impossible to separate news from community or, over time, even more specifically from democratic community.

A FREE PRESS IN A NETWORK-CONNECTED AGE

Today, information is so free that the notion of journalism as a homogeneous entity might seem quaint in a world where everyone may at some point produce it. Perhaps the First Amendment itself is an artifact of a more restricted and elitist era.

Certainly, the notion of the press as a gatekeeper—deciding which information the public should know and which it should not—no longer defines journalism's role. If *The New York Times* decides not to publish something, one of countless other websites, talk radio hosts, social media networks, blogs, or partisans might. The rise of Facebook, Twitter, Instagram, YouTube, and Reddit has transformed the essential transmission of news—how information becomes public—from "one to many" to "many to many." Countless works in the early years of the Web made this point, from Dan Gillmor's *We the Media* and Clay Shirky's *Here Comes Everybody* to Meredith Clark's essay "How Black Twitter and Other Social Media Communities Interact with Mainstream News."

These changes have profoundly altered the information life of everyone, even those who do not tweet, post, or offer comments online. As we use Google to search for information, graze across a seemingly infinite array of outlets, share stories or links with friends, or "like" things on Facebook, we become our own editors, researchers, and even news gatherers. What was called journalism is now only one part of our information diet, and journalism's role as intermediary and verifier, like the roles of other civic institutions, has become relatively smaller and thereby a weaker influence on the whole. We are witnessing the rise of a new and more active kind of American citizenship—with new responsibilities and new vulnerabilities. The journalism of the twenty-first century must recognize this shift, or democracy will continue to suffer. Journalists must organize their work in a way that helps arm the public with the tools it needs to perform this more active form of citizenship. And it must begin to understand far better than it has in the past the way audiences receive information. In the new environment, if journalism simply becomes another form of argument, it will wither further.

In the gatekeeper metaphor, the press stood by an imagined village guardhouse and determined which facts were publicly significant and sufficiently vetted to be made public. In a networked world, the organized press plays that gatekeeper role over a far more limited sphere of information—those stories over which they have exclusive, or practically exclusive, access, including their own enterprise's reporting and some range of local information. And in the age of presidential Twitter feeds and webcast government meetings, the press's role as gatekeeper has shrunk even more.

For some, the end of the gatekeeper metaphor might suggest the end of journalism. Here comes everybody. Who needs paid observers?

We arrive at a different conclusion. We believe the end of the press's monopoly over mediating information to the public offers the opportunity to elevate the quality of journalism, not weaken it. For that to happen, however, those who produce journalism must acquire a better understanding of what people need from their news, what citizens and the machinery of the digital network can contribute to that, and what tasks are necessary for trained journalists to organize, verify, contextualize, and add to these contributions.

What do we mean by a better understanding of the tasks of journalism? At a rudimentary level, this means understanding the functions that journalism plays in people's lives so that you are developing new and better practices to perform those functions. Rather than interviewing people to get quotes for stories, for instance, journalists should be thinking about developing the skills to really listen to and understand people—more ethnography and less simple journalistic routine.

At a higher level, it means understanding the larger role that journalism and journalistic reporting play in the modern news environment. John Seely Brown, the former director of Xerox PARC, the legendary think tank in Silicon Valley, saw early on in the digital era that rather than rendering the democratic public service notion of journalism moot, technology had changed how journalists fulfill it. "What we need in the new economy and the new communications culture is sense making. We have a desperate need to get some stable points in an increasingly crazy world." This means, Brown explained, that journalists need "the ability to look at things from multiple points of view and the ability to get to the core" of matters.[26] Futurist Paul Saffo described this task as applying journalistic inquiry and judgment "to come to conclusions in uncertain environments."[27]

Thus the new journalist is no longer deciding *what* the public should know—the classic role of gatekeeper—but working with sources and technology to help audiences make order out of it, and potentially take action. This does not mean simply adding interpretation or analysis to news reporting. It involves instead performing a series of different and more discrete tasks that, if understood more carefully, news producers should begin to perform better than they have before.

In a sense, while the press still sometimes plays the role of *gatekeeper over what people should know,* more often today the press is *an annotator over what the public has already heard.*

What does this annotator role involve?

In our 2010 book, *Blur: How to Know What's True in the Age of Information Overload,* we began to explore that role by identifying various functions that the public required from journalism: functions hidden behind or embedded in the gatekeeper metaphor. And we argued that if those functions or public needs were recognized and understood more clearly, journalists were more likely to perform them more effectively. Unpacking the old gatekeeper metaphor could help journalists better understand how to collaborate with citizens and employ technology to create a better journalism. We have called this journalism collaborative intelligence. Others have called it open journalism or engaged journalism. We will get into more detail about it later. But in the decade since we began to discuss these transformations, the annotative functions of the press have only grown.

One primary task of the new journalist, as with the old, is to verify what information is reliable, to play the role of *Authenticator*. In the networked world, audiences may have heard differing assertions about an event before they encounter a formal journalistic account. The role of the new journalist, more than the old, is to work with audiences to sort through these different accounts, to know which of the information they may have encountered they should believe and which they should discount, and to be strategic about knowing when doing so matters.

A second task of anyone trying to report and present news is to be a *Sense Maker*, to put events in context in a way that turns information into knowledge. One value of making these tasks more distinct is that the responsibilities and the presentation will shift subtly when the task changes. It is important for those who report news and information, for instance, to know when they have moved from authenticating facts to synthesizing and contextualizing them. The analysis of events crosses into another level of subjectivity, and it requires making that shift clear, both by acknowledging it to the audience and by sharing different evidence for why this particular contextual analysis is valid. This role of sense making, it is important to point out, is quite different from simply offering an opinion or, even more intrusively, telling people what events mean. Contextualizing implies doing more reporting, adding facts, widening the lens and perspective. It is not argument or persuasion. Nor is it telling people what to think. As we will discuss more later, scholars have learned over the last half century that the news is not hypodermic. The public does not simply hear or see or read something in the press and absorb it like a drug into their system. People bring their own experience and meaning to the news. They adjudicate what they encounter. The more journalists try to tell audiences what things mean—or how to think about them—the more large sections of the public will resist and feel they are being manipulated.

A third role is to *Bear Witness* to events. Witness bearing occurs when the person functioning as journalist is the sole observer of an event. Recognizing this as a distinct journalistic role, even in a world in which journalists no longer so regularly play the role of the gatekeeper, is useful. Those engaged in journalism are not simply interpreters who comment. Being monitors, sentinels who ask questions and dig, remains vital. Valuing the role of witness bearing also means that it is important to cover events that no one else is covering—so that there *is* a witness—and then to convey to readers why the event matters. It implies that institutional news organizations should not deploy their resources only where there is already a crowd and already an interest. Doing so makes a publisher less useful, even if it is the easiest way to generate traffic. For a citizen who finds him- or herself at an event that a citizen considers important, and where no press appear to be present, it may mean suddenly deciding to act journalistically, to tweet or take pictures or video—so there is a record. This, too, has become a vital part of our civic lives, particularly when crimes are committed or police or other authorities act in ways about which there may be questions, or laws broken, and the public should know.

A fourth role, closely related to witness but also different, is *Watchdog*. This is the classic role of investigative reporting, uncovering wrongdoing. But it is sufficiently different in practice and organization from the more common but often undervalued role of witness bearing that it is important they be distinguished from each other. The more routine monitoring performed by a witness bearer may lead to the watchdog investigation. But the two tasks are not the same.

In addition to these four roles hidden within the gatekeeper concept are at least six other distinct functions that the public requires of journalism, which have become more important as the internet age has matured. Readers of this list may well conceive more—and that will only help. The key here is to isolate the functions we need from news to help our lives. Interestingly, we often find many of these being performed by new outlets more strongly today than by legacy outlets:

INTELLIGENT AGGREGATOR (OR CURATOR): Picking the best of other accounts, perhaps comparing the conflicting ones, recommending them to your audience—playing editor, in effect, of the rest of the information available.

FORUM LEADER: Organizing public discussion in a way that reflects your journalistic values. This can also be thought of as structured engagement. (We will have more on this in a later chapter.)

EMPOWERER: Providing audiences tools and information so that they can act for themselves. This involves making information interactive, providing dates when action needs to be taken, explaining how to get more involved. It may go even further and involve organizing events that bring the community together to solve problems.

ROLE MODEL: In a networked news environment, journalism is an even more public act than before. How one gathers the news, one's conduct and decision-making, is being watched. That behavior must be exemplary, for it is, in a more explicit way than was once true, part of the brand.

COMMUNITY BUILDER: In older models of journalism, the news spoke for itself, and what citizens did with that news and information was beyond the sphere of the news provider. That is no longer the case. The purpose of news is to help people self-govern, but that only begins with giving them the information they need to do so. News must also be about solving the problems that confront individuals and the community. There are lines between news and advocacy, but helping solve problems is different from advocacy.

ESSENTIAL INFORMATION PROVIDER OR SERVICE JOURNALIST: Once, newspapers survived in large part by curating information from other sources and putting it in one convenient place. Newspapers thrived by offering sports, stock tables, TV listings, entertainment calendars, and more. That information today is easily and more efficiently retrieved elsewhere online. But there is still a role for service journalism in providing essential information that is not so easily retrieved, often because it is confusing or not easily accessible. During the pandemic, quickly shifting information about what was safe was a classic example. During the 2020 elections, how and where to vote was another. Publishers found the demand for this information high and their fulfillment of it much appreciated. Journalism will not survive if this is all it provides. But it will also fail to serve the public if it does not identify and provide essential information people need in real time.

JOURNALISM AS ORGANIZED COLLABORATIVE INTELLIGENCE

Some advocates of the digital disruption argued early on that professional journalists in organized settings had become largely unnecessary, or that their role could be reduced to a narrower zone of activity, because no one controlled information anymore. "The Internet has solved the basic distribution of event-based facts in a variety of ways; no one needs a news organization to know what the White House is saying when all the press briefings are posted on YouTube. What we do need is someone to tell us what it means," blogger Jonathan Stray wrote, epitomizing the argument in a post for Harvard's Nieman Journalism Lab in 2013.[28]

Stray was building on arguments of a host of writers who formed what was dubbed the Future of News Movement. Perhaps no clearer expression of the ideas of the group was articulated than in the "manifesto" authored under the title *Post-industrial Journalism* by three academics, C. W. Anderson, Emily Bell, and Clay Shirky. Their argument was even broader than Stray's: "The journalist has not been replaced but displaced, moved higher up the editorial chain from the production of initial observations to a role that emphasizes verification and interpretation, bringing sense to the streams of text, audio, photos and video produced by the public."[29] The argument that journalism can largely move beyond fact gathering and toward synthesis and interpretation might be called the Displacement Theory of News.

Some journalists tilted too far the other way, viewing the benefits of citizens and technology with excessive suspicion and romanticizing old methods. "The civic labour performed by journalists on the ground cannot be replicated by legions of bloggers sitting hunched over their computer screens," Bill Keller, then executive editor of *The New York Times,* said in a 2007 public lecture in London.[30]

Both views went too far. Citizens and machines should not try to "replicate" the role of professional journalists. At the same time, and in much the same way, the notion that the public and machines can "displace" the factfinding role of professional journalists in this collaboration is too constricted.

We need journalists to do more than bring sense to the streams produced by the public or technology. This idea of displacement or implied obsolescence or movement away from essential factfinding does not grasp the reality of how powerful institutions work or how to cover them. In the end, the notion that journalists as fact finders have been displaced is too theoretical, even dangerous, and in hindsight naive in a time of rising global despotism and rising doubts about democracy. It leaves the government, corporations, and other institutions with far too much power to control the supply of public facts. The fact that the White House now has a YouTube channel, a Twitter feed, and an Instagram account should not be mistaken for any administration being open or transparent. Nor is journalism enhanced if journalists begin to limit themselves largely to material officially released rather than going out and digging for a more complete version of the truth. The Web may have given everyone publishing tools, but it does not enforce distribution of all facts that matter or structure them in a way that citizens can use.

Perhaps even more important, technology has not "solved" the problem of knowing the essential facts of events. Many, if not most, of the events that affect the public do not occur in public. Even the decisions revealed at most public meetings are made, more often than they should be, away from public view, in executive session or in even smaller, more private meetings. Far too little of what we need to know is on YouTube. Yet if more of our civic proceedings moved there (which we support), there is no doubt much of the real decision-making of news would then move further behind closed doors. C-SPAN did not magically make Congress work better. And the events in Afghanistan, or the impact of major healthcare legislation, or a country's response to a pandemic requires far more shoe-leather and access than "bringing sense to the streams . . . produced by the public." We cannot assume the facts of civic life to be a commodity, the gathering and submission of which are taken care of by the network.

For most stories, learning the facts of an event is a multidimensional process of discovery—an official action, event, or revelation, followed by inquiry, reaction, and observation, new questions, then more inquiry—a process that repeats itself and involves direct investigation as well as making sense of the streams produced by officials and the public.

The discussion about technology and the network displacing factual reporting also tends to focus on a limited range of topics, often just national affairs. "Not all journalism matters," Anderson, Bell, and Shirky wrote in their manifesto, suggesting that a broad range of arts, sports, lifestyle reporting, and more did not. "Much of what is produced today is simply entertainment or diversion." They are wrong. As we will describe in detail in the chapter on comprehensiveness and proportion, the reporting of culture, social events, trends, sports, and much more forms a vital part of how we come to understand community and civil society and how, as citizens, we navigate our lives. Journalism that narrows itself to accountability of government agencies will limit its value, its engagement, and its chance to sustain itself.

We see the future of news in the middle, between the skeptics and the utopians. Rather than displacing journalists, the network and citizens make possible a new and enriched kind of journalism in which citizens, technology, and professional journalists work together to create a public intelligence that is deeper and wider than any one of these could produce alone.

Machines bring the capacity to count beyond anything previously imaginable—to make the news more empirical and more accurate.

Citizens bring expertise, experience, and the ability to observe events from more vantage points—knowledge and expertise that are deeper than can be found in any newsroom or in a traditional reporter's "Rolodex" of sources.

Journalists bring access, the ability to interrogate people in power, to dig, to translate and triangulate and verify incoming information, and, more important, a traditional discipline of open-minded inquiry.

Working in concert, these three contributors can create a new kind of journalism, one that might best be understood as an organized collaborative intelligence.

We need journalists of the future, in other words, to embrace the potential of the network and to vet and organize its input, while also providing the elements that skilled journalists at any given moment are best disposed to offer. This is the way to a deeper and wider foundation of facts and community understanding.

Journalists in this vision will do much more now than produce narrative stories and the graphics that illustrate them. Instead, they will help gather and organize and structure this community intelligence, combining the technology of the machine network with the knowledge and input of the broader citizenry and other sources, and adding the reportorial, evidentiary, and vetting skills they possess as journalists. Journalism, in this view, is much more than a static product. It is, as we said, a kind of organized community intelligence.

But this better journalism, one that fulfills the promise of creating community and improving the lives of citizens, does not reside in an either/or view of journalism and technology. In this view, journalists are not displaced, replicated, confined, or elevated to becoming synthesizers of meaning. This view does not denigrate the power of narrative, or the significance of witness-bearing reporting, or the importance of simply finding out what happened. It is a vision of journalism's future that doesn't denigrate its past.

Instead, this new vision of a new journalism depends on the networked media culture committing itself, as the old system did, to establishing verified and truthful information and building out from that foundation of facts toward meaning. The driving force of the Age of Enlightenment, out of which grew the notion of individual worth and a public press, was the search for truthful information. This information freed the public from the control of centralized dictatorial or dogmatic power. We see parallels to that kind of control today forming in new places, corporate and governmental rather than monarchical or religious. If the Journalism of Verification is to survive in the new age, then it must become a force in empowering citizens with the information they need to effectively take part in self-government.

THE JOURNALIST'S THEORY OF DEMOCRACY

Historically journalists didn't tend to think about theories of news. They were focused on craft, on the daily, even hourly effort to cover and present news as a product. Many would find it amusing or even slightly ridiculous if they were asked, "What is the theory of democracy that drives your TV news operation or your newspaper?"

Still, the question of what people need and want to know has always been critical. If the public is uninformed, the press has a responsibility to figure out why and what to do about it. But it has become more of a challenge in recent years for journalists to fulfill this responsibility. And in the wake of the Trump administration, the coronavirus pandemic, and the national reexamination over race and social justice, journalists have begun to reexamine their role even more deeply. That means journalists have a greater need than ever to understand and potentially reexamine the theory of news implicit in their work and in the role journalism plays in people's lives.

With only a few ways to deliver news—newspapers, magazines, radio, and TV—journalists in the twentieth century thought mostly about quality of production—the writing, photography, design, story craft—and about getting the news out on time in a seamless package. They also didn't think about outside pressure. Having little or no challenge to their role as mediators over information or to the profitability of their companies, most journalists were content to think the answer to good editorial judgment was found in remaining insulated from commercial pressure. They were content to let something called "news judgment," a subjective and wildly unscientific notion, dictate their decisions about what determined the news. As long as it was independent of pressure from advertising, it was considered ethical.

There was always a reason to be concerned about how well this trust in subjective news judgment worked. We may have had the freest press imaginable, yet over the last third of a century the number of Americans who could even name their congressperson was as low as three out of ten, and not many more, 39 percent in 2019, could name the three branches of government.[31]

Little more than half of the American electorate voted in presidential elections—fewer than in countries without a First Amendment (it rose to 58 percent in 2016 and nearly 65 percent in 2020).[32] Until recently, local television news was the source people relied on for news more than any other, a medium that has largely ignored coverage of government and politics. But particularly among the young, its top position is being overtaken by the internet and social media, which contain even less local news and information.[33] Maybe, when you look hard, the idea that the press provides the information necessary for people to self-govern is an illusion. Maybe people don't care. Maybe we don't, in reality, actually self-govern at all. The government operates, and the rest of us are largely bystanders.

This argument has ebbed and flared throughout US history, but it found its most famous articulating during the 1920s in a debate of ideas between journalist Walter Lippmann and philosopher John Dewey. It was a time of pessimism about democracy. Democratic governments in Germany and Italy had collapsed. The Bolshevik revolution loomed over the West. There was a growing fear that police states were employing new technology and the new science of propaganda to control public will.

Lippmann, already one of the nation's most famous journalists, argued in a bestselling book called *Public Opinion* that democracy was fundamentally flawed. People, he said, mostly know the world only indirectly, through "pictures they make up in their heads." And they receive these mental pictures largely through the media. The problem, Lippmann argued, is that the pictures people have in their heads are hopelessly distorted and incomplete, marred by the irredeemable weaknesses of the press. Just as bad, even if the truth were to reach the public, the public's ability to comprehend it would be undermined by human bias, stereotyping, inattentiveness, and ignorance. In the end, Lippmann thought citizens were like theatergoers who "arrive in the middle of the third act and leave before the last curtain, staying just long enough to decide who is the hero and who is the villain."[34]

Public Opinion was enormously influential and gave birth, according to many, to the modern study of communications.[35] It also deeply moved the nation's most famous philosopher, Columbia professor John Dewey, who called Lippmann's analysis about the limits of human perception "the most effective indictment of democracy . . . ever penned."[36]

But Dewey, who later expanded his critique in his own book *The Public and Its Problems,* said Lippmann's definition of democracy was fundamentally flawed. The goal of democracy, Dewey said, was not to manage public affairs efficiently. It was to help people develop to their fullest potential. Democracy, in other words, was the end, not the means. It was true that the public could only be an "umpire of last resort" over government, usually just setting the broad outlines of debate. That, however, was all the founders ever intended, Dewey argued, for democratic life encompassed so much more than efficient government. Its real purpose was human freedom. Rather than giving up on democracy because of its problems, we needed to try to improve the skills of the press and the education of the public.

Dewey a century ago sensed something that is easier to grasp in today's networked news culture, when citizens are producers, critics, consumers, and editors as well as audience, and where scholars are wondering whether democracy worldwide is in twilight. Dewey believed that if people were allowed to communicate freely with one another, democracy would be the natural outgrowth of the human interaction. It was not a stratagem for making government better.

A hundred years later, the Lippmann-Dewey debates still constitute the essential arguments over the viability of a free press in democratic society. For all that the world has changed, Lippmann's skepticism and Dewey's optimism are echoed in the impassioned disputes today between those worried about the demise of the professional press and those who see something superior in the wisdom of the crowd.

For all that citizens can decide—what they want to know and when, for instance—the role of journalists as agenda setters signaling to the audience what news is important, the top stories, has not disappeared, even if trust in the press has become highly polarized and partisan. Those who cover the news professionally still have to decide how to deploy resources, which stories to cover, which to cover at length, which to handle in brief, and a thousand more matters every day.

Today, however, the judgments about these journalistic choices are voiced publicly and in real time—and can be measured in the analytics about what is read, viewed, shared, commented on, liked, and tweeted. The agenda itself has become a dialogue, and—after missteps along the way—increasingly a healthy one when informed by the right data.

For journalists, the challenge is how to respond so that they continue to play a constructive agenda-setting role that helps their community, and their different publics, and makes the journalism they produce useful to their fellow citizens. How, for instance, do news publishers use metrics thoughtfully, rather than employing them self-destructively, shallowing their content in an effort to maximize page views with slideshows and quick posts about celebrities or shallow crime incident coverage that is often thoughtlessly racist? How do they use metrics to understand the public while adding a sense of significance to the news, to indicate to citizens, "This story matters; you should pay attention"? (We will discuss this at length in the chapter on comprehensiveness and proportionality. For the moment it is sufficient to note that, as the advertising model has collapsed and publishers are looking to generate revenue by creating higher-value content that consumers will pay for, the industry has moved to better and more meaningful measures of audience engagement. The page view alone was a flawed metric that led to poor choices.)

Journalists have always been engaged in something more impor- tant than merely the production of news. Whenever editors lay out a page or website, or reporters decide what angle or element of an event or issue to emphasize and explore, they are guessing at what audiences want or need to know on the basis of their personal interactions in daily life. As they do so, they are, however unconsciously, operating by some theory of democracy—some theory of what drives politics, citizenship, and the formation of judgments. And as they choose the metrics they will now use to measure engagement or value to the audience, they are also touching on an implicit theory of how information works in people's lives and making inferences from the data that are as much a mix of their personal values as anything that could be called math or science.

If news is not organic, if it is created by journalists on the basis of their assumptions about the public and their own personal values, what kind of theory of democracy should they be using? Our purpose here is to lay out a theory that we think lies implicit, and often unrecognized, in the journalism that serves us best as citizens.

A number of critics have argued that Lippmann's view dominated too much of how journalists operated over the next hundred years.[37] Studies show that newspapers and TV aimed their coverage at target markets that were designed to sell advertising rather than trying to inform a broad citizenry. Some publications, particularly newspapers, were tailored to elite demographics, usually white, that were most attractive to some kinds of advertisers. Other publishers, such as local TV newscasts, were aimed at wide audiences that bought cars and beer but did little to offer civic news.[38] Policy and ideas were ignored or presented as sport, or were couched in the context of how a certain policy position was calculated to gain someone power over a rival.[39] Even the practice of interviewing voters in political campaigns, reporters admit, became a vanishing art, replaced by the perceived science of public opinion polling in which the public was merely a responder to questions invented by media. Even the representation of the public was incomplete, as surveys often screened out nonvoters, leaving results that gave no voice to an important segment of the population. As he saw the rise of polling, scholar James Carey wrote that we had developed "a journalism that justifies itself in the public's name but in which the public plays no role, except as an audience."[40] Citizens had become an abstraction, something the press talked about but not to.

No doubt the rise of citizen media and the empowering of consumers have helped address the problem of the public becoming an abstract construct in our public debates. The public is forcing itself into the conversation. Traditional journalism was always better at covering official debate that occurred in public spaces than at covering real public debate that occurred around the kitchen table.

The journalists who claim to know what citizens care about through today's discourse in social media will quickly find they are misled. Social media are not a good proxy of actual public sentiment. And public opinion polling, as the 2016 and 2020 elections demonstrated, faces structural problems over response rates, trust, inaccurate voter models, and political polarization that have placed the future and accuracy of the field under a cloud.

Yet this does not solve for journalists the problem of discerning what citizens want and need. It calls instead for the press to develop an even clearer theory of its role in relation to democracy and citizenship.

As we examine the interactive relationship between journalists and citizens in the new public and networked sphere online, we see a more complicated and fluid vision of the public than the traditional debates usually offer. We think this vision holds a key to how both citizens and many journalists really operate.

THE THEORY OF THE INTERLOCKING PUBLIC

Dave Burgin, a newspaper editor who worked in venues from Florida to California, had a theory about news audiences that he passed on to young staffers when he taught them the art of print page layout. Imagine, he would say, that no more than say 15 percent of your readers will want to read any one story on the page. A journalist's job, he said, was to make sure each page of a newspaper had a sufficient variety of stories so that every member of the audience would want to read at least one of them.[41]

Implicit in Burgin's theory of a diversified menu of news on each page is the idea that everyone is interested and even expert in something, but almost no one is expert in everything. The notion, in other words, of information elites and paupers, that some people are simply ignorant while other people are highly informed, is a myth.

Most Americans no longer consume news in broadsheet print pages—or even in newscasts (which would operate by the same principle as Burgin's pages). Yet the concept of diversified interests is even more relevant. Our modern news landscape makes more clear than ever that the public is made up of people with different interests and levels of knowledge in different subjects, whose interests and expertise woven together become a fabric.

In the first three editions of this book, we called this the theory of the interlocking public. The theory of the interlocking public was the assumption, unarticulated but widely practiced, that journalists used when they laid out newspaper pages, assembled radio shows, and created lineups for their nightly newscasts. It was a kind of pluralistic and optimistic view of the public square: Create a wide enough mix of topics, and write about them in a way that both the informed and the less informed will get something from, and you create a public square with common facts.

Clearly old notions of how the public square operated in the twentieth century are obsolete in the twenty-first. One of the biggest questions facing the notion of democratic republicanism—and also journalism—is whether a public square with a common set of facts even exists. And if so, how does it work?

If there is a public square, it is more like a vast public park where people are huddled in their own ideological groups, stewing over separate facts, concerned with different stories, buzzing with their own rumors, occasionally looking outward to call other groups names across the long expanse of green. A spin across the TV dial at the parallel universe most days on cable TV, or a dive into the alternate universe of hashtags, might suggest so. The different groups in this new public square often do not share the same facts, let alone the same level of interest. Conspiracy theories abound. And the media are often perceived as biased or even part of a conspiracy.

How does information flow today in this more polarized and fragmented imagined landscape, and to what extent, in this imagined public park, do we share common facts? The answers to these questions are fundamental to whether journalism, and democratic republican government, can survive.

To unpack how this information polarization works, it is still important to recognize that people are interested in different things—and this was the core notion of the interlocking public theory. For any given news story, there is an involved public with a personal stake in the issue and a strong understanding. There is an interested public that has no direct role in the issue but that is affected and responds with some firsthand experience. And there is an uninterested public that pays little attention and will join, if at all, after the contours of the discourse have been laid out by others. In the interlocking public, we are all members of all three groups, depending on the issue.

An autoworker in suburban Detroit, for instance, may care little about agriculture policy or foreign affairs and may only sporadically buy a newspaper or watch TV news. But he will have lived through many collective bargaining debates and will know a good deal about corporate bureaucracy and workplace safety. He may have kids in local schools and friends on welfare, and he may know how pollution has affected the rivers where he fishes. To these and all other concerns he brings a range of knowledge and experience. On some matters he is the involved public; on others, the interested; and on still others, remote, unknowledgeable, and unengaged.

A partner in a Washington law firm will similarly defy generalization. She is a grandmother, an avid gardener, and a news junkie who looks from a distance like a classic member of the involved "elite." A leading expert on constitutional law who is quoted often in the press, she is also fearful of technology and bored by and ignorant of investing and business. Her children grown, she no longer pays attention to news about local schools or even local government.

Or imagine a stay-at-home mom in California with a high school education who considers her husband's career her own. Her volunteer work at children's schools gives her keen ideas about why the local paper is wrong in its education coverage, and from her own life she has an intuitive sense about people.

These sketches are obviously made up, but they bring the complex notion of the public down to earth. The sheer magnitude and diversity of the people are the public's strengths. The involved expert on one issue is the ignorant and unconcerned citizen on another. The three groups—who themselves are only crude generalizations—work as a check on one another so that no debate becomes merely a fevered exchange between active interest groups. In a hopeful imagining of the interlocking public, this mix of publics is usually much wiser than the involved public alone. To a large degree, this was the public, and the public square, that journalism in the twentieth and early twenty-first centuries was trying to communicate with.

In the early days of the Web, a young CUNY professor named C. W. Anderson wrote perceptively about the fragmenting effect of the internet on audiences. He suggested an even more complex series of publics than we had outlined. And he thought that a public square with common facts was dynamic—that it could come together at times around certain subjects and then split apart again. He viewed the public, in other words, as interlocking, but also as fluid and complex, coming together only occasionally. "Online, all publics appear fragmentary," Anderson wrote.[42]

Now, nearly a decade later, publics around the world are more polarized, particularly in the United States. The public square is made up of people huddled in groups who are barely in sight of one another; and now we have entered the hyperpolarized atmosphere of a post-Trump presidency, one in which political actors pass on absurd conspiracy theories and brazenly lie, doubling down on the falsehoods when challenged. Foreign governments try to seed discord through social media platforms, actively trying to fragment the public square further—in effect they are antijournalistic forces. And at least some political figures are still trafficking in former White House counsel Kellyanne Conway's concept of "alternative facts," implicitly scoffing at the notion that the truth of anything can actually be understood.[43]

How are journalists, dedicated to trying to understand the nature of problems of a community and the efforts to solve them in public life, supposed to engage a public that is fragmented rather than interlocking?

We asked Anderson in 2020 to imagine this new public square. He told us he now sees two key factors influencing or shaping his idea of a fluid or changing public square. The first is that people can come together in curiosity and enlarge the public square, perhaps just temporarily, around a specific topic—a sports team, a weather incident, an economic crisis, or a pandemic.

The other factor that influences how and whether people congregate and learn about news is tonal, Anderson argues. An important part of Donald Trump's appeal, he points out, had to do with the way he communicated, not just what he said. He spoke as president in a kind of tribal code—one laced with humor, sarcasm, and a thick layer of resentment—that his most ardent supporters loved. They knew what he meant and were delighted; those outside the tribe were appalled and outraged, which made it all the better. To his supporters, Trump's tonal style, his code, sounded refreshingly true and authentic precisely because it was unpresidential, unpolitical, unelevated, and untechnical. He "got" his audience, and they got him because he talked like them. He was one of them.

To Anderson's two factors—topic and style—influencing this fluid but still occasionally interlocking public square, we would add a third: timing. When events are newer, and opinions have not formed or deepened, there is a chance for the public square and the common set of facts to be enlarged for a time around a topic. The pandemic offered just such a chance for Donald Trump in 2020. He chose not to embrace an approach to the pandemic that would have enlarged the public square by rallying people to unify around protecting one another, fighting the virus, and learning a common set of science-based facts about how to do this. He chose instead to politicize the disease, to suggest that mask wearing and shutdowns were for people who lacked courage and wanted to hurt him politically.

Leaders in other countries, in Italy and Germany, for example, took different approaches and unified their countries far more, enlarging the public square and the common set of facts, and embracing the role of media in helping them do that. Trump's approach, by contrast, empowered the divisive tendencies of the Web, animating the political differences that already polarized the country. It probably cost him reelection. Had Trump embraced the science of mask wearing and a coordinated national response to the virus, would the conservative media echo chamber have followed his lead? We believe it would have.

The press also bears some responsibility for creating the polarization that now threatens it. It ventured down this road, in part, through business strategies meant to enhance revenue. Newspapers in the 1970s and 1980s, for instance, began to aim at more elite demographics; local TV became a more blue-collar medium aimed in particular at stay-at-home moms. In the process, the press advanced an early kind of civic fragmentation. The segmentation was not partisan; it was demographic. But these strategies were a precursor to the media and political fragmentation that would follow. The trend was then fueled by the deregulation of media begun in the 1980s under Ronald Reagan and advanced in the 1990s under Bill Clinton. Reagan-era deregulation eliminated a series of rules over electronic media, such as the equal time rules and the Fairness Doctrine, which taken together required broadcasters to include differing points of view. Their end made possible the explosion of partisan talk radio in the 1980s and early 1990s. That was then carried forward during the Clinton era into cable and the Web. Cable news became partisan. Internet companies were all but unregulated.

But the notion of an interlocking public, in which people cannot be simply categorized as elites versus mass, informed versus uninformed, or even left versus right, suggests that the press can have a role in partially rebuilding a public square—even if, as Anderson suggests, it is transitory, forming around a given issue and then vanishing.

For that to happen, however, we believe it is critical for some part of the news media to still try to serve the interests of the widest community possible, eschewing partisanship and focusing instead on common facts, common interests, and community as a civic and geographic concept. That approach can work even for media that focus on a single subject, such as education or science, entertainment or sports. One way to take it is to imagine and serve gradations of interest and knowledge in covering events, one dimension of the interlocking public. Another is to try to focus on issues of common concern to one's audience that cut across demographics. Still another is to build newsrooms that are as diverse ethnically and ideologically as the communities they serve.

It is hard work. The press, largely, has failed at it. The networked media of the digital age have struggled to understand or create a coherent narrative for the fault lines in the American electorate, other than to label the country as "polarized" into pro-Trump and anti-Trump, conservative and liberal, or perhaps right-wing, conservative, liberal, and progressive factions. The press largely failed to see the conservative wave of the first two elections of the twenty-first century, as well as to anticipate or understand the rise of the Tea Party movement or, later, Trumpism. The press similarly failed to anticipate the countermovements: the election of Obama in 2008 and, with a handful of exceptions, his relatively easy reelection in 2012, fueled by what the media would almost instantly label as the inevitable result of changing demographics. It also misunderstood, or at least oversimplified, public resentment toward Hillary Clinton, which it tended to see in terms of a backlash to Obama and as an evidence of misogyny. The results of the 2016 election were largely a surprise to the media. So, too, were the close results in many states of the 2020 election. When the outcome of a race strikes journalists and the public as inexplicable, that is a failure of journalism.

Some media are taking steps to consciously enlarge the public square that bear watching. One of those steps is a growing number of "news collaboratives." In cities such as Cleveland, Oklahoma City, and Philadelphia, publications that serve different audience segments are sharing their work. In Cleveland, fourteen publishers take part in the Neighborhood and Community Media Association of Greater Cleveland. They share reports with one another and attend meetings together. They learn what's happening in one neighborhood from one publication, which helps a different publication pursue a similar story in another. They also coordinate advertising sales and submit grants together for foundation support.[44]

Such collaboratives offer hope that a fragmented media landscape can be also pluralistic. We want vibrant ethnic presses, strong Black publications, a Jewish press, a Catholic press, highly professional neighborhood publications, and more. They need not be isolated, however. When journalists from differently focused publications come together, the whole community can learn.

Imagine a curated newsletter or app that pulls the strongest reporting or the most important stories from all fourteen Cleveland community publications. In one spot you may not only see the news for the publication you most identify with, say the publication for Cleveland's Hispanics, but also scan over the headlines and be exposed to stories from the Chinese- and Arabic-language publications, neighborhood newsletters across the town, and more.

While the era of the newspaper as a general store where everyone goes, and where every page should strive to have something of interest to everyone, may be gone, the notion of collaboratives may approximate Dave Burgin's notion of a shared space in the digital era. It takes work. But we can see opportunity.

So can others, including a series of start-ups that started email newsletters or mobile apps curating many sources of local information. One example is 6AM City, a company focused largely in midsized towns in the US Southeast. There is no collaborative, per se, in many of these cities. But there are still many news sources. And people appear to appreciate a source that manages the information load for them. What they may not know is that approaches like these could also put back together an interlocking public.

Nationally, such efforts would be more complicated. It is hard to imagine any coming together of the *National Review* and *The New York Times,* or Fox News and CNN. Yet curated services still exist on the national stage. Pieces are there. The conservative *Dispatch* could include pieces it considers interesting from liberal publications. *The Nation,* from the left, could do the same.

But strong forces pull in the other direction, especially nationally. In an increasingly crowded media environment, the most precious commodity of all becomes attention. To gain it, and hold it, some publishers have resorted to the political version of sensationalism: fear-mongering and the use of stereotypes and labels that marginalize and demean antagonists.

Often in coverage of the great social issues of the latter half of the twentieth century—civil rights, the sexual revolutions, anti–Vietnam War sentiment, immigration, and globalization—traditional media employed such generalizations and pigeonholing and depended on spokespeople from the extremes. These stereotypes and labels became the lingua franca of the public debate and pulled the news media away from stopping to ask to what extent these positions were widely held, or even what they meant. In many ways, the press's elevation of Donald J. Trump as a candidate in the early stages of the 2016 race for president—as a candidate who made for good TV but couldn't win—was an example of this kind of sensationalism. In the open culture of the Web, where the most passionate and organized interests can marshal voices that look like "the public," the tendency toward extremism and polarization has only increased. For their part, the platform companies have profited from that. Elevating a definition of what they call "meaningful engagement" or "likes" and "shares," they created places where extremist rhetoric thrived. Virality increased ad revenue. The platform companies, in turn, evaded editorial and civic responsibility and tried to make doing so sound like a civic virtue. In truth, they hid behind the twin but empty slogans "free speech" and "the open Web" (the idea that if the Web is open to all, truth and civil discourse will win out naturally). In doing so, either naively or cynically, they demeaned both concepts. The free speech amendment to the Constitution applies to Congress abridging free speech, not to commercial entities making money from it. These are near monopolies whose predatory practices in an all-but-unregulated industry have allowed them to seize effective control over the internet and its revenue. Whatever values to an open Web these companies once believed in have now been subsumed by the inevitable momentum corporations take on to protect and grow revenue and build shareholder value.

It is similarly a mistake to imagine that discourse in social media is somehow more real, or closer to the true public, because it is unmediated. It is an illusion, and not just because only a fraction of Americans are active in social media (only 22 percent of Americans with internet access used Twitter in 2019, and 10 percent of Twitter users accounted for 80 percent of tweets, according to Pew Research Center data).[45] When the Pew Research Center monitored the discourse on Twitter over the course of a year and compared it to scientific samples of the public answering survey questions on the same issues, it found little correlation. The sentiment in social media tended to be unrepresentative, dominated by whatever side was outraged at a given moment.[46]

That poses a whole new set of challenges for understanding the public, as Anderson has said. And it raises the responsibility. If our new journalism is to work for citizens of a democratic society, then it must begin to facilitate the understanding that allows the sort of compromise on which governance of a complex interlocking public depends.

THE NEW CHALLENGE

At the beginning of the internet age, more traditional media companies saw the future in terms of size. That led to a wave of consolidations and mergers—and nearly all of these concentrations failed. As these companies consolidated, however, they began to move their interests further away from journalism and further toward commercial gain—away, in a sense, from mission and toward profit as a reason for being.

In the twenty-first century, the word *media* is now used to describe companies that create little content of their own and are larger and more powerful than any of the media companies of the previous century. They also have little commitment to creating the public service and accountability reporting that journalism has historically laid claim to. By 2018, two companies—Google and Facebook—controlled roughly 60 cents of every dollar of digital ad revenue in the United States.[47] Add Amazon to the mix and the number is 70 percent. As the Web matured (largely unregulated), it became the most monopolized industry in American history. Google, Facebook, Apple, and Amazon were richer and more powerful than most countries. It is no surprise their corporate self-interests began to ignore the democratic good.

Writer Dan Gillmor has suggested that Google's power has become so great the company is in effect the "Internet overlord."[48] And writer Rebecca MacKinnon has argued that Google, Facebook, and a handful of other companies have such power over our lives that they operate as de facto sovereigns. "Our desire for security, entertainment and material comfort is manipulated to the point that we all voluntarily and eagerly submit to subjugation." She ends with a rallying cry: "We have a responsibility to hold the abusers of digital power to account, along with their facilitators and collaborators. If we do not, when we wake up one morning to discover that our freedoms have eroded beyond recognition, we will have only ourselves to blame."[49]

Those companies are dissociated from geography, civic space, and even nation. The implications of that fact raise another level of uncertainty about the concept of corporate citizenship or social responsibility in the context of news.

Some, such as Nicco Mele, author of *The End of Big*, have suggested that these large companies may be short-lived. To create new innovation, the conditions of the networked economy favor the nimbleness of individuals loosely connected. We are not so sure. The facts would suggest that regulatory action, the approach European countries are taking ahead of the United States, or even the breakup of these companies, may be more likely to reduce their power. But even if Mele is right, in the current environment these large companies seem likely to be replaced by other short-lived giants. The currency of the new media economy may lean more heavily on stock options, public offerings, getting in, getting out. And in this world, corporate responsibility and values seem antiquated, even irrelevant.

If the distribution companies begin to buy up news, or create it themselves, the managers of the news subsidiaries will fight and protest for their independence, but history suggests they will suffer from a minority position. Journalism scholar Jim Carey worried about this at the dawn of the Web. "We look at the 1930s and we see steel and chemical industries starting to buy up the journalism of Europe." That altered how the press of Europe saw the rise of fascism. Militarism was good business. Carey worried that American journalism was beginning to be "bought up by the entertainment business—and e-commerce. Entertainment and e-commerce are today what the steel and chemical industries were in the 1930s."[50] Two decades later, news companies are not being bought up as assets inside entertainment. They are viewed as declining commodities in a failing market being acquired by hedge funds who will strip the remaining assets.

The notion of freedom of the press is rooted in independence and diverse voices. The founders believed that only a press free of government censors could tell the truth. In the modern context, that freedom was expanded to include independence from other institutions as well—parties, advertisers, business, and more. One by-product of the economic collapse of news is that the press as an independent institution is now threatened. Not only can news not stand alone as a business as it once did, but its production is increasingly intermingled with that of other products (the rental of financial terminals at Bloomberg News) or with political causes (advocacy groups producing their own journalism). And while technology has created an unprecedented free flow of information and opinion, shrinking newsrooms have also meant a decline in accountability journalism. It is a fact, and one about which all citizens should worry.

In the end, the question is this: Can journalism sustain in the twenty-first century the purpose that forged it in the three and a half centuries that came before?

Answering this question begins with identifying what journalism's purpose is. The next step is understanding the principles that allow those who gather the news to sustain that purpose on behalf of the rest of us.

2

TRUTH: THE FIRST AND MOST CONFUSING PRINCIPLE

A few days after John F. Kennedy was murdered, the man who succeeded Kennedy as president, Lyndon Johnson, sent for his secretary of defense. Johnson wanted to know what was really going on ten thousand miles across the globe, in a tiny country called Vietnam. Johnson didn't trust what he'd been told as vice president. He wanted his own information. Press reports at the time suggested the situation in South Vietnam had deteriorated in recent months following the takeover of a new government in a coup d'état. How bad was it? Defense Secretary Robert McNamara flew to Saigon and spent three days talking to all the generals and touring the various battle zones.

On his way back, McNamara gave a press conference at Tan Son Nhat Airport. The enemy activity had eased, he announced, and he was "optimistic as to the progress that can be made in the coming year."[1] When he landed at Andrews Air Force Base the next day, McNamara took a helicopter to the White House to report to Johnson personally. Afterward, in brief remarks to White House reporters, he described his meeting with the president: "We reviewed in great detail the plans of the South Vietnamese and the plans of our own military advisors for operations during 1964. We have every reason to believe they will be successful. We are determined that they shall be." As Benjamin C.

Bradlee, executive editor of *The Washington Post* at the time, would put it many years later, "And the world heard nothing more about the secretary's visit or his report to President Johnson."[2]

Eight years later, *The New York Times* and *The Washington Post* published a secret government-written history about what the leaders really knew and thought about the Vietnam War. Among the mountain of documents, which came to be called the Pentagon Papers, was the substance of what McNamara in fact had reported to the president that day. "The situation is very disturbing," McNamara's private memorandum to Johnson warned. "Current trends, unless reversed in the next 2–3 months, will lead to neutralization at best," he wrote, using the term at the time for a stalemate, "and more likely to a Communist-controlled state," in other words, utter US defeat in Vietnam in early 1964. The new South Vietnamese government was "indecisive and drifting." The US team helping them "lacks leadership, has been poorly informed, and is not working to a common plan." The situation with the enemy "has been deteriorating in the countryside since July to a far greater extent than we realized."

It was a startling appraisal, utterly at odds with everything McNamara had said publicly, starker and more alarming than anything that the American public would know.

The seriousness of the situation in Vietnam was hardly a mystery to reporters on the ground. Two days after McNamara's report to the president, David Halberstam of *The New York Times* authored a detailed assessment of the situation there. The struggle in Vietnam had reached "a critical point," wrote Halberstam, who had just returned from fifteen months in the country. His thesis in some ways even mirrored McNamara's private memo.[3] Halberstam's sources, however, were anonymous, described in the couched language of "experienced Western observers" and unnamed "officials." United Press International reporter Neil Sheehan went even further. His story about McNamara's visit to Vietnam suggested that the defense secretary had been blunt with Vietnamese leaders about how badly things were going. Yet Sheehan's sources were also unnamed, and he made no mention, or apparently had no idea, of how stark an assessment McNamara would give to Johnson.

"What might have happened," Bradlee would wonder two decades later, "had the truth emerged in 1963 instead of 1971," about what McNamara really thought and what he had really told the president?[4]

We use the words every day—*truth* and *lies, accurate* and *false*—and we think they convey something meaningful. McNamara *lied* during his press conferences. The Pentagon Papers revealed the *truth* of what he really thought and reported to Johnson. The press reported accurately what McNamara said in his press conferences. Some reporters even tried to convey, using unnamed sources, the sense that McNamara might have been more worried than he was letting on. But they did not get at the truth of what he had written and told the president. The Pentagon Papers would be a sensation eight years later, so much so that the Nixon White House would try—and fail—to use the Supreme Court to stop their publication. The war would go on another decade before the defeat McNamara had predicted finally occurred.

Over the last three hundred years, news professionals have developed a loose set of principles and values to fulfill the function of providing news—the indirect knowledge by which people come to form their opinions about the world. Foremost among these principles is this:

Journalism's first obligation is to the truth.

On this there is absolute unanimity and also utter confusion: Everyone agrees journalists must tell the truth, yet people are befuddled about what "the truth" means.

When we worked with the Pew Research Center for the People & the Press and the Committee of Concerned Journalists to ask journalists in 1999 which news values they considered paramount, 100 percent answered "getting the facts right."[5] Two decades later, working with the Associated Press and the National Opinion Research Center at the University of Chicago, the American Press Institute found the numbers unchanged. Fully 99 percent of journalists surveyed said it was "extremely" or "very important" to "verify and get the facts right."[6] The commitment was unchanged.

In long interviews with our university research partners, journalists from both old and new media similarly volunteered "truth" overwhelmingly as a primary mission.[7] In forums, even ideological journalists gave the same answer. "What we're saying is you cannot be objective because you're going to go in with certain biases," said Patty Calhoun, the editor of the alternative weekly paper *Westword*. "But you can certainly pursue accuracy and fairness and the truth, and that pursuit continues."[8]

The desire that information be truthful is elemental. Since news is the material that people use to learn and think about the world beyond themselves, the most important quality it can possess is that it be usable and reliable. Will it rain tomorrow? Is there a traffic jam ahead? Did my team win? What did the president say? Truthfulness creates, in effect, the sense of security that grows from awareness and is at the essence of news.

This basic desire for truthfulness is so powerful, the evidence suggests it is innate. "In the beginning was the Word" is the opening line of the Gospel of John in the New Testament. The earliest journalists—messengers in preliterate societies—were expected to recall matters accurately and reliably, partly out of need. Often the news these messengers carried was a matter of survival. The chiefs, among other things, needed accurate word about whether the tribe on the other side of the hill might attack.

It is interesting that oppressive societies tend to belittle literal definitions of truthfulness and accuracy, just as postmodernists do today (although for different reasons). In the Middle Ages, monks held that there was actually a hierarchy of truth. At the highest level was anagogical truth: what events portended about the fate of the universe, such as whether heaven existed. Next came moral truth: what events taught us about how to live. This was followed by allegorical truth, which explained what events signified. Finally, at the bottom, the least important, was the literal truth of what happened. As one fourteenth-century manual explained, using logic similar to what we might hear today from a postmodern scholar or a Hollywood producer, "Whether it is truth of history or fiction doesn't matter, because the example is not supplied for its own sake but for its signification."[9]

Modern political operatives are enamored of similar notions and often preach the idea that in public life perception is reality. The operatives around Richard Nixon in 1968 extolled such notions to aggrandize their role in that election, for instance, as would operatives for politicians as diverse as Bill Clinton and Mitt Romney.[10] In 2004 an anonymous adviser to George W. Bush told reporter Ron Suskind (of *The New York Times Magazine*), that "[journalists] are in what we call the reality-based community. . . . That's not the way the world really works anymore. . . . When we act, we create our own reality. While you are studying that reality . . . we'll act again, creating other new realities, which you can study too."[11] That was twelve years before Donald J. Trump was elected president and began to systematically label any accounts he didn't like as "fake news" and describe reporters as "the enemy of the people."

The tools for such information management have never been stronger. The technology that inspired utopian hopes of a more truthful and tolerant world has now endowed political officials with the power to lie on social media platforms without any filters, or for foreign governments to disrupt elections and pass on disinformation. A 2013 study of Twitter messages from reporters at fifty-one US newspapers found that "politicians were quoted in tweets 12 times more often than citizens, and along with government employees, accounted for 75 percent of quotes," reflecting the extent to which new communications technology has opened the public mind to special-interest messages.[12]

If the press offers inconvenient facts that differ with the narrative of those in power, leaders have more tools than ever today to deliver "alternative facts" of their own invention.[13] And if they repeat them often enough, they will predominate. As president, Donald Trump so often repeated claims that had been proven to be falsehoods that *The Washington Post* created a new category of political lying that seemed immune to fact-checking, "The Bottomless Pinocchio."[14]

Repetition is critical. Hearing a lie repeated over and over makes it seem more plausible by making it more familiar. As Hannah Arendt put it in her essay on political lying, "Lies are often much more plausible, more appealing to reason, than reality, since the liar has the great advantage of knowing beforehand what the audience wishes or expects to hear. He has prepared his story for public consumption with a careful eye to making it credible."[15]

Yet simplicity is almost always a signal of incompleteness. An accurate understanding of the day is almost always full of contradiction and dissonance to orthodoxy. Or as Arendt says, "Reality has the disconcerting habit of confronting us with the unexpected, for which we were not prepared."

As the modern press began to form with the birth of democratic theory, the promise of being truthful and accurate quickly became a powerful part of even the earliest marketing of journalism. The first identifiable regular newspaper in England proposed to rely "on the best and most certain intelligence." The editor of the first paper in France, though his enterprise was government owned, promised in his maiden issue, "In one thing I will yield to nobody—I mean in my endeavor to get at the truth." Similar promises to accuracy are found in the earliest papers in America, Germany, Spain, and elsewhere.[16]

The earliest colonial journalism was a strange mix of essay and fact. The information about shipping and cargoes was accurate. The political vitriol was less so, yet it was also obviously more opinion or speech than strict information. Even James Callender, the notorious scandalmonger who made his reputation with sex exposés of Alexander Hamilton and Thomas Jefferson, did not make his stories up; he trafficked in facts mixed with rumor.[17]

In the nineteenth century, as it disentangled itself from political control, journalism sought its first mass audience in part by relying on sensational crime, scandal, thrill seeking, and celebrity worship, but also by writing the news in plain language for regular people. The move away from party affiliation began with *The New York Sun* in the 1830s, and journalism reached new heights of popularity and sensation at the end of the nineteenth century. These were the years of William Randolph Hearst, Joseph Pulitzer, and "yellow journalism." Yet even the Lords of the Yellow Press sought to assure readers that they could believe what they read, even if the pledge was not always honored. Hearst's *Journal,* which was guilty more of sensationalism than of invention, claimed it was the most truthful paper in town. Pulitzer's *World* operated under the motto "Accuracy, Accuracy, Accuracy" and was more reliable than is usually credited.[18]

To assure his readers they could believe what they read, Pulitzer created a Bureau of Accuracy and Fair Play at the New York *World* in 1913. In a 1984 article in the *Columbia Journalism Review,* Cassandra Tate described how the *World*'s first ombudsman noticed a pattern in the newspaper's reporting on shipwrecks: Each such story featured a cat that had survived. When the ombudsman asked the reporter about this curious coincidence, he was told:

> One of those wrecked ships had a cat, and the crew went back to save it. I made the cat a feature of my story, while the other reporters failed to mention the cat, and were called down by their city editors for being beaten. The next time there was a shipwreck, there was no cat but the other ship news reporters did not wish to take a chance, and put the cat in. I wrote the report, leaving out the cat, and then I was severely chided for being beaten. Now when there is a shipwreck all of us always put in the cat.[19]

The irony, of course, is that the embellishments were all put there to create a sense of realism.

REALISM VERSUS TRUTH

By the beginning of the twentieth century, journalists began to realize that realism and reality—or accuracy and truth—were not so easily equated. In 1920, Walter Lippmann used the terms *truth* and *news* interchangeably in his book *Liberty and the News.* But in 1922, in *Public Opinion,* he wrote: "News and truth are not the same thing. . . . The function of news is to signalize an event," or make people aware of it. "The function of truth is to bring to light the hidden facts, to set them into relation with each other, and make a picture of reality upon which men can act."[20] By 1938, journalism textbooks were beginning to question how truthful the news could really be.[21]

Over the next fifty years, after decades of debate and argument, sometimes by political ideologues and sometimes by postmodern deconstructionist academics, we came to the point where some denied that anyone could put facts into a meaningful context to report the truth about them. An epistemological skepticism began to pervade every aspect of our intellectual life, from art, literature, law, and physics to history. Columbia University historian Simon Schama suggested that "the certainty of an ultimately observable, empirically verifiable truth" was dead.[22]

With the digital age, some have suggested that what we considered truth was merely "consensus" arrived at by an oligarchical press system canvassing the opinions of a limited number of establishment sources, something changeable and far less solid than what we imagined. "Truth is a judgment about what persuades us to believe a particular assertion," NYU professor Clay Shirky argued.[23] All this was before Donald Trump became president and the United States experienced the most sustained, systematic, and continuous assault on journalism, facts, science, and empirical research-based understanding from a national leader in US history.

The arguments doubting that there is anything such as truth, in other words, are long-standing. Truth, it seems, is too complicated for us to pursue—in our journalism or anything else. Or perhaps it doesn't even exist, since we are all subjective individuals. These are interesting arguments—maybe, on some philosophical level, even valid. But where does that leave what we call journalism? Is the word *truth* now something adequate for everyday conversation but something that doesn't hold up to real scrutiny?

Clearly, there are levels. "The journalist at *The New York Times* told us the other day that the New York Giants lost a football game by a score of 20–8," journalist and press critic Richard Harwood told us at one of the original forums we organized to research this book. "Now that was a small piece of truth. But the story of why the Giants lost can be told in a hundred different ways—each story being written through a different lens that is fogged over by stereotypes and personal predilections."[24] Harwood's observation is still a good starting place for wrestling with the question.

As we imagine moving beyond an initial accounting of facts—the score of that game—to something that includes more contextualized understanding, how far can we go? Or put it this way: What does journalism's obligation to the truth mean?

The usual efforts to answer this question, at seminars or in philosophical tracts, end up in a muddle. One reason is that the conversation is usually not grounded in the real world. Philosophical discussions of whether "truth" really exists founder in semantics.

Another reason is that journalists themselves have never been very clear about what they mean by truthfulness. Journalism by nature is reactive and practical rather than philosophical and introspective. The serious literature by journalists thinking through such issues is not rich, and what little there is most journalists have not read. Theories of journalism are left to the academy, and many newspeople have historically devalued journalism education, arguing that the only place to learn is through the osmosis of practice on the job. As Ted Koppel, the highly respected and thoughtful network TV journalist, once declared: "Journalism schools are an absolute and total waste of time."[25]

The conventional explanations by journalists of how they get at the truth have tended to be quick responses drawn from interviews or speeches or, worse, marketing slogans, and they often have relied on crude metaphors. The press is "a mirror" of society, said David Bartlett, former president of the Radio-Television News Directors Association, echoing a common phrase of the 1990s. Journalism is "a reflection of the passions of the day," famed author and network anchor Tom Brokaw told our academic research partners. News is whatever is "most newsworthy on a given day," said a CNN producer.[26] These explanations made journalists seem passive—mere recorders of events rather than investigators, selectors, or editors.[27] It's as if they thought truth was something that rose up by itself, like bread dough. Rather than defend their techniques and methods for finding truth, journalists tended to deny that they existed—let alone that their subjective experience, culture, age, gender, or race had any hand in the choices.

Whether it was secrecy, idealism, or ineptness, the failure by journalists to articulate what they were doing left citizens suspicious that the press was either deluding itself or hiding something. This is one reason the discussion of journalistic objectivity became such a trap. The term is so misunderstood and battered, the discussion mostly goes off track. It is also one of the reasons that a new era of digital pioneers, as they tried to contemplate the journalism they were disrupting, have tended to dismiss journalistic professionalism. They imagined journalists were largely stenographers, with random lists of sources, using fairly crude notions of balance to get at accuracy. Many if not most journalists were doing much more. But they had little vocabulary, let alone standard method, and even less journalistic literature, to explain themselves.

As we will discuss in more depth in chapter 4, on verification, originally it was not the journalist who was imagined to be objective. It was his or her method. Today, however, in part because journalists have failed to articulate what they are doing, our contemporary understanding of objectivity is mostly muddled and confused. Most people, as we noted earlier and will detail more later, mistake objectivity to mean neutrality.

Despite the public's confusion, there is little doubt that journalists believe themselves to be engaged in pursuing truth, not just free speech or commerce. They have to be—for this is what society requires of them.

And, as we will see, "journalistic truth" means more than mere accuracy. It is a sorting-out process that takes place between the initial story and the interaction among the public, newsmakers, and journalists. This first principle of journalism—its disinterested pursuit of truth—is ultimately what sets journalism apart from other forms of communication.

JOURNALISTIC TRUTH

To understand this sorting-out process, it is important to remember that journalism exists in a social context. Out of necessity, citizens and societies depend on accurate and reliable accounts of events. They develop procedures and processes to arrive at what might be called "functional truth." Police track down and arrest suspects on the basis of facts. Judges hold trials. Juries render verdicts. Industries are regulated, taxes are collected, and laws are made. We teach our children rules, history, physics, and biology. All of these truths—even the laws of science—are subject to revision, but we operate by them in the meantime because they are necessary and functionally they work.

This is what our journalism must be after—a practical or functional form of truth. It is not truth in the absolute or philosophical sense. It is not the truth of a chemical equation. Journalism can—and must—pursue the truths by which we can operate on a day-to-day basis. "We don't think it's unreasonable to expect jurors to render fair verdicts, or teachers to teach honest lessons, or . . . scientists to perform unbiased research. Why should we set any lower goals for poor journalists?" Bill Keller, then editor of *The New York Times,* told us. "Whether true objectivity is ever possible—I don't think that is what we're here for. . . . We strive for coverage that aims as much as possible to present the reader with enough information to make up his or her own mind. That's our fine ideal."[28]

Does this suggest that journalism should stick simply to accuracy, getting the names and dates right? Is that sufficient? The increasingly interpretative nature of most modern journalism tells us no. A journalism built merely on accuracy fails to serve contemporary civil society.

In the first place, mere accuracy can be a kind of distortion all its own. As long ago as 1947, the Hutchins Commission, a group of scholars who spent years producing a document that outlined the obligations of journalism, warned of the dangers of publishing accounts that were "factually correct but substantially untrue."[29] Even then, the commission cited stories about members of people of color that, by failing to provide context or by emphasizing race or ethnicity pointlessly, reinforced false stereotypes. "It is no longer enough to report the fact truthfully. It is now necessary to report the truth about the fact," the commission concluded.

Mere accuracy is also not what people are looking for. In his book *News Values,* journalist Jack Fuller described how philosophers imagine there are two tests of truth: One is correspondence, the other is coherence. For journalism, these tests roughly translate into getting the facts straight and making sense of the facts. Coherence must be the ultimate test of journalistic truth, Fuller decided. "Regardless of what the radical skeptics argue, people still passionately believe in meaning. They want the whole picture, not just part of it. . . . They are tired of polarized discussion."[30]

Common sense tells us something similar. A report that the mayor praised the police at the Garden Club luncheon seems inadequate—

even foolish—if the police are entangled in a corruption scandal; the mayor's comments are clearly political rhetoric, and they come in response to some recent attack by his critics, or the mayor has a record of passing along unfounded rumors and gossip.

This is far from suggesting that accuracy doesn't matter, that facts are all relative—just another form of fodder for debate. On the contrary, accuracy is the foundation upon which everything else is built: context, interpretation, debate, and all of public communication. If the foundation is faulty, everything else is flawed. A debate between opponents arguing with false figures or purely on prejudice fails to inform. It only inflames. It takes the society nowhere. It is more helpful, and more realistic, to understand the truth we seek or can expect from journalism to be a process—or a continuing journey toward understanding—that begins with the first account of an event and builds over time. For instance, the first news accounts signal a new situation or trend. They may begin with reports of something simple—an accident, a meeting, an inflammatory statement. They may come in the form of a brief alert with few details. The time and place of the accident, the damage done, the types of vehicles, arrests, unusual weather or road conditions—in effect, the physical externalities of the case—are facts that can be recorded and checked. Once they have verified the facts, those engaged in reporting the news should strive to convey a fair and reliable account of their meaning, valid for now, subject to further investigation. Journalist Carl Bernstein has described this as reporters striving to provide "the best obtainable version of the truth."[31] Journalist Howie Schneider has called it "conditional truth," subject to revision with new information. The principles of *The Washington Post*, drafted by Eugene Meyer in 1933, describe telling "the truth as nearly as the truth may be ascertained."[32]

An individual reporter may not be able to move much beyond a surface level of accuracy in a first account, particularly if that account is written in real time as a blog post or an alert or a running "live" story. And these first accounts are often the most vulnerable to distortion or inaccuracy because less is known.

But the news is not a static product. The first account builds to a second, in which new details emerge, sources react, news outlets correct initial mistakes and add missing elements. The second account builds to a third, and so on. Context is added in each successive layer. In more important and complex stories, there are subsequent contributions on editorial pages, in blogs, in social media discourse, in official responses—the full range of public and private conversation. This practical truth is a protean thing that, like learning, grows like a stalactite in a cave, drop by drop, over time.

The truth is a complicated and sometimes contradictory phenomenon, but if it is seen as a process over time, journalism can get at it: first by stripping information of any attached misinformation, disinformation, or self-promoting bias and then by letting the community react in the sorting-out process that ensues. As always, the search for truth becomes a conversation.

This definition helps reconcile the way we use the words *true* and *false* every day with the way we deconstruct those words in the petri dish of a philosophical debate. This definition comes closer to journalists' intuitive understanding of what they do than the crude metaphors of mirrors and reflections that are commonly handed out.

We understand truth as a goal—at best elusive—and still embrace it. We embrace it the same way as Albert Einstein did when he said of science that it was not about truth but about making what we know less false. For this is how life really is—we're often striving and never fully achieving. As historian Gordon Wood has said about writing history: "One can accept the view that the historical record is fragmentary and incomplete . . . and that historians will never finally agree in their interpretations" and yet still believe "in an objective truth about the past that can be observed and empirically verified." This is more than a leap of faith. In real life, people can tell when someone has come closer to getting it right, when the sourcing is authoritative, when the research is exhaustive, when the method is transparent. Or as Wood put it, "Historians may never see and present that truth wholly and finally, but some of them will come closer than others, be more nearly complete, more objective, more honest, in their written history, and we will know it, and have known it, when we see it."[33]

Those who have worked in news or in public life say much the same thing: Getting news that comes closer to a complete version of the truth has real consequences. In the first hours of an event, when being accurate is most difficult, accuracy is perhaps most important. It is during this time that public attitudes are formed, sometimes stubbornly, by the context within which the information is presented. Is it a threat to me? Is it good for me? Is it something I should be concerned about? The answers to these questions determine how carefully I follow a new event, how much verification of the facts I will look for. On the basis of his experience, Hodding Carter, the longtime journalist who served as assistant secretary of state for public affairs in the Carter administration's State Department, said that this is the time in which the government can exercise its greatest control over the public mind: "If given three days without serious challenge, the government will have set the context for an event and can control public perception of that event."[34] Internet researcher danah boyd has similarly found that the time when events are just forming is the time when bad-faith actors have the most influence to introduce false information and false narratives—including by elevating them in searches. These efforts then shape the perception of events by those curious enough to look them up.[35]

The digital age adds pressures in both directions to this process of searching for functional or conditional truth. The first pressure is speed. In the context of gathering news, speed is almost always the enemy of accuracy. It offers those who seek to report less time to check facts. This is why cable news channels that report continually (such as CNN and Fox News) tend to report more erroneous information than the broadcast channels (NBC, CBS, or ABC), which have hours to vet their reports for a single network evening newscast. Posting news in real time on Twitter or elsewhere online thus tends to make all news organizations as vulnerable as cable.

And if a first account is incomplete or prone to the reporter's preconceptions, critics will move faster, too, to create a counternarrative about media bias. Consider the viral video of Covington Catholic High School students' encounter with a Native American elder at the Lincoln Memorial in 2019. *The Washington Post, The New York Times,* and others reported on the video clip, which seemed to suggest that the mostly white and male students—particularly one boy named Nicholas Sandmann, who was wearing a red pro-Trump Make America Great

Again cap—were harassing the Native elder, Nathan Phillips. Additional video and reporting showed the truth was more complicated. Phillips had approached the students, not the other way around. And an entirely third group, made up of Hebrew Israelites, known for public conflict, appeared to provoke everyone. When the initial stories suggested only a single view, a wave of conservative sentiment in social media saw proof of Trump's claim that the news media were purveyors of a false and biased narrative against America. It is just one case of the risk of technology: that reporters, influenced by what they expect or simply moving too fast, can fan flames of existing tensions with poor initial accounts.[36]

Automation and the values of the platform companies add to that pressure. Researchers are finding that algorithms built at social media platforms often raise up emotional content—sensationalism, commentary, and likely misinformation—rather than more fact-emphasizing, calm, likely truthful content. Computational social psychologist William J. Brady and colleagues in 2017 looked at the reach of half a million tweets. They found that each moral or emotional word used in a tweet on average increased its virality by 20 percent. The Pew Research Center found something similar in the same year. Facebook posts expressing "indignant disagreement" received double the engagement (i.e. likes and shares) of other types of content on the platform. The results of what algorithms often have favored keep users engaged but distort collective senses of reality. Worse yet, for citizens and journalists alike, the design of platforms invites these reactions. As Yale psychologist Molly Crockett has found, digital spaces that ask for reactions and retweets give little room for normal human behavior that inhibits outraged response, such as time to reflect or seeing another person's face.[37]

This outraged emotionality is also driving news consumption. In 2018, researchers at *The New York Times* assessed what emotions certain words in articles induced in readers. "Hate drives readership more than any of us care to admit," one employee on the business side told a reporter at *New York* magazine.[38]

The third pressure is the growing orientation toward commentary and argument. As people compose polemics, they are focused on persuading or inflaming the public, not informing them. Thus such advocates naturally tend to choose facts that help them make their case. Over time they also learn what the algorithms favor, and they build their inflammatory point to succeed there too. This all pushes the emphasis by degrees away from the work of journalists, of testing initial impressions, empathizing with different points of view, adding context to make things more complete or fair, getting to the bottom of what happened, and arriving at the most complete understanding of the facts.

An open networked media environment also means that more rumors and more misinformation are passed along in public—creating more confusion for users and more pressure on news organizations.

Add to that the virulent attitude toward facts and penchant for advancing false rumors embraced by Donald Trump and some in his administration, as well as similar attitudes by a raft of authoritarian leaders in other countries. After Trump seized control of the Republican Party in 2016, he began to normalize racist views, conspiracy theories, proven falsehoods, and false rumors as a way of animating his base, diverting attention from scandals, and intimidating critics. When fact-checked, he doubled and tripled down on repeating the falsehoods in the self-evident conviction that repetition of a lie would make some people either believe the lie or at least doubt the truth. Trump's disdain for facts, and his political success springing from it, represent the most blatant and broad-based attack by an American president on the notion that the publics and officials in democratic republics are guided by facts, beyond anything seen during the Vietnam War under Lyndon Johnson or Watergate under Richard Nixon. The legacy of this dishonesty will take years to sort through, the body blow an indeterminate amount of time to heal. But heal we believe it will. For the practical consequences of real problems like pandemics or war eventually require facts to redress.

The pressures pulling against truth and accuracy are also balanced against others brought by the digital age that move in a different and more positive direction. While the utopians were clearly wrong that the internet would automatically fact-check itself, it is true that the opening of the civic conversation to more voices has the potential to strengthen the process of verification. Fact-checkers from around the world now share listservs to help each other verify false claims.[39]

New technology has been developed to identify if pictures have been manipulated and whether an image attributed to one event was really of somewhere else and another time. And the crowd, as early Web enthusiasts like Dan Gillmor and Clay Shirky promised, can operate as citizen sentinels to help fact-check events. During political speeches, people on Twitter and other platforms point out and share inaccuracies in almost real time. During the pandemic, medical professionals were correcting misleading information released by Trump's administration and reacting to the conflicting accounts of his own doctor when the president himself became ill with the disease.

As powerful and profound as the network is, however, it is still naive to think that in the networked culture the sorting-out process always works efficiently—that the internet, as some have put it, will ever be "a self-cleaning oven." In addition to the speed, a variety of other factors get in the way. In a fragmented media culture, as we discussed in the previous chapter, more people may be operating in their own bubbles of self-selected interests and sources. We may, as we scatter to our own sources for information, lack a central gathering place or a common understanding of the basic facts. The initial account of an event is always the most important, and the more hastily it is put together, the more inaccurate it is likely to be. And bad actors, as we noted above, know that influencing first impressions with disinformation can be effective. That problem is added to by the phenomenon of our simply moving on, deciding we have learned what we needed about something and are on to the next thing, like the student paying only partial attention in class and getting a general sense of the topic but botching all the details. Only there is no test at the end of the unit to tell us we got it about half-wrong.

TRUTH REQUIRES PROCESS: VERIFICATION

The more compelling sense is that truth requires commitment, a dedication to a process of verification, and that the search is made more powerful when journalists and the public are knit together in a way that mixes the structure of traditional journalism techniques and authority with the power of the networked community.

There are some inspiring examples of how this organized collaborative intelligence can work. Consider the case of Ian Tomlinson, a newspaper vendor who died after being caught in the middle of a protest over the G20 meeting in England in April 2009. The initial police account held that Tomlinson suffered a heart attack while walking home and that protesters were culpable for getting in the way of medics whose treatment might have saved his life. The next day's *Evening Standard* newspaper, the paper Tomlinson sold, bore the headline "Police Pelted with Bricks as They Help Dying Man."

The Guardian newspaper, skeptical of that version and of police secrecy surrounding the case, pursued two lines of inquiry to go deeper. One, traditional shoe-leather reporting, had journalists covering the protest go through their notebooks of interviewees to identify possible eyewitnesses; the paper also pored over its photos to see if anyone had inadvertently caught a glimpse of the incident. The effort found one eyewitness and photographic evidence that seemed to prove Tomlinson had fallen to the ground at the feet of police, one hundred yards from where he would later fall again and die.

The second line of inquiry reached out to readers on the internet. After taking four days to conclusively establish that its photos indeed proved Tomlinson had fallen earlier, near police, *The Guardian* put its photographic evidence online and asked if anyone knew more. The paper thus became part of the online conversation questioning the circumstances of Tomlinson's death. Via Twitter, *Guardian* reporter Paul Lewis discovered photo albums on another social media platform, Flickr, that contained more images raising doubts about Tomlinson's death. But all of this was circumstantial evidence, feeding online speculation, Lewis thought, not yet proof of any wrongdoing. The crowd, like *The Guardian,* in other words, was uneasy, but it did not really know what had happened.

One member of that crowd was Chris LaJaunie, an investment fund manager in New York who had been in London during the protest. LaJaunie had shot video that he thought might be explosive; it showed a policeman pushing Tomlinson. He had considered releasing it on YouTube but had had second thoughts. It might go unnoticed. It might be challenged. It would also lack any context, a lone video posted by an unfamiliar source. Believing *The Guardian* had been the most effective interrogator of the police version of events, he contacted Lewis. The paper verified his account, triangulated his footage with other evidence, and eight days later overturned what in effect was a police cover-up, establishing that Tomlinson had died as a result of actions by police.

The Tomlinson case, Lewis argues, illustrates the synergy of what *The Guardian* then called "open journalism," and what we call journalism as "organized collaborative intelligence." By whatever name, this approach combines the professionalism of journalists and their access to the observations and knowledge of public witnessing and experience.[40]

More recently, perhaps no one has employed the concept of collaborative intelligence, combining traditional reporting, input from the public, and technology, more effectively than David Fahrenthold, the Pulitzer Prize–winning reporter at *The Washington Post*, particularly in covering Donald Trump's charities. The story of how Fahrenthold discovered that Trump's foundation had violated the law to buy a portrait of Trump that was hanging in his Doral Country Club is an example worth retelling. Fahrenthold received a tip one morning that the portrait existed, along with the suggestion that he could find it using a particular Google search for art. He used Google technology to identify what the portrait might look like. He then turned to his expanding universe of Twitter followers, asking them if anyone knew where the painting was located now. If it was being used in a commercial rather than charitable setting, that would be a violation of the law.

It was 10 A.M. in Washington at that point. A woman who followed Fahrenthold on Twitter guessed the portrait might be hanging in a Trump golf club somewhere and began searching by looking through photos from the clubs that guests had posted on Tripadvisor. Around 8 P.M. she found it among 385 guest photos posted on the Tripadvisor page for Trump's Doral Country Club in Miami. The picture was from February 2016, several months earlier. Fahrenthold tweeted to his followers asking if anyone knew if the portrait was still there at the club. An anchor at the local Univision affiliate in Miami named Enrique

Acevedo, whose offices were just blocks away from Doral, decided to book a room at the club for the night to answer Fahrenthold's query. He got off work at midnight and checked in. Once there, he began wandering the grounds, asking housekeeping workers and maintenance crews if they had seen the portrait. One let him into the now-closed Champions Bar & Grill, where the portrait hung. Acevedo took a picture and tweeted it at Fahrenthold. As the reporter put it, unless the Champions Bar & Grill was used as a soup kitchen in its off-hours, having the portrait, which was purchased by Trump's foundation for $10,000, hanging in his for-profit golf club was a violation of the law. "What might have taken me a year, if ever, I was able to verify in a day," Fahrenthold explained. And the process had occurred in public, fully transparent, and in a way that was bulletproof.[41]

One striking feature of this engaged or collaborative journalism is that parallels with how journalists discovered facts in earlier eras reveal just how much the means of getting at the truth have changed, while the goal of pursuing it has not.

Fifty years earlier, in Orangeburg, South Carolina, three students were killed and more than twenty others injured in what police described as "an exchange of gunfire" with state troopers during a protest over civil rights. After hearing about the shootings, reporter Jack Nelson, the Atlanta bureau chief of the *Los Angeles Times,* flew to South Carolina to check out the story. While most reporters were gathered at press conferences, Nelson went to the Orangeburg Regional Hospital, where twenty-seven wounded students were being treated. He stuffed two reporter's notebooks into the inside pocket of his jacket, creating a bulge that resembled a shoulder holster bearing a handgun, and walked into the office of the hospital administrator, Phil Mabry. Nelson identified himself "as being from the Atlanta bureau" and said he wanted to examine the medical records of the wounded students. Mabry assumed Nelson was from the Atlanta office of the FBI. Nelson did not disabuse him.

The dutiful hospital administrator laid the medical records out on his desk. The records showed what had really happened. Most of the wounded students, and the ones who had died, had been shot in the back, caught in the cross fire as they were running away. Nelson corroborated the medical records with eyewitness interviews and other official records to prove the police account was false. He wanted his story to be airtight. His account proved the state police were lying and added momentum to the civil rights protests.[42]

Nelson began with suspicions offered by eyewitnesses. Paul Lewis at *The Guardian* and Fahrenthold at the *Post* sought the help of the public in their reporting, working with remarkable transparency in the process. Increasingly, the network of collaborative intelligence is triggered by the public itself, often by offering evidence of wrongdoing in the form of video. The media in turn can press authorities for answers. The deaths of George Floyd in Minneapolis, Michael Brown in Ferguson, Missouri, and jogger Ahmaud Arbery in Georgia are only three in a far-too-long list of cases. The key point here is that journalists once worked largely alone. Today, journalists seeking the truth have millions of citizen sentinels strengthening our ability to get to the bottom of things. One does not replace the other. They work together to get the public closer to the truth. In all of these cases across the years, truth was a process—but within reach.

NEW JOURNALISTIC NORMS EMERGE CHALLENGING TRUTH

Over time there have been people, even inside traditional journalism, who were unsure if truth was a practical goal for news. At different times, some journalists have suggested substitutes. Probably the two most common of these have been fairness and balance. If newspeople cannot know the truth, they can at least be fair and balanced. But both of these concepts, under scrutiny, are inadequate. Fairness is too abstract and, in the end, is more subjective than truth. Fair to whom? How do you test fairness? Truthfulness, for all its difficulties, at least can be tested.

Balance, too, is subjective. Balancing a story by being fair to both sides may not be fair to the truth if both sides do not, in fact, have equal weight. And in those many cases where there are more than two sides to a story, how does one determine which side to honor? Balance, if it amounts to false balance, becomes distortion. Both-sidesism can lead to political stenography, in which the press becomes a purveyor of lies or exaggeration.

Technology has added obstacles to the process before. By the late 1990s, as we detailed in our book *Warp Speed*, various forces were converging to weaken journalists' pursuit of truthfulness, despite the continuing allegiance most journalists professed to it. With the advent of the continuous 24-7 news cycle, which began with cable and grew with the Web, the news became more piecemeal or partial; what were once the raw ingredients of journalism began to be passed on to the public directly.

As audiences fragmented, different news outlets began to adopt differing standards of journalism. In the continuous-news culture, news channels trying to shovel out the latest information had less time to check things out. Amid growing competition and speed, there emerged what we called a new Journalism of Assertion; it overwhelmed the more traditional Journalism of Verification, which had moved more slowly and put a higher premium on getting things right first. (We will offer much more detail on this in chapter 4.) For now, suffice it to say that in the Journalism of Assertion, reporters had less time to check things out. News accounts did not build upon themselves toward a more accurate whole. They often just moved on. What you learned depended on when you tuned in. News was less a finished product and more a constant stream of raw components.

The Journalism of Assertion was also part of another often little-recognized but important change in news. It brought with it a power shift in the dynamics between sources and journalists. As the number of news outlets proliferated, the sources who talked to the press and wanted to influence the public gained more relative power over the journalists who covered them. More outlets, in effect, made for more of a seller's market for information. Newsmakers had more ability to cherry-pick which outlets and which reporters they wanted to talk to. So, too, the format favored in the Journalism of Assertion, live interviews versus edited stories or "packages," handed over more power to the interviewee, who could dissemble, filibuster, and mislead. The journalist interviewer was in a much weaker position. There was no time to fact-check and little time to add context; doing so involved interruption, looked rude, and usually got nowhere. Live interviews in the end were more performance than news gathering, a fact that too many in TV still do not fully recognize.

With the advent of the Web, as audiences further fragmented and a proliferating number of news outlets competed to get the attention of that audience, we saw the rapid rise of a third model of media that we call the Journalism of Affirmation. It is epitomized by talk show hosts like Rush Limbaugh, Sean Hannity, and Rachel Maddow, who attract audiences through reassurance, or the affirming of preconceptions. With each new outlet, and each new political faction, there can come a new channel to affirm it. In the era of Trump we saw the birth of channels like One America News Network, TruNews, and the ascendance of so-called alt-right websites like Breitbart and Newsmax. (We will talk more about this in chapter 4 as well.)

In short, what had been a fairly homogeneous notion of journalism that was grounded in reporting, even if it had somewhat differing styles in alternative weeklies versus daily newspapers or nightly local TV, was giving way to different models built on speed and convenience in one model and reassurance in another. The changes were subtle. Even some of the journalists who worked in these new media barely recognized that their news values were shifting. Cable TV journalists did not readily acknowledge that they put less of a premium on verification. They just imagined they did it differently. But recognized or not, the shift in the core appeal to the audience represented, however subtly, a critical shift in ethics.

With the internet, there emerged yet a fourth model of news—a Journalism of Aggregation—in which publishers such as Business Insider, *The Skimm,* and *Huffington Post,* search engines such as Google, and, with the rise of social media, individual citizens themselves recommended and passed along content that they had no direct role in producing and, often, had made no effort to verify. Google became one of the most powerful institutions on earth by aggregating for users the material produced by others, with the assurance that its computerized algorithm was ranking its searches on the basis of the reputational record of the source. There is no doubting the incomparable richness of a curated news environment. The experience of sorting through numerous accounts of an event effortlessly in minutes offers a depth, context, and control that the reading of the single account in the past could not come close to. But it is also important to recognize that we now operate in a distributed media environment where publishers, platforms, the public, and sometimes even journalists themselves are passing along work they cannot possibly vouch for—and may make no effort to—and that we accept this now without a second thought. The burden of verification has been passed incrementally from the news deliverer to the consumer.

It was in this rich mulch of vulnerability that we have seen the rise of conspiracy theories such as Q-Anon—which claims that a Satanist cult of pedophiles is deeply embedded at the highest levels of government; deepfake videos that are designed to deliberately mislead; false theories such as "Plandemic," which posits that the coronavirus pandemic was invented by Microsoft founder Bill Gates so he could profit from it; and political actors such as Trump, who rise to power in part by appealing to factions of the public who believe such theories.

Add to this pressure the shrinking resources in newsrooms dedicated to direct reporting, as the advertising dollars in legacy platforms were replaced by digital dimes. It is a world in which an initial error in reporting or editing or interpretation can turn into a kind of original sin that influences us forever.

JOURNALISTIC TRUTH TODAY

The instinct for truth is no less important today—but it is under more pressure. Peter Viereck, professor emeritus in history at Mount Holyoke College, has argued that in a networked and connected world, the value of a group dedicated to pursuing truth is now greater. "I can think of nothing more gallant," Viereck says, "even though again and again we fail, than attempting to get at the facts; attempting to tell things as they really are. For at least reality, though never fully attained, can be defined. Reality is that which, when you don't believe it, doesn't go away."[43]

Thus we have, once again, technology pulling us in two directions. In practical terms, more information makes truth more challenging. At the end of the process, however, the truth we arrive at will likely be more accurate. The problem is that the process of truth telling has become dramatically more demanding and more difficult. Call it the paradox of knowledge in the information age. When information is a commodity in oversupply—when there is so much more input—knowledge becomes more difficult to acquire because one must sift and synthesize more information to set things in order. The knowledge acquired may be deeper and better, but it is also more elusive and likely will be more specialized. Not everyone will have the energy to acquire it.

This paradox may be the most daunting tension affecting our ability today to know what's true, and one of the pressures that has put democracy under threat. In his book *Black Swan,* essayist and scholar Nassim Taleb argues the abundance of information facing people today may actually be making us worse at discerning the truth of things, not better. Against a background of so much complex information, Taleb argues, we tend to cling to our preconceptions and biases to help us navigate; we are also more likely to employ specialized methods we learned in specialized careers, which can make us less open to random or unexpected events and explanations. "The problem is that our ideas are sticky: once we produce a theory, we are not likely to change our minds—so those who delay developing their theories are better off. When you develop your opinions on the basis of weak evidence, you will have difficulty interpreting subsequent information that contradicts these opinions, even if this new information is obviously more accurate."[44]

Taleb's arguments offer a basis for why people would be more inclined to believe reassuring falsehoods and conspiracy theories today.

This is an existential challenge for those who want to help people know what has really happened. When the media become a cacophony of conflicting accounts, our capacity to focus is diminished. It becomes more difficult to rise above the din. If Winston Churchill was correct that "a lie gets halfway around the world before the truth has a chance to get its pants on," greater technology has only speeded up the process.[45] One study by MIT researchers in 2018 indeed found that fake news spreads six times faster than real news—and that number was derived after the authors controlled for the presence of robots spreading it even faster.[46] All this helps explain why the new partisan journalism of the twenty-first century, the Journalism of Affirmation, is even more appealing for some audiences. It makes things easier. It is a way of achieving order in a more confusing world, without so much sifting and heavy lifting. It offers comfort. They tidied up our mental rooms for us. The neopartisans, be they Sean Hannity, Tucker Carlson, Don Lemon, Lawrence O'Donnell, or a growing array of ideological websites, create the impression for audiences that they are sense makers.

Rather than rush to add interpretation, we need to ensure that we also have a journalism that first establishes what has truly happened— a journalism that first concentrates on context and verification. We should look for news that makes transparent how it was produced— the sourcing, evidence, and journalistic decision-making that went into it. We should look for journalism that has explicitly tried to sift out rumor, innuendo, and spin and that shows evidence of that effort. We need a journalism, in other words, that allows us to answer the question "Why should I believe this?" rather than "Do I agree with it?" And the more journalism, through its transparency, encourages consumers to think about how the news was put together, the more it will increase their skills for making informed judgments about what constitutes reliable news.

What we need from our journalism in the twenty-first century, in short, is not so different in concept or function from what we needed in the twentieth. What that journalism looks like, however, how it is presented, and even the routines that journalists use to achieve those goals are very different. If you take little else from this book, this concept is important: The underlying function of journalism, the service it must provide for the public, and thus the goals that journalists aspire to, the elements of journalism, have not changed. Truth is still the first and most important of those goals. But how a journalist goes about fulfilling that goal must change dramatically.

The new journalism cannot presume anymore to be the only content its audience sees. It cannot present itself as a singular omniscient account of events. It must assume that we have seen other, more partial information in real time, but it also must provide a coherent account on its own in case we have not. It must be conscious of false information that has previously been presented and try to correct it, particularly if there is a reason to think that misinformation has resonated in the marketplace of ideas. It also must be strategic about when and how to address false information, taking care not to amplify lies unwittingly. Put more simply, if the best new journalism will compete in the marketplace of ideas, it must be more deeply reported and more transparent than before, it must correct the record for audiences that have been misinformed, and it must answer questions other accounts have left unclear. It must be a service that listens to and understands audiences and the science of how audiences process information. It must help people learn, not just provide information.

The impact of this new journalism, in turn, will extend beyond its direct audience, for it will influence and change the work others produce about the same news events. And if it is produced by smart managers, they will spend more effort than they once did marketing this work to elevate its impact both on the public and on other news producers and analysts.

We will explain the new ways in which this journalism must be created and presented in subsequent chapters. But it all begins with the recognition that the new journalism, even in a networked era, must be built on a foundation of truth—and that truth cannot be assumed to appear automatically from the presence of more sources. The pursuit of truth is a process that requires an intellectual discipline and vigilance. It also requires memory—not forgetting about misinformation simply because the discussion has quickly moved on. And the need for this is greater, not less, in the new century, because the likelihood of untruth has become so much greater.

For truth to prevail, journalists must make clear to whom they owe their first loyalty. That is the next step.

3
WHO JOURNALISTS WORK FOR

n most businesses, accountability is tied to fairly straightforward metrics. Usually, success is measured in dollars. The bonuses of lawyers, doctors, businesspeople, and most of upper management are tied to how much money their operations bring in.

What is the best mark of value for someone producing journalism?

For years, journalists were evaluated mostly on the basis of highly subjective judgments about the quality of their work. The number of stories reporters produced might be part of the mix, but that varied widely by beat and was not necessarily relevant to how their bosses, the editors themselves, were judged.

At the end of the twentieth century, a new trend emerged: As the industry began to worry more about efficiency and profit, under the assumption that it now was a mature industry whose audience could not grow, it began to tie the performance of top news managers to the profitability of the news enterprise rather than the quality of the content produced under their watch, just as it had previously done with its advertising and circulation executives. Quality factors started to make up half or less of the decision criteria about the performance of news executives and how much they should be paid. The bonuses, at least for managers, began to be based in large part on how much profit their companies made.[1]

These business incentive programs formalized a new theory of newsroom management. In deed if not in name, by 2000 America's journalistic leaders had been transformed into businesspeople. Half of newspaper newsroom leaders reported that they spent at least a third of their time not on journalism but on business matters.[2]

At a minimum, the shift in focus did not have the desired effect. The effort to turn newsroom leaders into cost managers was part of the collective failure of the news industry to adapt to disruption. Ensuring that everyone was focused on maximizing profit and share price only broadened and reinforced the defensive fortress mentality in news companies, which became concentrated on protecting revenue rather than innovating the product. It made it more difficult for newsroom leaders to advocate for the public interest within their companies and to push for risky, expensive experiments in coverage that might hurt short-term profitability. Publishers and executives talked openly about trying to "blow up the culture of the newsroom" because it resisted these business imperatives. These changes in the culture of news companies, not coincidentally, showed up in the data about why citizens began to lose their faith in and connection to the news. The public began to see the news as much more of a business and much less of a public service—precisely when the industry tied the compensation of newsroom leadership to those business demands.

Perhaps it made no difference. The fortress mindset that blocked innovation, and led more digitally sophisticated people into industries other than news, might have occurred anyway. But the move to make those who produced the news accountable not for the quality of their journalism but for the profit they helped generate came just at the moment the industry needed to reimagine its product, not protect its revenue.

That cycle of declining revenue caused by audiences shifting to new platforms, by the way, is about to occur in television news. As audiences "cut the cord" to cable and move fully to streaming, the ties to TV newscasts will be largely broken, a process that has already largely occurred with audiences under age forty.

Today, in the networked news environment, evaluating success in journalism is even more complicated than it was before. Many emerging media outlets do not expect to generate revenue at the outset as much as build audience and create a brand, which means getting attention, getting on the map. This pulls innovation toward the most ephemeral and meaningless forms of measurement, page views, and toward the practices that generate them, sensationalism, speed, extremist speech, sexual exploitation, and controversy. TikTok experiments are often likely to generate more page views than the work of the reporter whose enterprise has revealed critical problems with the city's water supply. The investigative reporter covering the CIA and the NSA, whose profile must be low to protect his often anonymous sources, is not likely to want to compete at promoting himself in social media with the film critic who appears on television, blogs avidly about movies and celebrities, and is highly visible on Twitter.

A number of people trying to contemplate the metrics of the Web have also begun to think that a better measure of journalism value should be "impact." In a morass of numbers, where page views, unique visitors, and time on site seem to create a muddle of conflicting opinions, with each rating company offering conflicting data, can the criteria of whether journalism has value—and will build brand—be measured by the good it does for democratic society? This new discussion is highly idealistic. And those pushing this argument are quick to admit that the task is complex and that any metrics are only proxies, just the beginning of the quest.

There are now pressures in a different and more positive direction. As the business model for journalism shifts away from advertising to revenue that comes directly from consumers (subscriptions, membership, donations), how value is measured on the Web is changing—for the better. Page views are becoming less important. Whether an article builds audience loyalty, was shared, or correlates to subscriptions and new subscribers, are becoming more important. We will discuss this more in a moment, but the shift toward consumer revenue is aligning the mission of journalism and the business of journalism in new and powerful ways, demonstrating for the first time in generations that what newspeople consider good journalism—deep, original reporting that breaks new ground and is well told—is also a path to sustainability.

Wherever this comes out, the struggle over how to assess the value of a work of journalism goes to the heart of an underlying issue: We established in the previous chapter the idea that journalists must seek out the truth. But what conditions are necessary for those who practice journalism to be able to get at the truth, and also to communicate that truth to the public in such a way that their citizens will believe it? The answer—the second principle of journalism—is loyalty.

No one questions that news organizations answer to many constituencies. Community institutions, local groups, parent companies, shareholders, advertisers, and many more interests must be considered and served by a successful news organization. Yet what newspaper publishers gradually came to understand in the nineteenth century—and what generations of news publishers across other technologies refined with significant hardship and later, under duress, began to forget in the twentieth—is that those who produce news in an organization (whether the ultimate motive is profit, prestige, community building, authority, audience reach, or some mix) must have one allegiance above all others. And this commitment forms the second element of journalism:

Journalism's first loyalty is to citizens.

A commitment to citizens is more than professional egoism. (Again, we use the term *citizen* not in a legal sense but in the sense of a member of the public in a civic context, regardless of legal or immigration status—citizen as opposed to consumer, audience member, or someone whose attention you are seeking so you can leverage it for money.) This commitment to the public is the implied covenant between someone producing a work of journalism and those who consume it. This commitment requires that the producer demonstrate that the work is honest. In some cases, this commitment involves citizens themselves to be transparent about who they are and why they are sharing or creating content. Whoever produces the news, it is an understanding about purpose that tells the audience that the movie reviews are straight, that the restaurant reviews are not influenced by who buys an ad, that the coverage is not self-interested or slanted on behalf of friends or underwriters or political allies—that the work is not a veil whose real purpose is something different than it is presented to be.

The notion that those who report the news are not obstructed from digging up and telling the truth—even at the expense of the owners' other financial interests, the funders' political agenda, or the sponsors' products—is a prerequisite of telling the news not only accurately but also persuasively. It is the basis for why citizens believe what they are seeing or hearing or reading. They know they are not being misled or lied to. In short, loyalty to the public is the most important asset any publisher that claims to produce journalism can possess. It is what makes the news content trustworthy. And that, in turn, is what makes the publication's advertising more credible. It makes the e-commerce transactions readers engage in on the site seem safer. It makes the events that generate revenue seem more worth attending. It also means that any new experiments to make advertising messages more compelling, whether they are called "native advertising" or "sponsored content" or something else, must be designed in a way that does not undermine the credibility of the news enterprise. All of this begins with the idea of loyalty to the citizen, to the concept that the public is being served rather than exploited—or, worse, deceived.

People who produce journalism have different loyalties than employees engaged in other kinds of work. They have a social obligation that at times overrides employers' or financial sponsors' immediate interests, and yet this obligation is the source of their employers' financial success.

Allegiance to citizens is the meaning of what we have come to call journalistic independence. As we will see, it is not a self-serving or disinterested form of independence. It is, rather, a form of civic commitment. This, too, is something people get confused by. The phrase *journalistic independence* has often been used as a synonym for other ideas, including disengagement, disinterestedness, detachment, or neutrality. These other terms, ironically, have tended to create a fuzzy understanding of what the intellectual independence of journalism really means. Professional journalists have contributed to their woes by passing that confusion on to the public, and citizens have understandably become skeptical, even cynical and angry, as a result.

That journalists' primary commitment is to the public is a deeply felt tradition among both journalists and citizens. In a survey on values by the Pew Research Center for the People & the Press and the Committee of Concerned Journalists that we designed when we began this work, more than 80 percent listed "making the reader/listener/viewer your first obligation" as a "core principle of journalism."[3] In open-ended, in-depth interviews with developmental psychologists, more than 70 percent of journalists similarly placed "audience" as their first loyalty, well above their employers, themselves, their profession, or even their families.[4] "I always worked for the people who turned on the television set," said Nick Clooney, the father of the actor George Clooney, who was a former newscaster in Los Angeles, Cincinnati, and elsewhere. "Always. Whenever I was having a discussion with a general manager or a member of the board of directors, my bottom line was always, 'I don't work for you. You're paying my check, and I'm very pleased. But the truth of the matter is, I don't work for you, and if it comes down to a question of loyalty, my loyalty will be to the person who turns on the television set.' . . . When I made that position clear, [it was] never questioned."[5]

This sense that the journalist has a loyalty beyond and above that to his or her employer is so deeply held that it manifests itself at the very best news organizations in dramatic, public rebellions of a sort inconceivable in other industries. In 2003, when reporters and editors at *The New York Times* felt that the two most powerful people in their newsroom—the executive editor and the managing editor—had violated this loyalty in condoning the conduct of and then trying to avoid responsibility for Jayson Blair, a reporter who plagiarized and fictionalized, the newsroom's anger effectively forced the publisher to remove these editors.[6]

The revolt was not unique. The *Los Angeles Times* had a similar response from its newsroom over a sweetheart deal with a local sports arena, which toppled the editor and publisher. *The Washington Post* backtracked on an ill-conceived plan for private dinners between lobbyists and lawmakers. (Various newsroom revolts in 2020 over race and default culture in journalism are examples as well and will be discussed more in chapter 4.)

Has the mission been weakened? Is a commitment to the public a luxury that the business of journalism can no longer afford now that it is struggling to turn a profit? The evidence was less clear a decade ago. As we enter the third decade of the digital age, the answer appears more promising. American newspapers once made about 25 percent of their revenue from subscriptions and 75 to 80 percent from advertising, and television news made virtually 100 percent from ads. Today, as advertising has declined and publications like *The New York Times* and *The Wall Street Journal* have shifted their focus to consumer revenue, those numbers have come close to reversing. (The same thing will happen to television news when it converts to streaming platforms in the next ten years. Consumers will have to choose it.) The question of whether smaller local publications can replicate the success with subscriptions that national publications are enjoying is unclear. But this model shows that at the national level at least, journalistic loyalty to audience and the business of journalism may be aligning in ways we have never seen before. It may even be the kernel of a journalistic resurgence.

The sense of loyalty to the public in the broadest sense—not to faction but to community—is also an impulse that the evidence suggests goes deep into the motivations of journalists across cultures. It is an almost spiritual sense of mission for journalists and one we have heard countless times from journalists we have met, from countless countries. "I see journalists all around the world as soldiers in an army of truth," Idriss Njutapvoul, a journalist from Cameroon who then wrote for the website Journal du Cameroun, told us in 2013.[7] Everyone in the room nodded. The same sentiment resonates years later in rooms of wildly diverse kinds of journalists. You can see it in organizations like the International Fact-Checking Network, in which hundreds of journalists who fact-check governments around the world share a listserv and meet annually in a different country each year. As Filipino journalist Maria Ressa has written, "In a battle for truth, in a battle for facts, journalism is activism."[8]

There is something in the act of trying to find out the truth of events, and relate them in a way that connects to the public, that binds those who gather the news. The similarities among journalists working in different countries, in different traditions and media, are far more important than their differences.

The public also expects this commitment from those who provide news, particularly professionals. For years, the Pew Research Center for the People & the Press has asked people whether they want news that reflects their point of view or news that reflects all sides. While trust, accuracy, and a host of other metrics have fallen, the numbers have never significantly wavered. More than six in ten Americans, roughly two-thirds (64 percent), in 2012 preferred news that was not aligned with a particular point of view.[9] In 2019, 83 percent of Americans considered one-sided news to be a "big problem" in social media, now the rival of local TV news as the dominant place where news is consumed.[10] More worrisome, in 2020 only about half of Americans (48 percent) had even a fair amount of confidence that journalists acted in the public interest, according to the Pew Research Center data, and only 9 percent had a great deal of confidence.[11]

Though news produced on behalf of the public rather than a party first began to emerge in the 1830s, it was not until the latter part of the nineteenth century that a large number of leading daily newspaper publishers began to replace political ideology with this new notion of editorial independence. The most famous declaration of intellectual and financial independence came in 1896, when a young publisher from Tennessee named Adolph Ochs bought the struggling *New York Times*. Ochs was convinced that a good many New Yorkers were tired of the tawdry sensationalism of William Randolph Hearst and Joseph Pulitzer and that they would welcome a more tasteful—and accurate—style of journalism. Under the simple headline BUSINESS ANNOUNCEMENT, Ochs published on his first day as owner the words that would become his legacy. It was his "earnest aim," he wrote, "to give the news impartially, without fear or favor, regardless of party, sect or interests involved."

Other publishers had made similar claims to independence, but as authors Alex Jones and Susan Tifft put it in their history of the *Times*, Ochs "actually believed what he wrote."[12] In that moment, as the yellow journalism era was waning, Ochs caught something in the zeitgeist. Newspapers across the country reprinted his statement in full. As the *Times* went on to become the most influential paper in New York and then the world, others followed the Ochs model, staking their business plan on the idea that putting the audience ahead of political and immediate financial interests was the best long-term financial strategy. After buying *The Washington Post* in 1933, Eugene Meyer crafted a set of principles that stated, among other items, "In pursuit of the truth, the newspaper shall be prepared to make sacrifices of its material fortunes, if such a course be necessary for the public good."[13]

As owners began trumpeting editorial independence in their marketing, journalists seized on it to upgrade their professionalism. A generation of early press critics emerged, such as Will Irwin, a former newspaper reporter and editor of *McClure's Magazine,* who in 1911 published a bracing fifteen-part series in *Collier's* chronicling in bold detail the abuses of the press. Seizing on the new technology of the lightbulb, Irwin called on a new public service role for journalism, "an electric light in a dark alley."[14] Newspaper editors in turn reacted to the rhetoric of their bosses and the rebukes of the critics, and they tried to professionalize as a group. Malcolm Bingay, a columnist for the *Detroit Free Press,* has traced this development to the genesis of the American Society of Newspaper Editors, the primary trade association for those who run America's newspaper newsrooms, now called the News Leaders Association. In 1912, a group of editors had gathered to preview the newly established Glacier National Park one summer night in the Rockies: "As they sat around a campfire they heard [Casper] Yost [editorial page editor of the *St. Louis Globe-Democrat*] discuss an idea which possessed him. His dream was the creation of an ethical organization of American newspaper editors. . . . Little Casper, tagged Arsenic and Old Lace by his contemporaries, might more appropriately be remembered as creating the modern concept of responsibility of the press."[15]

The organization's code of ethics placed editorial independence above all: "Independence: Freedom from all obligations except that of fidelity to the public interest is vital," it stated. "Promotion of any private interest contrary to the general welfare, for whatever reasons, is not compatible with honest journalism. . . . Partisanship, in editorial comment which knowingly departs from the truth, does violence to the best spirit of American journalism; in the news columns it is subversive of a fundamental principle of the profession."

In the commercial era, at the height of its monopoly over audience attention, news organizations were periodically tested to see how seriously they took these statements of public commitment. When one of its columnists, Foster Winans, was caught engaging in insider trading in the 1980s, *The Wall Street Journal* felt compelled to publicly reexamine and rewrite its code of conduct. "The central premise of this code is that Dow Jones' reputation for quality and for the independence and integrity of our publications is the heart and soul of our enterprise." This was a financial premise, not a purely journalistic one, just as it is for other news organizations. "Dow Jones cannot prosper if our customers cannot assume that . . . our analyses represent our best independent judgments rather than our preference, or those of our sources, advertisers or information providers."[16]

Newspapers became monopolies in the 1960s and tended to tone down such declarations, except generally—as was the case with the *Journal*—in moments of crisis. There was always the question, too, of which "public" the outlet was supposed to serve. As newspapers became focused on demographics, and newsrooms lacked diversity, the notion of public interest was constrained by who inhabited the newsroom and who bought the paper. (We will discuss race and newsroom culture at greater length in chapters 9 and 10, where we address comprehensiveness and conscience.) Television journalism, which is far more commercially competitive, continued to market itself in the public's name. Throughout the 1990s, for instance, at the very time of rising suspicions about the press, "On Your Side" and "Working 4 You" were two of the most popular slogans in local television news. Internal station research, as well as focus groups conducted by the Project for Excellence in Journalism, suggest they were also the most effective slogans.[17] These kinds of slogans in the twenty-first century have been adopted by the nonprofit journalism movement.

FROM INDEPENDENCE TO ISOLATION

Like so many professional ideas, editorial independence began over time in some quarters to harden into isolation. As journalists tried to honor and protect their carefully won independence from party and commercial pressures, they sometimes came to pursue independence for its own sake. Detachment from outside pressures could bleed into disengagement from the community. Flawed and simplistic notions of what objectivity meant—thinking that it implied some kind of blank slate consciousness rather than a method of reporting the news—added to the confusion.

In part, ironically, this was a result of journalism's becoming professionalized. As journalists became better educated and the press organized itself into chains, companies began to use their newspapers and TV stations as farm systems to train journalists in small markets for later assignments in bigger ones. By 1997, two-thirds of newspaper journalists, according to one survey, had not grown up in the community they were covering.[18] The majority of them felt "less involved" in their communities than other people who lived there, a trend up markedly from only eight years earlier.[19] Journalists were becoming transients—residents only of the community of journalism, a class of "news Bedouins."

A second factor in the growing isolation was a change in journalism's tone. After Vietnam and Watergate, and later the advent of twenty-four-hour cable news, journalism became noticeably more subjective and judgmental.[20] Coverage was focused more on mediating what public people were saying than simply reporting it. One notable study found that on television, for instance, the length of time for each candidate quote, or sound bite, on network nightly news programs during election years began to shrink, from an average of forty-three seconds in 1968 to a mere nine seconds in 1988.[21] At the same time, the stand-up closes, in which the reporters summarized the story, became longer and more judgmental.[22] In newspapers, as various studies have found, stories began to focus less on what candidates said and more on the tactical motives for their statements.[23] A study conducted by one of the authors of the front pages of *The New York Times* and *The Washington Post* found that the number of "straight news" accounts decreased, and the number of interpretative and analytical stories grew. Often, these analytical stories were not labeled or identified as analysis.[24] Phrases designed to pull back the curtain of public life, including terms like *spin doctors* and *photo op,* began to emerge in the press. In time this engendered a new jargon about the objectionable behavior of journalists—terms like *feeding frenzy* and *gotcha journalism.*

Even some journalists became concerned that too many of their colleagues had crossed a line from skepticism to cynicism, or even a kind of journalistic nihilism, the philosophy of believing in nothing. Phil Trounstine, then political editor of the *San Jose Mercury News*, was moved to write an essay on the subject for the Committee of Concerned Journalists. "It seems the worst thing a reporter or commentator can be accused of in certain circles is not inaccuracy or unfairness but credulousness."[25]

A key part of the problem, University of Pennsylvania professors Joseph N. Cappella and Kathleen Hall Jamieson argued in *Spiral of Cynicism: The Press and the Public Good,* was the growing journalistic focus on the motives of public officials rather than their actions. By shifting from the "what" of public life to the "why," they argued, journalists "interiorized" public life, making it about the psyche and self of politicians and also making it less about the outcomes of public policy that actually affected citizens. This cynical focus tended to further disconnect journalists from citizens.

Finally, creeping journalistic isolation coincided with a business strategy at many newspapers and later television stations to enhance profits by going after the most affluent or efficiently targeted audience rather than the largest. In television, that meant designing the news for women ages eighteen to forty-nine, who made most household buying decisions. In newspapers, that meant limiting circulation to the more affluent zip code areas, which cut the cost of production and distribution if papers were not printed and delivered to readers whom advertisers were not trying to reach. Targeting the news meant a news company theoretically could get more out of less—higher advertising rates with a smaller audience. It also meant the paper or TV station could ignore parts of the community in its coverage—usually poorer communities and communities of color—which also saved money. Not only was this a failure of journalistic responsibility. It has proven, as the advertising model has collapsed a generation later, to be a costly business mistake.

Isolation, in other words, became a business plan. After the Minneapolis *Star Tribune* dropped in circulation by 4 percent in three years in the mid-1990s, publisher Joel Kramer told *The New York Times*, "We are a healthier business because we are charging readers more and accepting a somewhat smaller circulation."[26] Perhaps nothing illustrated the thinking better than the story of a Bloomingdale's executive who told Rupert Murdoch that the store did not advertise in his *New York Post* because "your readers are our shoplifters." Though it was probably apocryphal, the story became an urban legend within the newspaper business because it so succinctly framed the industry's prevailing modus operandi.

A BACKLASH AGAINST DETACHMENT

Though few realized it at the time, there began in the 1990s what amounted to a reconsideration of the independence of the newsroom. The initial cause was that the business strategy of targeted demographics began to backfire. Making money without growing circulation had worked because the journalism business was such a monopoly that it had been able to take its advertising base for granted. By 1989, with transformative shifts in American retailing and communications technology, that situation began to unravel. Grocery and department stores—the financial backbone of newspapers—were being rocked by bankruptcy, mergers, and debt. The discount retailers that replaced them didn't buy newspaper advertising; since everything was discounted every day, they didn't need to announce their special sales. In the eleven years between 1980 and 1991, the amount of advertising space in big-city dailies dropped by 8 percent, according to Sanford C. Bernstein.[27] In 1991 alone, the industry suffered a 4.9 percent drop in retail advertising—the steepest one-year decline in history to that time. A similar dislocation was affecting television, where the audience began to slip away to pseudonews programs, cable reruns, and eventually the internet.

In short, the business of journalism was starting to suffer a structural decline—a decade before the internet. Managers began to refashion how they operated. For newspapers, that largely meant cutting costs and not investing more in the news to try to build more audiences. Between 1992 and 1997, a period of still-high profitability, smaller newspapers cut the percentage of their news budgets by 11 percent, and larger papers by 14 percent.[28]

As they cut costs, business managers also began to expect newspeople to begin justifying their journalism in terms of short-term financial gains. The businesspeople had market research and all kinds of new technology—minute-by-minute ratings data in TV, focus group data, even infrared glasses that would track reader eye movements across a page. The hope was that if journalists somehow used the technology more, they could do more to build circulation and not be so unpopular with the public.

A gulf began to form between businesspeople and newspeople—and worse, between reporters and news managers. Journalists saw the business side as challenging their journalistic independence and feared that the word *accountability*, as it was being used inside companies, was a code word for letting advertisers shape the news. The business side began to believe that if the newsroom was so intransigent about change, maybe the fabled detachment of the newsroom was the root of its stagnation. A culture war began to break out in the news business.

Journalists who made a case for the public interest obligation inside their companies could be labeled as naive, old-fashioned, and difficult. "If you mention 'public service' with corporate, you will be branded as an idealist, as an unrealistic person, and you will not be listened to," John Carroll told the authors. Carroll won a record thirteen Pulitzer Prizes in five years at the helm of the *Los Angeles Times* from 2000 to 2005 and then resigned after fighting with his corporate bosses at the Tribune Company in Chicago.

The real fight was less over values than over the nature of change. The advocates of change saw themselves as fighting for the industry's survival. The resisters saw themselves defending a professional ethic that was the basis of the industry's success.

Regardless of the side you were on, some business practices were put into the newsroom that ran counter to everyone's best interests. One of the most basic techniques to create more newsroom accountability was the incentive program called Management by Objectives, or MBO, that we described at the beginning of this chapter. The concept, pioneered in the 1950s by management guru Peter F. Drucker, was simple: set goals and attach rewards for achieving them, and a company can create a coherent system for both coordinating and monitoring what its executives are doing. The problem was, the industry was creating the wrong incentives for its newsroom leaders. Too often, the goal wasn't quality or innovation. It was short-term profitability.

By the early part of the new century, the vast majority of news executives in TV and print worked under an MBO program.[29] A good many of these programs were structured in a way that distorted and undermined the role of journalists or the needs of communities. In a survey by the State of the American Newspaper Project in 1998, 71 percent of editors said their companies managed by objectives. Of those that did, half said they got 20 to 50 percent of their income from the programs. And the majority of these editors said that more than half of their bonus was tied to their paper's financial performance.

Tying a journalist's income to his or her organization's financial performance during the advertising era changed the journalist's allegiance. Companies were explicitly saying that a good portion of the journalist's loyalty must be to the corporate parent and to shareholders—ahead of readers, listeners, or viewers—just when journalism needed to invest in innovation to face the coming disruption of the Web. What if an advertiser made it clear that more income would come if the coverage of an issue began to ease off, or if a certain reporter was fired or moved off a beat? When has an advertiser ever urged more coverage of business corruption or price-fixing? How do you tell the news without fear or favor when you are explaining to the editor that one of his or her key goals is making money this quarter? Editors still would resist. But MBOs tied to the bottom line divided that loyalty.

Sandra Rowe, while editor of Portland's *Oregonian*, captured the problem well. She said it was fine to teach your journalists about business. The question was, as she put it, What religion are your journalists practicing? Are they journalists who understand business? Or are they businesspeople who understand journalism? The distinction is a matter of loyalty. Is the corporate culture based on the belief that devotion to serving the citizens will lead to solvency? Or is the corporate culture based on a dedication to maximizing profit, most of which comes from advertising revenue, even at the expense of what the citizens require?

In retrospect, MBO efforts at creating accountability in the newsroom can be seen as too simplistic—and too imitative of other industries. They failed to recognize how the news business, particularly in the advertising era, was different. And they incentivized the news industry to the wrong things at just the wrong moment on the eve of disruption. The incentives of newsroom managers should have been tied to innovation, to growing their audience on new platforms, to new ways of storytelling, to reaching younger and underserved audiences, not to profit. But it is easier to see that now. And the shift toward consumer revenue that is transforming the news industry today has meant that, at least for that portion of a news operation's funding that is coming directly from the public, the separation between news and revenue is disappearing. Creating better journalism of higher value may be the path to sustainability, not a threat to profit.

ARE CITIZENS CUSTOMERS?

Bringing business accountability to the newsroom brought the language of business as well. In some cases this meant applying the language of marketing to news, with readers and viewers becoming "customers," and with understanding them becoming "marketing."[30]

Few would argue that journalists shouldn't market the services they offer the public, but precision in language matters, especially in times of change. Providing news in a commercial setting is far more complex than simply delivering eyeballs to advertisers—a fact that is more obvious as the financing of news shifts toward consumers paying for content online. The essential product of journalism is trust—the deeply felt sense that the content one receives is honest, intelligent, and useful to helping the user live his or her life. Key to that trust is the sense that the editorial decisions, however flawed, are made independent of revenue, politics, or other hidden considerations, that what one is encountering is not unacknowledged product placement or commercial or political manipulation.

People who provide news build a relationship with their audience based on a mix of qualities that the audience senses—a combination of values, judgment, authority, intellect, experience, courage, and commitment to the community. Providing this service creates a bond with the public.

In the old advertising model, the news enterprise then rented its bond with the public to sellers of goods and services that wanted to reach those members of the public. In short, the business relationship of journalism in the era dominated by advertising was different from traditional consumer marketing. And in some important ways it was also more complex. It was a triangle, with the news provider forming one line, the public another, and those trying to reach the public to sell them goods and services the third. In this triangle, the public was dominant—they formed the longer line of the triangle—even though the revenue they provided was historically less than that provided by advertisers. Even entrepreneurial business magnates such as Henry Luce understood this relationship. "If we have to be subsidized by anybody, we think that the advertiser presents extremely interesting possibilities," he told top aides in 1938. His goal was not to compromise "more than a small fraction of our journalistic soul."[31] Luce's boast was that "there is not an advertiser in America who does not realize that Time Inc. is cussedly independent." Key to Luce's model was to have so many advertisers that no one advertiser could exercise too much leverage.

THE WALL

If journalists are committed to the citizen first, what about the rest of the people who work in news companies—the ad salespeople, the marketing department, the circulation department at newspapers, the publishers or division presidents, the CEO, the shareholders, charitable funders, board members? What should citizens expect of them? What should their relationship be to the independence of the news products? The answer to that is changing, just as the economic model for news is changing.

Traditionally, journalists in the twentieth century often talked about there being a firewall between the news and the business sides of news companies. Editors at Time Inc. often praised Henry Luce's assertion of a separation in their company between church (news) and state (the business side). Robert McCormick, the famous and notorious publisher of the *Chicago Tribune*, early in the twentieth century created two separate banks of elevators inside his ornate Tribune Tower overlooking the Chicago River. He didn't want his advertising salesmen even to ride with his reporters.

Unfortunately, that notion of the journalist cloistered behind some wall in service to the audience while everyone else was committed freely to profit was a misguided metaphor. First, it encouraged an isolation from and willful ignorance about business among newspeople that made them vulnerable to being outmaneuvered, as we have described. Second, if the two sides of a news-providing organization are really working at cross-purposes, the journalism tends to be what gets corrupted.

The scandal involving the *Los Angeles Times* and the STAPLES Center sports arena in 2005 revealed how weak the wall metaphor really was. The paper arranged to share profits with arena owners in exchange for help selling ads. The arena owners sent stern letters to their subcontractors insisting that ads be bought. The stories assigned and written at the paper for the magazine about the arena were all positive. The newsroom was not told of the arrangement. The wall, in other words, was kept intact. When the arrangement was discovered, both reporters and readers were outraged.

More than two hundred letters, emails, faxes, and phone messages poured onto the desk of reader representative Narda Zacchino in less than a week. When Sharon Waxman of *The Washington Post* went to interview Zacchino, she saw a log of phone messages lying on the desk, the main ideas from each one highlighted with a yellow marker. "Basically, readers are saying that this shakes their faith, their trust in the paper," Zacchino told Waxman. "People are questioning a lot of things. They are asking whether advertisers have influence in our stories. Questioning our integrity. What concerns me are these questions over whether our reporting is honest: 'Does such and such corporation have a deal with you?'"

Eventually, L.A. *Times* media reporter David Shaw would discover a growing pattern by *Times* management of exploiting the readership on behalf of its advertisers, all without letting the newsroom know. All of this had occurred after a former cereal company executive named Mark Willes, with little background and a shallow understanding of the economics of journalism, took over the Times Mirror Company that owned the paper. The mythical wall, in other words, did little to protect anyone. The business side was selling the newsroom out and had enough power to do so without the newsroom knowing.

Tensions between the newsroom and the business side of news companies had been building for years. In retrospect, the simmering predigital war over whether good journalism was good business was grounded in a question about the future. Were legacy media operations such as print newspapers or broadcast television "mature industries" that could no longer grow their audiences? If so, then it made sense to manage costs and pay more attention to advertisers. But that approach also tacitly acknowledged inevitable decline. Such operators were not saving newspapers. They were harvesting them—a preview of the behavior of many hedge fund owners a few years later. Or were legacy news organizations still businesses that, if they adapted, could continue to reach new audiences in new ways, with new content and products? Wall Street had largely decided these media could not grow. And on balance it rewarded media companies that got tough with costs and reduced inefficiency.

That vision of the future—that most traditional media were mature industries—became a self-fulfilling prophecy. Rather than invest in R&D to figure out new ways to deliver quality and reach audiences, the newspaper industry focused heavily on managing costs on the one hand and raising the price of its advertising on the other, making the argument that in a fragmented news environment, advertising had become a singular way to reach elite audiences. The industry did not change its business model as much as it changed its argument about why it was a good business. So, as its foundation weakened, the industry raised prices. Newspaper revenues reached their peak in 2005, after all of the structural elements that would shrink the industry were well in place.[32]

As the business side began tightening its grip, a series of academic studies continued to find evidence the strategy was misguided, identifying a strong correlation between financial investment in the newsroom and improvement in the bottom line. Supporting news gathering, the studies found, would create quality journalism, which in turn would drive up circulation. But it would also have another financial benefit.

Econometric modeling by Esther Thorson at the University of Missouri established that more investment in news, which presumably translated into more quality, was also correlated with newspapers being able to charge more for advertising. The argument was never popular in boardrooms, however, where most of the debate occurred. For years this dispute was little but background noise for journalists and their public. Some scholars, such as Phil Meyer at the University of North Carolina, argued that the industry was committing suicide, placing itself on the path toward a death spiral of cuts to the product to maintain high profit margins. The cuts would only drive away more readers who had other choices for news, which in turn would lead to further cutbacks. It was, whether conscious or not, a strategy of liquidating the industry.

The news industry was barely aware of the research. At the dawn of the digital disruption, instead of investing in digital innovation, the newspaper industry focused on managing costs to protect profit margins. And the business began to quickly erode.

The issue wasn't so much loss of audience. Between 2006 and 2012, for instance, daily print newspaper circulation in the United States fell 17 percent and Sunday circulation 16 percent, according to data from the Newspaper Association of America. Many of those lost print readers, however, had simply migrated to the Web version of the same papers, not abandoned the content. Total newspaper readership, which included online readers, held relatively steady. According to data from Scarborough Research, between 2007 and 2016, the percentage of American adults who read newspaper content in print or online dropped a few percentage points, from 74 percent in 2007 to 69 percent in 2016.[33]

But the financial side of the industry suffered far more. Newspaper advertising revenue between 2006 and 2018 fell more than 70 percent, roughly triple the rate of print readers, and about five times the rate of total readership. The problem, to be precise, was that advertising dollars failed to migrate to the Web along with readers. There were a variety of reasons, among them the fact that people don't respond well to pop-up and banner ads, and that there is no scarcity of websites, so the cost of advertising fell.[34]

The revenue losses, in turn, had a devastating effect on the newsgathering power at many news organizations. From 2006 to 2018, the reporting and editing ranks of newspapers fell by 50 percent, and by more at many major metropolitan newspapers, which were hit hardest financially, according to estimates by the Pew Research Center.[35]

The news divisions of the three major broadcast networks were cut by more than half from the 1980s, in the wake of the advent of cable. While some of the journalists who left legacy media moved to alternative news operations, most left the profession or moved to public relations, think tanks, or other fields. An analysis of Census Bureau data has found that the ratio of public relations workers to journalists grew from 1.2 to 1 in 1980 to the point in 2018 that public relations professionals outnumbered journalists by 6 to 1.[36]

Broadcast television news, the dominant news platform of the late twentieth century, had its own version of loss of confidence even earlier. In the 1990s, as it began to feel the impact of cable news and syndicated infotainment programming, network evening newscasts became increasingly focused on tabloid crime and celebrity. The number one topic on network evening newscasts for the decade was crime, even though crime rates nationally were plummeting during the period. Making their newscasts more entertaining became the focus of broadcasters, rather than investing in new platforms such as cable and later online platforms. The one exception at the time was NBC, whose news division has thrived largely because of revenue from its cable news operations, particularly CNBC, and which amortizes its healthier news division across all its platforms.

In short, the long decline that would be accelerated by the internet was already in place twenty years ago. In 2000, Peter C. Goldmark Jr., then chairman and chief executive of the *International Herald Tribune,* suggested in a meeting at the Aspen Institute that corporations needed to do something "to cement the value of the journalistic enterprise within these huge corporate empires. . . . Every CEO understands they have a fiduciary obligation to their shareholders. In terms of journalism, I put more faith in corporate leadership that understands that they have an equally solemn fiduciary responsibility arising from their ownership of a news organization—that they hold a public trust."[37]

Goldmark offered four suggestions: have the CEO meet annually with those of similar organizations to assess the journalistic health of their companies; designate a member of the board of directors to assume special responsibility for protecting the independence of the news organization; invite an annual review or audit of the independence and vigor of the company's news function; jointly, with similar companies, fund an independent council to track, promote, examine, and defend the independence of the press.

A few years later, when the economic impact of the Web was clear, the battle at the top of many legacy media companies between the idealists and the accountants was over. The idealists had lost. Shrinking revenue made notions of focusing on audience and quality seem an unaffordable vanity to many business managers—at just the moment that consumers were about to have more power to make decisions over where and how they wanted to get news.

An executive at one of the three broadcast networks told senior staff in a meeting in 2005, "The ethical anvil has been lifted," meaning the producers could dispense with traditional notions of journalistic propriety.[38] The most cogent explanation for why journalism in the public interest had lost leverage was probably offered by Polk Laffoon IV, the corporate spokesman of Knight Ridder, a company that had managed itself to the point that it was about to vanish altogether: "I wish there were an identifiable and strong correlation between quality journalism . . . and newspaper sales," he said. "It isn't . . . that simple."[39]

There were some notable exceptions to the loss of the faith in quality journalism as a business proposition. To a large degree, they were in organizations where there was no wall, where the business side embraced the values of the newsroom as the soul of the operation. In these companies, independent public interest journalism was the product the company was selling, with profit as a predictable by-product that was strategically and necessarily required for long-term health.

In 2002, the Guardian Media Group in the United Kingdom responded to the challenge when it launched a major effort in transparency, creating an annual audit called "Living Our Values." The purpose of the independently produced audit was to make clear to readers the special nature of the relationship between a commercial news organization and citizens. The annual audit would report to the public in documented detail on the social and ethical behavior of the company and its promise to produce a "liberal, progressive, internationalist newspaper," as well as its behavior as a commercial business in such areas as its relationships with its employees, its business partners, and other institutions in the community and the world. *The Guardian* audit would describe how the values shared by the business and the news sides combined to serve a public interest.

Though it had ups and downs, *The Guardian* proved to be among the more nimble early responders to new technology and the ability to turn audience into a community and even part of the eyes and ears of the staff. It embraced data journalism—or the inclusion of large databases as a new form of reporting—more rapidly than most legacy media. It was early to employ social media tools, such as Twitter and Facebook, to collaborate and gather information from its community of readers, rather than just to market its traditional content to them.

Despite ups and downs of its own, *The New York Times* also generally has maintained a commitment to quality journalism, best reflected by the flagship newspaper. Analysts even expressed a worry that the Times Company was too focused on newspapers and did not look to diversify its revenue by investing in other products. "We are a company committed to journalism," Arthur Sulzberger Jr., the company chairman and publisher of *The New York Times*, told Ken Auletta of *The New Yorker* in 2005. "That is our core strength. That is our hedgehog. We are not in the education or cooking business. You are going to see us make journalism investments."[40] The *Times*'s subsequent CEO, Mark Thompson, would echo the same sentiments numerous times, often saying that he, in effect, worked for the editor of the paper, not the other way around. But it became increasingly clear that meant adhering to journalism values, not producing the same old journalism. The product would need to change dramatically. The values were the bedrock. Listen to Thompson, for instance, in 2014, when the notion of being a cooking company that Arthur Sulzberger had dismissed in 2005 was now an important part of *Times* journalism. "Cooking has successfully built on many of our learnings with our other new products this year. It's evidence of the approach we're taking to digital product development: grounded in The Times's great strengths in journalism and design, but increasingly user-centric and data-driven, unashamedly experimental and willing to adapt."[41]

To a significant extent, the *Times* was scorned when it decided to charge for online content in April 2011. (Until then, only financial newspapers purchased for business reasons had succeeded in charging for content.) Yet the *Times* proved doubters wrong. By 2013, the paper had roughly seven hundred thousand digital-only subscribers, and by November 2020 the company had exceeded six million digital-only paid subscribers to its apps and news, close to ten times the number of its print subscribers.[42]

The *Times* also shifted its economic model. Whereas in 2011 it made roughly 80 percent of its revenue from advertising, by 2020 it had inverted that; close to two-thirds of its revenue came from subscriptions.[43]

Some doubters continued to insist that the *Times* was unique, a national paper of such distinct quality that it could charge when others couldn't. The doubters were wrong about this, too. By 2016, 78 percent of US papers with a circulation of fifty thousand or more sold digital subscriptions.[44] By 2019, an international study found, 69 percent of larger papers worldwide were doing so.[45]

In 2020, another argument against the *Times* began to surface, promoted incoherently in part by the *Times*'s own media writer, Ben Smith, that the *Times*'s success was helping to weaken local news institutions around the country because it was diverting potential local subscribers to its national publication. That argument, too, is specious.

The shift from advertising to subscription revenue that the *Times* pioneered with the meter in 2011 also seeded the ground for a series of other subtle but in many ways profound shifts in how we have come to understand journalism in the digital age. In an advertising-dominated model, the page view is the most important metric of registering audience "engagement"—or how many people are reading. Once your revenue moves to subscribers, other metrics become relatively more important. How many visits did a person make in a month? How long did that person read something? Did he or she share it with friends? Did the same person visit on multiple devices? Did the person subscribe to the newsletter or ask for news alerts?

When you begin to look at audiences more holistically in this way, you begin to see a different kind of interaction with news online. Subscribers read different kinds of stories. They read them longer. They like opinion columns and stories about government. Once you move past examining page views, a series of long-held notions about the Web— including the idea that no one reads anything for very long, that people are largely interested in listicles and stories about celebrity and what child movie actors look like when grown up, evaporate. And if you have someone's email, so you can track him or her across different devices (measuring people, not just so-called unique visitors), you discover you have a smaller but a much more loyal audience than page views alone can tell you.

The move that began in 2011 to charging people for content online also had other impacts. The newsroom shifted from being a cost center—something that took money but brought nothing in—to being a revenue generator—where smart, data-driven decision-making about what created subscribers was an investment that more than paid for itself. Some newspapers began to reinvest some resources back into editorial quality. The Gannett Company, one of the pioneers, under former CEO Al Neuharth, of creating in the late twentieth century an expectation of quarterly profit growth, invested tens of millions of dollars in new news-gathering resources after 2011. While cutbacks were soon to come again, newsrooms this time were more insulated relative to other parts of the publications. The line of reasoning was one the fallen idealists had argued and lost with years earlier: If you are going to charge people a fair price for the content, the content has to improve. Quality was a business strategy after all. The move to charging for digital content, pioneered for general audiences at the *Times*, represented a significant shift back toward the concept that the core of the business of media was that journalism must deliver value to the audience—rather than that the audience was something to be leveraged to advertisers. To grow, journalism had to change and the audience had to grow. The advocates of that financial innovation were those, it turned out, who did not stop believing in the journalism.

The metaphor of the wall was always a myth—and in the end it failed journalists instead of protecting them. Top news managers and top business managers always conversed. The so-called wall was never anything more than an easy way to assure readers that journalists were independent, with the added benefit of avoiding contact at lower levels so that managers would not have to officiate the conflicts.

FIVE KEYS TO INDEPENDENCE

In reality, other characteristics historically have defined the culture of organizations where the news could be trusted, and those characteristics have had more to do with journalistic commitment at the top than with insulation at the bottom. We identify five keys to a news company or organization maintaining its commitment to citizens:

1 • THE OWNER MUST BE COMMITTED TO CITIZENS FIRST

Rather than the newsroom being cloistered from the rest of the organization, journalism works best when both sides are committed to the values of honest independent news, not one side to business or ideology or some other cause and the other to public service. History suggests that this works only when the owner of the operation believes deeply in these core journalistic values.

Even some of the so-called defenders of the wall were, in reality, practitioners of this joint philosophy, with journalism being the predominant value. Contrary to legend, there is scant evidence that Henry Luce actually talked about church and state, according to historian Tom Leonard. Rather, Luce believed the whole company needed to be "cussedly independent."

As he looked back on his own career, Tom Johnson, former publisher of the *Los Angeles Times* and then president of CNN, came to the same conclusion as Luce had a generation earlier, and Ochs a generation before that:

> Media owners, or in the case of publicly traded companies, the board-elected CEO, ultimately decide the quality of the news produced by or televised by their news departments. It is they who most often select, hire, fire, and promote the editors, and publishers, top general managers, news directors, and managing editors—the journalists—who run

their newsrooms. . . . Owners determine newsroom budgets, and the amount of time and space allotted to news versus advertising. They set the standards of quality by the quality of the people they choose and the news policies they embrace. Owners decide how much profit they should produce from their media properties. Owners decide what quality levels they are willing to support by how well or how poorly they pay their journalists.[46]

The historical protection for journalism, the benevolent patriarch, has largely disappeared, although there are some exceptions. Now, in the wake of the disruption of the Web, the corporation culture has given up significant ground to private equity firms, billionaire private owners, and a small but growing movement toward nonprofit or public benefit corporations. Glen Taylor in Minneapolis, Jeff Bezos in Washington, D.C., Patrick Soon-Shiong in Los Angeles, and John Henry in Boston appear to be operators who want to invest in the newsroom and do not generally own the paper to advance personal agendas. On the other hand, the hedge fund called Alden Global Capital, which by 2020 had bought through its MediaNews Group a major stake in some one hundred newspapers, is widely viewed as "the grim reaper" of the newspaper industry, in the words of *Vanity Fair,* operating its papers so that it can harvest profits and by all evidence pillaging them and their communities in the worst way.[47] Some nonprofits, such as the Lenfest Institute for Journalism, which owns *The Philadelphia Inquirer,* have provided some stability where there was managerial chaos on the business side of some news enterprises. Others, such as at the *Tampa Bay Times* (owned technically by the Poynter Institute), have until recently performed below the mean in adapting to the Web and innovating online. Being a publicly traded corporation, with a two-tier stock system, has been a success at *The New York Times.* It was a failure at the Times Mirror Company, which gave way to the Tribune Company, which sold to a succession of charlatan or questionable owners who now may have given way to the hedge fund Alden.

It has become popular to imagine that nonprofit ownership might be the path to the future. That is naive and wishful thinking. History, past and present, is abundantly clear: What matters are the values of the owner, not the structure of ownership. Nonprofits can be enlightened or they can be insulated and naive or driven by political motives, sometimes in ways well-meaning nonprofits do not even recognize. Corporations can be smart or gluttonous. Billionaires can be arrogant and political or they can be interested in community and in innovating a way to a new future. The assumption that one kind of owner is more committed to putting citizens first isn't borne out by the facts.

2 • HIRE BUSINESS MANAGERS WHO ALSO PUT CITIZENS FIRST

While the owner is the ultimate determiner of an institution's values, successful businesspeople also talk about hiring managers who share the mission, even if selling ads or building circulation is a different path from producing stories. Robert Dechard, chairman and chief executive of A. H. Belo, the owner of *The Dallas Morning News,* has said that commitment and understanding should flow down the organization. "It comes down to selecting people who have good news judgment and experience in journalism and are sensitive to potential conflicts. I would prefer to have a person with that sound judgment."[48]

3 • JOURNALISTS HAVE THE FINAL SAY OVER NEWS

As news organizations experiment with new revenue models, those in charge of news have an even larger role to play. They must guard the editorial integrity of the operations and protect the integrity of the commercial brand. Today they also have a central role in understanding the audience and driving the product that drives most of the revenue— which puts them at the heart of the business strategy. In all of these roles they must raise their hand and speak out when they think an organization is crossing the line—to make either economic decisions that are self-destructive or editorial decisions that are self-defeating because they will undermine a brand's quality, which is the key to winning subscribers. A decade ago, *The Washington Post*'s then publisher and then editor both earned early black eyes when the paper tried to generate revenue by hosting private dinners that served no news-making value, to provide access to lawmakers. In 2020, the editor of *The Salt Lake Tribune,* Jennifer Napier-Pearce, resigned abruptly, reportedly after chairman and publisher Paul Huntsman tried to influence the paper's coverage of the governor's race involving his brother, Jon Huntsman Jr.[49] Think of it this way: The leader of the newsroom in a modern news operation is, in effect, the protector of the brand.

4 • SET AND COMMUNICATE CLEAR STANDARDS INTERNALLY

Even if owners share the journalistic mission, and hire managers and editors who agree, those standards must be clearly articulated down the ranks to create an open atmosphere in which the businesspeople and newspeople, at least at certain levels, can talk to make sure they understand and appreciate one another's role. Particularly in an era when the editing process has been shortened, when the first version of a story might see little or no editing, when tweets are controlled by individual reporters, and when decision-making time has become truncated to seconds, it has become more critical than in the past that those who lead newsrooms articulate a clear vision and standards they want reporters to follow.

Marty Baron at *The Washington Post* has been a model for this in public speeches about the standards he sets, the importance of verification, and the maintaining of standards when covering challenging public figures such as Donald Trump. His contemporary at *The New York Times*, Dean Baquet, has become increasingly vocal and transparent as well, doing long interviews on philosophical questions like objectivity and being open about tribulations at the institution during the challenges of 2020.

5 • COMMUNICATE CLEAR STANDARDS TO THE PUBLIC AS WELL

The final key is to be clear with audiences—clearer than in the past—about how news organizations operate. Evan Smith, the founder and editor of the Texas Tribune media organization, believes so passionately in transparency that he publishes his operation's internal strategic plan. Richard Tofel, the head of ProPublica, produces a regular email for readers that provides insights about decisions at the investigative website. The public radio station KPCC in Southern California has created a space on the website Medium dedicated to discussing its many experiments to serve its community.

The movement toward more explanation gained force not initially to explain radical changes with technology but in response to the growing credibility crisis about news that had begun a generation earlier. In his address to the American Society of Newspaper Editors in 1999, Edward Seaton, the president of that group and editor of *The Mercury* in Manhattan, Kansas, advised that the best way for newspapers to rebuild trust and credibility was to "explain yourself. . . . As editors, we have to lead. We have to state our values. When we have standards, we have something that we can explain to the public and our staffs, something that everyone can hear and understand. We must do much more and better than we have. Our emphasis has to be on serving citizens, not our bottom line or technology."[50]

Some television stations have taken similar approaches. When he was news director at KGUN-TV in Tucson, the late Forrest Carr created and repeatedly broadcast a "Viewers' Bill of Rights" that outlined precisely what citizens in Tucson should expect from his station and his people.

The list of seven rights included such items as supporting the public's right to know (the station "asks tough questions and conducts investigations"), the right to ethical news gathering (the station will live up to the ethics code of the Society of Professional Journalists), and the right to solution-oriented journalism (the station will attempt to find or spotlight solutions, not just focus on problems).

The language of a bill of rights may strike some as corny. But focus groups conducted by the Project for Excellence in Journalism in Tucson around the time of the station's introduction of the program suggested that it connected with people. "It might go back to the station having some guidelines, something called ethics in reporting," said one man.

The station's share of the Tucson television audience continued a steady climb. Carr said the project had another benefit: making the values of the organization clear to those who worked there. Nothing he had ever done, Carr would say, helped him more in improving the culture of his own newsroom.

There is evidence that the "bill of rights" idea still has some resonance today. In June of 2013, the Louisville, Kentucky, Fox affiliate WDRB rolled out a "Contract with Our Viewers." The statement contained ten principles intended to convey its commitment to a set of core journalistic values and to the audience. The contract contained promises not to "hype our product," to "strive to present reporting that is bias free," and to use the term *breaking news* judiciously, not as a marketing gimmick. The contract promised not to take the viewer's time for granted.[51]

Whatever approach a news organization takes, the question of allegiance remains pivotal and is usually ignored or misunderstood. The reason it is so vital, however, is precisely that the press has become so unpopular. What is often missed in considering the decline in public trust of the press is that, at bottom, this credibility crisis is about motive. As citizens, we do not expect perfection of our journalists—or even a journalism with every word spelled correctly. The problem is more fundamental.

Journalists like to think of themselves as the people's surrogates, covering society's waterfront in the public interest. Increasingly, however, the public doesn't believe them. People see sensationalism and exploitation, and they sense that journalists are in it for a buck, personal fame, or, perhaps worse, a kind of perverse joy in unhappiness. When it was revealed that Bob Woodward had a practice of interviewing administration officials for his books and not letting much of the information obtained be part of the immediate record, readers challenged his allegiance. Was he an author working for himself or was he a *Washington Post* reporter working for the public? Some readers did not trust Woodward to decide whether something needed to be exposed immediately or could wait a year or two to make it into a book. The controversy, which has dogged Woodward for years, probably gained its most intense level of scrutiny in 2020 when critics wondered why he had not revealed until late summer that he had Donald Trump on tape in February acknowledging that the coronavirus was far more deadly and contagious than he was admitting publicly.

To reconnect people with the news, and through the news to the larger world, journalism must reestablish the allegiance to citizens that the news industry has mistakenly helped to subvert. Yet even this, ultimately, will not be enough. Truth and loyalty to citizens are only the first two steps in making journalism work. The next step is just as important: the method that journalists use to approach the truth and how they convey that method to citizens.

4

JOURNALISM OF VERIFICATION

s he sat down to write, the Greek correspondent wanted to convince his audience that it could trust him. He was not writing an official version of the war, he wanted people to know, or a hasty one. He was striving for something more independent, more reliable, more lasting. As he had gone about his reporting, he had been mindful of the way memory, perspective, and politics blur recollection. He had double-checked his facts.

To convey all this, he decided to explain the methods of his reporting right at the beginning of his story. This is the dedication to the methodology of truth that Thucydides drafted in the fifth century B.C., in the introduction to his account of the Peloponnesian War:

> With regard to my factual reporting of events . . . I have made it a principle not to write down the first story that came my way, and not even to be guided by my own general impressions; either I was present myself at the events which I have described or else heard of them from eye-witnesses whose reports I have checked with as much thoroughness as possible. Not that even so the truth was easy to discover: different eyewitnesses gave different accounts of the same events, speaking out of partiality for one side or the other, or else from imperfect memories.[1]

Why does this passage feel so contemporary more than two thousand years after it was written? Because it speaks to the heart of the task of nonfiction: How do you sift through the rumors, the gossip, the failed memories, the manipulative agendas, and try to capture something as accurately as possible, subject to revision in light of new information and perspective? How do you overcome your own limits of perception, your own biases and experience, and come to an account that more people will recognize as reliable? Strip away all the debate about journalism, all the differences among media or between one age and another. These are the real questions faced daily by those who try to gather news, understand it, and convey it to others.

While not following any standardized code, everyone who produces what is viewed as news, or even the broader range of nonfiction, operates by relying on methods of testing and providing information—his or her own individual discipline of verification. Practices such as seeking multiple witnesses to an event, disclosing as much as possible about sources, and asking many sides for comment are, in effect, tools for the discipline of verification, which is the essential process of arriving as nearly as possible at the truth of the matter at hand. These methods may be intensely personal and idiosyncratic: Writer Rick Meyer at the *Los Angeles Times* would splice his facts and interviews into note card–like snippets and organize them on his office floor. Or the methods may be institutionalized, like the fact-checking department of *The New Yorker*. But by whatever name, in whatever medium, these habits and methods underlie the third principle of journalism:

The essence of journalism is a discipline of verification.

In the end, the discipline of verification is what separates journalism from entertainment, propaganda, fiction, or art. Entertainment—or its cousin "infotainment"—focuses on what is most diverting. Propaganda selects facts or invents them to serve the real purpose: persuasion and manipulation. Fiction invents scenarios to get at a more personal impression of what it calls truth.

Journalism alone is focused on the process employed to get what happened down right. This is true whether it is the work of a network TV news division or the work of a lone citizen posting eyewitness accounts on social media, and it is the first criterion by which any work claimed as journalism should be judged for competence.

Those who produce journalism often fail to connect their deeply held feelings about craft to the larger philosophical questions about journalism's role. They know how to check a story even if they can't always articulate the role that checking a story plays in society. But verifying facts resides in the central function of journalism. As Walter Lippmann put it in 1920, "There can be no liberty for a community which lacks the information by which to detect lies."[2]

This is why journalists often become so upset with people from other media, such as dramatists or filmmakers, when they tell stories of real-life events. In 2012, the public radio program *This American Life* "retracted" a program it had aired about manufacturing in China after it discovered that the author of the program, dramatist Mike Daisey, had blended names and incidents, both from his own visits to China and from accounts by others. "We're retracting the story," Ira Glass, the host and executive producer of *This American Life*, said in a statement, "because we can't vouch for its truth."[3]

Daisey himself had no such doubts. "I stand by my work," he said in his own statement. "My show is a theatrical piece. . . . It uses a combination of fact, memoir, and dramatic license to tell its story, and I believe it does so with integrity. Certainly, the comprehensive investigations undertaken by the *New York Times* and a number of labor rights groups to document conditions in electronics manufacturing would seem to bear this out." But, he added, "What I do is not journalism."[4]

The Daisey/*This American Life* example is only one in a long line of collisions over the meaning of truth between journalists and those in other forms of communication. *60 Minutes* correspondent Mike Wallace was livid in 1999 when the movie *The Insider* put invented words in his mouth and altered the time frame to suggest that he was worried about his "legacy" when he caved in to the tobacco industry on a story. "Have you ever heard me invoke the word *legacy*? That is utter bullshit . . . and I'm offended."[5] The film's director, Michael Mann, countered that though things were changed to make the story more dramatic, the film was "basically accurate" to some larger definition of truthfulness, given that Wallace had indeed caved.

The antagonists in these two cases were speaking different languages. To Mann and Daisey, truth was found in the larger contours of the story, not in the minutiae of every fact. To Glass and Wallace, truth could never be detached from an accurate account of the details. Both arguments may be defensible. But the journalistic process of verification must take both of them into account. It must both get the facts right and report the truth.

Since the moment news became a commodity that was instantly and continuously available in almost unlimited outlets, the process of verification—the beating heart of credible journalism in the public interest—has come under new pressure. There are two principal sources of this pressure. The first is the temptation to publish immediately because something can always be corrected later. The second is the impulse to publish news simply because it's already "out there" and being talked about in the new, networked-media system.

The problem was made more complex in the new reality created by the war against terrorism that was declared in the aftermath of September 11. This new reality conflicted with the popular notion of "we media" culture, which suggested that since citizens could communicate with one another at will, they could be closer to real truth and more accurate information.

No doubt they can communicate more easily. Whether or not the end result sustains a Journalism of Verification depends on the degree of commitment to that goal by those who produce the information in competition with other powerful mediating institutions that produce information for persuasion or manipulation.

THE LOST MEANING OF OBJECTIVITY

Perhaps because the discipline of verification is so personal and so haphazardly communicated, it is also part of one of the great confusions of journalism—the concept of objectivity. The original meaning of this idea is now thoroughly misunderstood and close to being lost. And in 2020, amid the pandemic, the presidency of Donald Trump, and national protests over race and justice in the wake of the police killing of a man named George Floyd in Minneapolis, the principle became again the subject of reexamination, in which the word *objectivity* was seen as a synonym for a default culture in newsrooms that was largely white and male. Yet getting at the original intention behind objectivity, when the concept migrated from science to journalism in the early twentieth century, and finding new language that captures that lost meaning can help point a way for a better journalism in the future.

When critics, including many in journalism, reject the notion of objectivity, they usually do so on the grounds that no person can ever be objective. As Dan Gillmor, author of *We the Media*, wrote in a much-circulated 2005 essay called "The End of Objectivity," "We are human. We have biases and backgrounds and a variety of conflicts that we bring to our jobs every day."[6] Gillmor was advocating that journalists drop the word *objectivity* and replace it with *thoroughness, accuracy, fairness,* and *transparency*.

His is not the only voice to be so raised in nearly eight decades of skepticism about the notion of objectivity. What dominates the argument, however, is a general confusion. When the concept of objectivity originally migrated from social science to journalism, it was not meant to imply that journalists were free of bias. Quite the contrary.

The term began to appear as part of journalism early in the last century, particularly in the 1920s, out of a growing recognition that journalists were full of bias, often without knowing it. The call for objectivity was an appeal for journalists to develop a consistent method of testing information—a transparent approach to evidence—precisely so that personal and cultural biases would not undermine the accuracy of their work.

In the nineteenth century, journalists talked about realism rather than objectivity.[7] This was the idea that if reporters simply dug out the facts and ordered them together, the truth would reveal itself naturally. Realism emerged at a time when journalism was separating from political parties and becoming more accurate. It coincided with the invention of what journalists call the "inverted pyramid" structure, in which a journalist orders a story's facts from most important to least important, thinking it helps audiences better understand the events.

At the beginning of the twentieth century, however, some journalists began to worry about the naïveté of realism. In part, reporters and editors were becoming more aware of the rise of propaganda and the role of press agents. At a time when Freud was developing his theories of the subconscious and painters such as Picasso were experimenting with Cubism, journalists were developing a greater recognition of human subjectivity. In 1919, Walter Lippmann and Charles Merz, an associate editor for the New York *World,* wrote an influential and scathing account of how cultural blinders had distorted *The New York Times* coverage of the Russian Revolution, published in a special forty-five-page section of *The Atlantic* magazine.[8] "In the large, the news about Russia is a case of seeing not what was, but what men wished to see," they wrote. Lippmann and others began to look for ways for the individual journalist "to remain clear and free of his irrational, his unexamined, his unacknowledged prejudgments in observing, understanding and presenting the news."[9] In other words, they were worried about what today we could call "unconscious bias," precisely the critique critics of objectivity raise today.

Journalism, Lippmann declared, was being practiced by "untrained accidental witnesses." Good intentions, or what some might call "honest efforts," by journalists were not enough. Faith in the rugged individualism of the tough reporter—what Lippmann called the "cynicism of the trade"—was also not enough. Nor were some of the trends of the time to make the work slightly more transparent, such as bylines and columnists.[10]

The solution, Lippmann argued, was for journalists to acquire more of "the scientific spirit. . . . There is but one kind of unity possible in a world as diverse as ours. It is unity of method, rather than aim; the unity of disciplined experiment." Lippmann meant by this that journalism should aspire to "a common intellectual method and a common area of valid fact." To begin, Lippmann thought, the fledgling field of journalism education should be transformed from "trade schools designed to fit men for higher salaries in the existing structure." Instead, the field should make its cornerstone the study of evidence and verification.[11]

Although this was an era of faith in science, Lippmann had few illusions. "It does not matter that the news is not susceptible of mathematical statement. In fact, just because news is complex and slippery, good reporting requires the exercise of the highest scientific virtues."[12] In the original concept, in other words, the journalist was not objective, but the journalist's method could be.

This original understanding of objectivity also has some important implications that are crucial to a twenty-first-century understanding of media. First, it means that objectivity is not the absence of a point of view. Instead, the aim of objectivity as a disciplined unity of method transparently conveyed comes close to what Gillmor and others have advocated as an alternative. Another implication is that the impartial voice employed by many news organizations—that familiar, supposedly neutral style of news writing—is not a fundamental principle of journalism. Rather, it is simply a device many news organizations use to highlight the fact that they are trying to produce something obtained by objective methods. The third implication is that this neutral voice, without a discipline of verification, often is a veneer atop something hollow. Journalists who select sources to express what is really their own point of view, and then use the neutral voice to make it seem objective, are engaged in deception. This deception, this exploitation of journalistic style for another purpose, damages the credibility of all journalistic enterprise by making it seem unprincipled, dishonest, and biased. This is an important caution in an age when the standards of the press are in doubt.

This idea is worth repeating for emphasis. In this original understanding of objectivity, neutrality is not a fundamental principle of journalism. It is merely a voice, or device, to persuade the audience of one's accuracy or fairness. Nor does objectivity mean neutrality, or the obviously false notion that people can annihilate or deny that they have personal experience, feelings, or beliefs. To the contrary, this original and more sophisticated notion of objectivity defines objectivity as an observable and disciplined method of inquiry, one that can be learned and replicated so that the news becomes more accurate and truthful.

It is interesting that those in the commercial press, on both the left and the right, who produce opinionated journalism often deny that they are peddling opinion and claim fairness and accuracy instead. Fox News's first marketing slogan was "fair and balanced." On the right, commentator Ann Coulter offered to expose the "lies" of the Left. Al Franken, when he was a liberal commentator, marketed his book as "truth." They echoed Hearst and Pulitzer and the yellow press of the nineteenth century, who claimed that their sensationalized reporting was more accurate than their competitors'. Rarely do people in journalism—even on the opinion end of the craft—market themselves as better arguers; instead, they present themselves as more accurate or closer to the truth.

Another implication of the original meaning of objectivity as method is that it reconciles how various other forms of American journalism fall inside the broad principles of a single discipline, one that well accommodates the citizen contributions of today, the alternative press that typically came from the Left in the 1960s and 1970s, and the magazine Journalism of Opinion from all sides of the political spectrum. If producing news starts with accuracy, a careful method or discipline of verification made transparent, and some unity of method to this process of verifying facts, then it can encompass a range of presentations. (We will discuss this in greater detail in the next chapter, on the meaning of the concept of independence from faction.)

Unity of method rather than aim, as Lippmann put it a hundred years ago, is the one unity that can be assessed in a diverse culture. And that method relates to the gathering of information, not the style of presentation. Lippmann was not alone in calling for a greater sense of professionalization, though his arguments were the most sophisticated. Joseph Pulitzer, the great populist journalistic innovator a generation earlier, had just created the Graduate School of Journalism at Columbia University for many of the same, though less clearly articulated, reasons. The Newspaper Guild was founded in large part to help professionalize journalism.

Over the years, however, this original and more sophisticated understanding of objectivity was utterly confused and its meaning to a large degree lost. Writers such as Leo Rosten, who authored an influential sociological study of journalists, used the term to suggest that the journalist was objective. Not surprisingly, he found that idea wanting. So did various legal opinions, which declared objectivity impossible. Many journalists never really understood what Lippmann meant.[13]

Over time, journalists began to reject the term *objectivity* as an illusion. They remained largely "accidental witnesses."

People in the alternative press often felt antagonistic toward so-called mainstream journalists for their faith in objectivity, when really what divided them was their positions about neutral voice, not how they went about gathering and verifying information. Newspaper people often move effortlessly to magazine work such as *The New Yorker,* where they produce journalism in a voice not dissimilar to what the alternative press might be employing or even the more subjective forms of TV news.

In the early part of the twenty-first century, NYU professor Jay Rosen famously criticized a straw man definition of objectivity as neutrality by calling it "the view from nowhere," implying that trying to have no point of view was worse than useless. Rosen has called this definition of objectivity "a bid for trust that advertises the viewlessness of the news producer," and "the attempt to acquire authority by constructing an artificial impartiality," one that is performative rather than real.[14]

Ironically, Rosen borrowed the phrase "view from nowhere" from the title of a 1986 book by philosopher Thomas Nagel that is one of the most eloquent philosophical defenses of objectivity as method ever written. In *The View from Nowhere,* Nagel, like Lippmann, writes that "objectivity is a method of understanding," and his aim in the book is to "defend the possibility of [this] objective ascent and to understand its limit."[15]

And how do people pursue this objective method? "To acquire a more objective understanding of some aspect of life or the world, we step back from our initial view of it and form a new conception which has that view and its relation to the world as its object." To do that, to understand one's initial view in relation to the world, requires inquiry, or making the effort to understand the views of other people, so that we can place our own view in a fuller, more comprehensive context. In other words, rather than claiming neutral consciousness or denying the subjective, Nagel says we must start with it, recognizing what he calls "our initial view." We must become conscious of that initial view, our personal reaction to the thing we are observing, to acquire some humility about its limits. Then we expand our understanding by trying to understand the views of others. That is how we can acquire what Nagel calls "an expanded consciousness that takes in the world more fully."

In short, Nagel uses the term "the view from nowhere" to mean, not "viewlessness" (as Rosen means it), but something closer to empathy. He wants to know "how limited beings like ourselves can alter their conception of the world so that it is no longer just the view from where they are but in a sense a view from nowhere, which includes and comprehends that the world contains beings" with different viewpoints "and explains why the world appears to them as it does and explains how they arrive at [their] conceptions."[16] Put another way, in Nagel's view, one's personal experience and predilections are where the journalistic inquiry begins, not where it ends.

Nagel is a philosopher, not a reporter, but his advice about method applies to journalism. The characteristics of an objective method in journalism involve Lippmann's notion of a scientific spirit, consulting multiple sources, gathering and weighing evidence, asking tough questions, making sure we are being open-minded to the arguments that we do not initially understand or agree with, and then being equally sure we are asking tough questions of the viewpoints we tend to personally lean toward—and making that process as transparent as possible to the people we are reporting for.

And it is critical to keep in mind the purpose of these journalistic efforts. Unlike the aims of the propagandist or advocate, the point of this journalistic inquiry is to get closer to an expanded understanding of the events we are portraying—to get closer to a more accurate, comprehensive, and truthful account—not to justify or buttress one's preexisting point of view. Far from being viewless, this notion of objectivity is deeply self-conscious.

Those who dismiss objectivity as neutrality are being unfair to the concept. Objectivity as a method of gathering, weighing, and understanding evidence does not mean both-sidesism, political stenography, false equivalency, or the denial of self. Nor does it mean that the journalist, after conducting sufficient reporting, has no point of view. At the same time, those who hide behind a neutral voice, who employ false balance and look mindlessly for equivalency (as Rosen warns too many do), are not being objective. In many cases, they are just lousy journalists—advocates hiding in journalists' garb.

The debate over the meaning of objectivity comes from thoughtful people on the right and the left. *The Dispatch,* a conservative online publication that strives for rigorous independent inquiry, notes in its description of itself: "Some of the best journalism is done when the author is honest with readers about where he or she is coming from, and some of the very worst journalism hides behind a pretense of objectivity and the stolen authority that pretense provides."[17] We agree. But being honest about one's biases does not make something good journalism. There is far more to it than that. That is what this book is about. And the fact that some bad journalists or propagandists will steal the authority of journalism by adopting a neutral pretense and will use the voice of independent inquiry while cherry-picking quotes and using straw man arguments does not denigrate the aspirations of genuine inquiry. It shows, rather, that genuine inquiry still generates respect.

OBJECTIVITY OR MORAL CLARITY?

Every generation by degrees reinvents its own journalism, a cycle that history suggests occurs about every twenty years. In the summer of 2020, amid the pandemic, the campaign and protests over the killing of George Floyd in Minneapolis, and the conduct of some police officers nationwide, Pulitzer Prize–winning reporter Wesley Lowery helped spark such a reexamination when he wrote a column in *The New York Times* connecting the question of journalistic norms with the failure of mainstream newsrooms to understand racism in America and cover people of color.

"The failure of the mainstream press to accurately cover Black communities is intrinsically linked with its failure to employ, retain and listen to Black people," he wrote. "The mainstream press has allowed what it considers objective truth to be decided almost exclusively by white reporters and their mostly white bosses. And those selective truths have been calibrated to avoid offending the sensibilities of white readers. . . . The views and inclinations of whiteness are accepted as the objective neutral." But "no individual journalist is objective, because no human being is." Perhaps most sweepingly, Lowery wrote, "Neutral objectivity trips over itself to find ways to avoid telling the truth."[18]

Adopting a term in growing use already, Lowery suggested that in place of "neutral objectivity," journalists think of "moral clarity." As he put it, "Moral clarity would insist that politicians who traffic in racist stereotypes and tropes—however cleverly—be labeled such with clear language and unburied evidence."

Lowery's column gave a more public voice to a debate already simmering over whether the goal of telling the truth was being stifled by a default culture dominating newsrooms that was largely white, male, and older. Much of Lowery's diagnosis was correct. A default culture does exist in many newsrooms, one too many newsroom leaders cannot see, and it is not only white and male but also elitist and liberal. For fifty years, newsrooms have paid lip service to creating more diversity in their ranks. As we will discuss in subsequent chapters in more detail, they have utterly failed at the goal, proof that the commitment was shallow and poorly understood. One number stands out. In the early 1970s, just 3.9 percent of journalists in America were Black. Forty years later, after decades of supposed effort at creating diversity in newsrooms, the number was virtually unchanged, 4.1 percent.[19] And this default culture is an important element, though not the only one, that has driven the crisis of trust in journalism among large portions of the American public.

At the root of this default culture, as Lowery says, is homogeneity—the persistent and in some cases worsening failure of newsrooms to diversify culturally, ethnically, by class, and by perspective, especially at the top. People of color in newsrooms, women, members of an LGBTQ community, and any group that is not well represented at the top, who have felt like outsiders, have a harder time speaking freely and bringing their experience to bear on the news. The cultural homogeneity of American newsrooms makes them intellectually narrow, full of blind spots that undermine their fundamental obligation to recognize, let alone tell, the truth.

But part of the solution Lowery offers will not solve the problem; it may well make it worse. For if you understand authentic objectivity as we have defined it above as a method of verification, a blind default culture in newsrooms is a failure of objectivity, not a result of it.

Lowery calls for a devotion "to accuracy, that we will diligently seek out the perspectives of those with whom we personally may be inclined to disagree and that we will be just as sure to ask hard questions of those with whom we're inclined to agree." But in trying to explain why journalists do not always live up to that goal he mixes two different ideas. Like Rosen, he conflates objectivity with neutrality. (He even joins them into a single term, *neutral objectivity*.) This, as we have discussed, is a mistake that leads us away from understanding a better journalistic process. The irony here is that the diligent process Lowery advocates for finding truth is precisely the objective method of reporting that Lippmann, Nagel, and we have described.

"The best of our profession already does this," Lowery acknowledges. "But we need to be honest about the gulf that lies between the best and the bulk." Lowery attributes that gulf largely to cultural factors, and to journalists not wanting to offend audiences whom they imagine only as white. Yet this discounts years of work, often led by journalists of color, to define multiple audiences for news, using new listening techniques. Ethnic identity is also not the only cause of hasty, sloppy journalism. Journalism is a reflection of the culture of its creators and also of the technology that produces it, the haste of a digital news environment, the resources that can be devoted to it, the economic model that is hollowing out newsrooms, and the reduction in the number of journalists in America. Bad journalism is a wicked problem created by a complex convergence of forces. Genuinely solving the problem requires that we also define it well.

Perhaps most important, Lowery's suggestion that journalists abandon the goal of journalistic objectivity and replace it with "moral clarity" as their aspiration risks moving journalism away from, not nearer to, the deep, open-minded inquiry he endorses. And that would accelerate, not reduce, the terrifying loss of trust in journalism that threatens not only the profession but prospects for democracy.

If moral clarity is the goal, neo-Nazis would claim they have it; so would jihadists. Indeed, moral clarity is a hallmark of extremism. For clarity means a lack of ambiguity. It implies certainty. And certainty is no sibling of inquiry. Certainty, to the contrary, will move us away from the kind of open-mindedness that leads us, as Nagel has written, to a more comprehensive and inclusive understanding of the world. For the more fully one understands something, the more complex it becomes. The more we see gray. The more we must appreciate uncertainty. Rather than being the result of more knowledge, certainty is the bridge we build to jump the abyss we cannot understand. As the philosopher Reinhold Niebuhr puts it, "It is when we are unsure that we are doubly sure."

If clarity and certainty are the only guides—without evidence, empiricism, verification, transparency, and method—journalism will descend even further into a shouting match of opinion and bloviation, in which facts are marshaled to support argument rather than to discern the truth. The public square will shrink further. Our common set of facts will become even smaller.

The term *objectivity* is fraught with problems. Its antonym is *subjectivity*, which only confuses people further. But *moral clarity*, we fear, lacks the clarity Lowery is seeking. We can think of many better terms. *Comprehensive journalism* is one. *Moral inquiry* is another. At bottom, however, the debate should not be about terminology. It should be about journalistic process.

We welcome reexamination of what is required of journalism. We were part of that kind of reexamination when we first undertook this work twenty years ago. We were inspired by earlier reexaminations of journalistic responsibility, such as the Hutchins Commission in 1947 and the debate over journalistic responsibility led by Lippmann and Dewey in the 1920s. We admire Lowery's powerful arguments in 2020. But if journalists engaging in just such a reexamination in the twenty-first century reduce objectivity to a stereotype and a straw man of political stenography and both-sidesism—and abandon the aspiration of deeply reported open-minded inquiry—we risk making journalism just another form of advocacy. And if we replace one confusing term, *objectivity*, with another, *moral clarity*, we fear that journalism, rather than a process for helping people learn about the world, will take one step closer to becoming just another means for people to justify their own preconceptions.

THE OBJECTIVE METHOD LIVE AND IN PRACTICE

While the debate over objectivity has raged on now for more than a century, reporters have gone on to refine the concept Lippmann and Nagel had in mind, developing objective methods in their reporting. They have usually done so privately, and in the name of technique or reporting routines rather than journalism's larger purpose. Still, in these techniques the notion of an objective method of reporting lives, often in pieces, handed down by word of mouth from reporter to reporter.

Developmental psychologist William Damon at Stanford University, for instance, identified various "strategies" that journalists have developed to verify their reporting. Damon asked his interviewees where they learned these concepts. Overwhelmingly the answer was that they had learned them by trial and error, on their own, or from a friend. Rarely did journalists report learning them in journalism school or from their editors.[20]

Many useful books have been written on the subject. For instance, one group calling itself Investigative Reporters and Editors tried to develop a methodology for how to use public records, read documents, and produce Freedom of Information Act requests.

But by and large, the differing approaches and strategies for verification have never been pulled together into a unified method, let alone a curriculum or an intellectual discipline. Although journalism may have developed various techniques and conventions for determining facts, it has done less to develop a system for testing the reliability of journalistic interpretation.

Most important, in the twenty-first century, the notion that journalists or anyone else can arrive at a truthful account of things or follow an objective method of verification seems even more eroded in the public mind. And the platform companies, with their emphasis on what they like to refer to as an "open Web" rather than on editorial responsibility, have encouraged this erosion. This amounts to a threat not only to the notion of journalism but also to the possibility of civil society's confronting and solving its problems. The public sphere becomes an arena solely for polarized debate, not for compromise, consensus, or solution.

If journalists are to make a case for journalistic accuracy and truth telling, they must understand the principles and methods of first getting the facts right, and they must reveal that method to the public. And in a fragmented world where people already have partial facts from social media platforms before they encounter a journalistic account, many members of the public seem to want affirmation from their media as much as or more than they want information. That desire by the audience for affirmation may, along with confusion by journalists themselves, be the biggest new threat that journalism, and by implication democracy, now faces.

Seen in this light, ideas such as fairness and the notion of gathering multiple points of view in stories take on new meaning. Rather than high principles, they are, as we have said before, really just techniques— devices—that can help guide anyone trying to gather and verify an account of an event. Fairness and the gathering of multiple points of view should never be pursued for their own sake or invoked as journalism's goal. Their value is in helping get us closer to more thorough verification and a reliable version of events. But like any technique they need to be used carefully, not overvalued.

Balancing multiple points of view, for instance, can lead to distortion. If an overwhelming percentage of scientists believe that global warming is a scientific fact, or that some medical treatment is clearly the safest, it is a disservice to citizens and truthfulness to create the impression that the scientific debate is equally split. Indeed, it is a journalistic habit that liars and purveyors of disinformation will easily exploit. Unfortunately, all too often journalistic balance is misconstrued to have this kind of almost mathematical meaning, as if a good story is one that has an equal number of quotes from two sides. As journalists know, often there are more than two sides to a story. And sometimes giving equal space to opposing views does not produce a true reflection of reality; instead it leads to false balance. If there are many more sides to an issue being ignored, or if the opposing views do not represent the views of the scientific community on an issue, or if one of those views is based on false information, this balancing becomes a distortion of the truth, not a method for getting closer to it.

Fairness, in turn, can also be misunderstood if it is seen to be a goal unto itself. Fairness should mean that the journalist is being fair to the facts and to a citizen's understanding of the facts. It should not mean "being fair to my sources, so that none of them will be unhappy." Nor should it mean asking, "Does my story seem fair?" These are subjective judgments that may steer the journalist away from the need to do more to verify his or her work. Fairness, in other words, is also an aim, not a method, and ultimately it is subjective. Some journalists like the term because *objectivity* is so misunderstood. But fairness as a method doesn't take you very far.

Trying to create the appearance of fairness can also lead to presenting false equivalencies, the idea that different perspectives have equal moral weight. Consider CNN's coverage in March 2013 of the conviction of two high school football players, Trent Mays and Ma'lik Richmond, for raping a sixteen-year-old girl at a party. The two young men were sentenced to one to five years in juvenile detention. The two teenagers were anguished at the verdict.

In a segment covering the trial, CNN anchor Candy Crowley and legal analyst Paul Callan seemed to lose sight of who was the victim as they tried to convey the emotional scene to viewers. "A sixteen-year-old just sobbing in court. Regardless of what big football players they are, they still sound like sixteen-year-olds," Crowley said. "When you listen to it and you realize, that they could stay [incarcerated] until they are twenty-one. They are going to get credit for time served. What's the lasting effect though on two young men . . . ?"

Trying to be sympathetic to the emotion of the scene is one thing. Losing a grip on the context of the story is another.

THE JOURNALISM OF ASSERTION VERSUS THE JOURNALISM OF VERIFICATION

Well before the arrival of the Web, changes in the modern press culture were weakening the methodology of verification that journalists had developed, even if that method was not adequately named or codified. In the age of the twenty-four-hour news cycle, journalists spent more time looking for something to add to the existing news, usually interpretation, than trying to independently discover and verify new facts. Facts had become a commodity, easily acquired, repackaged, and repurposed. "Once a story is hatched, it's as if all the herd behavior is true," Geneva Overholser, a journalist who has watched changes in media as an editor, ombudsman, and then educator, observed. "The story is determined by one medium—one newspaper or TV account. . . . Partly because news organizations are being consolidated and partly because of electronic reporting, we all feed at the same trough."[21] And this was before the full impact of the Web was felt, which only accelerated those influences.

Simply put, the Web makes redistributing content so convenient, and accelerates the pace of news flow so much, that the combination increases the potential that erroneous information will be passed on.

Each new breaking news story seems to bring new examples. In 2012, CNN and Fox mistakenly reported that the Supreme Court had struck down healthcare reform because their reporters were so eager to get on the air a moment before their rivals that they did not read further into the court's decision. The suspects in the Boston marathon bombings were reported to have been killed or captured when in fact they had not been. One of the most regrettable cases involved mistakes made in reporting the killing of twenty schoolchildren in December 2012 in Newtown, Connecticut.

At approximately 9:30 A.M. on December 14, Adam Lanza entered Sandy Hook Elementary School and began shooting. At 11:17 A.M., on its Twitter feed @CNN reported, "CNN's @SusanCandiotti reports the suspect is Ryan Lanza and is in his 20s." Candiotti would repeat the mistake on the air shortly after 2 P.M., although she acknowledged it had not been confirmed by state police. At 3 P.M. the AP said it had confirmed Ryan Lanza's identity. Some news organizations, following CNN's lead, showed Ryan Lanza's Facebook photo and published some of his posts.

This was not the only mistake. A number of news organizations, including *The New York Times*, would report that Lanza's mother was a teacher at the school and that she had been killed there by her son.

The problem was that Ryan Lanza was not the shooter. His brother Adam was. And their mother was not a teacher at the school, nor was she even present there at the time of the shooting. Adam Lanza had already killed her in her home.

Not all of the mistakes could be attributed to haste. The mistake about Lanza's mother may also reflect a felt need by some reporters for the story to have a logic or motive. "It's hard for us to accept the idea that something so horrible was completely random," said W. Joseph Campbell, the author of *Getting It Wrong: Ten of the Greatest Misreported Stories in American Journalism,* a study of media-driven myths. "The idea that she had little or no connection to the school makes it harder to wrap your mind around such a horrific and senseless act."[22]

At times, the breakdown in verification can be the result not simply of erroneous information being passed along but of journalists expecting certain facts because they fit a larger popular master narrative. A master narrative, or metanarrative, occurs when journalists coalesce around a general view of a political actor or news event and then begin to look for stories that illustrate that master narrative. There are countless examples.

One of the more enduring cases where we can identify precisely how it works was the popular narrative that Vice President Al Gore, then the Democratic Party nominee for president in 2000, continually exaggerated his past accomplishments to impress people. One account referred to Gore's "Pinocchio problem," another called him a "liar," and a third "delusional."[23] A key bit of evidence was Gore's supposed assertion that he had discovered the Love Canal toxic waste site in upstate New York, which helped change federal policy. The problem is, Gore had never made any such assertion. He had told a group of New Hampshire high school students that he first learned about hazardous waste dangers when a constituent told him about a polluted town in Tennessee called Toone, and Gore wanted to hold hearings. "I looked around the country for other sites like that," he told the students. "I found a little place in upstate New York called Love Canal. Had the first hearing on the issue, and Toone, Tennessee—that was the one that you didn't hear of. But that was the one that started it all."[24]

The next day, however, *The Washington Post* misquoted Gore completely as saying, "I was the one that started it all." In a press release, the Republican Party changed the quote to "I was the one who started it all." *The New York Times* printed the same misquote as the *Post.* Soon the press was off and running, relying on the faulty accounts ingrained in the databases of the two papers. It didn't catch anyone's attention that the AP had the quote correct. The matter was not cleared up until the high school students themselves complained. Today, more people probably remember the false account of what Gore said than the real one.

As journalists spend more time trying to synthesize the ever-growing stream of data pouring in through the new portals of information, the risk is that they can become more passive, more receivers than gatherers. To combat this, a better understanding of the original meaning of objectivity as a discipline or method could help put the news on firmer footing. We are not the only ones to advocate for this. "Journalism and science come from the same intellectual roots," said Phil Meyer, the legendary University of North Carolina journalism professor, "from the seventeenth- and eighteenth-century enlightenment. The same thinking that led to the First Amendment led to the scientific method. . . . I think this connection between journalism and science ought to be restored to the extent that we can. . . . I think we ought to emphasize objectivity of method. That's what scientific method is—our humanity, our subjective impulses . . . directed toward deciding what to investigate by objective means."[25]

THE "SHOW ME" ERA OF NEWS, NOT THE "TRUST ME" ERA

In a networked world where consumers have more control, and content may be distributed in ways in which it is disassociated from its institutional source (a chart or graphic, for example, might be shared on Twitter without the accompanying article), employing a more rigorous method of gathering the news, and then being more transparent in communicating that method in each piece of content, not only comes closer to the original meaning of objectivity but also empowers the news consumer with the tools necessary to make good decisions about what to trust.

In the old order, people relied on responsible gatekeepers to identify what stories they should know about and what facts they should hear. The journalists at these trusted brands—which in the case of many newspapers by the end of the twentieth century were monopolies—were not trained to make their presentation all that transparent. A lot of explanation about how the news was gathered might make the narrative unwieldy. It was enough that the brand was trusted. And that was how we encountered the content. We read the story in the newspaper or watched it inside the newscast. This was, as we have described elsewhere, the "Trust Me" era of news.

Now, as power has shifted to the consumer of news in our information system, we have entered the "Show Me" era of news. In a world where we rely on recommendations from friends, search results, references from social media, emailed stories, and curated and aggregated distribution, it now becomes far more important for each piece of content, each work of news, to have its own internal integrity, for the evidence and the choices that went into producing that content to be clear.

We have entered an era in which the consumer does not say, "I believe this because I trust everything from this source." The citizen should demand to be shown why he or she should believe any particular piece of content. The news has been atomized, broken into stories away from institutions. Each atom of news must itself demonstrate its trustworthiness.

In this sense, clarifying common misunderstandings about concepts like fairness and balance, along with improving the discipline of verification employed in the production of news, may be the most important step in improving the quality of news we receive and the public discussion we build from that news. In the end, a discipline of verification is what separates journalism from other fields of communication and creates an economic reason for it to continue.

A JOURNALISM OF OBJECTIVE METHOD IN PRACTICE

What would this journalism of objective *method*—rather than merely good intention—look like? What should citizens expect from the press as a reasonable discipline of reporting? What should we expect to see from news that comes from unfamiliar sources, from fellow citizens, or even partisan producers, for us to be able to consider it reliable and useful? As we have listened to and studied the thoughts of journalists, citizens, and others concerning the news, we began to see a core set of concepts that form the foundation of the discipline of verification. They are the intellectual principles of a science of reporting:

1. Never add anything that was not there originally.
2. Never deceive the audience.
3. Be as transparent as possible about your methods and motives.
4. Rely on your own original reporting.
5. Exercise humility.

Let's examine them one at a time.

An important parallel to the new Journalism of Assertion is the rise of fiction posing as nonfiction. It has had different names in different areas. On television, producers have called it docudrama. In the publishing world, some—such as author James Frey—have hijacked the memoir genre to pass fiction off as biographical truth. In 2006 Frey was exposed for having fictionalized much of his memoir *A Million Little Pieces.* But all of it is making stuff up. In some cases it is just lying. Some writers who practice narrative nonfiction, such as John Berendt, the author of *Midnight in the Garden of Good and Evil,* argue that, in order to hold a reader's attention, some details—such as subjects' thoughts, or pieces of dialogue—can be invented in order to add color to the story.

Perhaps John McPhee, a *New Yorker* writer noted for the strength of his narrative style, best summarized the key imperative: "The nonfiction writer is communicating with the reader about real people in real places. So if those people talk, you say what those people said. You don't say what the writer decides they said. . . . You don't make up dialogue. You don't make a composite character. . . . And you don't get inside their [the characters'] heads and think for them. You can't interview the dead. Where writers abridge that, they hitchhike on the credibility of writers who don't."

In 1980, John Hersey, the Pulitzer Prize–winning author of *Hiroshima,* the story of the effects of the first use of the atomic bomb in World War II, attempted to articulate a principle to help make journalism compelling without crossing the line between fact and fiction. In "The Legend on the License," Hersey advocated a strict standard: never invent. Journalism's implicit credo is "Nothing here is made up."[26]

Today, we think Hersey's standard of "never invent" needs to be refined.

Along with Roy Peter Clark, the senior scholar at the Poynter Institute in St. Petersburg, Florida, we developed an updated pair of ideas for navigating the shoals lying between fact and fiction.

DO NOT ADD

Do not add things that did not happen. This goes further than "never invent" or make things up, for it also encompasses rearranging events in time or place or conflating characters or events. If a siren rings out during the taping of a TV story, and for dramatic effect it is moved from one scene to another, it has been added to that second place. What was once a fact becomes a fiction.

Usually, when people do add or embellish, they hide it—a tip-off in itself that invention is not acceptable. And when authors of nonfiction have invented and admitted it, critics and readers have generally reacted poorly. This was the point of Hersey's original essay, which challenged author Tom Wolfe, among others. Biographer Edmund Morris discovered this when he wrote *Dutch,* his authorized biography of Ronald Reagan, in which he made himself a character in the book witnessing Reagan in his early life, before the author was actually born. Morris said he was trying to make a point about how Reagan himself created fictional reality. Yet this intermingling of fantasy and reality did little to illuminate Reagan and much to damage the credibility of the book. "Why would I want to read that?" former *Washington Post* editor Benjamin C. Bradlee exclaimed in reaction.[27]

DO NOT DECEIVE

Never mislead the audience. Fooling people is a form of lying, and it mocks the idea that journalism is committed to truthfulness. This principle is closely related to the first one. If you move the sound of the siren and do not tell the audience, you are deceiving them. If acknowledging what you've done would make it unpalatable to the audience, then it is self-evidently improper. This is a useful check. How would the audience feel if they knew you moved that sound to another point in the story to make it more dramatic?

"Do not deceive" means that if you are going to engage in any narrative or storytelling techniques that deviate from the most literal form of eyewitness reporting, the audience should know. On the question of quoting people, a survey that we conducted of journalists found broad agreement: Except for word changes to correct grammar, some signal should be sent to audiences—such as ellipses or brackets—if words inside quotation marks are changed or phrases deleted for clarity.[28]

If someone reporting events reconstructs quotes or events that that person did not witness, the audience should know that these specific quotes were reconstructed and be told they were verified. A vague author's note at the beginning or end of a book or story that tells audiences merely "some interviews involved reconstruction" is not adequate. Which interviews? Reconstructed how? These kinds of vague disclosures are not disclosures at all, they are excuses.

We believe these two imperatives—"Do not add" and "Do not deceive"—serve as guideposts for navigating the line between fact and fiction. But how, as citizens, are we to identify which journalism to trust? Here, some other concepts are necessary.

BE TRANSPARENT

If those doing journalism are truth seekers, they must be honest and truthful with their audiences, too—truth presenters. If nothing else, this responsibility requires that those engaged in journalism be as open and honest with audiences as they can about what they know and what they don't. How can you claim to be seeking to convey the truth if you're not truthful with the audience in the first place?

In practice, the only way to level with people about what you know is to reveal as much as possible about your sources and methods. How do you know what you know? Who are your sources? How direct is their knowledge? What biases might they have? Are there conflicting accounts? What don't we know?

Call it the Spirit of Transparency. We consider this idea the most important single element in creating a better discipline of verification.

Most of the limitations journalists face in trying to move from accuracy to truth are addressed, if not overcome, by their being honest about the nature of their knowledge, why they trust it, and what efforts they make to learn more.

Transparency has a second important virtue: It signals one's respect for the audience. It allows the audience to judge the validity of the information, the process by which it was secured, and the motives and biases of the persons providing it. This also makes transparency the best protection against errors and deception by sources. If the best information one has comes from a potentially biased source, naming the source and acknowledging the source's perspective will reveal to the audience the possible bias of the information—and may inhibit the source from deceiving as well. It will also compel the reporter to find the most authoritative sources possible.

Transparency also helps establish that the journalist has a public interest motive, which is the key to credibility. The willingness to be transparent is at the heart of establishing that the reporter is concerned with truth. The lie, or the mistake, is in pretending omniscience, or claiming greater knowledge than one has.

How does the Spirit of Transparency work? It starts at the top, where it may mean public meetings, speeches, or editors' columns, especially during controversy. It flows down to individual stories, where it may demand specificity. If a piece reports that "experts say," how many experts did the reporter actually talk to? Perhaps the most valuable thing about transparency is that its natural ally is the open architecture of the internet. In a digital landscape, the consumer is also a critic, who may comment on stories, ask questions of the news producer, research additional sources, or offer his or her own commentary on a piece of content in social media. This dialogue of news has empowered the consumers of news to ask the most important question one can pose about the credibility of the information one is offered: "How do you know that?" Asking that question of a news provider can encourage a clear accounting of the original sources of assertions, conclusions, labels, and facts. News organizations should welcome these questions, responding to both public comments and private messages. But they should also anticipate them, creating a culture in news that first strives to show audiences how they know what they know, rather than doing so only when asked.

Clear and detailed identification of sources is one of the most effective forms of transparency news publishers have at their disposal, and it forms the basis of a more open relationship with the public. While journalists were in many ways slow to embrace the Web, they did recognize this new relationship with audiences, and how the higher level of transparency and proof made possible by digital distribution was an empowering tool in the production of news. In 2002, for instance, the *Los Angeles Times* employed extensive footnotes detailing the sources of quotes, facts, scenes, and other information in "Enrique's Journey," a six-part Pulitzer Prize–winning series about a Honduran teenager journeying to the United States to find his mother. More than seven thousand words of footnotes kept the narrative clean of overattribution but also provided detailed information about sourcing to the reader.

If you can be transparent with audiences about how many sources are eyewitnesses and how many are offering hearsay, whether a police source is a public spokesman or the investigating officer, or what the background and expertise are of the professor you quoted, you are sharing more with your audience and getting closer to the truth. If you can state that an account is based on a video recording rather than someone's recollection, or that the studies cited have been peer reviewed, you are offering the audience more evidence on why they should believe you.

The Web also created scores of new ways of presenting news and information that made the legacy forms of television or print seem paltry, from data visualization and interactive graphics to archives, multimedia, curation, and much more. In our book *Blur*, we noted that in covering a news event in print, a news provider could offer roughly seven elements to convey the story—a headline, a narrative story, a chart or graphic, a photo, a map, a sidebar (second story), and perhaps a pull quote (taking an interesting quote from a story, blowing it up, and using it as a graphic element to pull people into reading the story). In a digital form, a news publisher had perhaps ten times as many elements to choose from—databases, original documents, audio and video interviews with sources or reporters, visual forensics of user-generated videos, the code behind a computer-assisted project, answers to reader questions in chats or comments, corrections sent to users who shared on social media a now out-of-date story, and much more.[29] All of these tools empower transparency, encourage engagement, and can make news more credible. Strategies for using these tools to make news transparent are still evolving. Yet to see these tools as a threat, or more work to be burdened by, is a mistake. The key is to see them as opportunities.

The Spirit of Transparency first involves the journalist asking for each event, *What does my audience need to know to evaluate this information for itself?* The answer includes explaining as much as is practical about how the news organization got its information.

A second element of transparency involves answering the question, *Is there anything in our treatment of this that requires explanation? Were any controversial decisions made to leave something in or take something out?* In an age of incredulity toward journalists, it is critical to explain editorial decisions that might be misconstrued.

As Joy Mayer, who runs an organization called Trusting News, puts it, "Journalists spend a lot of time discussing and debating editorial decisions. It's important to remember that all thoughtful decision-making is invisible to the audience unless it is publicly described."

When making decisions about transparency elements, journalists should start by anticipating the user's or audience's curiosity. What will the audience assume or misconstrue about your motivations, ethics, or process? What are you likely to get pushback on? What do you wish the audience knew about how you reported this story? The answers to those questions can form the basis for decisions about transparency.

If something was a tough call in the newsroom, it is probably worth explaining publicly how and why you made that decision and how you thought it through. By being open about the difficulties of making these decisions, you will not only increase trust. You will also help your audience become more discriminating news consumers.

A third element of the Spirit of Transparency involves something that may seem counterintuitive for most journalists: *Those who produce news should acknowledge the questions they cannot answer.* Traditionally, journalists were trained never to raise a question the story could not answer. They were told to write around the holes in the story and to make stories seem airtight, even omniscient. In the twenty-first century, when journalists cannot control everything the public knows about public events, when they are no longer gatekeepers, that view is no longer sensible—if it ever was.

These ideas about transparency can solve myriad problems. Consider the case of Richard Jewell. *The Atlanta Journal-Constitution* broke the story that police briefly thought Jewell might be the bomber at the 1996 Olympics. The story came from law enforcement sources who wished to remain anonymous and said that Jewell, who was initially hailed as a hero for alerting police to the pipe bomb, had become a suspect in the investigation. The story also said Jewell fit the profile of a "lone bomber."

To make matters more complicated, the paper had to deal with its own rules, which prohibited the use of anonymous sources. So how did the *Journal-Constitution* handle the story? It used what the paper called a "Voice of God" approach, in which the journalists did not attribute this information but simply stated it as their own understanding of the facts.

The piece never mentioned all the things police did not know. It did not include the fact that police had no physical evidence linking Jewell to the crime. The police had also not interviewed Jewell as a suspect. Nor had they yet worked out a time line to see if Jewell could have called in the tip to the police and still gotten to the place where he found the knapsack in the time allotted.

The paper insists it didn't get anything wrong. It simply reported what police were thinking. However, had the news organization noted all the things that police had not yet done to establish their unfounded suspicions of Jewell, the story might have been less explosive but far more complete—and accurate. It also would have avoided sparking the years of litigation that followed publication.[30]

The Spirit of Transparency is the same principle that governs the scientific method: explain how you learned something and why you believe it, so the audience can do the same. In science, the reliability of an experiment, or its objectivity, is defined by whether someone else can replicate the experiment. In journalism, only by explaining how we know what we know can we approximate this idea of people being able, if they want, to replicate the reporting. This is what is meant by objectivity of method in science, or in journalism.

Even as he began to develop doubts about whether journalists could really sort out the truth, Walter Lippmann recognized this:

> There is no defense, no extenuation, no excuse whatsoever, for stating six times that Lenin is dead when the only information the paper possesses is a report that he is dead from a source repeatedly shown to be unreliable. The news, in that instance, is not that "Lenin is Dead" but "Helsingfors Says Lenin is Dead." And a newspaper can be asked to take responsibility of not making Lenin more dead than the source of the news is reliable. If there is one subject on which editors are most responsible it is in their judgment of the reliability of the source.[31]

Unfortunately, even two decades into the digital age, too much journalism fails to reveal anything about methods, motives, and sources. Television newscasts, as a matter of course, will say simply "sources said," a way of saving valuable time on the air, yet most of these sources are hardly confidential. Similarly it has been a standing rule in most offices on Capitol Hill that staffers be quoted anonymously at all times, that only the representative be on the record.

Withholding information from the public in ways like this is a mistake. As citizens become more skeptical of both journalists and the political establishment, such disservices to the public bring journalism under greater suspicion.

DON'T MISLEAD SOURCES:
A COROLLARY TO BEING TRANSPARENT

The Spirit of Transparency also suggests something about the way those engaged in journalism deal with their sources. Obviously journalists should not lie to or mislead their sources in the process of trying to tell the truth to their audiences.

Unfortunately, journalists, without having thought the principle through, all too often have failed to see this. Bluffing sources, failing to level with them about the real point of the story, even flat-out lying to sources about where one is heading with a story, are all techniques many journalists have applied in the name of truth seeking. While at first glance candor may seem a handcuff on reporters, it won't be in most cases. Many reporters have come to find that it can win them enormous influence. "I've found it is always better to level with sources, tell them what I'm doing and where I'm going," concluded Jill Zuckman, who worked as a political correspondent for *The Boston Globe* and the *Chicago Tribune* before going into government and public relations. *Washington Post* reporter Jay Mathews long made a habit of showing sources drafts of stories. He believed it increased the accuracy and nuance of his pieces.[32]

REVEAL DELIBERATELY MISLEADING SOURCES

At the same time, those engaged in journalism should expect similar veracity from their sources. Indeed, we would go one step further. If a source who has been granted anonymity is found to have deliberately misled the reporter, the source's identity should be revealed. Part of the bargain of granting a source anonymity is that in exchange the source tells the truth. If the source has lied, and used the shield of anonymity to do so, the source should be exposed. That source has broken the covenant. Journalists should not only employ this technique on behalf of the public. The practice should be common enough that sources know it—and fear it.

MASQUERADING: ONLY UNDER SPECIAL CIRCUMSTANCES AND EXPLAINED TO AUDIENCE

A special category of misleading that journalists practice with sources is called masquerading. This occurs when journalists pose as someone else to get a story. The "undercover" reporting technique is nothing new. At the beginning of the twentieth century, muckrakers like Nellie Bly, who among other remarkable achievements posed as an inmate in an insane asylum to expose mistreatment of the mentally ill, used masquerade. Television is particularly inclined to use masquerade and tiny hidden cameras to expose wrongdoing.

What do avoiding deception and being transparent with audiences and sources suggest about masquerade? These ideas do not preclude journalists' use of masquerade. Rather, they suggest that journalists should use a test similar to the concepts justifying civil disobedience in deciding whether to engage in the technique. Citizens should also apply this test in evaluating what they think of it. There are three steps to this test:

1. The information must be sufficiently vital to the public interest to justify deception.
2. There is no other way to get the story.
3. Journalists should reveal to their audience whenever they mislead sources to get information, and should explain their reasons for doing so, including why the story justifies the deception and why this was the only way to get the facts.

With this approach, citizens can decide for themselves whether journalistic dishonesty was justified or not. And journalists, in turn, have been clear with the citizens to whom they owe their first loyalty.

We have dealt at length with this notion of a more transparent journalism because it will help over the long run to develop a more discerning public. This is a public that can readily see the difference between journalism of principle and careless or self-interested imitation. In this way, journalists can enlist the new power of the marketplace to become a force for quality journalism. This transparency means embedding in the news reports a sense of how the story came to be and why it was presented as it was.

Mayer's group Trusting News, which works on using transparency to build trust, and the Center for Media Engagement, a team of scholars at the University of Texas that studies media experimentation, have done research together showing that news consumers particularly appreciate when news organizations explain why they did a story in the first place—because story choice itself is such a common form of bias. (Interestingly, people tended to have a negative reaction to the claim that a story was an "exclusive," a norm that apparently is more important to journalists than to the public.)

WCPO TV used that research to explain to viewers why they

devoted so much time to the pandemic—a choice some might easily assume was self-explanatory but that the station realized was not. WCPO's Mike Canan wrote a blog acknowledging that he had encountered people, including friends, who thought "the whole coronavirus thing" was "being overblown by the media. I've seen and heard people say journalists are salivating over the virus because it will drive pageviews and TV ratings. The reality could not be further from the truth for our newsroom. . . . I don't know whether the coronavirus coverage would increase TV ratings. . . . Our journalists cover the news we think is important for our community. . . . Our goal with our coverage is not to scare anyone or create a panic. Instead our goal is to equip you with information that can help you understand what is happening and how to keep you and your family healthy."

Whether that messaging helped or hurt ratings was not the objective. Canan, the senior director of local content at the station, wanted to explain that himself, and wanted the community to understand his motivations as a person. He did not hide behind a lot of journalistic rhetoric.[33]

ORIGINALITY: RELY ON YOUR OWN REPORTING

Beyond demanding more transparency from journalism, we also should look for another quality from the news we produce and consume: originality. When he was Washington bureau chief of *The New York Times*, Mike Oreskes offered this deceptively simple but powerful idea in the discipline for pursuing truth: Do your own work. This idea has become even more important as technology has made the distribution of others' work easier and more common—and turned facts into a seeming commodity of diminished value.

One of the first major stories to break at the dawn of the digital age was the sex and legal scandal involving President Bill Clinton and White House intern Monica Lewinsky. The story is instructive precisely because news organizations were then less familiar with the concept that stories were already, in the phrase that became popular at the time, "out there." Throughout the scandal, news organizations found themselves in the uncomfortable position of trying to decide what to do with often-explosive exposés from other news organizations that they could not verify themselves. To make matters more complicated, these stories usually were based on anonymous sources, meaning that the news organization had to take even greater responsibility for the veracity of the story than if they were quoting someone. On the basis of such sourcing, three different news organizations reported that a third-party witness had seen the president and Lewinsky in an intimate encounter—stories that were later found to be inaccurate. Should a news organization have reported these exposés because they knew that others might, and that in the newly proliferating world of media the story would be public anyway somewhere else?

Oreskes concluded that the answer was an adamant no. "The people who got it right were those who did their own work, who were careful about it, who followed the basic standards of sourcing and got their information from multiple sources. The people who worried about what was 'out there,' to use that horrible phrase that justifies so many journalistic sins, the people who worried about getting beaten, rather than just trying to do it as well as they could as quickly as they could, they messed up."[34]

Originality is a bulwark of better journalism, deeper understanding, and more accurate reporting. An ancient axiom of the press says much the same thing: "When in doubt leave it out." In the era before curation and aggregation, the tradition of "matching" stories was rooted in the same idea. Rather than publishing another news outlet's scoop, journalists tended to require one of their reporters to call a source to confirm it first. This tradition of matching was a way for news organizations to avoid having to credit their rivals, which in this earlier era was considered an embarrassing admission of being scooped. Yet the tradition of matching had another, more important and salutary effect. Stories that couldn't be independently confirmed would not be repeated.

This concept of originality dovetails with the notion of transparency. There are levels of knowledge in reporting, and those who produce news should be aware of them and consider acknowledging them to their audience. Journalism is first concerned with the physical externality of events. A dump truck ran a stoplight and crashed into a bus. The president said these words. This many people died. The document said this. The closer you are to this physical and external level of information, the easier it is to verify the information.

Even here, of course, there are levels. Documents or facts that a reporter can see and verify for him- or herself are at the highest level of solidity. If one is relying on others to convey these facts, it then becomes important to know how those intermediary sources know what they are relaying. Were the sources eyewitnesses? Or are they second-hand sources (such as a press secretary who was briefed on a meeting but not present) or someone even further removed (a police public relations officer who did not interview witnesses but who was in turn briefed on what was said)?

But as reporting moves toward the interior world, trying to report on what someone believes or what motivates the person, journalism necessarily becomes more speculative. What was the truck driver thinking when he ran that light? Why did the president say these words? What motivated the shooter in Newtown, Connecticut?

Interior thoughts may be something the journalist feels the audience should know, but it's more difficult to obtain solid proof for these kinds of details. There may be multiple interpretations and different levels of knowledge. This softer level of proof should be signaled to the audience. If the newsroom decided the best way to address motive and answer the "why" was through an expert, it should make clear to the public why the expert was chosen and describe his or her expertise in or involvement with the topic. Newsrooms should not hide behind experts to abdicate their responsibility for getting as close to the truth as possible.

Why do we suggest this? Because the more honest the journalist is with the audience about what he or she knows and doesn't know, the more the audience will be inclined to trust the story. Level with people. Make no claims to an omniscience you cannot justify. Acknowledging what you don't know gives you more authority, not less.

Some public figures become so familiar that the press is even more likely to assume a motive; President Donald Trump is the most dramatic example of this, in part because the extensive use of his Twitter feed seemed to invite the public into a personal ongoing conversation with him. Even here, the press needs to be scrupulously transparent about what it can prove versus what it is only speculating about. It is one thing to describe patterns of behavior, another to ascribe political, let alone psychological, motives to that behavior.

EXERCISE HUMILITY

A fifth and final concept to keep in mind for those engaged in developing a science or method of reporting is that they should be humble about their own skills. In other words, not only should they be skeptical of what they see and hear from others, but just as important, they should be skeptical about their ability to know what it really means. Jack Fuller, the late editor-publisher of the *Chicago Tribune*, suggested in his book *News Values* that journalists needed to show "modesty in their judgments" about what they know and how they know it.[35] Journalists benefit from practicing humility in many ways. A starting point may be language in stories. Findings from psychology by Harvard researcher Julia Minson and others show that linguistic features that acknowledge some uncertainty—such as "sometimes," or "occasionally"—help people believe you are engaging thoughtfully with material, including someone's perspective on an issue. It helps people hear you, even across ideological divides.[36]

Moreover, a key way to avoid misrepresenting events is a disciplined honesty about the limits of one's knowledge and of the power of one's perceptions. An incident described to us by veteran religion writer Laurie Goodstein illustrates the point. The event was a Pentecostal prayer revival on the steps of the US Capitol. The gathering featured faith healings, calls for school prayer, condemnations of abortion and homosexuality—a fairly typical revival meeting. A reporter for a newspaper covering the event related all this but added this sentence: "At times, the mood turned hostile toward the lawmakers in the stately white building behind the stage." Then the reporter quoted a Christian radio broadcaster speaking from the stage: "Let's pray that God will slay everyone in the Capitol."[37]

The reporter assumed the broadcaster meant *slay* as in "kill." But Goodstein explained, "Any Pentecostal knows that asking God to slay someone means to slay in spirit, slay in the sense of Holy Spirit, praying that they are overcome with love for God, for Jesus."

The problem was the reporter didn't know, didn't have any Pentecostals in the newsroom to ask, and was perhaps too anxious for a juicy story to double-check with someone afterward whether the broadcaster was really advocating murder of the entire Congress. "It made for a very embarrassing correction," said Goodstein. It also makes a strong case for the need for humility.

Humility also means that you are open-minded enough to accept that the next person you talk to could change the entire meaning of your story or even convince you that you have no story.

Together, these five ideas amount to a core philosophy that frames the discipline of verification and could guide a science or method of reporting. They also establish a closer relationship between the journalist, by which we mean anyone producing news, and the citizen—a relationship that is mutually beneficial. By employing the powerful tools of transparent, narrative storytelling, those gathering and reporting news engage citizens with important information. At the same time, by being more open about their work, those engaged in journalism are encouraged to be more thoughtful in acquiring, organizing, and presenting the news.

THE CHALLENGE OF VERIFICATION IN THE DIGITAL AGE

In the nearly twenty years since the first edition of this book was published, we have been asked one question more often than any other: Is a discipline of verification still possible in an age when the rumors, gossip, innuendo, and misinformation may flow through the virtual public square in real time before there is any journalistic notice? How does one play the role of steward over facts after the fact—when false information has already spread?

There are new examples every day, from presidential tweets to fake videos of Speaker of the House Nancy Pelosi manipulated to make her appear drunk, to filmmaker Michael Moore's claim on Facebook that Donald Trump's COVID diagnosis and hospitalization were a fake contrived to create sympathy for his candidacy. They can even occur at in-person events where the intentions are far loftier. A symposium at the Newhouse School of Journalism at Syracuse University was a case in point. The subject of the event was how the press should deal with child molestation accusations. Bernie Fine, a basketball coach at the school, had been the subject of those accusations. The local paper had investigated and decided it couldn't prove them. Years later the press decided the charges needed to surface. The case was explosive and ongoing. During one of the symposium's afternoon sessions, a therapist who treated molestation victims in Syracuse declared suddenly that though he could provide no details, there was another coach at the school who was still actively molesting children and the school was protecting him. Other panelists were aghast.

A reporter for the local paper came up to us as soon as the session ended. What was he supposed to do with this utterly unsubstantiated allegation, he asked. The panel was being live-tweeted and livestreamed online. The accusation was already out there—with the press having no part in it. Should he ignore it because it was unsubstantiated? Or report it was said? Or what?

The best way forward in a case such as this, we believe, is transparency and humility. There was no way the reporter could simply ignore the allegation. It was already "published" by tweet and webcast. So the first step, in whatever reporting time existed before publication, was to seek corroboration. Track down the man who had made the statement and demand what evidence there was to substantiate or justify making this allegation public. (He refused further comment.) Ask the police if any complaints had been filed. Find out if the university had heard the allegation before (though note that the university and police had been implicated in not acting quickly in the case that was the subject of the symposium).

The next step was to contextualize the now-public allegation as much as possible for the audience. Explain that the accuser had offered no evidence to substantiate his claim. Report that other therapists on the panel were appalled that such an unsubstantiated accusation had been made public. In other words, the journalist's obligation to verification required that he put the public allegation in context. Don't just repeat it. And don't just stop by saying it was unsubstantiated. That would be insufficient. Take the steps to corroborate or knock down the unsubstantiated allegation, and share what you have learned with the audience. Again, be transparent. Bring them into the process of verification.

The third step was to share with the public what would need to be established to prove the accusation. Doing so would show how careful the public would need to be. In effect, in a networked media environment, the journalistic responsibility involves arming the public with as much information as possible so that people can determine for themselves whether to believe the public allegation. The audience, in other words, must be treated as adults, informed rather than protected. (Some who have worked through this problem with us have suggested monitoring social media to see how large an impression the accusation has made before publishing anything more.)

In a predigital world, in short, a news organization could justify ignoring unsubstantiated allegations on the grounds of not dignifying them. In a digital world, the answer is not nearly so simple. Particularly in the age of disinformation and fragmentation, investigating the unsubstantiated that is already public—particularly at the moment that it has reached critical mass—has become a critical part of the journalistic art. The modern news provider has to inform the public what elements of that allegation still need to be substantiated for a citizen to know what to think about it; then it should lead the community in the search to find the answer. The process of verification thus has become more public, and more collaborative. But it has not vanished.

At the same time, it is now clear that the open nature of the Web makes it easy for bad actors to game or manipulate, with false information, bot-driven virality, deepfakes, false accusations, and more. What follows are some ideas for coping with an environment in which political actors and even foreign governments may want to sow confusion and doubt over facts.

COPING WITH MISINFORMATION: TECHNIQUES

STRATEGIC AMPLIFICATION

If something is unsubstantiated—meaning there is genuine doubt about whether it is true—journalistic responsibility dictates that journalists should do whatever they can to verify whether the allegation is true or not. If it is deemed to be unsubstantiated, a journalist may decide the allegation has not become widespread enough to publish anything more. In other words, if something is "out there" in a limited way, and a journalist determines only enough to say it can't be proven, he or she might determine to leave well enough alone. The risk of amplifying the allegation is too high, given that the allegation seems to have not spread very far. But the journalist still should have done everything possible to substantiate or knock it down, and be ready to act quickly if the allegation reaches critical mass. If the allegation resurfaces and becomes more widespread, the journalist will then be ready to provide the truth.

This issue of amplification becomes even more complicated if something is posted online that is known to be false—or is even intended as a deepfake to confuse people. In short, when should a news organization take steps to call something false if doing so might amplify the lie? This gets into the question that researcher danah boyd has called "strategic amplification," or deciding when it is necessary to repeat a lie to repudiate it and when it is wiser strategically to let it disappear on its own.

The calculus in deciding when and if you can simply let something rest is never simple. One of the most interesting cases involved a fake video that was posted of Speaker of the House Nancy Pelosi that had been manipulated to make it appear as though she was drunk. *The Washington Post* made the decision to prove the video was a fake. And it was careful in doing so.

It did not publish when it first spotted the video. It waited until it was convinced that the doctored Pelosi video had reached a certain level on Facebook—that it had crossed a tipping point. It was influenced by Facebook's refusal to take down the video—in contrast to YouTube's decision to remove it. It also believed the video was a cautionary tale for what was coming for the election—there would be more of this kind of manipulated video, and it was newsworthy to explain how it worked. The *Post*'s David Cho told us that they considered the possibility that doing a story would attract even more viewers. They believed their story would create awareness of the video being a fake, not confuse people and make the fake more viral.[38]

Weighing the evidence, we're convinced that the *Post*'s coverage, while it made more people aware of the video, helped expose the fake, not enlarge its effect. The reporters and editors made it clear that this was a story about a fake video, not one about Pelosi. The first word in the headline was "faked" and the first word in the story was "distorted"— useful techniques both for influencing the audience's first impression and for search engines. The evidence suggests most of the people who downloaded the video after the *Post* story were viewing it as a fake manipulation rather than believing it. The *Post* drowned the video, in effect, in a wider pool of context and repudiation.

THE SUCCINCT BUT DEFINITIVE KNOCKDOWN

Strategic amplification is only one tool for reacting to misinformation, and sometimes deciding to ignore a claim isn't enough. Some allegations simply require more effort to prove false. Ignoring them is insufficient.

In the 2020 election, Donald Trump's erratic lawyer and former New York mayor Rudolph Giuliani began peddling allegations that Hunter Biden, son of Democratic Party nominee Joseph Biden, had abandoned at a repair shop in Delaware a laptop that contained information suggesting that Hunter had passed bribes to his father from the Chinese. The *New York Post* published it. Most of the press simply ignored it as unsubstantiated, trying to avoid the trap of taking the bait, as it had four years earlier by publishing in weekly doses largely trivial emails from Hillary Clinton's campaign chairman John Podesta, stolen by Wikileaks and a Russian security agent. Twitter then made it difficult for people to share the Hunter Biden article because it was unsubstantiated, a decision the platform company later called a mistake.[39] But the claims about Hunter were spreading widely through right-wing media, including in talk programs on Fox.

The Wall Street Journal made a different decision. Just as columnist Kimberley Strassel was writing something on the editorial pages promoting the false theory, reporters from its news section took the time to look into the claims. Conservatives were furious that the larger press had simply turned its back on the allegations. But the *Journal* story, succinct and definitive, was something else. They didn't print the allegations in the *New York Post*. They met with the people in the Trump campaign peddling the allegations. They looked into them. Then they published a story establishing they were unsubstantiated, even repudiating Strassel on the other side of their operation. The *Journal* story had the force of the final word.[40]

After the election, Hunter Biden announced that he had been informed he was under investigation by the Justice Department, but there were no details and no hint that they involved his father. In December, the attorney general announced that the case did not require a special counsel investigation.

There are other ideas for how to approach misinformation and disinformation.

THE TRUTH SANDWICH

While some decisions focus on whether to report on falsehoods at all, others deal with how to portray falsehoods when knocking them down. During the Trump presidency, one approach for dealing with false or misleading claims stories gained attention, in part because it also took on a buzzy name: "truth sandwich." The idea is this: When dealing with a false claim they are trying to debunk, journalists should put the truthful account first, then the falsehood, then repeat the truth again. The reasoning is that people remember what they hear first, and journalists should prefer that this first impression be factual.

The concept was more easily understood than practiced in many news stories, but the main point resonated: Wherever possible, journalists should give primary treatment to facts, not falsehoods. The idea, not new, echoed the work of professor Kathleen Hall Jamieson in the early days of fact-checking in the 1990s, when she noted that television producers fact-checking campaign advertising should also sandwich the ads inside a television on the screen to make it visually obvious this was an ad being analyzed, not a real event.

WRITING HEADLINES ABOUT MISINFORMATION

Monitoring whether too much weight is given to falsehoods is a function that affects more than just the story text. It also matters when writing headlines or social media posts about stories—the first impressions you give people.

When many people absorb news from what they see while scrolling a social media feed, this is equally or perhaps even more important. If a newsworthy claim you must report on is false, you don't want the headline to merely amplify the falsehood. For example, it would be misleading to tweet, "Mayor Brown claims election fraud in Centerville, but the accusation is baseless." Search algorithms are likely to pick up the first part of the headline, not the end, thus amplifying the falsehood. The second problem is that people will be confused. The headline should be inverted: "Mayor Brown spreads false claim of election fraud in Centerville." And by no means should the headline simply repeat the falsehood: "Mayor Brown claims election fraud." During the Trump presidency, this form of headline writing was a constant challenge when the president of the United States daily made baseless claims about everything from rounding the curve on the pandemic to the pending election being the biggest fraud in American history. Dan Gillmor of Arizona State University has called such headline writing an example of giving a "loudspeaker to liars." Others have denounced it as stenography rather than journalism, as it is certainly a failure of verification.

The larger point is this: In the new discipline of verification, journalists are now often annotators of what the public has already heard rather than gatekeepers of what the public knows. They must be thoughtful in deciding when to engage and when not to. But annotating falsehoods is now a critical part of journalists' mission of knowing the truth.

Annotation is a game journalists will never "win," but they must continue to play it. Fighting misinformation and disinformation is not a problem like a leaky pipe that you simply seal and have fixed. It is more like a social condition, like crime or poverty, that requires constant and ever-adapting attention, for the bad guys will keep adapting, too, and the job is never really done.

BIAS

The discipline of verification, and particularly the concepts around being transparent as part of it, are among the most powerful steps journalists can take to address the problem of bias. By *bias* we don't mean simply political or ideological bias. Bias encompasses all kinds of predilections, both appropriate and troubling. We mean *bias* in a broader sense that covers all the judgments, decisions, and beliefs of those who gather and report news. This could include a bias for truth or facts or giving voice to the less powerful, as well as a bias toward one's own personal social, economic, or political leanings. The critics are right that we're all shaped by our personal history and the biases of the culture in which we live. Looked at this way, it becomes impossible to communicate without engaging some of these biases, including those that make a story compelling.

Understood in this broader, more realistic sense, bias is not something that can or even should necessarily be eliminated. Rather, the job of those engaged in journalism is to become more conscious of the biases at play in a given story and decide when they are appropriate and useful and when they are inappropriate. The journalist needs to become a manager of his or her own bias and the biases, if the setting is an institutional one, of the operation that is publishing the work.

Acknowledging or being aware of one's biases and initial reaction to events is obviously also the first step to a discipline of rigorous open-minded inquiry. (This is exactly what Nagel means in his approach, the opposite of denying one's initial views, or the illusion of "viewlessness.") What follows are ideas about how to do that in practice—how to avoid the problem of letting one's biases get in the way by acknowledging them rather than denying them.

Keep the following two ideas in mind. You may have biases that help you journalistically (a bias toward skepticism, for example, toward doubting yourself and double-checking all facts). You may have biases or preexisting attitudes that are negative (subtle racism that you are only vaguely aware of, or distrust of people you disagree with politically, or abject ignorance of religion). The biases that will hurt journalistic inquiry are the ones journalists fail to acknowledge even to themselves, the ones about which they are only vaguely aware or are too deluded to recognize. The biases people do not see are the ones most likely to enter their journalism and distort it. The only biases we can correct for are the ones we recognize.

We all have default biases. Being male or white or Asian or female or Black is a default bias. These are factors that shape our initial reaction to things. But as critics like Lowery rightly point out, whole newsrooms can become captive to default biases in a damagingly pernicious way if people fail to acknowledge that their personal experiences and backgrounds play a meaningful and sometimes-valuable role in the choices being made in those newsrooms. If people in newsrooms pretend they are objective—rather than acknowledging that they have an obligation to use objective methods for deciding and reporting the news—they fall into the trap of mistaking their good motives for actual professional method. In a newsroom that is trying to develop a genuine open-minded discipline of verification, managers must acknowledge that the personal experiences of the people in the newsroom are informing their choices; most important, they will encourage open constructive debate about newsroom coverage, about story choices, about assumptions inside stories and the way coverage may or may not be slanted. Fostering such an environment requires leaders to pay extra care to the way the newsroom's dominant culture can make it difficult for diverging viewpoints to be heard. Group dynamics can often override the perspective of the one or two people in the room who represent minorities' perspectives or backgrounds. Leaders must model seeking those perspectives out and not letting the majority view in the room be a false proxy for the debate in the world.

The only way to move beyond default biases that exist in a newsroom, in other words, is to first acknowledge that we are human, that our biases exist, to identify them, and then to take steps to expand the points of view that are involved in making choices. That is the first critical step toward moving past confusing one's good intentions about fairness and understanding with good execution and creating journalism that reflects the experience of the whole community.

A reporter's personal experiences and initial biases could be positive journalistically—a passion that government should be as transparent as possible, for example. Or they could be harmful: a view that all officials lie almost all the time or that all businesspeople are corrupt. The key is to examine what your biases are so you can move beyond them.

Imagine a reporter who is covering a childhood disease. Now imagine that her sibling had that same disease a few years earlier. That experience will no doubt enrich the reporter's understanding. Should it be part of the story? Perhaps or perhaps not. Whatever she decides, her knowledge of the emotional impact of being a family member of someone ill with the disease will make her reporting better.

Now consider a political reporter. Political writers almost certainly have their own thoughts and feelings about politics and policies. Now imagine a political writer who in his personal life always votes Democratic and is assigned to cover the day-to-day campaigning of candidates in both parties. He, too, must now address in his own thinking his personal preferences. But it would be a delusion to imagine that his personal preferences do not color how he tries to understand the race. He cannot, in other words, make the mistake of thinking that because he wants to be fair to the candidates in both parties he automatically will be. In fact, to be fair, he probably needs to work more diligently to understand the candidates he might reflexively disagree with. He needs to work harder to listen, to hear, and to learn. He might, in his interactions with the candidates, even admit that he grew up liberal and really wants to understand what a candidate is trying to say. In both cases, in other words, journalists' personal experience can positively inform their reporting. The only way it would not would be if they denied that any personal experience or attitude existed.

There is some validity to the axiom that bias is in the eye of the beholder—or that a biased story is just one you disagree with. The problem with this interpretation is that it too easily becomes an excuse to let everyone off the hook. You can't please everyone, so why worry about it? Problem solved. Dismissing the issue this way, however, doesn't address the frustrations of the audience, and it doesn't improve the reporting.

Managing bias involves several components that relate to the discipline of verification. The first task is to become more systematic and conscious about getting the facts right, using any number of the techniques we will soon describe below. Adopting a method of verification, rather than simply having faith in one's own and others' good intentions, is the most effective first step for those engaged in gathering and reporting news to overcome their preconceptions.

The second way to manage or curb bias is to move toward the Spirit of Transparency. This changes the relationship with the audience from one of talking down to one of sharing as equals. Explaining their decision-making forces those engaged in news to evaluate and sometimes reconsider what they are doing. If you cannot explain your decision-making, or if it looks awkward or embarrassing when you do, you will know there are problems in your decision-making. Journalists have also told us that more transparency has a remarkable impact in defusing assumptions that audiences would otherwise make about the motives of journalists.

But this third step may be the hardest. Cast a cold eye on yourself. Acknowledge your reflexive reactions to things. Recognize your default biases. And then take steps to address them. Do not just pick a side and become an advocate for where you began. That will make you a poorer journalist and a poorer learner and will narrow, not expand, the knowledge that a community requires of you.

TECHNIQUES OF VERIFICATION

Obviously, these concepts are not specific enough to constitute "a scientific method" of reporting—that is for individual journalists to refine. The key is that those who engage in journalism become conscious of the techniques they are employing to verify their reporting. They must check that the context they are trying to provide is fair and expansive, and be honest with themselves that they have taken steps to move beyond any initial or reflexive bias. But by way of illustration, we would like to offer some concrete methods from journalists around the country. While they are not encyclopedic, any journalist could fashion a superb method of gathering and presenting news from adapting the following few techniques.

EDIT WITH SKEPTICISM

When Sandra Rowe was editor of *The Oregonian* in Portland, Oregon, she employed a system at her paper that she and her successor, Peter Bhatia, call "prosecutorial editing." The term may be an unfortunately aggressive one. Reid MacCluggage, a former editor and publisher of *The Day* in New London, Connecticut, has suggested a better one, "skeptical editing."[41]

The approach involves adjudicating a story—in effect, line by line, statement by statement—editing the assertions in the stories as well as the facts. How do we know this? Why should the reader believe this? What is the assumption behind this sentence? If the story says that a certain event may raise questions in people's minds, who suggested that? The reporter? A source? A citizen?

Oregonian editor Amanda Bennett, who brought this idea from *The Wall Street Journal,* said the idea was designed for "rooting out not so much errors of fact but unconscious errors of assertion and narrative—to root out the things that people put in because 'they just know it's true.'"[42]

If a story said that most Americans now have a personal computer, the editor would ask for verification. If a story said "according to sources," the editor would ask, "Who are the sources? Is there more than one?" If there was only one, the story would have to say so. If a story said that candidate Smith's flip-flop on some tax bill proposal raised questions about his ideological consistency, the editor would ask, "What questions?" and "In whose mind?" If the answer was merely the reporter and the reporter's friends, the story would have to say so or that line would come out.

This kind of editing is designed to root out errors of assumption. It also is a way of rooting out default bias.

Whenever practical, said Rowe, this kind of editing involves the editor and the reporter sitting side by side, and the reporter producing original material. "The more of it we did, the more we were sending true fear" through the newsroom, said Rowe.[43] Bennett, who later ran *The Philadelphia Inquirer* and the Voice of America, began teaching it in the newsroom in front of groups of reporters and editors. "People didn't know it was okay to ask these questions," Bennett said. The purpose, in large part, is to "make that role of asking questions okay, and to make it conscious." Rather than more being included in stories, more was taken out, unless it could be absolutely verified.[44]

The technique, Bennett and Rowe believe, makes editors and reporters better and more thorough. The objective of *The Oregonian*'s skeptical editing was to create an atmosphere in which people can question a story without questioning the integrity of the reporter. It becomes part of an atmosphere of open dialogue in a newsroom, which goes bottom-up as well as top-down.

KEEP AN ACCURACY CHECKLIST

Several news organizations began to use accuracy checklists to remind their journalists of the importance of verification. Some of the checklists we collected are more conceptual and ask questions like:

- Is the lead of the story sufficiently supported?
- Is the background material required to understand the story complete?
- Are all the stakeholders in the story identified, and have representatives from each side been contacted and given a chance to talk?
- Does the story pick sides or make subtle value judgments? Will some people like this story more than they should?
- Have you attributed and/or documented all the information in your story to make sure it is correct?
- Do those facts back up the premise of your story? Do you have multiple sources for controversial facts?
- Did you double-check the quotes to make sure they are accurate and in context?

To these conceptual questions we would add another:

- Is it clear why you reported and ran the story in the first place? In other words, does the story choice itself need an explanation? Would some people think the choice itself reflects a bias? What is the reason this story is worth your effort and the public's time? And are there any risks in telling it?

Other checklists we have seen are more factual and concrete:

- Did you double-check the quotes to make sure they are accurate and in context?
- Have you checked websites, phone numbers, and unusual names?
- Did you check that all first references in your story have a first and last name?
- Have you checked ages, addresses, and titles to make sure they are correct? If so, have you written "everything else cq" above your byline to signal those things are correct?
- Do time references in your story include day and date?

Some editors consider such checklists too mechanistic, and if they are handled badly, we agree they can erode the confidence of reporters by seeming to quash the creative element of storytelling. But properly handled, such questions can bring reporters and editors together to make their work more accurate and credible.

COMPLICATING THE NARRATIVE:
OR MAKING CONFLICT INTERESTING AGAIN

After the 2016 elections, journalist Amanda Ripley felt her profession had fundamentally failed to understand voters and wondered if that reflected failures in the traditional ways that journalists tried to listen to people. She spent months with people with different listening skills, conflict mediators, psychologists, lawyers, clergy—people whose listening was less transactional (designed to get quotes) and more focused on helping people. The result was a beautiful and influential essay called "Complicating the Narrative."

Ripley's essay included the idea that oversimplifying conflict is a form of distortion that makes coverage less accurate. This simplification, which journalists have employed thinking they will make things easier to understand, actually makes them polarizing because people know it is a cartoon version of an important topic. Not only does making things more nuanced, more complicated, and less like a bumper sticker make them more accurate, it makes people more open to learning about positions different from their own.

To accomplish this, to make coverage of debate more truthful and accurate, Ripley suggested journalists need to learn some new techniques for listening. She also began to develop some new questions to probe beneath the short answers an increasingly distrustful public might offer to journalists.[45] Her work in turn inspired the Solutions Journalism Network to workshop and crowdsource some questions journalists might ask that would accomplish what Ripley was recommending.[46] Here are some of them.

AMPLIFY CONTRADICTIONS: Rather than cutting the details that don't fit the plot, Ripley called on journalists to raise those details up by showing that people are complicated. Don't oversimplify. The work that's emerged from her essay even advises asking people:

- "What gets oversimplified about this issue?"
- "Where do you feel torn?"
- "Is there any part of what you hear from the other side that makes sense to you?"

ASK QUESTIONS THAT GET TO MOTIVATION: Rather than asking people simply, "What's your position on this?" or "Why is the other side wrong?" which is transactional, try to open people up by asking them about motivations, or why they feel the way they do. Among questions that can do that:

- "Why is this important to you?"
- "What experiences shaped your views?"
- "What do you want the other side to understand about you?"
- "What would you like to understand about the other side?"

- "How has this conflict affected your life?"
- "What would change in your life if more people agreed with you?"

LISTEN MORE AND BETTER: Perhaps the richest parts of Ripley's essay are her suggestions for simply listening better—in effect listening rather than interviewing. In her essay, Ripley, using terminology from conflict resolution, refers to this as "looping." Some of her suggestions are simple and powerful.

After hearing someone talk, check what you heard by repeating it back to them and saying, "I want to make sure I have this right. Do you mean . . . ?" Then listen to their answer. If they are enthusiastic about your distillation of what they said, ask for more. If they sound hesitant, as if you didn't really get it, say, "I must be missing something. I haven't got this right, have I?"

That is listening, not interviewing.

In the subsequent work that the Solutions Journalism Network did adding to Ripley's essay, other journalists added further suggestions for the kinds of questions that move from interviewing to listening. Among them:

"Tell me more about that."

"How do you feel, telling this story?"

"What's the question nobody's asking?"

APPROACH INTERVIEW SUBJECTS WITH PERSONAL HONESTY, NOT VIEW-LESSNESS: To Ripley's methods we would add one other: Consider coming to such interviews in full transparency. Rather than saying, "I come from *The New York Times* or *The Daily Bugle* and want to ask you some questions," as if you had no opinion—as if you were that view-less journalist who doesn't exist—consider a more frank and personal approach. What if you said, "I write for *The Daily Bugle* and I want to ask you some questions. But, obviously, I am pretty different from you." Then be honest. "I am a young white liberal." Or "a Jewish kid from New York." Or "a Black person and I am frightened by you guys." Or "a young liberal gay woman. Help me understand you." Your honesty might just help get you theirs in return. It's a technique we have heard used by people covering extreme groups, often to very good effect.

TOM FRENCH'S RED PENCIL

If Ripley's method is comprehensive, Tom French's is wonderfully simple. French specialized in writing long, deep narrative nonfiction for the *St. Petersburg Times* in Florida. He won the 1998 Pulitzer Prize for feature writing. He also wrote on deadline.

French developed an easy but powerful test to verify any facts in his stories. Before he handed a piece in, he took a printed copy and went over the story line by line with a red pencil, putting a check mark by each fact and assertion to tell himself that he had double-checked that it was true.

BE CAREFUL WITH ANONYMOUS SOURCES

As citizens, we all rely on other sources of information for most of what we know. Those who produce journalism also most often depend on others for the details of their reporting. One of the earliest techniques journalists developed to assure audiences of their reliability was the practice of providing the sources of their information: Mr. Jones said so and so, in such and such a speech at the Elks Lodge, in the annual report, et cetera. Such dependence on others for information has always required a skeptical turn of mind. One axiom was: "If your mother says she loves you, check it out." If the source of the information is fully described, the audience can decide for itself whether the information is credible.

That isn't possible when a source is anonymous. At that point, audiences must invest more trust in the news provider that the source is believable and the information is true. As we argued above, one way to mitigate this scenario is for the journalist to share more information with the audience about the anonymous source, while still protecting the source. Yet over time this has become more complex.

As news sources have become more sophisticated in the art of press manipulation, confidentiality has shifted from a tool used by journalists to coax reluctant whistleblowers into confiding vital information into something quite different—a condition press-savvy sources impose on journalists before they even agree to an interview.

As dependence on anonymous sources for important public information has grown, journalists have begun trying to develop rules to assure themselves and their audience that they are maintaining independence from the anonymous sources of their news. What follow are two of the best sets of rules for how and when to trust anonymous sources. In a fractured media environment, where standards vary, these two sets of rules may be more important than they have ever been.

Joe Lelyveld, when he was executive editor of *The New York Times*, required that reporters and editors ask themselves two questions before using an anonymous source:

1. How much direct knowledge does the anonymous source have of the event?
2. What, if any, motive might the source have for misleading us, gilding the lily, or hiding important facts that might alter our impression of the information?

Only after they were satisfied by the answers to these questions could they use the source. And then, to the maximum degree possible, they had to share with the audience information to suggest how the source was in a position to know ("a source who has seen the document," for example) and what special interest that source might have ("a source inside the Independent Prosecutor's Office," for example). This effort at more transparency was a crucial factor in enlarging the audience's ability to judge for itself how much credence to give a report, but more important, it signaled the standards of the organization serving up their news.

The *Times* would add another important caveat in its use of anonymous sources—one that we see violated all the time. It created a rule against what it called the "anonymous pejorative." The anonymous pejorative occurred when an unnamed source was allowed to offer a negative opinion about someone personally without attaching their name to it. For example: "'Politician X was disorganized and didn't know what he was talking about, and whenever he was embarrassed about it, he would become abusive to his staff,' a former staffer said. 'I don't think they are just that smart.'" This is an opinion, and allowing someone to offer it publicly, without attaching their name to it, was considered under this rule to be unfair. We agree.

The late Deborah Howell, who worked as ombudsman of *The Washington Post*, Washington editor of the Newhouse newspapers, and editor of the St. Paul *Pioneer Press*, developed two other rules for anonymous sources that reinforced Lelyveld's and took the anonymous pejorative even further:

1. Never use an anonymous source to offer an opinion of another person. (In other words, use anonymous sources only for facts that you can independently verify.)
2. Never use an anonymous source as the first quote in a story. (In other words, never hang a story entirely on a claim that is anonymous. There must be more.)

Glenn Guzzo, a former editor of *The Denver Post*, had another set of questions he wanted reporters and editors to be able to answer when they requested approval for keeping a source anonymous to their audience. In a way, Guzzo blended Lelyveld's questions and Howell's rules into a single checklist.

1. Is the information essential to the story?
2. Is the information fact, not opinion or judgment? (He would not allow anonymity for judgmental statements.)
3. Is the source in a position to truly know—is this an eyewitness?
4. What other indicators of reliability are there (multiple sources, independent corroboration, experience with the source)?
5. What descriptors can you use so the audience can decide what weight to assign this source?

The three versions of these questions or tests also offer practical instructions for how to convey news, even after one has decided to use what an anonymous source is offering.

The point is not that anyone adhere rigidly to any one of these tests but that those engaged in practicing journalism apply conscious judgment when deciding to allow a source to remain confidential and that they share some of that reasoning with the audience. Public opinion surveys in 2020, by the way, revealed that while the public does not like anonymous sourcing, majorities of adults across the political spectrum support the practice when necessary.[47]

How would such a disclosure read? An example might be as follows: ". . . according to an attorney with access to the details of the case. The publication granted anonymity to the attorney because of the importance to the public of having this information and our belief that identifying him would put him in legal jeopardy."

Many publications now offer some kind of explanation for why they offer anonymity to sources. When we first published this book, almost none did so. There is no perfect method. Explaining why a source has been offered anonymity should not become boilerplate. It should be as specific to each case as it can safely be without risking identifying the source. It makes sense for publications to develop clear policies for using anonymity and to publish them from time to time and post them on their websites. The key is to create a "spirit of transparency," a sense that while you may not be perfect all the time, you are trying to level as much as you can with your community of readers, viewers, and listeners, that you respect them, and that you are thoughtful about your own methods. The more transparent and specific a news operation is about methods, the more it will distinguish itself from those operations that are not so thoughtful.

TRUTH'S MULTIPLE ROOTS

In the end, everyone in the journalistic process has a role to play in the journey toward truth. Publishers and owners must be willing to consistently air the work of public interest journalism without fear or favor.

Editors must serve as the protectors against debasement of the currency of free expression—words—resisting efforts by governments, corporations, litigants, lawyers, or any other newsmakers to mislead or manipulate by labeling lies as truth, war as peace.

Reporters must be dogged in their pursuit and disciplined in trying to overcome their own perspectives. Longtime Chicago TV newscaster Carol Marin put it to us this way: "When you sit down this Thanksgiving with your family and you have one of the classic family arguments—whether it's about politics or race or religion or sex—you remember that what you are seeing of that family dispute is seen from the position of your chair and your side of the table. And it will warp your view, because in those instances you are arguing your position. . . . A journalist is someone who steps away from the table and tries to see it all."[48] If philosopher Thomas Nagel, whose book *The View from Nowhere* defended objectivity as a method of understanding, were at Marin's dinner, he would wholeheartedly agree.

And, if journalism is conversation, in the end that conversation includes discourse among citizens as well as with those who provide the news. The citizens, too, have a role. They must, of course, be attentive. They also must be assertive. If they have a question or a problem, they should ask it of those who have provided the reporting: How do you know this? Why did you write this? What are your journalistic principles? These are fair questions to ask, and citizens deserve answers.

Thus those engaged in journalism must be committed to truth as a first principle and must be loyal to citizens above all so that citizens are free to pursue it. And in order to engage citizens in that search, they must apply transparent and systematic methods of verification. The next step is to clarify their relationship to those they report on.

5
INDEPENDENCE FROM FACTION

I n 1971, a few months after the historic confrontation between *The New York Times* and the federal government that the publication of the Pentagon Papers touched off, William Safire, a speechwriter for President Nixon, was seated next to *Times* publisher Arthur "Punch" Sulzberger at a fundraising dinner. During their conversation Safire mentioned that he was planning to leave government service.

Safire's comment fell on receptive ears. Since the election of Nixon in 1968, Sulzberger had been under pressure to find a conservative voice to balance the *Times* op-ed pages. The pressure was coming from Scotty Reston, the paper's Washington correspondent, former bureau chief, and executive editor, who worried about how the political world viewed the paper, as well as from members of the *Times* board of directors, who believed a greater balance of voices would ensure the success of a plan to launch a national edition. At the time, the op-ed page was dominated by liberals, including Tom Wicker, Anthony Lewis, Flora Lewis, and, more moderately, Reston himself. Sulzberger had come to the conclusion that he agreed: A strong conservative voice was a genuine need.

Safire was an appealing choice. He was raised in New York and still had many friends in the city. His clear and sometimes stinging prose included memorable criticisms of the press. The fact that Katharine Graham, the publisher of *The Washington Post,* had tried to hire Safire but couldn't agree on a salary made the idea even more attractive to Sulzberger.

Yet if the addition of Safire eased the pressure on Sulzberger from one side, it lighted a firestorm of criticism from longtime readers on the other, as well as from some in the *Times* newsroom. From both quarters came expressions of dismay that a presidential speechwriter could pass himself off as a journalist.

By what criteria could a partisan political activist suddenly call himself a journalist? Certainly something more than merely having a column was required to be a journalist at the *Times*. When Safire finally arrived three weeks before the Watergate scandal broke wide open, he recalled years later, he was thoroughly "ostracized by my Washington bureau colleagues as an unreconstructed Nixon flack. The only reporter who would even have lunch with me was Martin Tolchin, a long-before classmate at the Bronx High School of Science."[1]

Two unrelated events changed Safire's status. The first was personal. "At the annual bureau picnic, the three-year-old child of a reporter fell in a pool and started to drown," Safire said; "as the only adult standing nearby, I jumped in fully clothed to fish him out. The general opinion changed to 'he can't be all bad.'" The second was journalistic. *Times* reporter John Crewdson had broken a story on secret wiretaps placed on sixteen reporters and one Nixon aide. The aide was Safire. "That was a seemingly unprecedented assault on press freedom and was later made illegal; however, since I was the aide wiretapped, that made me 'one of them,' in Nixonian terminology, and when I blew my stack about secret taps in a *Times* column, that was reported in *Time* magazine as 'Safire Afire' and helped establish my independence. It was like getting a shower; I was no longer a pariah."

Thirty-two years later, Safire would retire from the *Times* with a Pulitzer Prize and the esteem not only of his colleagues in journalism but also of millions of readers. What earned him that acclaim? It certainly wasn't neutrality, or a tepid tone, or the desire to be evenhanded. Safire remained a dyed-in-the-wool conservative who could skewer adversaries, end careers, and be strident when moved to be.

What was it, then, that distinguished Safire from a partisan advocate or propagandist?

Put another way, what makes something opinion journalism as opposed to just someone's opinion—or distinguishes it from political advocacy and propaganda? The question is increasingly pertinent to the delivery of news and information in the twenty-first century.

Technology has opened media to millions of new voices; everyone on Facebook and Twitter is a publisher. And as commercial newsrooms have shrunk, think tanks, corporations, political activist groups, and nonprofits, all with clear social agendas, have become newsrooms and have moved to generate coverage for issues that affect them—sometimes with an eye to correcting the slant, shallowness, or other limitations they perceived in commercial media. As digital thinkers have noted, all the rest of us can publish, too.

Then add to that what has happened to politics. The question of whether we can distinguish journalistic opinion from political advocacy and propaganda has become all the more important as our politics has become so dysfunctional, our citizens so polarized, our media so partisan, and our public debate so debased.

Amid all this, then, what makes something opinion journalism?

Part of the answer is found in two of the values outlined in previous chapters. Journalists with a point of view must maintain the same fidelity to truthfulness and the same commitment to citizens as any other journalist. And, as we will describe in later chapters, journalists of opinion have a role to play in being a watchdog and providing a forum for public debate.

But for now let's deal with where the role of opinion fits in journalism.

News with a point of view cannot be discounted from being journalism. If it were, columnists and editorial writers would be excluded from the profession. Magazine writers such as Nikole Hannah-Jones (who led *The New York Times*'s Pulitzer Prize–winning 1619 Project) or Nick Lemann (who also served as dean of Columbia Journalism School) would be denounced for crossing a line when they drew conclusions in their reporting. Authors such as Robert Caro and the late David Halberstam, whose thoroughness elevated their work from journalism to history, would not have been honored for the depth, courage, and compassion of their reportorial judgment; instead, they would have been cast out for having it. Columnists such as Ruth Marcus and Michael Gerson of *The Washington Post*, essayists such as David Frum and Ta-Nehisi Coates at *The Atlantic*, and David Brooks and Nicholas Kristof at *The New York Times* would be castigated rather than honored. Some of the most celebrated work, known by some as "knowledge journalism" because its authors are experts who also report, would be denounced because it was too informed, too useful.

Every year the Pulitzer Board awards a prize for commentary under the heading "Journalism." And many have argued that the American alternative press is closer to the historical roots of journalism than large corporate-owned papers that profess to provide a neutral news account.

All of these precedents are worth remembering when people complain that contributions to new media made possible by the Web are not journalism because they are commentary. The fact that someone has formed a judgment and offered opinion after doing reporting does not, by any tradition or distinction, disqualify that work from being journalism.

But this doesn't mean all commentary is journalism.

The point is worth restating to make it clear. Being impartial or neutral is not a core principle of journalism. As we've explained in the previous chapter on verification, objectivity does not mean neutrality or balancing two sides equally, or being a political stenographer for public liars. But if neutrality is not a cornerstone of journalism, what, then, makes something journalism as opposed to propaganda? After all, propagandists publish. So do political activists. Scores from both sides of the political aisle write partisan blogs. Are they journalists? Is anyone who publishes or broadcasts a journalist?

The answer is no. There is a difference between journalism and advocacy, propaganda, or even just speech. If those distinctions are not grasped—if journalists cannot discern them—then the public cannot possibly hope to either. And journalism will be lost in a growing ocean of argument, disinformation, and misinformation, just as propaganda, with the advent of film and radio, became a new science a century ago.

After he retired from the *Times,* we asked Safire to ruminate on the qualities that had guided his thinking and had propelled that transformation from politician to journalist.[2]

A central issue, Safire agreed, had to do with allegiance.

> Where does loyalty lie—with your old personal friends and colleagues, with your political ideology or party, with your news medium, with the cold facts—or with The Truth?
>
> In real life, it's a fluctuating combination of all these. You don't burn a good long-term source to get a pretty-good story. You don't let your ideology turn you away from a good story. (You don't let a copy editor change "story" to "article" without a fight.) You don't let a series of hard facts lead you to a softly untruthful or misleading conclusion. You don't become a hero by joining a pack savaging your ideological soulmates. You don't quote from this paragraph selectively, reporting accurately but corrupting its whole meaning.

In other words, Safire held the same fidelity to accuracy and facts as does any other journalist, and that allegiance to hard facts and truthful conclusions separated him from his old partisan team. He was his own man, still conservative, but now working for his readers.

Safire also believed his experience in politics helped inform his second career as journalist. He believed just as clearly that this was a transformation one could not repeat. "Going back and forth every few years confuses the reader/viewer and must trouble the inveterate switcher as well," he said. Journalism is more than just having a perch at a TV station or on an op-ed page, although Safire believed political experience was good training for becoming a reporter.

> Having learned to skirt an issue or fuzz up a statement on the inside helps a journalist detect such manipulation of words when on the outside. When on the inside, you develop lifelong relationships with people you trust (and you remember those less trustworthy). After you have crossed the street, these friendships can lead to confidential sourcemanship: the art of getting information from insiders, or predecessors of insiders, that you as a journalist are not supposed to get. Nothing beats a confidential source with whom you have shared a

political foxhole. You know what to expect from that person, who knows how far you will go to protect a confidence.

Safire believed that opinion journalists had more liberty than other journalists to call things as they saw them without the qualifiers of a straight reporter. They might even have more obligation. "I like to think I helped launch a field called 'opinionated reporting,'" Safire said. "This was not the sneaky business of slanting a purported news story; it was the digging for a fresh fact that illuminated, or at least called attention to, a candidly labeled op-ed opinion column."

There was one other matter that bothered his new colleagues at the *Times* that Safire chose not to clear up. "[There] was still the 'nattering nabobs of negativism' problem," Safire would recall, referring to a speech he had helped write that would become one of the most famous denunciations of the American media ever delivered by a major political figure. "I wrote that phrase in a 1970 speech given by Vice President Agnew in San Diego denouncing defeatists in general, not the press in particular; but because it followed a televised speech he made, written by Pat Buchanan, excoriating the media for 'instant analysis' and other sins, my alliterative phrase, generously credited to me by Agnew, was associated with his caustic attack on the press. (I never tried to straighten that out, because having a reputation of media critic didn't hurt me a bit with readers.)" This, too, is revealing. Safire was less concerned with how his new colleagues perceived him than with how the audience reacted.

These qualities thus emerge as the fourth key principle of journalism:

**Journalists must maintain an independence
from those they cover.**

This even applies to those who work in the realm of opinion, criticism, and commentary. It is this independence of spirit and mind, intellectual independence rather than neutrality, that journalists must keep in focus.

Editorialists and opinion journalists are not neutral. Their credibility is rooted instead in the same dedication to accuracy, verification, and the larger public interest and the same desire to inform that all other journalists subscribe to. "Do you need to present both sides to be impartial?" Safire wondered. "Clearly no. Don't be afraid to call somebody a 'terrorist' who strikes terror into a populace by deliberately killing civilians. That killer is not a 'militant' or 'activist,' which are suitable terms for political demonstrators or firebrands, nor is he or she a 'gunman,' which is not only evasive but sexist. To be excessively evenhanded is to be, as the Brits say, kak-handed—clumsy."

Safire also felt phony evenhandedness was a disservice to his readers. "Playing it straight does not mean striking a balance of space or time. When one side of a controversy makes news—issues a survey or holds an event—it's not the reporter's job to dig up the people who will shoot it down and give them equal attention. Comment, yes; 'balance' by column inch or stopwatch, no."

That does not mean seeking out straw man arguments to knock down. For political activists and propagandists, facts are often stretchable and more selectable, and ideas tend to be tactics rather than the point of the exercise. The goal of the political activist or propagandist is not just to win an argument; it is to get to a particular political outcome. The goal of an opinion journalist is different. The aim is to explore ideas and to generate public consideration. This difference in purpose is essential.

Some of the best opinion journalists indeed like to engage the strongest arguments of their opponents, not knock down the weakest. Michael Gerson, who was a speechwriter for George W. Bush before becoming a columnist for *The Washington Post* Writers Group, has said that taking account of the arguments on the other side is a way of making his own ideas stronger and more interesting. And E. J. Dionne, whose column also appears in the *Post,* on the art of argument cites writer Christopher Lasch, who contended that when writers seriously engage in opposing ideas they are also prone to learn from them and change their own.

In some ways, this fourth principle—that journalists must be intellectually independent—is rooted more in pragmatism than in theory. One might imagine that one could both report on events and be a participant in them, but the reality is that being a participant clouds all the other tasks a journalist must perform. It becomes difficult to see things from other perspectives. It becomes more difficult to win the trust of the sources and combatants on different sides. It becomes difficult if not impossible to then persuade your audience that you put their interests ahead of those of the team that you are also working for.

INDEPENDENCE OF MIND

As we talked to journalists around the country from different fields, probing their motives and their professional goals, it became clear that Safire, Gerson, and Dionne had articulated key but subtle notions that are widely shared. The late Anthony Lewis, a liberal opinion columnist for *The New York Times,* said that the difference is grounded not only in a commitment to truthfulness but also in a kind of faith that this commitment implies. "Journalists who end up writing columns of opinion have a point of view. . . . But they still prize facts above all. C. P. Scott, the great editor of *The Manchester* (Great Britain) *Guardian,* put it this way: 'Comment is free but facts are sacred.' I think we tend to go from the particular to the general; we find facts and from them draw a conclusion," Lewis continued. Media "provocateurs like Ann Coulter or veteran conservative talk show host Sean Hannity are the other way around. All they care about are opinions, preferably shouted. Facts, if any, are incidental. They follow the advice of the Queen of Hearts, 'Sentence first—verdict afterward.'"[3]

Independence of spirit even reaches into opinion writing that is nonideological—the work of art critics and reviewers. John Martin, former dance critic of *The New York Times,* said that as he moved to judgment and opinion he believed he retained a kind of journalistic independence. "I feel that my first responsibility is to tell what happened, and secondarily, to express my opinion, let's say, or an interpretation, or, as briefly as possible, to put this particular performance in its place in the scene. And I think that, in a way, is reporting, too."[4]

It has become fashionable in recent years to wonder who is and who isn't a journalist. We think this is the wrong question. The question people should ask is whether the person in question is doing journalism.

Does the work proceed from an adherence to the principles of truthfulness, an allegiance to citizens, and an aim of informing rather than manipulating—concepts that set journalism apart from other forms of communication? Not every post by a journalist is a work of journalism. Pictures of grandchildren, for instance, do not usually qualify. But an eyewitness account by someone on vacation with her cellphone with pictures and her personal experience of witnessing the effects of a hurricane might well be journalism.

The important implication is this: Freedom of speech and freedom of the press belong to everyone. But *communication* and *journalism* are not interchangeable terms. Anyone *can* be a journalist. Not everyone *is*.

The decisive factor is not whether someone has a press pass or an audience. Phil Donahue, who had one of the first popular daytime talk shows on television, years before Oprah Winfrey, suggested to us long ago that the man who walked into the bar at Chernobyl and said, "The thing blew," at that moment had committed an act of journalism. If he was reporting an event he had witnessed or had checked out, not passing along a rumor, he was doing journalism. Donahue's hypothetical example would come to be borne out—again and again—when technology made public spaces something more than physical places such as bars. Consider IT consultant Sohaib Athar, who happened to be living in Abbottabad, Pakistan, at the time of the US raid on the compound where Osama bin Laden was hiding. Athar's tweets on that day in May of 2011—observing an unusual helicopter, noting the sound of an explosion, and surmising that the activity seemed to go beyond routine Taliban operations—go down as the first known reporting on the raid that killed Osama bin Laden.

These distinctions may be easily lost on the public, which we have seen increasingly duped by political propagandists pretending to be journalists, employed by websites that position themselves as legitimate sources of news. But these people and these outlets are something else. First, they lack the fidelity to facts (in recent years many have trafficked in conspiracy theories and deepfakes). They are not independent (usually they are paid for and staffed by partisan activists). And their purpose is not to inform; it is to amass an audience for political purposes.

Yet the growing cohort of partisan propaganda outlets posing as news is doing enormous damage to the reputation of real journalists who aspire to accuracy, independence, and the goal of informing rather than manipulating audiences.

There may be little that can be done to stop such pretenders from spreading. But we can clarify what genuine Journalism of Opinion looks like so that its practitioners can stand up and defend the model—or the distinctions will begin to disappear.

For it is one thing to understand the intellectual difference between an opinion journalist and a partisan propagandist. Living up to that distinction can be harder. Friendships, opportunities, and flattery all will conspire to seduce the opinion writer to cross the line.

THE EVOLUTION OF INDEPENDENCE

Ancient Greek philosophers understood that humans are political by nature and that an organized community requires some sort of political activity. It was in this crucible of political affairs that the first periodicals were born, inviting the broad public to become involved in the political decisions that affected their lives.

As we outlined in chapter 3 when discussing journalists' loyalty to citizens, the history of journalism over the last three hundred years, particularly in the American tradition, was distinguished by a move away from a fealty to political party toward a loyalty to the public interest. "Journalistically, the twentieth century can be defined as the struggle for democracy against propaganda, a struggle inevitably waged by an 'objective' and 'independent' press," journalism scholar James Carey of Columbia University wrote.[5]

In essence, the press, gradually and in a struggle that took more than half a century, swapped partisan loyalty for a new compact—that journalism would harbor no hidden agenda. Editorials and political opinion, which before had mixed with and sometimes even constituted the news on the front page, were now set apart by space or label. From these simple decisions, much of today's standard journalistic ethic was formed, especially those principles concerning political positioning by reporters.

Those ethics strengthened generally through the twentieth century as journalists aspired to greater professionalism and also as the number of competing newspapers in cities shrank, leaving the survivors to appeal to a more mass audience, something to which broadcast television news organizations also aspired before the spread of cable.

In the twenty-first century, one of the biggest questions is whether this notion of journalistic independence will survive. New technology and the audience fragmentation it spawned have led to the creation of niche media outlets built around ideology and the appeal of affirming the audience's preconceptions (a Journalism of Affirmation), such as Breitbart, One America News Network, and others. Increasingly, research has shown some of these outlets are guilty of publishing information that is simply false, perhaps knowingly so. Some of these partisan outlets are owned by corporations, and their purpose is commercial, not strictly partisan. (Fox News, MSNBC, websites such as The Daily Caller, and the internet operations of conservative pugilist Glenn Beck are a few examples.) For now, there is no fully analogous market for ideology at the local level, though it is growing. Sinclair Broadcasting, whose clearly partisan programming and dictates from above about editorials that all its stations must air have made it an object of deep skepticism and concern, by 2020 owned close to two hundred stations in nearly ninety markets.

A growing number of state-oriented online news sites are also appearing, sometimes funded by nonprofits, some of them with untraceable dark money, both liberal and conservative. Courier Newsrooms is a network of progressive websites in swing states that contend, "Facts and first-hand sources are [their] north star," yet it also purchases ads in social media to boost its most partisan content. At the same time, a network of 1,300 local sites that aggregate public information, while at least in many cases slipping in right-leaning partisan content, is also ballooning.[6]

This is already throwing into doubt the future of the American press tradition of independence from faction. It will also further weaken the economic possibilities of the mass markets that encouraged nonpartisan journalism in the first place. As the sorting-out process of the new media system goes on, the question is whether audiences in the twenty-first century will continue as they did in the twentieth to respond more to news that is produced with genuine intellectual independence. The platform companies have an influential role to play here. They could help consumers see those distinctions if they wanted to.

The evidence is not encouraging. After two decades in the internet and cable age of a proliferation of partisan outlets, Americans are far less likely to see the press as independent from faction than they once were. The perception that people see bias in news coverage has steadily been growing since the internet began. As of 2019, almost half of Americans (46 percent) saw a "great deal" of bias in news coverage, up an alarming 15 percentage points since 2007. Another 37 percent saw "a fair amount" of bias—meaning a total of 83 percent see significant bias in the news.[7] Perhaps even more troubling, the youngest Americans, those who grew up in this new partisan media age, are the least likely trust the press. Just 19 percent of American adults under age thirty have a generally favorable view of the news media. Only conservative Republicans are more distrustful.[8]

INDEPENDENCE IN PRACTICE

The rules have been modified and strengthened over time, to the point that reporters and editors at many traditional news organizations have been forbidden from participating in such political action as public rallies on politicized issues. In 1989, *New York Times* Supreme Court reporter Linda Greenhouse was famously criticized for participating in a "Freedom of Choice" demonstration in support of abortion rights. She called her participation anonymous activism and made note of the fact that she did not call attention to herself. "I was just another woman in blue jeans and a down jacket," she said afterward. But the *Times* said her marching jeopardized the appearance of her reporting and reprimanded her.[9]

The Greenhouse incident came at a time when journalism was becoming more sensitive to the charge of liberal bias. The nature of the political debate had been changing since the 1960s, stimulated in part by the creation of an active network of conservative think tanks injecting new ideas into the public debate. And Republican lawmakers were more vocal in asserting press bias.

The advent of new digital publishing platforms has refueled the debate about what journalists can and cannot do or say in their private lives. In April 2004, Rachel Mosteller was fired from the Durham *Herald-Sun* for keeping a blog, *Sarcastic Journalist,* in which she talked about newsroom life. Her blog did not identify the company or her coworkers. In January 2006, the weekly *Dover Post* fired a reporter because his personal blog contained, among other things, disparaging references to people who sought coverage from the newspaper. In 2010, CNN parted company with Octavia Nasr, a senior editor for Middle Eastern affairs, after she posted a tweet in response to the death of a Shiite cleric: "Sad to hear of the passing of Sayyed Mohammed Hussein Fadlallah . . . one of Hezbolla's giants I respect a lot." Among the prominent cases was the departure from *The Washington Post* of Wes Lowery, the Pulitzer Prize–winning reporter whose column we talked about at length in chapter 4. Lowery tweeted that *The New York Times,* in a retrospective on the rise of the Tea Party movement in the early 2010s, had failed to declare the movement to be "essentially a hysterical grassroots tantrum about the fact that a black guy was president." In a private meeting, *Washington Post* editors reportedly told Lowery his tweets violated the paper's social media rules and undermined the *Post*'s ability to cover conservatives. Soon thereafter, Lowery left the paper.

As newsrooms began a reckoning over race in 2020 amid the protests over the death of George Floyd, the issue of what journalists could say in their personal social platforms became an even more intensely debated issue, mixed in some cases with the issues Lowery had raised in his *New York Times* column over the default culture in newsrooms and the idea that journalists of color, in order to get along, were expected to behave as if they were white. The issue was hardly resolved. But it led many newsrooms to reexamine policies on social media and participation. We were part of conversations in which newsroom editors acknowledged usefully that they stood for certain values—they were not neutral. They stood, for instance, for equal rights under the law, for racial justice, for government transparency, and more. Each news organization could make its own list (though many of the same concepts would likely show up on many of the lists). And different newsrooms could arrive at slightly different conclusions about what was allowed. The editor of one paper told us her reporters could say "Black lives matter" in their social messaging, as long as they did not capitalize the L in lives and the M in matter. For that would be endorsing a group. Other organizations said their staff could march in protests for racial justice, as that goal should be not controversial. The distinction may strike some as subtle. That makes it no less important to recognize and understand. It is one thing for a news organization to stand for a set of principles such as equality under the law, social justice, factualism, and government transparency. It is another to endorse the particular policies or solutions of one group in the arena over another on issues of controversy over those principles. The difference is not neutrality. It is independence.

INDEPENDENCE REEVALUATED

Even as the rules of independence became stricter in the past decades, there were always those who challenged or evaded them.

In the lead-up to the Iraq War in March 2003, conservative George Will wrote a column dismissing the conventional idea that America should seek approval from its allies before invading the Middle Eastern country. To support his view that multilateralism was foolish, Will quoted at length from a speech by British House of Lords member and newspaper owner Conrad Black. In his speech, Black said American foreign policy was successful because when its objective was threatened, America swiftly removed the threat.

Will's column did not disclose that he had been paid for years to sit on the international advisory board of Black's newspaper company, Hollinger International. *The New York Times* said that for every meeting Will attended, he received $25,000; Will said he did not remember how many meetings he was present at. Will had also failed to inform *The Washington Post* Writers Group, which syndicated his column, of the conflict. Asked by the *Times* if he should have told readers about receiving money from Black, Will replied: "My business is my business. Got it?"[10]

The Conrad Black episode was not the first of its kind for Will. In 1980, then a strong backer of Republican presidential candidate Ronald Reagan, he coached Reagan to prepare the candidate for his debate with President Jimmy Carter. Will then took to the airwaves after the debate as an ABC commentator and hailed Reagan's performance, saying Reagan was a "thoroughbred" under pressure.

Such secret counsel to politicians had plenty of precedent. Among others, Walter Lippmann wrote speeches for various presidents, including Lyndon Johnson, and the belated discovery of the secret work tarnished Lippmann's reputation.

What was new in the Will case was the columnist's continued insistence that he didn't care. When news of the coaching of Reagan eventually surfaced, Will dismissed the criticisms as nitpicking. "Journalism (like public service, with its 'conflict of interest' phonetics) is now infested with persons who are 'little moral thermometers' dashing about taking other persons' temperatures, spreading, as confused moralists will, a silly scrupulosity and other confusions."[11]

Will was not making an ideological argument. He was implying something else, something that others, regardless of ideology, would echo: that the morality or ethics of journalism are subjective and invalid.

There was only one problem with Will's argument, the same one that reveals why the concept of independence is grounded in pragmatism rather than theory. Will had kept his coaching of Reagan (and his money from Conrad Black) secret. He did not want to tell his readers that he had helped produce the performance by President Reagan that he then glowingly reviewed. If he had, his praise of Reagan would have been discounted. Not by ethicists. By the audience.

For in reality Will's business, as it turns out, isn't entirely his own business. He is in the business of public discourse.

Will's pattern is an old one. Cable news, for example, has also become a hazy and discouraging netherworld of conflict of interest disguised as expertise. All of this has contributed to the growing sense among the public that journalists are not acting in the public interest but are just another group of actors working for interested parties, often to enrich themselves.

With each campaign cycle, the cable networks continue to blur the line and damage journalism's reputation. In 2008, Chris Matthews, Paul Begala, and Donna Brazile presented themselves as unaligned commentators when in private they were supporting or advising either Barack Obama or Hillary Clinton in the race for the Democratic nomination. In 2020, MSNBC announced that journalist-turned-historian Jon Meacham "would no longer be serving as a MSNBC contributor" after *The New York Times* reported that he had been working on speeches for Joe Biden and then appearing as a presidential historian on MSNBC commenting on Biden's speeches, usually in tones of great authority. Meacham could still appear on MSNBC, whose programming was consistently anti-Trump, but his involvement with Biden would be noted and he would no longer be paid.[12] The problem is endemic on cable. In 2020, CNN contributor Ana Navarro did events for Joe Biden. David Urban and strategist Steve Cortes advised the Trump campaign. Tucker Carlson's and Laura Ingraham's relationships with Donald Trump cross so many lines it is difficult to know where to begin. (We will get to Sean Hannity in a moment.) The cable channels all have workarounds, including that their "contributors" should not formally endorse candidates. But these rules are symbolic and serve little purpose other than offering a loincloth over the networks' exposed breach of ethics.

Another erosion of journalistic independence happens when political candidates woo commentators by "consulting" with them for their ideas. In 2005, the Bush administration consulted with various journalists on drafts of the president's second inaugural speech, among them *Weekly Standard* editor William Kristol and syndicated columnist Charles Krauthammer. Both said they had offered general consultations about policy, not speech preparations, and contended that as such they had done nothing wrong.[13] Yet both also praised the speech after it was delivered as if they were independent voices.

The failure to disclose the relationship is one mistake, though it's obvious why they didn't. It would have hurt their reputations as independent conservatives if it was known they had consulted on the speech they were praising. But there is another problem with journalists "consulting" with those they are supposedly covering. The journalists are deluding themselves about what is really going on. As a rule, politicians are far less interested in what any journalist might actually contribute to a speech; they have more speechwriters than they need. Instead, they are far more interested in making the journalist imagine that his or her rhetorical and intellectual powers are so magical, policy makers had no choice but to seek the journalist's indispensable wisdom. When politicians seek the advice of journalists, the effort is far more likely a gambit to ensure good press than to solicit the wisdom of the pundit.

In the new landscape, the double-dealing is barely a secret. Sean Hannity advises President Trump in private phone calls, then interviews Trump on his program as though he were a journalist, a pose that damages all those real journalists who try to conduct interviews on television. In the end, Hannity has become neither a presidential aide who can be held accountable nor a journalist whose questions are genuine inquiry. And a company that calls itself a news organization perpetrates and perpetuates the fraud. To call it opinion journalism—or even just opinion—is a stretch. It is propaganda, often drenched in lying. The damage to both journalism and the republic is still being calculated.

TRANSPARENCY, INDEPENDENCE, AND DECEPTION

Besides the fairly obvious and self-defeating double-dealing, there are other challenges to the notion of journalistic independence that deserve more consideration. One of these is the worry that journalistic independence has wandered into a kind of self-imposed solitary confinement from society at large. As Elliot Diringer, a former reporter with the *San Francisco Chronicle* who later joined the Clinton White House, told our academic research partners, "There is this notion that you should be disinterested to the point . . . that you should withdraw from civic affairs if you are a journalist. And I find that somewhat troubling. I don't know why being a concerned citizen should be antagonistic with being a journalist."[14]

There have been two major responses to correct this sense that those operating by traditional news conventions have become too distant and alienated. One was the movement called public or civic journalism, which gathered steam in the 1990s before new technology created much more powerful ways of creating an interactive relationship with community. These movements argued that journalism should not just point out problems but also examine possible answers and help communities arrive at those solutions. Proponents of the movement did not see this approach as a rejection of the journalistic principle of independence. Critics, on the other hand, argued that it put journalists in a position of advocate because they identified with outcomes. But that divide, in the end, was more an argument over careful execution than an argument over philosophy.

More recently the Solutions Journalism Network has been more effective at getting journalists to recognize that the work of news should do much more than spotlight problems; it should also explore solutions. The group trains journalists and encourages learning from like-minded peers; it also helps news organizations to develop content that highlights solutions and to form collaborations with other news organizations around specific topics. In addition, it helps college educators teach a new generation of journalists the skills of covering solutions and not just problems.

The focus on solutions is in no way an abridgement of journalistic independence. To the contrary, it makes journalism more accurate. It also makes it more useful and relevant. News that talks only about problems is incomplete, lacks context. It is a poorer journalism.

Remember, too, that the purpose of journalism is more than reporting the news. At a deeper level, as we noted in chapter 1, the function of news is to create community. And in addition to establishing a common set of facts, creating community involves creating channels and forums that help people working through those problems connect with one another. Community creation has always been at the heart of news—from the earliest days of newspapers growing out of the conversation that occurred in coffeehouses to the communities of citizens and journalists that form and re-form around breaking news stories or communities of interest on social platforms such as Twitter. The difference between a path forward or a path into the ditch is in the execution, and in the intent of the people operating in the role of journalist. Are they posing as journalists, pretending to provide news and information, when in fact their real motive is to manipulate others toward a predetermined outcome? Or are they genuine information providers and forum communicators who do not presume to have the answers but want to present information and then help convene the community to address problems together and work on those problems?

The other reaction to the sense that the independent news provider is somehow not to be trusted has been to abandon the principle of independence altogether, reaching out to the audience by arguing from one side or the other. During the Trump presidency, more people also began to suggest journalists should do this and embrace journalism as a kind of advocacy. (While Wes Lowery says he is not advocating abandonment of independence, his rhetoric may invite others to head down that road.)[15] Frighteningly, one need only turn on cable news to see a preview of this dystopia.

The model was refined to an art by conservative media mogul Rupert Murdoch and political consultant Roger Ailes at Fox News. Murdoch's aim was in part to make money. But he and Ailes also wanted to reshape the Republican Party. By 2020, after nearly a quarter century on the air, Fox, however, had become the old guard of propagandistic partisan cable news programming. And with Lear-like inevitability, it had spawned even-more-Far-Right offspring and competitors, among them One America News Network (OANN), Newsmax TV, Sinclair Broadcasting, and the Blaze. All, in different ways, were trying to cater to an even angrier and more extreme base than Fox.

The network's first marketing campaign featured the slogan "We report, you decide," which it later dropped in favor of "Fair and balanced." Developed by Ailes, a political consultant in his prior life to Richard Nixon, Ronald Reagan, and George H. W. Bush, this was classic campaign pugilism. Claim the strength of your rival (the old broadcast networks like CBS or even, at the time of Fox's 1996 launch, CNN), even if the claim is absurd; doing so puts your competitors on the defensive and makes a bid, however specious, that your flaw does not exist. One could hear in Fox News's claims the echoes of Ailes's political campaigning, which included ads claiming that Massachusetts Democrat Michael Dukakis was bad for the environment and that he was a radical who would put murderers back on the street.[16]

Fox's claims "Fair and balanced" and "We report, you decide" also echoed Hearst's and Pulitzer's advertising of themselves not as they were but as they wanted people to imagine them: as accurate and fair, not simply as a source one was likely to agree with. It was an appeal to each audience member's sense of him- or herself as reasonable. If you like us, that is because we are more accurate, more complete, not because you agree with us.

The channels that have emerged in Fox's wake also engage in this linguistic violence. They, too, tend to rely on innuendo and claims of independence rather than acknowledging their partisanship. OANN has broadcast conspiracy theories ranging from the suggestion that high school shooting victims are trained actors to the idea that the coronavirus is a globalist conspiracy concocted by George Soros, the Clintons, Bill Gates, the Chinese government, and Dr. Anthony Fauci. Yet in its promotions, a pretty blond newscaster walks toward the camera and says, "It's time for a new way of looking at news. It's time for a network that cares about a strong America. . . . If you're looking for credible news, you've come to the right place. One America is ready. Are you?" Newsmax similarly peddles conspiracy theories and falsehoods. During the COVID-19 crisis, it sent an email to its subscriber list asserting that "the Worst thing you could do is get a vaccine when it becomes available" because "vaccines are one of the biggest health scares of our lifetime—a scam perpetuated among the American people." Instead, it suggested it would be "far more effective" to subscribe to its newsletter for forty dollars a year. Subscribers in turn got pitches for dietary supplements that would supposedly boost immune health. Newsmax TV's marketing slogan: "Real News for Real People."[17]

The appeal of this new partisan press rests on reinforcing the preconceptions of the audience while insisting, to the contrary, that it is simply being accurate and independent. OANN, for instance, promises an "honest assessment of our nation's leadership." The partisanship is adamantly denied. It's the rest of the media that's biased, the slogan suggests. We tell you the truth.

The problem is not just that this is inaccurate. Whenever public institutions engage in this kind of distortion of language and twisting of the meaning of words, there is a degrading effect on the culture.

Words begin to lose their meaning. Belief begins to ascend over fact. It becomes by turns easier to call true things fake or facts hoaxes. When a journalistic institution engages in this kind of Orwellian dishonesty, it is a special kind of sin. Accuracy and precision are fundamental requirements of the profession. To abandon them, or to clothe hucksterism, conspiracy theories, and propaganda in the apparel of news, is to move toward despotism and tyranny.

This new Journalism of Affirmation is different from the old American partisan press, which was controlled by the parties with the explicit purpose of advancing the parties' goals, educating and persuading. It also stands in stark contrast to the Journalism of Opinion, which grew up in the twentieth century in publications like *The New Republic* on the left or the *National Review* on the right. This Journalism of Opinion still exists, though not much anymore on television, in journals such as *The Bulwark*, a conservative online publication founded by veterans of *The Weekly Standard*; in *The Nation*, the liberal magazine whose roots go back to the abolitionist movement; and in the work of conservative writers like Jonah Goldberg at *The Dispatch* (who founded the site with colleagues from the *National Review*) and Conor Friedersdorf at *The Atlantic*, liberals like Elizabeth Bruenig at *The New York Times*, and writers who are harder to categorize such as Christine Emba at *The Washington Post*. In the networked age, there are also voices who are known online but not affiliated with traditional publications, such as Matt Yglesias (a liberal but hardly a partisan), Thomas Chatterton Williams (also leaning left), and Glenn Loury (on the right). What distinguishes the Journalism of Opinion from the new Journalism of Affirmation on cable news and elsewhere is that it is more transparent about its partisanship. It is also more intellectually independent from party. And it adheres steadfastly to the same aspirations of accuracy as other realms of journalism. The Journalism of Opinion also doesn't tend to engage in conspiracy theories and invented facts. The reason is simple. *The Dispatch* and *The Nation*, at bottom, are concerned with exploring ideas and inspiring public consideration of issues, not in manipulating the public to particular outcomes—or, as in the case of Newsmax, selling diet supplements associated with the channel's other business interests.

Here's how *The Dispatch*, which promises "fact-based reporting and commentary on politics," describes itself: "When we provide analysis, we will endeavor to describe the opposing view with honesty and charity. When we report, we will do so without concern for whether the facts prove inconvenient to any party or politician. We'll test our own assumptions and, we hope, challenge our readers to do the same. We expect people to disagree, but we hope they will see that we come to our positions honestly, without some unstated agenda."

The Dispatch, like the Journalism of Opinion more generally, exists squarely inside the realm of responsible journalism. It is clear and honest about its purpose: It is a journal of opinion exploring ideas and is clearly ideological in nature. Such publications do that best, indeed, when they challenge the strongest arguments of those with whom they disagree. They are trying to advance ideas, not outcomes.

By contrast, the Journalism of Affirmation, as it has evolved in the last quarter century, purports to be one thing—neutral and factual—while being another. It has become a new form of propaganda, a discipline where facts are often inconvenient and usually are employed in the service of one party over the other.

This distinction between the Journalism of Opinion (like *The Dispatch* or the *National Review*) and the propagandistic advocacy and conspiracy peddling of the Journalism of Affirmation (like Fox or OANN) is critical. Open in its intent, the Journalism of Opinion is also transparent in its allegiance to a set of intellectual principles, which it holds above faction or party. David Brooks describes himself as a libertarian, in the same manner that George Will in *The Washington Post* calls himself an American Tory and Victor Navasky at *The Nation* refers to himself as a progressive. The Journalism of Affirmation, claiming fairness, balance, and neutrality, lacks both the agility and the candor for such distinctions. Its proponents are loyalists. Watch these commentators carefully—Rachel Maddow, Rush Limbaugh, Sean Hannity—or online, writers at sites such as Breitbart.com. Their currency is emotional mobilization. Much of their conversation focuses on the wrongness of the other side, or the anticipation that there lies trouble ahead for the obviously misguided opponent. This is the essence of the affirmation: be afraid, or be angry, or be assured they will get their comeuppance. As one talk radio host told us after we finished a segment on his program one evening: "My show isn't really about ideology. It's about outrage."

There is another difference as well. The Journalism of Opinion, be it in the column of a conservative or a liberal, is not fundamentally about reporting the news but about making sense of it. It assumes that the reporting occurs elsewhere and that interpretation is the primary concern. While the Journalism of Opinion may involve reporting, there is no claim that this reporting occurs outside the realm of the gathering that information to make an argument. Historically, the Journalism of Opinion does not claim to be the primary or first news source.

The new Journalism of Affirmation, by contrast, makes more claim to straight reporting (We report, you decide). Yet in prime time and increasingly throughout their day, Fox, MSNBC, and others have opened the door to using political operatives and celebrities as paid contributors and even show hosts because these people are popular and have an audience. They are no longer newsmakers to be interviewed. They are part of the team, paid for their affiliation. So former White House press secretary Dana Perino is now a Fox host, and political aide and PAC activist Karl Rove is a commentator. Civil rights activist Al Sharpton and former Democratic operative Lawrence O'Donnell have shows on MSNBC. Chris Cuomo on CNN regularly interviews his brother, Andrew, the governor of New York.

The notion that there is no such thing as accuracy or truth, or that the only authentic approach to information is through opinion, is appealing to some people because it requires no professional discipline or technique or even idealism. There is a simplicity to it, like a faith in pure markets or the idea that any emotion is valid if it is strongly felt. But it is further shrinking, not enlarging, the public square.

INDEPENDENCE AND CLASS OR ECONOMIC STATUS

The question of independence is not limited to partisan press and opinion journalism. In fact, it may be easier to recognize and reckon with what independence means in journalism in the area of partisan TV networks and commentary than in other areas of news. The solution to bias, as we outlined in chapter 4 on verification, is to develop a clearer method of reporting. Yet to fully understand the role intellectual independence can play in gathering and reporting news, it is important to look at other kinds of conflicts and interdependencies that journalists might have besides partisanship.

As journalists in the twentieth century became better trained and educated (and in certain quarters better paid), another complication to the concept of independence emerged. Journalism became more elitist, which only complicated its coverage of issues like race and ideology. New York journalist Juan González, who worked as a columnist for the New York *Daily News* and was president of the National Association of Hispanic Journalists, spoke often about the impact of class on journalistic perspective. "The biggest problem . . . is that the American people feel there is a class divide between those who produce the news and information and those who receive it. That the class divide manifests a class bias toward most Americans whether they are conservative or center or liberal: if they're working class and they're poor, they're considered less important in the society. I think that's the principal bias."[18]

Richard Harwood, who held many top jobs at *The Washington Post*, including being its ombudsman, agreed. "Journalists, as members of [the] cognitive elite, derive their worldviews, mind-sets, and biases from their peers. Their work is shaped to suit the tastes and needs of this new upper class. I must say there's a lot of evidence that the mainstream press is staking its future on this class because it's increasingly going upscale . . . and rejecting or losing working people, lower-income people."[19]

Tom Minnery, a former journalist who later became vice president of Focus on the Family, an evangelical Christian organization based in Colorado Springs, Colorado, has argued that this class bias helped accelerate commercialization of the news. "The direction of coverage . . . is a distortion of the way life is lived in the United States by a vast, broad middle of the country's population," Minnery explained. "In the United States, 1 percent of the population owns 35 percent of all the commonly traded stock. You would think from watching the evening news or reading newspapers that we are all at home watching the streaming ticker across the bottom of CNBC." Or, he continued, watch the morning network shows "and see extensive, lovingly detailed coverage of the latest gizmos and gewgaws. . . . The confluence of commerce and news coverage is now so deep and profound that we can't even see the edges of it anymore."[20]

In short, Harwood, Minnery, and González were arguing, the commercialized advertising-driven media had begun to serve consumer society rather than civil society.

Some idealists hoped the Web would largely fix this, democratizing information by reducing the barriers to publishing, auto-correcting falsehoods, creating a wiki culture of accuracy, fairness, and contextualization and diversity of voices. That didn't happen.

Technology, as it turned out, was not a magical solution. There remain digital divides, class divides, digital competence divides, and divides in how active and influential different people are in different spaces. For all that we imagine the world has changed, for instance, as of 2019 just 22 percent of internet-connected American adults were on Twitter, yet a majority of journalists were active there. (Revealingly, just 10 percent of those accounts—just 2 percent of Americans—accounted for 80 percent of the tweets produced, and 66 percent of links posted on Twitter came from bots that were not real people, according to data from the Pew Research Center.)[21]

This potential class isolation is reinforced by strategic targeting of elite demographics, and it will only intensify as online media increasingly try to use targeting based on online behavior to identify audiences. As the Web has matured, digital publishers have also increasingly been expected to make a profit—not simply to attract a crowd. That is also influencing which Web ventures are launched and financed. And nonprofit news sites, which depend on rich donors and foundations with agendas and also increasingly are trying to get membership and donation money from people, aren't immune.

The biggest exception to media demographic isolation in news may be localism. It is one thing for a national outlet to target demographically. It is more of a challenge and an economic threat for local publications to do so. There is also less of a trust problem locally. People tend to distrust the media. Yet what they have in mind when they imagine media are national media, and particularly cable news. For instance, research that the authors designed for the American Press Institute, the Associated Press, and the National Opinion Research Center at the University of Chicago found that while only a quarter of Americans (27 percent) thought the media were willing to admit mistakes, that number almost doubled (to 47 percent) when people were asked about the media they used, which tended to be local newspapers and television. The biggest jump was when we asked if people thought the press was moral. Just 24 percent thought the news media in general were moral. But more than double that number (53 percent) believed the media they relied on were.[22]

While localism may be a way to mitigate against the tendency toward elitism in news, another pressure is pulling journalism in the opposite direction. Local journalism is the form of our news gathering most threatened by the Web. There are several reasons for that. Local news outlets used to be the way that Americans got national news. Technology changed that. As people had more access to national news, first through twenty-four-hour cable and then through the Web, interest in local news began to decline and interest in national news rose. That also shifted people away from local issues tied to civic geography. The definition of community began to be tied less to place than to interests, be they political or otherwise. But the effects of this were far-reaching. Politics became nationalized. Political figures everywhere used the same talking points. The decline in local media, in turn, then reinforced that trend. As local newsrooms shrank, interest in local news shriveled further. One study, for instance, found that as local newspapers closed, polarization appeared to increase in ways that were measurable at the ballot box. If a newspaper closed before the 2012 election, the share of split-ticket voting went down and down-ballot voting went up. The authors pointed to substitution of local news with national news as a factor.[23]

The solution is not to repudiate the concept of journalistic independence and replace it with more ideological content. Instead, the way to create a journalism that serves the public interest, and the interests of a more robust democracy, is to recruit more people from a diversity of classes and backgrounds to combat insularity in newsrooms. The journalism that people with different perspectives produce together is better than what any of them could produce alone.

Before the Web disrupted the revenue base of most publications, this was precisely where those interested in making news better were heading. "If you're going to change the composition of the journalistic workforce there has to be some kind of a program that takes people that are already in other careers . . . [and] offers them an opportunity to help diversify in a class way," González suggested.[24] More recently, this notion, of recruiting people with more diverse life experiences into journalism, has animated some of the more innovative efforts in journalism education. It was a key idea of Steve Shepard, the founding dean of the City University of New York's new journalism school, now the Craig Newmark School of Journalism at City University of New York, created in 2006. It is at the core of the Fellowships in Global Journalism, an idea developed by Rob Steiner, a former *Wall Street Journal* reporter, at the University of Toronto's Munk School of Global Affairs. Steiner's idea was to attract professionals with deep expertise in other fields and train them as journalists, to elevate the substance and expertise of the journalism being created.

The move to more fragmented media, while it may seem inevitable in a crowded marketplace, threatens this kind of pluralistic media creation. And if journalists want to combat that, they must begin to construct news spaces with more diverse perspectives. The most promising place to do that is locally. But for that to happen, journalists must first begin to better understand and embrace the role that experience and identity play in the creation of news—beyond class.

That is what we turn to next.

DIVERSITY AND JOURNALISTIC INDEPENDENCE

What does diversity in a newsroom mean? What role does personal background play in the choices someone makes about what is news and what is not, whom to interview, what voices to seek out, how to frame stories? It is one thing to say it matters. It is another to allow those forces to come into play—to create a newsroom where people's backgrounds and their differences inform the news. A default culture begins to harden in a newsroom when everyone is supposed to think the same way—not when their differences are encouraged to broaden how the news is created.

In what was clearly an acknowledgment that personal identity and experience influence journalistic decision-making, the news industry began to formally embrace the idea of diversity in the latter part of the twentieth century. The most public move in this direction came in 1978 when the American Society of Newspaper Editors formally stated that the number of people of color working at American newspapers should reflect the percentage in the general population.

More than forty years later, that effort can only be described as a failure. According to the best academic research, the American Journalist Project, headed by David H. Weaver, Lars Willnat, and G. Cleveland Wilhoit, in 1971 just 3.9 percent of people working in newsrooms across media were Black. By 2013 that number had barely budged, at 4.1 percent.[25]

Beneath those numbers was a more complex story—hiring programs, mentorship programs, culture clashes, and talented people of color leaving newsrooms in frustration. There was also progress made and then regression. But as newsrooms shrank because of economic disruption, and the media landscape fragmented into more partisan outlets, the problem of newsrooms lacking class, race, ethnic, and cultural diversity only worsened.

And as efforts to make newsrooms more diverse along racial and ethnic lines failed, the question of political or ideological diversity—another dimension of our human culture—was largely ignored. This failure, in turn, is now connected to another profound challenge facing news and democracy—the breach of trust between journalists and the roughly half of the American population who consider themselves conservative.

American newsrooms do not just lean toward an older, white, and male default culture. Over the last two generations, they also have become increasingly liberal—largely because conservative voices have departed. The same researchers who found no progress on racial diversity, Wilhoit, Willnat, and Weaver, found a retreat when it came to political identity. Over the last two generations, conservatives began to leave local newsrooms. In 1971, fully 26 percent of US journalists identified themselves as Republicans, 36 percent as Democrats, and 33 percent as independents. By 2013, only 7 percent of those working in newsrooms identified themselves as Republican, a drop of almost fourfold. The number of self-described Democrats had fallen slightly, to 28 percent. Independents had swelled to 50 percent. Asked differently, 39 percent in 2013 described themselves as "leaning left," 44 percent as "middle of the road," and only 13 percent as "leaning right."[26]

The reasons why newsrooms became narrower ideologically are the same ones that led to their failure to diversify along racial and ethnic lines. In practice, on the crush of deadline, journalists often expect everyone in the newsroom to think the same way rather than embracing debate inspired by personal background. Except in the case of political perspective the problem is worse.

While newsroom leaders, at least in theory, will acknowledge that a person's gender, ethnicity, geography, and class inform his or her journalistic decision-making, political preference has been more of an untouchable third rail of personal identity. It has been safer to default to a vision of journalistic consciousness that pretends politics doesn't enter into it. The result is that the default culture in newsrooms—liberal and elitist, as well as largely white—has largely gone unacknowledged, let alone perceived.

THE MEANING OF INDEPENDENCE

As we discussed in the chapter on verification, the biases that we do not recognize—our unconscious biases—are the ones that pose the greatest threat to accurate, comprehensive, and open-minded inquiry. And although we cannot quantify how identity and background influence the way news is created, the solution to the problem is nonetheless clear: We can broaden the news and enlarge the public square only by broadening the range of people who sit in the newsroom and have a voice in the decision-making that goes on there. What's more, the definition of diversity cannot be reduced to matters as obvious as race, ethnicity, and gender. It must embrace more subtle questions of background, such as class, culture, and politics. If it does not, the meaning of diversity will become constricted and distorted.

Above all, as we will discuss in more detail in the chapter on personal conscience, diversity must mean allowing the debate over newsroom decision-making to become more open, a challenging matter that also requires that the debate be respectful and constructive. Anything else risks replacing one default culture with another—and will defeat the purpose of embracing diversity in the first place.

Embedded here is another question about diversity, identity, and journalistic independence. It is the question of the degree to which ethnicity and gender and other markers can be equated with identity or expertise. If personal background matters, what does it imply? To be a white journalist or a Black journalist or a male or female journalist is not all-defining. Do we think that only Black journalists can capably cover Black Americans, or should? What about Asian Americans, or Latinos, Jews, or Catholics? If experience and background bring expertise, how do we think of identity as expansive and varied rather than limiting?

"The argument for diversity based on representation . . . at its core, presupposes that persons of the same race and gender think alike because of their shared experiences of racism and sexism," Black business executive Peter Bell has argued. "The argument, I believe, ignores and/ or minimizes the influence of class, education, region, family, personal psychology and religion in shaping our personal ideas and beliefs. . . . Observable traits such as race and gender . . . serve as a proxy, and I would argue a crude proxy, for ideas. . . . What is the Black position on any given issue? The answer, of course, is there isn't one."[27]

Many journalists, even those in minority groups, have had similar doubts.

At the same time, identity and background can drive how a reporter understands a story in ways that are powerful, positive, and transformative. *New York Times Magazine* writer Nikole Hannah-Jones, a Black woman who writes about racial inequality in America, says she became "hooked" by journalism because of the power of storytelling: "And not just the power of storytelling but the power of being able to tell your own stories and not allowing someone else to frame how you are seen to the world, but to do that framing for yourselves. That's how I came to be a journalist." She wrote a column in her high school paper called *From the African Perspective*. "I think one of my first columns was about whether or not Jesus was Black, and I can tell you my early investigation found I couldn't prove he was Black. But I certainly could prove that he didn't have blond hair and blue eyes, so I figured that was a win."[28]

Hannah-Jones does not use the word *objectivity*, though she cites deeply reported "meticulous" historical research with high levels of evidence and transparency as the hallmark standards she aspires to in her work (in other words, our reading of the true, historical definition of *objectivity*). "What drives me is rage," Hannah-Jones says. "My work is trying to shift the way that we're thinking about things, to shift conventional wisdom."

Some publications might be intimidated by Hannah-Jones's motivations, including her "rage." But if the journalist has fidelity to the core principles we have outlined in this book, to accuracy, to intellectual independence, to informing citizens, this kind of activism through storytelling will fall squarely in the best traditions of journalism—particularly the kind of long-form journalism Hannah-Jones pursues. Her background and her identity powerfully drive that work. The space between these two perspectives—the businessman Bell's, who worries that representation based on race is oversimplified, and Hannah-Jones's, for whom race is an essential motive behind her transformative storytelling—offers a wide expanse of thinking about identity and how it influences journalism.

People's background brings expertise and passion to their work. Professional training, ethics, and mission also guide that work. And race, gender, geography, and class alone may shape but do not entirely define personality. Yet if those who cover events are chosen simply by ethnic heritage or skin color, that can be just another kind of racial and ethnic stereotyping. It suggests that there is such a thing as a single Black perspective or a single Asian perspective.

Somewhere between hiring quotas and the fears of a new "politically correct" orthodoxy lies a richer terrain of possibility. There is ample evidence that newsrooms lacking diversity are unable to do their jobs properly. If you have no one in a newsroom who understands or has any connection to large parts of the community, you simply cannot cover the community competently. Newsrooms that lack diversity are almost certain to suffer from ignorance. As journalist Clarence Page has recalled: "One editor in northern Illinois tried to beg off [of minority coverage] saying that he really didn't have much of a minority population in his town, even though I knew for a fact that his town has a 17 percent Latino population—17 percent. . . . A rural Wisconsin editor told me that he really didn't have any minorities in his area, even though his newspaper was just down the road from a major Indian reservation."[29]

Independence from faction suggests there is a way to produce journalism without either denying the influence of personal experience or being hostage to it. The key is whether one maintains allegiance to the core journalistic principles that build toward truthfulness and informing the public. Just as it should be with political ideology, the question is not neutrality, but purpose. This journalistic calling for independence from faction should sit atop all the culture and personal history a reporter brings to an event he or she is covering and trying to understand. Whatever adjective attaches itself to someone who is described as a journalist—*Buddhist, Black, disabled, gay, Latino, Jewish, WASP,* or even *liberal* or *conservative*—it becomes descriptive but not limiting. He or she is a journalist who is also Buddhist, Black, WASP, or conservative—not Buddhist first and a journalist second. When that happens, racial, ethnic, religious, class, and ideological backgrounds inform the journalist's work but do not dictate it.

The journalist is committed to society. The model is not disinterested. It is not cynical. It is not disengaged. The journalist's role is predicated on a special kind of engagement—being dedicated to informing the public but not to playing a direct role as an advocate for one side or the other or for particular policy outcomes. We would put it this way. Journalism is a form of activism but not advocacy. The journalist is a searchlight, as Lippmann described, directing attention on matters of public interest, noting problems, spotlighting potential solutions, shaping the agenda of public discussion. But journalism is different from advocacy or propaganda. The journalist's goal is public consideration of civic matters. The political advocate or propagandist's goal is persuasion—trying to convince or manipulate people to support a particular policy or political outcome. He or she is in the arena, a member of a team, armed with talking points and bound by party strategy decisions. The journalist is an activist on behalf of the story, of discovery, of the facts, with the goal of public awareness. Journalism is an "engaged independence."

Gil Thelen, who worked as a newspaper editor and educator, was an early experimenter with the concept of civic journalism, which developed ideas designed to reconnect journalists with community. He also fought the publishers to protect the principle of journalistic independence. He ultimately left a newspaper in the Knight Ridder organization over the separation of news and business interests.

Thelen has described the journalist's role in the community as that of a "committed observer." Journalists' needs, he explained, are "interdependent" with those of their fellow citizens. If there is a key issue in town that needs resolution and is being explored by local institutions, "we have a commitment to reporting on this process over the long term, as an observer." It would be irresponsible to cover the issue haphazardly or ignore it because it seems dull. The journalist should be committed to helping resolve the issue, Thelen argued, and the way he or she does that is by playing the role of the responsible reporter.

In this sense, the term *observer* is not passive. It is not neutral. It implies that someone is acting as a connector, translator, contextualizer, interpreter, and investigator. It is, we would argue, a form of civic activism. But it distinguishes the journalist from other community actors, such as political advocates and combatants. The focus of those engaged in journalism is to uncover and inform, to accurately understand and convey events and what people are saying and doing—not to persuade or manipulate the public to embrace a particular policy solution or outcome. That difference makes the journalist a more reliable observer—more open to the truth, to fidelity to fact.

Thelen's ideas are echoed in the words of other journalists, who talk about the press creating a common language, a common understanding, or being part of the glue that defines and holds a community together. This is the proper understanding that many journalists have about the role of engaged independence. It is echoed in Hannah-Jones's desire to make the invisible visible about race in America.

The notion that journalists should be engaged in the community as observers, translators, and connectors is also expressed in the writings of people exploring the potential of social media. Among the most dynamic of these voices is Mónica Guzmán, who cofounded *The Evergrey* in Seattle and is writing a book about engagement, community, and polarization. "In a world where everyone can participate in newsgathering, cultivating self-informing communities is itself an act of journalism," she has written. "To accomplish it, we need to not only learn the language of these spaces, but also smart ways to join, respect and inspire the voices within."[30] In this way, Guzmán has argued, community is not a means to an end for journalism. It is the end.

"Journalists play the role not just of informers but also conveners," Guzmán explains. To do that today, they must be "fluent in the delicate art of creating contexts where people come together productively." In that sense, "They must know how to cultivate stronger working relationships not just between themselves and the communities they serve, but among the members of those communities."

What Guzmán describes is journalism's role in its essence. Journalists always convened, moderated, listened, and translated. That is what the newspaper and the television newscast were—limited by the constraints of print or broadcast. Now they have even more inputs for doing it; the result can be interactive more quickly (than say, printing letters to the editor); and their "product" is not limited to one format.

But, Guzmán points out, not all interaction is the same. "There is one and only one context where human beings can use 100 percent of the tools we have to make ourselves well understood in live conversation: in-person interaction. Every other platform for discussion limits people's full capacity to talk or listen—video chats, phone calls, social media threads, texting, etc."

That makes it even harder for journalists in a fast-paced, urgent, digital environment to help people understand each other. They must take that into account when they design public interaction, she adds, particularly when they decide whether to lean their efforts toward scale or impact.

"Yes, you reach more people when you convene them on Facebook, Twitter, or some other asynchronous, text-based platform with no faces, gestures, or consistent, committed presence," Guzmán said. "But how well will those people reach each other?"

In the early years of the Web's impact on journalism, no one was more innovative about using the community of voices to create a new connected journalism than Andy Carvin. When the Arab Spring began in 2011, Carvin was NPR's social media strategist. He quickly began to monitor the information being shared on Twitter by people on the ground in Cairo's Tahrir Square and elsewhere—and then to triangulate, highlight, and redistribute it, tapping those same people to help verify the reports of others. Some sources he knew. Others he checked out. Carvin curated the collection in a way that was thoughtful and transparent, and his Twitter feed, @acarvin, became a kind of news service of a growing number of authentic, credible voices few others could find. As Guzmán put it, "Carvin turned the random chatter into collected wisdom and gave that wisdom right back to the people who needed it most. All without writing a single traditional news story."

Every day, there are new examples of journalists who connect with their communities in order to better serve them, while maintaining the independence that allows journalism an authenticator's perspective. *The Guardian*'s belief in open journalism, in which the community participates in the process of news gathering, is one. Open journalism may have been the first to come close to the notion we have advocated of journalism as collaborative organized intelligence that combines the experience and diversity of the community, the power of machines, and the skills, access, and discipline of open-minded inquiry that journalists are trained to perform. Today there are now others.

The Guardian's editor at the time, Alan Rusbridger, said the approach involved ten core ideas:

- It encourages public participation.
- It is not inert (the journalist to the public), in short not a static product.
- It involves the public in the preproduction process.
- It forms communities of interest.

- It is open to the Web, links to it, collaborates with it.
- It aggregates and curates.
- It recognizes that journalists are not the only voices of authority.
- It aspires to achieve and reflect diversity.
- Publishing is the start, not the end, of the process.
- It is open to challenge, correction, and clarification.

At KPCC, in Southern California, leadership has steered the organization to emphasize engagement throughout reporting processes. Staff have even referenced themselves as a "help desk" for the community, taking as one example more than 4,000 questions local residents had about challenges in the pandemic, answering more than 3,900 questions personally, and using the process to inform overall reporting priorities. The emphasis on community driving questions exists even on the individual reporting level, where reporters like early education reporter Mariana Dale interviewed various stakeholders related to educating kids up to five years old and redesigned the beat to attend to what they said mattered to them and how they got information. The list of KPCC's engagement approaches could fill an entire chapter, but the important thread is that the diverse community informs reporters' questions and that journalists still produce journalism through open-minded inquiry.[31]

Guzmán, *The Guardian*'s Carvin, KPCC, and the work of Fahrenthold at the *Post* mentioned earlier all demonstrate this new journalism of collaboration, of journalism as organized intelligence, of listening, of recognizing the strengths of the network of community and machines. All of it represents a powerful shift in the way journalists do their work. But it also supports, rather than repudiating, the elements of journalism. It is, in other words, a strong reflection of the idea that the principles that the public requires of journalism haven't changed but that the ways those principles are fulfilled in the network age have.

These new ideas of connection and observation as the qualities of the reliable journalist also put in clear relief the way in which journalism is a form of participation—but one that demands commitment to accuracy and is distinct from other types of activism, even for those producing journalism in settings that are not otherwise journalistic. Those functioning as translator, observer, and communicator at a think tank, in an activist special-interest group, or in a corporate setting are not relieved of these obligations because of the funding source. Their work will lose its credibility and authority if they are not willing to engage in the same level of transparency and faithfulness to accuracy and verification. In the twenty-first century, journalistic independence, as it has always been for the opinion journalist, is intellectual. In this sense, we consider independence a core principle of producing journalism no matter where that journalism is produced.

TECHNIQUES FOR TESTING PRECONCEPTIONS

PAUL TAYLOR'S HYPOTHESIS TEST

Some journalists have developed highly personal techniques for testing whether they are maintaining the kind of intellectual independence this participation demands. Paul Taylor, former chief political correspondent at *The Philadelphia Inquirer* and *The Washington Post*, who went on to create the Social and Demographics Project at the Pew Research Center, used a before-and-after method to check himself when he was a journalist. When he was assigned to a story that involved substantial reporting and research, Taylor used to write a lead before he had started his information gathering—in effect his hypothesis of what he would find in his reporting. He was, in other words, writing down what philosopher Thomas Nagel would call his "initial view" of an event, or where he was starting from. At the end of the reporting process he would look at what he had written when he had started. If the two leads were too similar, he would know that he hadn't learned very much—he might not have done enough reporting, might not have been listening enough, and might have been simply rewriting his own preconceptions.

Taylor's technique, simple as it is, is a first step at identifying self, not denying it, in the process of becoming independent. It acknowledges, implicitly, that journalists start with preconceptions. That hypothesis or presumptive lead was probably arrived at from a discussion with an editor about what the journalist and the editor expected to find. Whatever the limits of the journalist's and the editor's experiences and perspectives, culturally, intellectually, because of class or race, they might be hinted at or reflected in that initial set of expectations. If you haven't advanced beyond them, what have you done?

One useful idea embedded in Taylor's approach is that rather than denying that he had an initial view of the story, influenced by his personal biases, it memorialized those biases so he could be sure he was not captive to them.

There are other techniques journalists can use to move beyond their own initial response to events. Amanda Ripley's ideas about complicating rather than simplifying conflict, and the questions journalists posed that we cited in chapter 4 on making news more accurate, fit well here.

Here are some other concepts that can help.

WORK IN TEAMS

Kim Bui, an editor in Arizona, writes that some stories, particularly those that try to understand many different points of view and require real empathy, "shouldn't always be assigned to a single person." A team approach can help reporters critically evaluate their stories, check their biases, and expand beyond the limitations of their own thinking. *The Boston Globe* used this idea to produce a series called *68 Blocks*, in which people spent months in a neighborhood of Boston beset with trouble. "There were enough people on that project to keep you honest," said one of the project's reporters, Andrew Ryan. The benefits of a team approach extend beyond reporting in the field. NPR's Code Switch team, which covers race through a mix of audio and digital reporting, holds wide-ranging pitch meetings, where journalists sharpen their ideas and get ideas about how to report them.[32]

AVOID LABELS—WHICH CAN TRIGGER "METAPERCEPTIONS"

A lot of journalistic shorthand now can be alienating. Labels such as "Democrats say" or "Republicans say" can come off as attempts to simplify, hide contradictions, and invite stereotyping. A third of voters, for instance, no longer identify with any party. Rather than simplifying matters, these common phrases can activate what neuroscience calls "metaperceptions," which are the views people believe other people harbor about them, often negatively. When Hillary Clinton in 2016, for instance, described half of Trump's supporters as "a basket of deplorables," she was confirming a metaperception—that elite liberals like her looked down on Trump supporters as less intelligent and less moral than she was.

Through stereotyping and labeling, journalists can increase polarization reinforcing metaperceptions, often unwittingly. But they are far more likely to do so, we would argue, when they are talking about groups and communities about whom they know little, where the journalists themselves are more prone to shallow understanding and fall victim to stereotyping. In short, if you're using a label in a story, check yourself. Have you thought about the connotations that label implies? Do you know how someone in the context in which you are using it would react? Are you using that shorthand out of ignorance? Is that shorthand accurate? When describing someone, try capturing him or her accurately with fine brushstrokes, not a broad brush.

In the end, no rigid prohibition against any kind of personal or intellectual engagement will guarantee that a journalist remains independent from factions, political or otherwise. It is good judgment, a professional discipline of verification, and an abiding commitment to the principle of working to inform rather than to fight for a particular policy outcome that separate the journalist from the partisan. Having an opinion not only is allowable and natural but may be the first step in the process or method of transparent and objective reporting. And journalism that arrives at a point of view, such as investigative reporting, explanatory journalism, or opinion journalism, is often the highest form of reporting. When done properly, the reporting is so complete that the journalist can draw conclusions from what he or she has found, not simply pass along the reporting in context. But journalists must be smart and honest enough to recognize that the point of view they reach at the end of the process must be based on something more substantial than their personal beliefs if it is to be of journalistic use. It cannot be their "initial view" backed up by reporting that was designed to justify their view. That is not inquiry. It is argument.

Journalism is the act of trying to expand one's own understanding of events so that one can expand the understanding of others in a community. But its goal is to inform, not persuade people to back a particular political outcome, or parrot party talking points like the member of a congressional delegation or a party hack. It is a profession, a craft, and an art that is elevated by knowing the skills of open-minded inquiry, of listening, learning, understanding, translating, and educating. Creating barriers to this process of discovery is, in the end, being disloyal to the public. It is, as philosopher Nagel describes, a professional discipline of moving beyond one's initial view or standpoint and learning about the views of others so that the citizens themselves can, as they encounter the new facts of the news, put their own views "in relation to the world." As that happens, we will inevitably discover inconvenient facts that challenge some of what we thought initially.

The importance of this independence becomes even more obvious when we consider the next special obligation of journalism, its role as watchdog.

6

MONITOR POWER AND ADD
VOICE TO THE LESS POWERFUL

n 1964, the Pulitzer Prize went to the Philadelphia *Bulletin* in a new reporting category. The award honored the *Bulletin* for exposing police officers in that city who were involved in running a numbers racket, a kind of illegal lotto game, out of their station house. The story presaged what would become a new wave of scrutiny about police corruption in American cities in the 1960s and 1970s. The award had one other significance as well. It marked formal recognition by the print establishment of a new era in American journalism.

The new Pulitzer category was called "Investigative Reporting." The newspaper executives from around the country who ran the Pulitzer under the auspices of Columbia University had added it in place of an older designation that they decided no longer required special recognition, "Local Reporting."[1] They were putting new emphasis on the role of the press as activist, reformer, and exposer.

In doing so, the journalism establishment was acknowledging a kind of work they saw increasingly being done in recent years by a new generation of journalists. Reporters like Wallace Turner and William Lambert in Portland and George Bliss in Chicago were reviving a tradition of pursuing and exposing corruption that had largely been absent from reporting during World War II and the years immediately following. The war years featured storytellers like Ernie Pyle of the

Scripps Howard wire service, who evoked the heroic spirit of the Allies at war, the sturdy British people, and the simple but gutsy American GI. After 1964, that began to change. Eight years after the introduction of the investigative reporting category to the Pulitzers, when Bob Woodward and Carl Bernstein of *The Washington Post* helped uncover the Watergate scandal inside the Nixon White House, investigative reporting would suddenly gain celebrity and cachet, redefining the image of the profession.

All of journalism was changed, especially Washington journalism. A. M. Rosenthal, then executive editor of *The New York Times,* was so disturbed by the way *The Washington Post* dominated the Watergate story that he ordered a reorganization of his newspaper's Washington bureau to create a formal team of investigative reporters. So long as Rosenthal was executive editor, the job of Washington bureau chief would be only as secure as the strength of the bureau's investigative reportage. CBS News launched its own investigative news show, *60 Minutes,* which became the most successful news program network TV had ever produced. Local television news, not to be left out, was soon awash in investigative teams—or "I-teams"—of its own.

Some old-timers grumbled. Investigative reporting, they harrumphed, was little more than a two-dollar word for good reporting. In the end, all reporting is investigative. While that is an oversimplification—investigative reporting is qualitatively different from other kinds of work in various ways—the critics were correct in one sense. What the Pulitzer Prize board formally recognized in 1964 had been, in fact, more than two hundred years in development.

And today it thrives in the work of a new generation of investigators and a broader definition of what gets investigated. In the work of investigative reporters and editors Julie K. Brown at the *Miami Herald*, Ron Nixon at the Associated Press, Jeremy B. Merrill at New York University's Ad Observer, which has investigated Facebook's targeting of political ads to particular demographics, and Wendi Thomas of MLK50, we are seeing journalists meet the challenges of uncovering abuses of power in today's world.

Investigative reporting's roots were firmly established in the very first periodicals, in the earliest notions of the meaning of a free press and the First Amendment, and in the motivation of journalists throughout the profession's history. These roots are so strong, they form a fundamental principle:

Journalists must serve as an independent monitor of power.

This principle is often misunderstood, even by journalists, to mean "Afflict the comfortable." Moreover, the watchdog principle is being threatened in contemporary journalism by overuse and by a faux watchdogism aimed more at pandering to audiences than at doing public service. The principle is also clouded when political operatives conduct opposition research designed to denigrate and attack political rivals and release it to the public as investigative journalism. That work, which inevitably casts information in the worst possible light to persuade rather than inform, is political pugilism, not journalism.

But in its true form, investigative journalism is a special category of journalistic enterprise, one in which the principles of independent inquiry and social advocacy blend into the highest form of journalistic public service.

When print periodicals first emerged in Europe in the early seventeenth century, they already saw their role as investigatory. During the English Civil War, when press freedom in England seemed to flicker to life, periodicals immediately began to promise that they would investigate what was going on and tell their readers. The *Parliament Scout*, which began publication in 1643, "suggested something new in journalism—the necessity of making an effort to search out and discover the news."[2] The next year a publication calling itself *The Spie* promised readers that it planned on "discovering the usual cheats in the great game of the Kingdome. For that we would have to go undercover."

These early efforts at investigative work became part of the reason the press was granted its constitutional freedom. Periodicals like *Scout* and *Spie* were, for the first time, making the affairs of government more transparent. They marked the ambition of the press to be what would later be called the fourth estate, and stated publicly that the affairs of government should be known to all, not just to the privileged. Until the journals appeared, the internal workings of government were primarily the knowledge of limited elites—those with business before the state or those directly involved in the administration of government. The general public's information on its rulers largely came from uninformed gossip or official government messages. Suddenly, in contrast to the proclamations and town criers who provided the information those in power wanted distributed, these new periodicals aspired to tell people what the government actually did. Though government often clamped down on these early printers, as it would so often throughout the world, they established investigative reporting as one of the earliest principles that would set journalism apart from other means of public communication. It was the watchdog role that made journalism, in George Mason's phrase in the Virginia Declaration of Independence, "a bulwark of liberty," just as truth, in the case of John Peter Zenger's challenge to English libel law, became the ultimate defense of the press.

These early efforts were often frustrated. The British government forbade note-taking during parliamentary debates. People had to remember what was said and then run outside to recall or paraphrase the event before the paper went to press. These early journalists were dismissed as "newsmongers," and historians look back on that early parliamentary press as often dishonest and corrupt. Yet the instinct toward transparency and the watchdog function that they represented, however crudely, proved enduring and ultimately would triumph.[3]

In the years to come, as conflict between a protected press and government institutions increased, it was this watchdog role that the Supreme Court fell back on time and again to reaffirm the press's central role in American society. Beginning with the case of *Near v. Minnesota*, which forbade the government from restraining publication of any journal except when the story threatened "grave and immediate danger to the security of the United States," the Court has generally built a secure place within the law where journalists are protected so that they may aggressively serve the public's need for information concerning matters of public welfare.[4] A full two hundred years after the American Revolution, Supreme Court Justice Hugo Black continued to focus on the press's watchdog responsibilities when he wrote, "The press was protected so that it could bare the secrets of government and inform the people. Only a free and unrestrained press can effectively expose deception in government."[5] With support from state and federal legislatures during the 1960s and 1970s, the press gained greater access through the Freedom of Information Act and the so-called sunshine laws, which provided public access to many documents and activities of the government.

Beginning in the twenty-first century—especially during the administration of George W. Bush and intensified under the administrations of Barack Obama and Donald Trump—unprecedented efforts were launched to withhold government information from the public and even to criminalize the efforts by the press to publish it. It is unresolved how the courts, newly stocked at the federal level with conservative judges by the Trump administration, will react to these efforts.

The watchdog principle means more than simply monitoring government; it extends to all the powerful institutions in society, governmental, nongovernmental, and commercial, anything that plays an influential role in people's lives. Today, obviously, that includes the platform companies that at times represent themselves as trying to help journalism, creating grants and other programs that can make journalism organizations financial partners with them. And this monitoring of institutions was true early on. Just as *The Spie* went "undercover" in order to discover the "cheats in the great game of the Kingdome," nineteenth-century journalist Henry Mayhew stayed out in the open to document the plight of that same kingdom's unknowns. Mayhew roamed the streets of Victorian London reporting on the lives of street people for the London *Morning Chronicle*.[6] By so doing, he gave the watercress girl and the chimney sweep individual faces, voices, and aspirations. He revealed their humanity to a population that regularly passed them unnoticed.

Combining the search for voices that went unheeded and cheats that went undiscovered, the earliest journalists firmly established as a core principle their responsibility to examine the unseen corners of society. The world they chronicled captured the imagination of a largely uninformed society, creating an immediate and enthusiastic popular following.

At the end of the twentieth century, nearly nine out of ten journalists believed the press "keeps political leaders from doing things they shouldn't do." The watchdog role was second, after informing the public, among the answers journalists volunteered as to what distinguished their profession from other types of communication.[7] As trust in the press declined, the watchdog role has remained one of the few elements of journalistic enterprise that the public tends to favor. A Knight Gallup survey from 2020 found that 82 percent of Americans felt holding public and business leaders and institutions accountable was critical or very important, a level of support basically unchanged in two decades.[8]

Even at the height of digital disruption, news organizations considered their watchdog responsibility one that, while expensive, could not be abandoned. On the eve of the company heading toward bankruptcy, the McClatchy newspaper chain offered full support to reporter Julie Brown and more than $100,000 in legal expenses to uncover the sexual crimes of financier Jeffrey Epstein, a horrendous record with more than eighty victims and associations with rich and powerful people around the world. And as the economics of journalism shift from advertising toward consumer revenue in the form of membership, donations, or subscriptions, investigative reporting has even more tangible benefit. Data from the American Press Institute, which built software that analyzes what kind of content drives audience engagement, show that deep investigative reporting is correlated not only with making readers more loyal but also with winning them over as subscribers.

Investigative reporting is expensive. James Hamilton, an economist who specialized in studying media at Duke and now at Stanford, did an analysis of the cost of investigative reporting at *The News and Observer* in Raleigh, North Carolina. He determined that an investigative series on the probation system had cost the paper $216,000 to produce in time and resources. Yet among the intangible benefits of such a series—in the case of a *News and Observer* series exposing problems in the North Carolina probation system—were not only a better-functioning probation system but saved lives as well.[9] Hamilton estimated that in the first year after the reporting, changes in probation policies in the community resulted in "net benefits" of $62.1 million, after deducting the costs of putting those probation policies in place ($11.7 million).[10] As

Hamilton puts it, "Each dollar invested by a newspaper in an investigative story can generate hundreds of dollars in benefits to society from changes in public policy. Stories costing thousands to produce can deliver millions in benefits spread across the community."[11]

As firmly as journalists and the public believe in it, and as much as research suggests it helps both the bottom line of journalism and the health of communities, investigative reporting is rare. In a study spanning from the 1950s to the early 2000s, scholars Katherine Fink and Michael Schudson found that investigative reports never made up more than 3 percent of the front-page stories in the *Milwaukee Journal Sentinel*, *The New York Times*, and *The Washington Post* (a high-water mark reached in 1991).[12] Original investigative reporting similarly represents about 1 percent of news stories on local TV, according to a multiyear content study we conducted at the Project for Excellence in Journalism, and less than that if one looks at stories about civic and political institutions.[13]

As firmly as journalists believe in it, moreover, the watchdog principle is often misunderstood. At the turn of the century, Chicago journalist and humorist Finley Peter Dunne translated the watchdog principle to mean "Comfort the afflicted and afflict the comfortable."[14] Dunne was half kidding; the remark was satirical, but the maxim stuck. On the day the St. Paul *Pioneer Press* won the Pulitzer Prize in 2000 for uncovering a cheating scandal on the University of Minnesota basketball team, for instance, the paper's sports editor in a speech cited his boss's fondness for repeating the phrase.[15]

Unfortunately, the notion that the press is there to afflict the comfortable and comfort the afflicted misconstrues the meaning of the watchdog role and gives it a liberal or progressive cast. The concept is deeper and more nuanced than the literal sense of *afflicting* or *comforting* would suggest. As history showed us, it more properly means watching over the powerful few in society to guard, on behalf of the many, against tyranny. The public also responds more to the idea of holding the powerful accountable than it does even to metaphors about watchdogs that people may not understand. Data from the American Press Institute and the Associated Press/National Opinion Research

Center find that Americans support the idea of "holding the powerful accountable" by 20 percentage points more than they do that the press should "act as a watchdog" (74 percent vs. 54 percent consider it extremely or very important).[16]

The purpose of holding the powerful accountable also extends beyond simply making the management and execution of power transparent, to making known and understood the effects of that power. This logically implies that the press should recognize where powerful institutions are working effectively as well as where they are not. How can the press purport to monitor the powerful if it does not illustrate successes as well as failures? Endless criticisms lose meaning, and the public has no basis for judging good from bad.

Like a theme in a Bach fugue, investigative reporting has swelled and subsided through the history of journalism but never disappeared. It has defined some of the most memorable and important eras in US history:

- The press in colonial America found its purpose as tribune of a people chafing under a distant government that interfered with the energy of its development. James Franklin's *New England Courant* established a role as watchdog over both governmental and religious institutions, and the colonies had their own *Spie*—Isaiah Thomas's *Massachusetts Spy* exposed those who trafficked with the enemy.

- The revolutionary press gave way to a nation-building press in which the issues of the shape and character of the new government were reported. Federalists and antifederalists each created their own newspapers to inform and encourage the public debate over the fundamental principles on which the new country would be built. One of the most important roles of this partisan press was to serve as a watchdog over the opposition party, a process of discovery and disclosure that at times became so virulent that the government with limited success tried to legislate against the practice.[17]

- Following the Civil War, journalism began to shine a light on still-present sins. Born into slavery in Mississippi in 1862, Ida B. Wells was freed by the Emancipation Proclamation and went on to become a teacher and then journalist known nationally for documentation of racial injustice. Her monumental contributions in journalism, including her investigations on lynching and its patterns—unlikely to appear in predominantly white newspapers—began after three friends were lynched by a white mob. Through investigative journalism Wells advanced justice for Black Americans and gave a model of the importance of personal experience, even tragic, in motivating the uncovering of horrific crimes.[18]

- At the same time, other new journalists experimented with methods for this investigative work and bringing it to other unexamined institutions. In a famous and early example of undercover investigative journalism, Nellie Bly imitated insanity to get committed to the Women's Lunatic Asylum on Blackwell's Island. While there, she uncovered detestable conditions and abuse of women, documented it for a series of articles and later a book, and forced asylum reforms.[19]

- By the dawn of the twentieth century, a new generation of journalists dubbed "muckrakers" gave voice to reform at the local, state, and federal levels. Their detailed investigation and exposure of corrupt power, ranging from child labor abuses to urban political machines and railroad and oil trusts, led to a progressive movement in national politics.

- As a fledgling effort at nonprofit journalism began to flower at organizations such as the Center for Public Integrity and its International Consortium of Investigative Journalists, one of the most successful was dedicated to investigative reporting, with an annual budget of $10 million. ProPublica, started by *Wall Street Journal* editors Paul Steiger and Richard Tofel, recognized a powerful reality: While it

might be difficult to cover a major metropolitan city with
such resources, that amount of reporting talent could
powerfully augment the investigative might of partner news
organizations around the country and serve as a signal
reminder to those in power that while the press itself was
scaling back, as an investigative force it was still here.

As the practice of investigative journalism has matured, several
forms have emerged. Today three main forms can be identified: original investigative reporting, interpretative investigative reporting, and
reporting on investigations. Each bears some examination.

ORIGINAL INVESTIGATIVE REPORTING

Original investigative reporting involves reporters themselves uncovering and documenting activities that have been previously unknown to
the public. This is the kind of investigative reporting that often results
in official public investigations about the subject or activity exposed, a
classic example of the press pushing public institutions on behalf of the
public. It may involve tactics similar to police work, such as basic shoe-
leather reporting, public records searches, use of informants, and even,
in special circumstances, undercover work or surreptitious monitoring
of activities.

Original investigative reporting would include the work of muckrakers like Lincoln Steffens, whose *Shame of the Cities* series in 1904
led to wide-ranging reforms in local government, or Rachel Carson,
whose revelations of the effects of pesticide poisoning in her 1962 book
Silent Spring launched an international movement to protect the environment. It would also include the reporting of Marcus Stern and
Jerry Kammer, whose Pulitzer Prize–winning investigation in 2005
and 2006 for the San Diego *Union-Tribune* led to the resignation from
office and eventual criminal conviction on corruption charges of Congressman Randy "Duke" Cunningham.[20] Using his own unique system
that he called a "lifestyle audit," Stern became suspicious of relationships between some of the congressman's travel and his style of living.
Digging into campaign contributions from defense contractors, Stern

uncovered other suspicious financial exchanges. He enlisted Kammer's help, and the two eventually pulled on these strings to unravel what was later described by the US Attorney's Office in San Diego as "the most audacious bribery scheme" in congressional history.

In modern original investigative reporting, the power of computer analysis often replaces the personal observation of the reporter. In 2018 a partnership of three different organizations, Centro de Periodismo Investigativo, Quartz, and the Associated Press used computer data, survey work, and interviews to identify hundreds of people who had died in Hurricane Maria in 2017 because of government neglect and who were never counted. The team used a survey combined with official records and hundreds of interviews to uncover the massive undercount of fatalities. The results, which were later confirmed by another investigation, have become a model for preventing such deaths in the future.

INTERPRETATIVE INVESTIGATIVE REPORTING

The second form of investigative reporting is interpretative reporting, which often involves the same original enterprise skills but takes the interpretation to a different level. The fundamental difference between the two is that original investigative reporting uncovers information never before gathered by others in order to inform the public of events or circumstances that might affect their lives. Interpretative reporting develops as the result of careful thought and analysis of an idea as well as dogged pursuit of facts to bring together information in a new, more complete context that provides deeper public understanding. It usually involves more complex issues or sets of facts than a classic exposé. It reveals a new way of looking at something as well as new information about it.

One early example is *The New York Times* publication of the Pentagon Papers in 1971. The papers themselves were a secret study of American involvement in Vietnam written by the government. Reporter Neil Sheehan went to great lengths to track down a copy. Then a team of *New York Times* reporters and editors expert in foreign policy and the Vietnam War interpreted and organized the documents into a dramatic account of public deception. Without this synthesis and interpretation, the Pentagon Papers would have meant little to most of the public.

In the summer of 2020, *The New York Times* obtained from anonymous sources Donald Trump's long-hidden tax returns going back more than twenty years. The president's fight in court to keep them private had broken with a decades-long tradition of presidents releasing them during their candidacies. Obtaining the documents was, however, only the beginning of the reporting process. The *Times* spent weeks working with experts to interpret them, putting them in context, and reconstructing decades of Trump's personal financial life, including recognizing to whom he was indebted and for what. The series answered years of questions and illuminated where Trump was financially vulnerable and explained his conduct in certain parts of his presidency.[21]

Some journalists have pushed the boundaries of interpretative investigative work to higher levels. Airliners and many other public spaces today have heart defibrillators because journalist John Crewdson while at the *Chicago Tribune* established conclusively that they would save lives—at a time when US airlines resisted the idea because they feared the liability of putting the equipment in the planes. At *The Philadelphia Inquirer* and, later, *Time* magazine, Donald Barlett and James Steele ambitiously explored the roots of elaborate social and economic conditions in America in projects such as *America: What Went Wrong* and *America: Who Stole the Dream?* Both of these multipart series probed how the US economic-political system had failed lower-income citizens. Both were the result of years of reporting, an intense examination of economic data, and hundreds of interviews. Both series operated under the premise that the country was leaving its poor behind.

The pieces were so interpretative that some journalists condemned them as polemics rather than journalism—suggesting the authors had abandoned the role of engaged, independent observers to become activists. *Newsweek*'s Bob Samuelson called *America: Who Stole the Dream?* "junk journalism" because it "does not seek a balanced picture of the economy—strengths as well as shortcomings."[22]

Yes, these pieces were not balanced in the sense of giving both sides equal space. Barlett and Steele were attempting to expose an aspect of economic trends that had gone largely unnoticed and unreported by others, who were recording the impact on those at the top of the economic ladder, active players in the economic boom. Even some journalists who praised the work believed the first series, *America: What Went Wrong*, had more documentary evidence than the second. Evidence that the disclosures in the first series were a revelation to many people could be found in the lines of people in the *Inquirer* lobby waiting for reprints. The paper received some ninety thousand calls in the first week. "We've never seen anything like it," said then-*Inquirer* executive Arlene Morgan. People were more critical of the second series, and *Inquirer* editor Maxwell King turned the editorial pages into a public forum for critics on all sides. While the first series was better than the second because of the level of documentation, both succeeded in stirring public conversation about enormously important subjects.

Seen in retrospect, the series and the criticism about the work raise fascinating and important questions about the future of journalism in the twenty-first century. The criticisms point out how important it is for people engaged in this level of interpretative investigation to provide sufficient outlet for alternative views.[23] When they appeared, opening up the opinion pages of the host newspaper in this way was considered an innovative break with the norm—and one that increased public engagement. Today, the Web makes the potential for this level of public reaction and criticism easier, richer, more typical—even expected. And, as we have highlighted in chapter 4, reporters can pave the way for richer discourse and strengthen reporting, even investigative, by complicating the narratives and accommodating alternative views in the stories themselves.

The bigger question is what news organization, if any, would have the resources to, or would allow two of its best reporters years to work on a single series. The answer is likely none. While Barlett and Steele were unusual even at the time, at the peak of their influence a number of top news organizations—*The New York Times*, the *Los Angeles Times*, and CBS News are just three examples—freed reporters for what today seem astonishingly long periods of time to dig into stories simply because they mattered. The expectation, assumed if not proven, was that such work would add to the "brand" of a news organization in the public mind. That notion can be documented now more easily, as publications with even a medium level of sophistication with analytics should be able to determine whether investigative stories increase reader loyalty (how often a reader engages with content each month) and whether investigative reporting is consumed by subscribers or even correlates to someone deciding to subscribe (that can be measured by whether the trigger was immediate or occurred within a week or even a month of reading an investigative series). Publishers can also track how much such work is shared and endorsed on social platforms.

In a subscriber- or member-driven journalism world, the benefits no longer need to be just theoretical or anecdotal. That is why various publications produce what scholar Matthew Nisbet at American University has called "knowledge journalism," work of such depth, expertise, and interpretative force that it reshapes the public debate on issues in the way that Barlett and Steele or Crewdson did earlier. Writers such as Bill McKibben, Andrew Revkin, and Ronan Farrow at *The New Yorker* or Ed Yong or Emma Green at *The Atlantic* combine deep reporting with significant subject expertise and produce work that is designed to change public knowledge. These knowledge journalists stand apart not only in the depth of their reporting and the level of their interpretation but also in the nature of that interpretation, Nisbet argued. "Knowledge journalists employ a unique orientation in their writing towards an 'expert logic' that analyzes problems deductively and a 'political logic' that criticizes the status quo and often seeks support for policy solutions. Moreover, they often distance themselves from the 'media logic' of their peers, criticizing the tendency of journalists to define problems in terms of conflict, drama, and personalities, to falsely balance claims, or to present policy options in terms of just a few choices."[24]

The work may come in the form of books, e-books, magazine articles, online projects, and more. In general, this work is highly personal. The commitment required involves a deep passion, expertise, and perseverance on the part of the writer, and often significant creativity about how to assemble the time and resources to do the work, whether it involves research grants, teaching positions, or other factors. McKibben, who writes about the environment, teaches at Middlebury College and lives in a place where his costs are much less. (McKibben also has engaged in advocacy work, operating a group called 350.org, trying to stop the Keystone oil pipeline, activity that pushes against the boundary of the committed observer.) Revkin left *The New York Times* in 2009 after fifteen years to become a senior fellow at Pace University and write a blog, *Dot Earth*, for the *Times* opinion pages, and later moved to ProPublica, one of the best-financed nonprofit news sites in the United States.

What is less clear is how often, or whether, any community-based news operation has the wherewithal to finance and sponsor such work as the Pentagon Papers or *America: What Went Wrong?*, as *The New York Times*, *The Washington Post*, and *The Philadelphia Inquirer* once did. Will the handful of emerging news institutions that have grown in the twenty-first century engage in such deep and expensive journalism? Or will watchdog journalism increasingly be the province of outlets that depend on charitable dollars, such as ProPublica and Inside Climate News?

The answer is still uncertain, but the trends suggest a lean toward nonprofits. Stanford economist James Hamilton in his 2016 book notes that the list of publications doing this kind of interpretative investigative work has shrunk, especially locally, and that new players are making up some but only some of the difference.[25] The world of nonprofit news, on the other hand, has grown since Hamilton published his work to include more state and local news organizations. The Institute for Nonprofit News, for instance, counted thirty-one new members between 2018 and 2019, more than a third local and a third focused on explanatory reporting. Collaboration between national and local outlets is also growing. Some of the national players in nonprofit news, including ProPublica, Reveal from the Center for Investigative Reporting, and others like Open Campus, a nonprofit that covers higher education, have expanded their programs that partner investigative reporters with existing local news organizations.

REPORTING ON INVESTIGATIONS

The third investigative category is reporting on investigations, a development that has become more common in recent years. In this case the reporting develops from a discovery or leak of information from an official investigation already under way or in preparation by others, usually government agencies. It is a staple of journalism in Washington, a city where the government often talks to itself through the press. But reporting on investigations is found wherever official investigators are at work. Government investigators actively cooperate with reporters in these cases for many reasons: to affect budget appropriations, to influence potential witnesses, and to shape public opinion.

Most of the reporting on President Clinton's affair with Monica Lewinsky was actually reporting on the investigation of Independent Prosecutor Kenneth Starr's office, augmented by counterinformation leaked by the White House or lawyers for those going before the grand jury. The reporting that security guard Richard Jewell had planted the bomb at the 1996 Atlanta Olympics was similarly based on anonymous leaks from police and FBI sources and proved to be mistaken. The reporting on the impeachment of Donald Trump was also largely reporting on investigations, mostly through information from inspectors general or from congressional staffs. In contrast, most of the work on Watergate, especially in the early critical months, was original investigative work in which the journalists were talking directly with principal sources about what had happened, not with investigators about what they theorized had happened.

Reporting on investigations proliferated after the 1970s. In part, this was because the number of investigations had grown, particularly in Congress, where investigating the misdeeds of the rival party became common, particularly if one of the congressional chambers was controlled by a different party than the White House. In part, this was because after Watergate, federal and state governments passed new ethics laws and created special offices to monitor government behavior. But it also spread because over time journalists came to depend on unidentified sources to the point where the practice became a concern among both journalists and a suspicious public. Relying on government officials to do the investigating seemed safer for some news organizations than cultivating unofficial anonymous sources.

In an article about the secretive National Security Agency (NSA), the primary collector of electronic intelligence for the US government, reporter Seymour Hersh, writing in *The New Yorker*, quoted anonymous intelligence officers about how the deteriorating quality of the NSA's work left it unable to meet the threats of sophisticated terrorist groups and rogue states. Whitfield Diffie, an encryption expert at Sun Microsystems, was quick to seize on the vulnerability of Hersh's anonymous methods: "What bothers me is that you are saying what the agency wants us to believe—[that] they used to be great, but these days they have trouble reading the newspaper, the internet is too complicated for them, there is too much traffic and they can't find what they want. It may be true, but it is what they have been 'saying' for years. It's convenient for NSA to have its targets believe it is in trouble. That doesn't mean it isn't in trouble, but it is a reason to view what spooky inside informants say with skepticism."[26]

The risk of this reporting, as Diffie pointed out, is that its value is largely dependent on the rigor and skepticism of the reporter involved. The reporter is granting the interview subject a powerful forum in which to air an allegation or float a suggestion without public accountability. This does not mean that reporting on investigations is inherently wrong. But it is fraught with sometimes unforeseeable risks. The reporters here usually are privy to only part of the investigation, rather than in charge of it.

The New York Times learned that lesson when it broke a story on nuclear espionage drawn from a secret congressional report. The *Times* story picked up the alarming language of the report and said that China was catching up with American nuclear technology because it had obtained data on building warheads from a Chinese American scientist, Wen Ho Lee. The *Times* did not name Lee, but it did allow authorities to characterize the scandal as the biggest in recent history. The story led investigators to rush into getting an indictment against Lee, who was eventually jailed for one year. Out of the fifty-nine counts brought against him, he pleaded guilty to one: illegally gathering and retaining national security information. He was sentenced to time served by a judge who issued a profound apology from the bench. The *Times* also printed a lengthy correction apologizing for taking so much of the report for granted and for not giving Lee the benefit of the doubt.[27]

The chance of being manipulated by investigatory sources is high. Instead of being a watchdog of powerful institutions, the press is vulnerable to becoming their tool. Reporting on investigations requires enormous due diligence. Paradoxically, news outlets often think just the opposite—that they can more freely report the suspicions or allegations because they are quoting official sources rather than carrying out the investigation themselves.

Tom Patterson, the Benjamin C. Bradlee Professor at the John F. Kennedy School of Government at Harvard, documented the shifting standards that gave rise to this new category of investigative journalism. "What we see in the studies," he told us, "is that by the late 1970s we find a substitute for careful, deep investigative reporting— allegations that surface in the news based on claims by sources that are not combined with factual digging on the reporters' part. That tendency increased in the 1980s, increased again in the 1990s, and the mix began to change. The use of unnamed and anonymous sources becomes a larger proportion of the total."[28]

Investigative reporter and author Jim Risen has argued that most investigative reporting involves elements of all three forms. Woodward and Bernstein, for instance, regularly checked in with government investigators as they worked on their own inquiry. Yet there are distinctions between whether a reporter's work is fundamentally original, interpretative, or about someone else's investigation, and it is important to recognize them—particularly for those engaged in the work. Each type of reporting carries its own distinct responsibilities and risks. Too often, though, journalists have not been sufficiently mindful of or careful about the differences. Mistakes come from failing to recognize when you have moved from the gathering phase to the interpretation phase, for instance. What if your evidence is incomplete? Are you ready to interpret it? What is missing? When you fail to realize that your investigation is fundamentally reporting on the investigative work of some official agency, and that you are not engaged in an original investigation, you are more vulnerable.

THE WATCHDOG ROLE LIMITED

If investigative journalism shines a searchlight on society's problems, what it chooses to shine the light on is a critical issue. Are investigative teams looking at corruption only in government? Do they explore other institutions of power, including major employers, universities, hospitals? Which communities or populations is their investigative work most concerned with?

Who holds the investigative searchlight thus is an important matter. Investigative teams, as small as they usually are, benefit from diverse backgrounds and experiences—particularly at the top—just as the rest of a newsroom does. Who is making decisions over the often limited investigative resources of a newsroom will inform what threads reporters follow, whom they decide to hold accountable, how stories are framed, and whom their stories are most likely to affect.

"You need people in the room when decisions are being made about stories or angles, or how to cover something, who are going to speak up when something feels off," Alissa Figueroa, the senior editor at Type Investigations, a nonprofit investigative newsroom, said of accountability reporting during the coronavirus pandemic. "You're seeing the numbers going up and you don't have anybody in that room who can think from a different perspective about why. You need those people in the conversation when stories are being assigned."[29]

The Ida B. Wells Society for Investigative Reporting, named after the pioneer Black female journalist and activist, is a prominent player working to increase diversity in investigative ranks. Cofounded by Nikole Hannah-Jones, Ron Nixon at the Associated Press, and Topher Sanders at ProPublica, the organization works to train, retain, and raise the profiles of journalists of color in investigative journalism, much like their cofounders.

"Journalism is getting better, but in many ways it hasn't changed," said Wendi Thomas, creator of the nonprofit news site MLK50. "Many of the people who are making decisions on what deserves scarce reporting resources are white men and they are not as likely, I don't think, to immediately identify some of the issues that are most challenging to [underserved communities], for example Black women."[30]

THE WATCHDOG ROLE WEAKENED

In the ebb and flow of the watchdog role over the last two centuries, we also reached a moment of diminution by dilution. The celebrity of

Woodward and Bernstein was followed by the success of *60 Minutes*, in which correspondents Mike Wallace, Morley Safer, Harry Reasoner, and Ed Bradley, succeeded by later generations, became the stars of their own reportage. People tuned in to see whom Mike, Morley, Harry, and Ed would catch this week. Investigative journalism, particularly on television, thus became a means both for public good and for commercial ratings. In the nearly fifty years since, the proliferation of outlets for news and information has been accompanied by a torrent of investigative reportage. With most local news stations in America now featuring an "I-team" and prime time newsmagazines offering the promise of nightly exposés, we have created a permanent infrastructure of news devoted to exposure.

Much of this work has the earmarks of watchdog reporting, but too often the stories focus on risks to personal safety or consumer pocketbooks, not to citizens' freedoms. Among some popular topics of local television I-teams over the years have been crooked car mechanics, poor swimming pool lifeguarding, housecleaning scams, and dangerous teenage drivers.

At the peak of network prime time newsmagazines in the late 1990s, for instance, a study revealed a genre of investigative reporting that ignored most of the matters typically associated with the watchdog role of the press. Fewer than one in ten stories on these programs concerned the combined topics of education, economics, foreign affairs, the military, national security, politics, and social welfare—or any of the areas where most public money was spent. More than half the stories, rather, focused on lifestyle, behavior, consumerism, health, or celebrity entertainment.[31] Victor Neufeld, then executive producer of ABC's *20/20*, told us, "Our obligation is not to deliver the news. Our obligation is to do good programming."[32]

Safety can often be an important target for intense and critical watchdog reporting. Yet too much "investigative" reporting was tabloid treatment of everyday circumstances. Local television news often employed its I-teams in such stories as "dangerous doors" (reporting on the hazards of opening and closing doors) or "inside your washing machine" (a look at how dirt and bacteria on the clothes consumers put in their washers get on other clothes). Consider the Los Angeles TV station that rented a house for two months and wired it with a raft of hidden cameras to expose that you really can't get all the carpeting in your house cleaned for $7.95—or the series of reports, popular in the mid-1990s, about a bra whose metal wires could poke the owner.

While this reporting frequently is presented in a way that makes it look like original investigative work, it often is not. First, much of it is what TV reporter Liz Leamy called "just add water" investigative reporting. These reports come from TV news consultants who literally offer stations the scripts, the shots, and the experts to interview, or the interviews themselves already on tape, and are specifically designed to generate ratings during sweeps periods. Some TV news producers call such exposés "stunting," an acknowledgment that they are playing tricks with viewers' appreciation of investigative work without actually doing the legwork required to deliver it. Another problem is that exposing what is readily understood or simply common sense belittles investigative journalism. The press becomes the boy who cried wolf. It is squandering its ability to demand the public's attention because it has done so too many times about trivial matters. It has turned watchdogism into a form of amusement.

The significance of this shift should not be underestimated. On television, which is still one of the most popular media for news, I-team segments and prime time magazines effectively replaced the documentary or any other long-form investigative reportage. As a consequence, some journalists began to question the expanded role of investigative journalism. Patty Calhoun, editor of *Westword*, an alternative newspaper in Denver, Colorado, wondered about the impact on a public that had no way of discerning between gossip and fact when she observed: "Talk radio . . . puts out rumors and now thinks they're doing investigative reporting—which is novel—but unfortunately, their listeners can't tell any better than the radio DJs that they're not."[33]

There is some evidence that local television news investigative reporting has improved in recent years. Gray Television has a national investigative unit, InvestigateTV, that has hired experienced journalists, many involved with the Investigative Reporters and Editors association, to produce in-depth pieces airing across its stations and to develop the investigative work specifically for an OTT channel.[34]

In 2020, Spectrum News was one of a handful of TV news stations to partner with the civically minded nonprofit Report for America, placing a fellow with investigative background to cover and explain topics like the housing crisis in Central Florida.[35] Tegna, the broadcast operation connected to Gannett, launched a fact-checking initiative called Verify. "Social media is proving to the bosses that people want [investigative journalism]," said Ellen Crooke, a VP at Tegna, at a 2018 media event on the state of TV news. "We have metrics that show great investigative work will bring in a younger audience." This trend of improving local TV investigative reporting will become particularly important as the broadcast industry is disrupted, as it inevitably will be, by streaming. For local TV news to survive, it will need to justify itself with content that is indispensably unique and local—which means meaningful investigative work. The convenience of traffic, weather, and breaking headlines will be lost to mobile digital devices. Few Americans under age forty have much relationship with local TV news. In 2017, just 18 percent of adults under thirty said they often got local news from TV compared to 47 percent of those between ages fifty and sixty-four and 57 percent of those over sixty-five.[36] If the medium has a future, it will need to include content worth seeking later on streaming services.

Public perceptions of the watchdog role tend to be complex. For years, the survey work of the Pew Research Center for the People & the Press found public support of the watchdog role remaining stable while the press in general began to become more unpopular. But the support was not unreserved. By 1997, it found the public objecting to techniques such as having reporters not identify themselves as reporters, paying informers for information, and using hidden cameras or microphones.[37] Over two decades, similarly, the public developed more doubts about press criticism of the military. The number of people who believed such reportage weakened the nation's defenses rose from 28 percent in 1985 to 47 percent in 2005. Yet as questions arose about the government's handling of the war in Iraq, public support began to rise for watchdog journalism that covered political leaders. By 2005, 60 percent of Americans thought news organizations kept political leaders from doing things they shouldn't, up from 54 percent in 2003.[38]

In 2017, the American Press Institute, the Associated Press, and the National Opinion Research Center at the University of Chicago had that number at 64 percent, but it, too, now has a significant partisan split.[39] In short, despite enormous misgivings about how the people engaged in journalism go about their work, and doubts about nearly every other dimension of press behavior, support for the watchdog role of the press remains remarkably high, if not unqualified.

INVESTIGATIVE REPORTING AS PROSECUTION

Although all reporting involves investigation, investigative journalism adds a moral dimension. It engages the public to make a judgment about the information disclosed and implies that the news organization considers it important—worthy of special effort. In that sense, investigative reporting usually involves not simply casting light on a subject but also making a more prosecutorial case, based on an observation that something is wrong. Here, journalists should be careful that they have enough evidence to do so, especially since pieces can be structured as either exposés or news stories. Playing fast and loose with the claim of exposing wrongdoing without the evidence to support the claim is an abuse of the audience for your work. This is particularly important in an age when various actors, from think tanks to nonprofits to independent websites, have entered the realm of investigative reporting but do not apply journalistic standards of verification and transparency.

The prosecutorial dimension of investigative reporting requires a higher level of proof, and this can be best seen by examining stories that fell short of that level. When questions arose about a state medical examiner who failed to thoroughly investigate the conduct of President Clinton's mother in a wrongful death case (she was a nurse), the *Los Angeles Times* wrote the story as an exposé. The story suggested that when Clinton was governor of Arkansas, he "refused for several years to dismiss a state medical examiner whose controversial decrees included a ruling that helped Clinton's mother . . . avoid scrutiny in the death of a patient." The problem was the story was inherently confusing and technical. Clinton, for instance, having been defeated for reelection as governor, was out of office at the time of the incident involving his mother. A good many reporters at the *Times,* even some involved in reporting it, believed the whole controversy could have been avoided if the paper had simply written the story as a feature about a curious piece out of Clinton's past instead of as an exposé. The *Times* failed to understand that an exposé is in effect a prosecutor's brief, and the case it sets forth must be unambiguous; if the story does not meet this test, it should be written as something else.

The incident points out an important issue that arises with the investigative model: The news outlet is taking an implied stance on the issue that some wrongdoing has occurred. That is why investigative journalism has been called advocacy reporting, or, as journalist Les Whitten said, "reporting with a sense of outrage," and why the acronym for the professional association called Investigative Reporters and Editors spells out the word *ire.*

To fulfill the watchdog principle responsibly, Bob Woodward has said, one key is to keep an open mind. "You might start a story thinking you are going to look at how the city health department administers vaccines, but . . . find that the story's really about the city's mismanagement in general. . . . Look at as much as you can in every direction." To do so, "some of the things I do are build a chronology, try to talk to everybody and interview them repeatedly."

Pulitzer Prize winner Loretta Tofani relied on the power of talking to potential sources face-to-face and spending a lot of time with them. In a story about a pattern of widespread rape inside a Maryland jail, which she wrote while at *The Washington Post,* she uncovered crimes that were occurring literally under the noses of law officers—crimes widely known to the police and judges. To get the story, she spent months of her own time in the evenings after work doggedly knocking on doors in order to convince some of the most reluctant possible witnesses to talk to her, and she was able to produce a series of stories that documented the prevalence of rape inside the Prince George's Detention Center in Maryland. In the end, Tofani produced what her editors thought impossible: a story documenting the crimes by quoting, by name and on the record, the perpetrators, the victims, and the responsible officials who should have acted to prevent the crimes from ever taking place.

As Tofani said, when the articles were published, all the needed documentation was "given to the government basically on a silver plat-ter. . . . It had everything. It had medical records. It had the victims' names. It had the rapists' names."[40] Public disclosure of the information forced the government to change the system that allowed the rapes to occur. In the end, the government convicted all the rapists.[41]

Investigative reporter Susan Kelleher also said that, before a source agrees to an interview, she tells the source up front everything that is involved in an investigative report. "I tell them how I work," she says. "I tell them they have to go on the record. I tell them I am going to be asking other people about them, that even though I find them really nice people, I am going to have to check them out. . . . I say to them, 'Once you agree to talk to me, that's it. You don't really have control, but you do have control to the degree you want to participate. And once you are on the record, if there's something you don't want me to know, then don't tell me because it's going to be on the record.'"

This level of honesty with sources allowed Kelleher to uncover some remarkable stories. One exposed abuses at an infertility clinic where some doctors were secretly, and illegally, taking extra eggs from their patients and selling them to other patients. Kelleher's story was meticulously documented with medical records and on-the-record in-formation by people involved in the process. And, like Tofani's report, this one won a Pulitzer Prize.

Technology has also strengthened the ability of journalists to ex-amine the effects of policy. The power of computational journalism to analyze large data sets represents an epochal shift in the ability of jour-nalists (and scholars) to understand and prove with data whether, for instance, public policy is having the effect intended, whether medical advances are working, or whether policing is fair. The ability of journal-ists to network with members of the community as their eyes and ears expands the scope of events journalists can monitor. Journalism as col-laborative intelligence, in other words, is a tool beyond the reckoning of news organizations when investigative reporting appeared to reach what we think of as its romantic peak in the 1970s after Watergate.

At the same time, even as revolutions in technology and economic organization create new opportunities, they also threaten an independent watchdog press. Newsrooms are shrinking, and the resources available for watchdog reporting—and the time it takes to do it well—have become scarcer.

Added to that pressure is the acquisition of new media by companies for whom journalism is a minor or even irrelevant concern. In some cases these are publicly traded corporations such as Disney (owner of ABC News) or Comcast (NBC News, and its related parts). For these companies, news is simply a small item in a large portfolio. Even more dangerous is the presence of hedge funds, whose interest in media appears to be cannibalistic, to harvest a declining industry in its final stages. The biggest example is Digital First, which is owned by the private hedge fund investment firm Alden Global Capital and which controls, by one count in 2020, ninety-eight daily and nondaily newspapers.

One of the important and often-overlooked elements of journalistic independence in America is that, historically, news was produced by companies whose primary business was journalism. The smaller the part of any company balance sheet or owner portfolio that news is, the more difficult it is, inevitably and by degrees, for those who work there to claim journalistic independence. It becomes more difficult for an ABC News producer to cover not only Disney but also any other Web, e-commerce, entertainment, cable, or telecommunications company that might be a competitor with ABC's owner.

The theory of a free press as we know it—that there should be an independent voice that can monitor the influence of powerful institutions in society—is put into question. "[These] mergers in the media business matter in ways that other takeovers don't," Rifka Rosenwein wrote in 2000, in an article examining a wave of media mergers prior to the first burst in the tech bubble. "Having five or six major widget companies may be enough to safeguard the price and product competition with which traditional economic theory and antitrust law have been concerned. But concentrating much of the power to create and distribute news and ideas in five or six media conglomerates with a vast array of interests raises all kinds of other issues. There is, after all, a virtue in diversity, lots of it, when it comes to expression that transcends widget economic theory."[42] Some of those first mergers, such as AOL Time Warner, failed, but they were replaced a decade later by another wave as new owners sought the refuge of bigness.

The level of concentration Rosenwein was worried about in 2000 looks paltry in 2020. The combination of the Gannett and Gatehouse companies has put 260 newspapers into the hands of one owner.

History promises that a market economy in an open society has the capacity to correct its mistakes organically. And there are signs of a market response to concerns about the loss of independence in American journalism. Consider that in 2013 the Pulitzer Prize Board awarded the coveted prize for national reporting to Inside Climate News, a seven-person website based in Brooklyn that relies on foundations and individual donations to fund its work. In 2020, ProPublica received the same prize for national reporting, and finalists in other categories came from nonprofits Kaiser Health News and Reveal from the Center for Investigative Reporting.

By most indications, the nonprofit ranks are expanding. The Institute for Nonprofit News in 2020 supported more than 250 nonprofit news organizations, double the number it had a few years earlier. The American Journalism Project, a new "venture philanthropy" organization, had raised tens of millions as of 2020 and made significant investments in twelve local and regional nonprofits to support their work on revenue and sustainability. The Texas Tribune, an earlier nonprofit news site focused on Texas politics and started in 2009, is now held up as a model for revenue diversification and has even contributed funds to help teach others lessons from its success in events and memberships and more. It's also a nonprofit that stands out for its ability to command its own audience.

As interesting as these new efforts are, though, many are still fragile and embryonic, especially when compared with mainstream journalism. The support of private philanthropy can disappear as quickly as it can be given, and while more news outlets appear set to follow and expand on the Texas Tribune's model, many outlets' ability to draw an audience depends on getting the attention of for-profit media to air their research.

The rise of new independent journalism outlets shows how the new technology could reorganize the way news is produced and communicated. Potentially, it suggests that if the old media abandon the watchdog role in any serious sense, others might take it up. Even a lone hacker rummaging through the databases now has the ability to shape or even dictate the flow of news, if what the hacker unearths is important enough (as in the case of Edward Snowden and the NSA).

But there are more practical economic questions still unanswered. Investigative journalism is distinct from the witness-bearing role of the press we outlined earlier, in chapter 1. It tends to require special reporting skills, experience, and temperament. More often than not, revelation comes, not from a single document suddenly found, but from discoveries slowly earned—winning the trust of sources, noticing a fragment of information, recognizing its possibilities, triangulating that with fragments from other information, fitting the pieces together, and establishing proof to a level that will satisfy lawyers. This work usually requires access, significant commitments of time and resources, independence from other interests, and also libel insurance. All of these special characteristics of investigative reporting combine to make it likely that it will remain primarily the product of organized professional journalism—not of the random or lone whistleblower.

In that sense, digital start-ups populated by professional journalists, such as ProPublica or Inside Climate News, seem more likely to be the new model for investigative reporting than crowdsourced models. ProPublica in particular has become an important American journalistic institution with more than one hundred journalists. It has also created an infrastructure of collaborations with local news and instituted large fellowship programs to support investigative journalism more broadly.

But it is no accident that the rise of investigative modern reporting in the 1960s coincided with the growing financial strength of news organizations in print and television. The collapse of that model raises substantial questions about the future of investigative journalism, especially at the local level.

The strongest possibilities lie in the new approach to journalism we have described, one in which the community plays a significant role as partner, not substitute, to the professional investigative journalist.

The community also has a significant role as sentinel over journalistic integrity. For that to happen, however, established news organizations must learn how to work with the worldwide audience with which they can now interact and learn from people about matters that need to be brought to light to which they can apply professional reporting. At the same time they need to help develop among that audience a deeper understanding of what constitutes journalistic integrity. If either the news organization or the participating audience confuses independent investigative reporting with propagandistic activism masquerading as investigation, then our new and deeper public discourse will inevitably slide toward endless argument. Facts, instead of helping form the foundation of our public discourse, will become elements that combatants use to confuse issues and create uncertainty rather than understanding.

JOURNALISM AS
A PUBLIC FORUM

When Jaron Lanier, an early digital pioneer and proponent of virtual reality technology in the 1980s, tries to get people to think about the impact of social media, he often tells them to think about Wikipedia, which is the user-produced and curated website where millions of people every day look up information about anything from classic movies, to food history, to economic theory.

"When you go to an entry," Lanier says, "you're seeing the same [information] as other people. It's one of the few things online that we at least hold in common."[1]

Now imagine, Lanier says, if Wikipedia offered each person a different custom answer or entry for the same search term.

"Wikipedia would be spying on you," he says. It "would calculate, 'What's the thing I can do to get this person to change a little bit on behalf of some commercial interest?' . . . And then it would change the entry. Can you imagine that? Well, you should be able to, because that's exactly what's happening on Facebook. It's exactly what's happening in your YouTube feed."

This, Lanier, suggests, is an enormous threat and challenge to democracy. Technology has shrunk, rather than broadened, the public square and our shared set of facts that can be found there.

Platform companies profit by monitoring and personalizing the content people see online. That monitoring allows them to sell targeted audiences to advertisers. It also keeps those audiences on their platforms longer, which in turn helps them sell more advertising. But there is a civic dimension to this ethos of personalization. Every click and interaction that is tailored to help the platforms sell more advertising also pushes us into smaller and more separate information spheres and makes us more tribal. Tristan Harris, a former Facebook design ethicist, puts it this way: "Even two friends who are . . . close to each other, who have almost the exact same set of friends, . . . see completely different worlds because they're based on these computers calculating what's perfect for each of them."[2]

The economic and technical architecture of the commercial Web offers a caution for understanding the next element of journalism. From its origins in the Greek marketplace to the colonial American taverns, journalism has always been a forum for public discourse. As far back as 1947, the Hutchins Commission placed this mission as an essential obligation of the craft, second only to telling the truth. "The great agencies of mass communication should regard themselves as common carriers of public discussion," the commission wrote.[3]

This is the sixth principle or duty of a free press:

**Journalism must provide a forum for
public criticism and compromise.**

New technology has made the forum more robust and journalism's role less paternal. But, as Lanier suggests, technology's promise of a larger public forum and a broader set of facts in common was mostly a fantasy. The Web has largely been organized in ways that separate us so we can be sold things. The forum's greater speed also has increased the power of bad actors to distort, mislead, and overwhelm whatever ability the Web had to self-correct. On Twitter, one study finds, false news stories are 70 percent more likely to be retweeted than true ones.[4]

How can journalism serve the role of a public forum in this environment? How can it exist when, as early Facebook investor and now critic Roger McNamee puts it, "each person has their own reality, with their own . . . facts"?[5] Journalism and democracy's survival rest on navigating that challenge.

Not all of this should be laid at the feet of technology, the Web, or social media. The challenges they pose reflect deep tendencies in human beings to believe what we want to and to organize in tribes. And the problems predated the Web.

Consider the story of the talk show host Chris Matthews and the journalist Cody Shearer.

The year was 1999, and the story dominating Washington was the potential impeachment of President Bill Clinton. At the center of the impeachment scandal, at least legally, was whether Clinton had lied to special prosecutor Kenneth Starr during a deposition probing whether the president had had sexual relations in the White House with an intern named Monica Lewinsky.

A Washington-based freelance journalist, Cody Shearer, had just returned from a trip to Europe. He sat down to watch television, cruised across channels, stopped on a cable news channel, and watched a few minutes of the talk show *Hardball* with host Chris Matthews.

Matthews's guest on his talk show that night was Kathleen Willey, a woman who claimed President Clinton had groped her in the White House. They were discussing Willey's claim that someone had tried to silence her by threatening her.

As he watched, Shearer suddenly realized that the topic of the interview was not the president or Willey's allegation—it was Shearer himself.

CHRIS MATTHEWS: When this man came up to you in—at dawn that morning, in Richmond five years after this incident, who was that guy? I'm gonna ask you again, because I think you know who it was.

KATHLEEN WILLEY: I do know. I think I know.

MATTHEWS: Why don't you tell me who it was? This is an important part of the story here, why would you want—come out and—on this program tonight on live television and not tell us who you think that person was? . . . Let me ask you a more careful way.

Were you ever led to believe who it might be, and who led you to believe it and what did they lead you to believe?

WILLEY: I was shown a picture and—

MATTHEWS: And who was in the picture?

WILLEY: I can't tell you. I'm not trying to be coy—

MATTHEWS: Would I recognize the picture?

WILLEY: Yes.

MATTHEWS: Is it someone in the President's family, friends? Is it somebody related to Strobe Talbott? Is it a Shearer?

WILLEY: I've been asked not to dis—

MATTHEWS: You've been asked not to admit that?

WILLEY: Yes, by—

MATTHEWS: OK.

With a sinking stomach, Shearer knew what Matthews was getting at. A rumor had been floating around Washington that it was Shearer who had approached Willey while she was jogging and that he had threatened her if she didn't drop her case against the president. The rumor was unsubstantiated. It was also untrue. Shearer had been in California when the encounter had supposedly taken place, but no one had bothered to check out that part of the story. Now he could only watch as Matthews made the false rumor public knowledge and made it sound like fact.

MATTHEWS: Let's go back to the jogger, one of the most colorful and frightening aspects of this story. You were confronted as you were out walking. You couldn't sleep, your neck was hurting—this guy came upon you that you never met before—You never met him before.

WILLEY: No.

MATTHEWS: And tell me about that—what he said, finish up that whole story.

WILLEY: Well, he mentioned my children by name. He asked how they were and, at the—at this point, I started asking him who he was and what he wanted. And he just looked me right in the eye and he said, "You're just not getting the message, are you?" And

I turned around and—and ran. I had no business running, and probably ran about 100 yards, I was so frightened, and I turned around and he was gone.

MATTHEWS: Who showed you the picture of the person you think might have been him?

WILLEY: Jackie Judd.

MATTHEWS: From ABC?

WILLEY: Yes.

MATTHEWS: And did you identify it positively?

WILLEY: Yes.

MATTHEWS: So it's Cody Shearer.

WILLEY: I can't tell you.

MATTHEWS: OK. But you identified it pos—Let's talk about a couple of other things just to tie up the loose ends here.[6]

The show had been over for only a few minutes when the first phone call came. It was an anonymous deep voice, and it was threatening Shearer's life. Shearer was shaken by the call, but he figured it was only a crank who had gotten charged up by the *Hardball* show. Then, however, came a second call. And a third. Shearer began to grow concerned.

The next day conservative talk radio host Rush Limbaugh broadcast the rumor: "She says Ken Starr asked her not to reveal the identity of the man who she says threatened her two days before her testimony in the Paula Jones case. . . . Here's who it is: It's Cody Shearer, S-H-E-A-R-E-R."[7]

Limbaugh had an even greater impact. Call after call came in that day to Shearer's house, nearly a hundred, nearly all of them threatening death or physical harm. Though the story was demonstrably untrue, that night on *Hardball* Matthews reprised some of the Willey interview and played a clip of his "scoop" for his panel of guests.

Shearer left town for a few days and tried to forget the incident. Washington was a town with attention deficit disorder, he figured. In a week or so, no one would care about this.

He was wrong. Sunday morning, back in Washington, Shearer was taking a shower when a houseguest ran into his bathroom and said there was a man in his yard with a gun claiming he had come to kill Shearer. Shearer thought it was a joke until he came out and saw the man, with a gun aimed directly at another friend and demanding to see him.

Suddenly, inexplicably, the gunman ran to his car and fled. Shearer and his friends copied down the license plate number and called the police. An hour later the police delivered the weird incident's even weirder denouement. The crazed gunman was Hank Buchanan, the brother of Patrick Buchanan, the former talk show host and GOP and Reform Party presidential candidate. Hank Buchanan had a history of mental illness.

Most of all, Shearer was appalled by Chris Matthews. "If I made a mistake like that, I would have sat down and written a letter explaining I was on a tight deadline and apologizing," Shearer said. "But I got nothing, not even from the producer. . . . And the most amazing thing is that nothing happened to him. He was back on the air the next night."[8]

The two met on a train a few days after the broadcast but before the Buchanan incident. They argued heatedly, according to Shearer, and he thought Matthews was unapologetic. After receiving letters from Shearer's attorney, Matthews made an on-air apology that included the attorney's assertion that Shearer "had nothing whatever to do with the events described by Ms. Willey."

"I now regret having spoken—not spoken—beforehand with him [Shearer] before I mentioned his name on the air. I should have never brought his name up till we had vetted it," Matthews said on his program. The words, however, were something less than a correction. They also failed to acknowledge that the story was untrue.

The Shearer story puts in frightening relief something it can be easy to lose sight of in an ocean of talk and opinion that now makes up our public forum: The forum has consequences and needs to be built on a foundation of facts.

In chapter 2, on truth, we examined the natural forum the first periodicals provided and its relationship to the creation of public opinion. With the reporting of the details of events, the disclosure of wrongdoing, or the outlining of a developing trend, news sets people to wondering. A modern media culture re-creates over long distances something akin to the face-to-face forum in the Athenian agora and the Roman markets where the world's earliest democracies were formed.

Today, the forum is so pervasive that it informs almost every aspect of gathering and reporting news. Editors across newsrooms keep Twitter open so they can track what others are delivering on their subject areas. Stories regularly include tweets as if they are interviews, and political actors in the post-Trump era now use social platforms, and Twitter in particular, as if they were press release services to issue their statements unfiltered.

In many ways the notion that there is something that can be called a general news cycle has become impossible. The real issue is not that the news cycle is continuous but that it is asynchronous: We do not learn at the same time. Each of us has a personal news cycle, and it may change day to day on the basis of our own behavior, our personal community of friends, the network of people we follow, and some element of randomness. And while this was to a lesser degree always true, now the speed and variation of our digital media culture create the sense that we never catch up and live in many ways in alternate universes. The concept of taking stock, of determining what facts are in evidence, established, and vetted, is complex to the point of seeming obsolete. Everything is in motion, since each of us is learning in a different individualized space and at a different time. Any stock taking must be personal and individualized as well. Our asynchrony is constant. This, in turn, can make the news seem to be something that only insiders are engaged in, or members of some deep state, which doesn't seem real—or at least can be described as "fake" and "a hoax." The largest of these is what has now become called in America "The Big Lie," the idea that somehow the election of Joseph Biden was stolen from Donald Trump.

None of this is lost on advocacy groups or political parties, which want to exploit this new political *Rashomon*. Every year millions of dollars are spent trying to sway public opinion, often with half-truths, sometimes with outright lies. That makes it all the more crucial that the news media play the role of honest broker and referee as they carry the common discussion—that role as annotator of what people already have heard. In the new age of media, it is more incumbent on those who aspire to provide us with a responsible journalism that serves the public interest to decipher the spin and lies of commercialized argument, lobbying, and political propaganda—to vet what is true and attempt to take stock, rather than simply to inflame or hitchhike on controversy to attract a crowd. We all have the ability today to be opinion writers in a public space, whether we work on the editorial pages of the newspaper, distribute our own opinions on a technology like Substack, appear on a talk show, write a point-of-view magazine essay, maintain a blog, or just engage in social media. But if the authors of this intelligence want to call their work journalism, then it follows that they should not misrepresent the facts—that they should hold to the highest standards of truthfulness and allegiance to public interest.

So journalism must provide a forum for public criticism, and in a new age it is more important, not less, that this public discussion be built on the same principles as the rest of journalism—starting with truthfulness, facts, and verification. A forum without regard for facts fails to inform, and a debate steeped in prejudice and supposition only inflames.

Just as important, this forum must be available to all parts of the community, not just those who are most vocal and thus most present in social media, or those who are demographically attractive to the sellers of goods and services.

Finally, there is another element to understand about the public forum that starts with news and that the platform companies' algorithms now amplify: A debate focused only on the extremes of argument does not serve the public and instead leaves most citizens out. Even as our news media and public discourse give airtime to the wide variety of opinions that reflect a society as pluralist as ours, we must not lose sight of the fact that democracies are, in the end, built on compromise. The public forum must include the broad areas of agreement where most of the public resides and where the solutions to society's problems are found.

Some people might consider this argument for stewardship anachronistic—and more than a little elitist—a leftover from an era when only a few outlets controlled public access to information. In a new century, with its new communications technologies, isn't it enough for Matthews to let Willey speak and then let Shearer respond? Why not get the journalist mediator out of the way and let the debate occur in the genuine public square, not the artificial one defined by NBC or CBS News? The Web is a self-cleaning oven. You need not worry about it. This is where the technology-versus-journalism debate comes to its clearest philosophical divide.

It is appealing to think that technology will do the fact-checking for us, that we can trust the larger marketplace of facts and ideas, not journalists, to sort out the truth now, without formal or paternalistic effort by journalists. Each one of us can now simply pass along what we have heard without checking it. If it's wrong, it will get found out somehow, by someone. The limitations of default cultures, flawed gate-keepers, establishment bias, and limited voices will be magically cured, as if it were a matter of simple mathematics.

Even if it were true—and it isn't—there is a problem with this dream of naturally occurring crowdsourced fact-checking. It is a form of passing the buck. It increases the likelihood that people will be mis-led, even if things are later corrected. And it is based on a theoretical hope in the network that the facts do not support. This frightening reality is clearer and clearer the farther we get into the digital age.

Finally, it does not absolve publishers or platform companies of responsibility for passing along false information. How will the media system self-correct if everyone feels it is someone else's job? By what criteria, for instance, is a TV interviewer freed of the obligation to en-gage in the discipline of verification as she conducts a live interview with someone making unchecked allegations? More channels? Inter-activity? The prospect of infinite links? While this notion might seem liberating—why do the hard work when technology will do it for me, especially when newsroom resources have shrunk and I have less time to report?—in the real-world marketplace of communication and po-litical culture, the hope in a crowdsourced truth cannot be relied on. Social science research on how information is shared in social networks makes clear that there are still influencers, those with more followers and more impact, and that their influence is often ideological and based on information that may or may not have been thoroughly vetted. We are beginning to discover that while old oligarchies are being displaced, newer ones are rising to take their place—often with little regard for verification.

The danger is that by assuming technology will replace responsibility, we have created a public square with a diminished regard for fact, fairness, and responsibility. Spin will replace verification. Right will become a matter of who has the greatest might, wattage, or rhetorical skill. In 2020, it may already have happened. Our idealism (which was also self-servingly convenient and profitable for the platform companies) may have, in fact, been our undoing.

The public forum presented on television and radio had already abdicated its responsibility to verify when it began to rely so heavily on live interviews as the primary method of news delivery. The live interview format, as any newsmaker will happily acknowledge, cedes power to the interviewee. The guests control what they say, with broad power to mislead, talk over the host, or even lie. The journalist host, for all intents and purposes, has a limited ability to check or correct all but the most obvious deceptions. Although TV journalists may not realize it, they have structured their programs in such a way that facts are effectively vulnerable to whatever the guests on these programs feel they can sell.

THE FIRST SOCIAL MEDIA

Public discourse lies at the heart of, and actually predates, formal American journalism. Before the printing press, as we have said, "news" was something exchanged over a pint of ale in publick houses. News accounts weren't static printed words, and they didn't exist in a void; they were part of conversation. And though conversations obviously involved the exchange of information, much of the point was the exchange of ideas and opinions.

With the arrival of the printing press, this tradition did not disappear but was carried forward into the essays that filled the earliest newspapers. Noah Webster (whose dictionary first defined the term *editorial*) described this function in an "ADDRESS to the PUBLIC," published in the inaugural issue of his *American Minerva* (December 9,

1793): "Newspapers are not only the vehicles of what is called news; they are the common instruments of social intercourse, by which the Citizens of this vast Republic constantly discourse and debate with each other on subjects of public concern."[9]

In the eras that followed, journalism worked to keep alive the idea of an open forum with the public. When newspapers began to hire reporters and had more "news" to deliver, the editorial page became a place for community discussion through published letters to the editor and later the page opposite the editorials, usually written by readers. Publishers also kept the forum concept alive in more elementary ways. In 1840 *The Houston Star* was among the first newspapers to make its lobby more than an entryway into the newsroom; it became an open salon for the public. Residents were encouraged not only to come by but also to help themselves to "a good glass, an interesting paper and a pleasant cigar." In many cities, the tradition of the newspaper lobby as an inviting public reading room and salon continued for more than another hundred years. The newspaper was not only part of the community but also in a very concrete way a place for the community to gather and talk, much as coffee shops like Starbucks are in the twenty-first century.[10] Before the pandemic, a few news organizations began to replicate this idea by setting up their newsrooms next to coffee shops, bars, and event spaces. In Chicago's South Side, the civic participation and news start-up City Bureau sat between an independent café and a bike shop. In small-town Marfa, Texas, the local paper's ownership bought an old dive bar and refurbished it.[11]

Arguably, at its peak of power and sense of responsibility, the industrialized press grew too restrained. Newspaper editorial pages in the latter part of the twentieth century tended to be tweedy spaces better known for their earnestness than their passion. The conservative *Wall Street Journal* editorial pages of the 1980s and 1990s stood out in part because they were fiery when most were dull.

In the years since, of course, the public forum around the news has grown more robust. But what we think of as the polarizing cacophony of social media platforms did not begin with the internet. It really began with the deregulation of media in the 1980s and the rise of talk radio, plus the move toward argument on cable.

By the 1990s, even before the Web, the media had helped develop what linguist and author Deborah Tannen described as the "Argument Culture." It was led by television programs such as *Crossfire* on CNN, *The McLaughlin Group* on commercial television, and talk radio, but it reflected deeper changes that were occurring in culture and politics. By 2000, in an average twenty-four-hour period, there were 178 hours of news and public affairs programming on television. About 40 percent of these hours were devoted to talk shows, many of them involving staged debates.[12] Scholarly experiments at the time affirmed that if the same ideas were conveyed through heated argument, or through more civil and dispassionate exchange, audiences preferred the drama of the argument.

But the rise of the Argument Culture was not grounded on social science research. It owed more to the fact that, quite literally, talk is cheap. The cost of producing a talk show is only a fraction of the cost of building a reporting infrastructure and delivering news.

Then there was the nature of the discussion itself that dominated the Argument Culture. The media's penchant for talk increasingly grew into a penchant for polarization and alarmism, instead of for journalism's mission of enlightening. On the theory that everyone likes a good fight, all problems began to be seen as unsolvable. Compromise was not presented as a legitimate option.

As far back as 1993, the late novelist Michael Crichton deconstructed the nature of the Argument Culture discourse: "We are all assumed these days to reside at one extreme of the opinion spectrum or another. We are pro-abortion, anti-abortion. We are free traders or protectionist. We are pro–private sector or pro–big government. We are feminists or chauvinists. But in the real world, few of us hold these extreme views. There is instead a spectrum of opinion."[13]

The news media thus became an early amplifier, enabler, and culpable partner in the political polarization a generation later it would decry.

For all its pyrotechnic appeal, moreover, the Argument Culture didn't expand the scope of public discussion. It narrowed it. The Argument Culture tended to limit itself to subjects where there was a good fight to be had. And as the Web began to replace cable news as a venue for breaking news, cable talk shows began to narrow their focus even further, dealing increasingly with a single subject: politics. The reason for this was the paradox of fragmentation. As the public forum grows, the tendency at any one website, Facebook group, chat room, or TV network is toward specialization.

The platforms, with their simple constructs of what they call "meaningful engagement"—namely likes and shares—naively added to this polarization. As people began to share more political content, they tended to like and share things that they already had strong feelings about. We are less likely to share something new, about which we know little, but that we find interesting and might be on the lookout to learn more about. Facebook and others then went further—purely to enhance advertising revenues—and tweaked their algorithms in 2016 to separate us further by our most passionate divisions. By building an advertising architecture around targeting, they prepared a rich, unregulated soil for bad actors to accentuate what separates us as a civic society—not what we hold in common. They became unwitting agents of polarization, unwilling to learn or incapable of knowing how to do anything else.

By 2006, the Argument Culture on television was giving way to something new. The media forum in legacy media was moving away from staged polarized debates and toward radio and television hosts who were no longer asking questions of guests as much as they were offering audiences the answers themselves. The Argument Culture, in which talk shows invited antagonists from both sides to argue, was giving way to the Answer Culture, in which the appeal of the host was to provide affirming answers to an ideologically uniform audience. The Answer Culture is at the heart of the Journalism of Affirmation, that part of the news industry that now builds its audience by affirming its audience's preconceptions rather than focusing on inquiry and reporting.

By 2020 the Answer Culture and the Journalism of Affirmation had fully taken command of cable news. CNN and MSNBC were offering answers, providing solace, and feeding the outrage of people dismayed by Trump's election. When a producer named Ariana Pekary resigned from MSNBC in the summer of 2020 and wrote a blog post about why she felt she had become part of something that was no longer healthy for the democracy, she quoted one of her bosses as telling her: "Our viewers don't really consider us the news. They come to us for comfort."

At the height of the Argument Culture, when CNN and syndicated political talk shows like *The McLaughlin Group* were staging polarized debates, at least viewers were seeing different points of view, offered by people who could at least be on the same TV set with each other, even if these debates had little nuance and denigrated moderation. By 2020, there was little exposure on television or online to even that level of debate.

The social consequences of the Answer Culture and the Journalism of Affirmation are obvious. The more time we spend in specialized forums, the more the public commons shrinks. This is the concept of the digital "filter bubble," the idea that with more diverse choices, we tend to dive into channels that we prefer, and the range of our learning shrinks. The reluctance of TV networks to broadcast key moments of public life, such as political conventions, instead leaving that job to cable television, is only one sign. Yet the result is that the mass media no longer help identify a common set of issues. One of the most distinguishing features of American culture—the nation's ability to summon itself to face great challenges, such as fascism and the Depression—becomes more doubtful. Dysfunctional breakdowns of government, such as the annual government shutdowns, the rise of Trumpism, and the notion that government expertise represents some kind of deep state manipulating the country for the secret private benefit of a handful of elites, become more common. Dysfunction becomes normal. The unthinkable becomes plausible.

The ironic effect of these characteristics of the new larger public—the diminished level of verification, the fragmentation of audiences into separate filter bubbles, the emphasis on affirmation, outrage, and comfort, and the amplification of all that on platforms such as Twitter, Facebook, and YouTube—is that they tend to prevent journalism from accomplishing its most important purpose: providing people with the information they need to self-govern.

"Democracy is based on a fundamental compromise between the majority and the minority," Robert Berdahl, the former chancellor of the University of California at Berkeley, noted at the height of the

Argument Culture era.[14] "Compromise, however, becomes impossible if every issue is raised to the level of a moral imperative" or "framed in a way to produce ultimate shock value." This, however, is what the press now typically does.

"I don't think for a moment that the media and newspapers are the sole source of cynicism in our society," Berdahl added. "But a wave of cynicism is upon us, and it is very damaging to the institutions of civil society. . . . For the kind of corrosive cynicism we are witnessing leads to apathy and indifference. It leads to withdrawal. It leads to the focus on the individual at the expense of concern for the larger community. . . . Cynicism, I believe, is corroding the quality of civil discourse in America and threatening the basis for democratic institutions."

Berdahl was issuing the warning before the first social media platform ever existed. Two decades later the world would see the attempted insurrection of American democracy live on television on January 6, 2021.

By then, after the rise of the Argument Culture on television, a decade after the triumph of the Answer Culture that replaced it, and the ascendancy of the platform companies that amplified it, America had changed politically. More of us held extreme views. Fewer of us considered ourselves moderate.[15] The public forum offered by the media was not the sole cause of this widening polarization, but it had become its enabler.

There was a discernible and in some ways ironic tipping-point moment in the transition from the public forum becoming a place for argument to a place of self-satisfied answers and moral outrage at the now invisible other. It came on October 15, 2004, with the appearance of comedian Jon Stewart on the CNN program *Crossfire*, the iconic example of Argument Culture media, which by then had been on the air for more than a decade.

Stewart, host of *The Daily Show* on Comedy Central before Trevor Noah, had become a critic of *Crossfire* and the argumentative way it dealt with political issues. It was the height of the presidential campaign between George W. Bush and John Kerry. Stewart was invited to the show by cohosts Paul Begala, representing the political Left, and Tucker Carlson, now a Trumpian populist Fox host, representing the Right of the political spectrum.[16]

"Well, he's been called the most trusted name in fake news," Carlson said with a broad smile that suggested the relish with which he looked forward to the conversation with Stewart and "his one-of-a-kind take on politics, the press and America." But it became obvious almost immediately that Stewart had not come on to the show to trade jokes.

STEWART: Why do you argue, the two of you? I hate to see it.

CARLSON: We enjoy it.

STEWART: Let me ask you a question.

CARLSON: Well, let me ask you a question first.

STEWART: All right.

CARLSON: Is John Kerry—is John Kerry really the best? I mean, John Kerry has . . .

STEWART: Is he the best? I thought Lincoln was good.

CARLSON: Is he the best the Democrats can do?

STEWART: Is he the best the Democrats can do?

CARLSON: Yes, this year of the whole field.

STEWART: I had always thought, in a democracy—and again, I don't know—I've only lived in this country—that there's a process. They call them primaries.

CARLSON: Right.

STEWART: And they don't always go with the best, but they go with whoever won. So is he the best? According to the process.

CARLSON: Right. But of the nine guys running, who do you think was the best? Do you think he was the best, the most impressive?

STEWART: The most impressive?

CARLSON: Yes.

STEWART: I thought Al Sharpton was very impressive. I enjoyed his way of speaking. I think, oftentimes, the person that knows they can't win is allowed to speak the most freely, because, otherwise shows with titles such as *Crossfire* . . .

BEGALA: *Crossfire*.

STEWART: Or *Hardball* or "I'm Going to Kick Your Ass," or . . . will jump on it. In many ways, it's funny. And I made a special effort to come on the show today, because I have privately, amongst my friends and also in occasional newspaper and television shows, mentioned this show as being bad.

BEGALA: We've noticed.

STEWART: And I wanted to . . . I felt that that wasn't fair and I should come here and tell you that I don't—it's not so much that it's bad, as it's hurting America. But I wanted to come here today and say . . . Stop, stop, stop, stop hurting America.

Carlson, sensing that he was no longer in control of the conversation, tried to regain it by challenging how Stewart had interviewed Kerry on *The Daily Show*.

CARLSON: Don't you feel like . . . you got the chance to interview the guy. Why not ask him a real question, instead of just suck up to him?

STEWART: Yes. "How are you holding up?" is a real suck-up. And I'm actually giving him a hot stone massage as we are doing it.

CARLSON: It sounded that way. It did.

STEWART: You know, it's interesting to hear you talk about my responsibility.

CARLSON: I felt the sparks between you.

STEWART: I didn't realize that . . . and maybe this explains quite a bit.

CARLSON: No, the opportunity to . . .

STEWART: . . . is that the news organizations look to Comedy Central for their cues on integrity . . . So what I would suggest is, when you talk about you're holding politicians' feet to the fire, I think that's disingenuous. I think you're . . .
[Crosstalk]

STEWART: But my point is this. If your idea of confronting me is that I don't ask hard-hitting enough news questions, we're in bad shape, fellows.

There was more crosstalk, and then Stewart got quite serious.

STEWART: You know, the interesting thing I have is, you have a responsibility to the public discourse, and you fail miserably.

CARLSON: You need to get a job at a journalism school, I think.

STEWART: You need to go to one. The thing that I want to say is, when you have people on for just knee-jerk, reactionary talk . . .

CARLSON: Wait. I thought you were going to be funny. Come on. Be funny.

STEWART: No. No. I'm not going to be your monkey.

BEGALA: Go ahead. Go ahead.

STEWART: I watch your show every day. And it kills me.

CARLSON: I can tell you love it.

STEWART: It's so . . . oh, it's so painful to watch. You know, because we need what you do. This is such a great opportunity you have here to actually get politicians off their marketing and strategy.

CARLSON: Is this really Jon Stewart? What is this, anyway?

STEWART: Yes, it's someone who watches your show and cannot take it anymore. I just can't.

CARLSON: What's it like to have dinner with you? It must be excoriating. Do you, like, lecture people like this or do you come over to their house and sit and lecture them: they're not doing the right thing, that they're missing their opportunities, evading their responsibilities?

STEWART: If I think they are.

CARLSON: I wouldn't want to eat with you, man. That's horrible.

STEWART: I know. And you won't . . . Why can't we just talk . . . please, I beg of you guys, please.

CARLSON: I think you watch too much *Crossfire*. We're going to take a quick break.

STEWART: No, no, no. Please.

CARLSON: No, no, hold on. We've got commercials.

STEWART: Please, please stop.

In January 2005, CNN president Jonathan Klein announced he was canceling the show. Announcing its demise, he told the press, "I guess I come down more firmly in the Jon Stewart camp."[17]

By then, Klein was hardly alone. Talk hosts like Rush Limbaugh on radio or Bill O'Reilly or Rachel Maddow on cable, websites like Free Republic on the right or Talking Points Memo on the left were offering ammunition for devoted followers instead of outlining even the vague parameters of civic argument.

If the era of Argument Culture appealed to extremism, and the Answer Culture that has replaced it put us into specialized channels with alternative realities, the platforms, led by Facebook, took us further. It narrowed our political discourse further by amplifying and celebrating what outraged us, things like metaperceptions, scorn for those who disagreed with us, and a sense that the future of the country was continually at stake. Psychologist Jonathan Haidt and writer Tobias Rose-Stockwell have noted just how social media changed our political interaction in ways that turned our separateness and tribal connections into something competitive. Communication in social media, they write, changes from a personal and two-way set of exchanges—two or three people laughing at each other's jokes and making reciprocal disclosures—into something more public and performative. It erects grandstands, in effect, on both sides of that street, and fills those grandstands with an audience of friends, acquaintances, rivals, and strangers who are passing judgment and offering commentary. Whatever meter we have that tells us how we are doing in the eyes of others—some call it a sociometer—has been put on public display. And that further incentivizes our becoming angry and polarized because it raises our score. As Haidt and Rose-Stockwell put it, "Social media, with its displays of likes, friends, followers, and retweets, has pulled our sociometers out of our private thoughts and posted them for all to see." And outrage, anger, and indignation help boost performance in ways that scholars can measure. "If you constantly express anger in your private conversations, your friends will likely find you tiresome," Haidt and Rose-Stockwell note, "but when there's an audience, the payoffs are different—outrage can boost your status."[18]

With numbing repetition and all of the passion of reciting talking points, the platform companies describe themselves as champions of free speech and an open Web. "I'm here today because I believe we must continue to stand for free expression," Facebook founder Mark Zuckerberg declared in a Georgetown University speech in 2019, one of countless statements he or the company has issued to portray themselves as champions rather than pillagers of healthy civil discourse.[19]

Whatever their original motives, platform companies' interests today are economic, not civic. Whatever they tell themselves, in reality they are avoiding editorial responsibility for the content they distribute because doing so serves their bottom line and protects them from legal exposure and political controversy. They dress up this abdication of responsibility in the name of it being a social good. In fact, this abdication has become a social ill.

The platforms could just as easily add other kinds of content to the mix of what they elevate. They could measure what people hover over without sharing. They could also add to our streams content that is deemed by editors to be in the public interest, that is highly local, that has overriding public safety importance, or that promotes any number of other values. They choose not to because it is not in their economic interest to do so, but they clothe those decisions in rhetoric about the public good. The platform companies could also do more to stop the spread of content that is clearly false. They choose not to except in extreme circumstances, usually when under broad attack, reactively and usually too late.

The late Jack Fuller, who rose from reporter to Pulitzer Prize–winning columnist, editorial page editor, editor, publisher, and eventually president of the newspaper division of the Tribune Company, eloquently explained how this kind of abuse of the public forum by a carrier damages a society and also wears itself out. He was discussing print, but the concepts apply across media and even across eras: "Here is the tension," Fuller told us. "A newspaper that fails to reflect its community deeply will not succeed. But a newspaper that does not challenge its community's values and preconceptions will lose respect for failing to provide the honesty and leadership that newspapers are expected to offer."[20]

To be at once the enabler and the goad of community action is a great challenge, but it is one that journalism has always embraced. It is a challenge that can be met by accepting the obligation to provide the members of the community not only with the knowledge and insights they need but with the forum within which to engage in building a community.

RECLAIMING AND REBUILDING THE PUBLIC FORUM LOCALLY

Journalists must find ways to replace the polarizing public forum they have helped build with a new one. This new public forum should be focused on finding common ground, identifying a common set of facts, explaining them in ways that people can accept, and identifying what people share, not what separates them.

To do this, the news industry must shift some of its definitions of news. And it must recognize the ways in which it has been complicit in the polarization that threatens the future of both journalism and democracy. Unwittingly, journalism has been sowing the seeds of its undoing.

At their best, newspaper opinion sections sought to provide a structured space for civil public discourse on important matters connected to place, to political geography—an arena where the platform companies have almost no presence. The question is whether this kind of space can be reconstructed online, innovated in format, and reimagined for today with a more diverse, inclusive, and equitable civic dialogue. Can local publishers use their convening power for new in-person and online engagement, refine content strategies for more inclusive or representative conversation, and take cues from psychology, neuroscience, and other fields to lead people to have empathetic, substantive dialogue with others?

There is some reason to be hopeful. Local models are emerging. In a small town in New Hampshire, as an example, *The Laconia Daily Sun* worked with a team connected to Amanda Ripley's "Complicating the Narratives" initiative (discussed in chapter 4) to train the writers of letters to the editor on how to make nuanced and thoughtful arguments. They aim to raise the quality of discourse in contributions to their opinion section but are also exploring offering the training to local residents broadly.

In Wisconsin, the *Milwaukee Journal Sentinel* has transformed its opinion section into an "Ideas Lab." Editorials are rare. Instead, resources focus on "solutions journalism" that explores responses to social problems. This forward-looking form of journalism serves as a backbone to community engagement, online and off, that helps people come together to discuss issues and in turn leads to more reporting.[21]

It's similar in Nashville, where the local newspaper, *The Tennessean*, has leaned even more into "civility," the Latin root of which, they point out, is *civitas*, referring to the duties of the citizenry. They are trying to "appeal both to people who were tired of the toxicity in politics and also to those whose believed that civility is used as a means to silence dissent," and are working with trusted partners in the community to help the movement. *The Tennessean* consulted nonprofits focused on better dialogue across division, such as Braver Angels, and psychologists such as Julia Minson, studying receptivity to opposing views, for insights. They've also used Facebook groups and other digital spaces to host ongoing conversations.[22]

There is also promising work occurring outside of opinion sections. Some news organizations have undertaken major initiatives that they hope can lead to and model civic compromise and progress. In Pennsylvania, for instance, the *Erie Times-News* led Erie Next, a nationally recognized engagement initiative that framed discussion on the kind of community the Rust Belt town wanted to become.[23]

In Kentucky, the Bowling Green *Daily News* worked with a polling outfit, Pol.is, to run a "civic assembly."[24] Through online voting, the effort uncovered common priorities across divisions and convened virtual town halls. And new nonprofits now exist, like Spaceship Media, that want to help news organizations pursue efforts that put community members in healthier dialogue across difference, in person or digital, and whether in opinion sections or not.

At the end of the day, the issue is what happens to our understanding if there is no space for civil discourse, for common ground. And as rich and diverse as the new forums of a networked media culture may be, their passion cannot replace the need for fact and context that the Journalism of Verification supplies. If those who gather and then deliver the news no longer spend time and money to report, verify, and synthesize—if they fear that applying judgment is an act of elitism, or that the technology now frees them from these old burdens of vetting, and of identifying points of consensus that define the public commons—then argument, magnified by the wide reach of the Web, is all we are left with.

Who will find out which assertions in the public conversation are true and which are not? Who will explore the backgrounds and motives of the various factions? Who will answer the questions that need to be answered?

In the future, we may well rely more on citizens to be sentinels for one another and in the process take on a watchdog role over their own exchanges and discussions. No doubt this will expand the public forum and enrich the range of voices. But unless the forum is intentionally constructed and based on a foundation of fact and context, the questions citizens ask will become simply rhetorical. The debate will cease to educate; it will only reinforce the preconceptions people arrive with, accelerated by the incentives of platform companies rather than civics, and the public will be less able to participate in solutions. And public discourse, instead of being something we can learn from, will dissolve into noise, which the majority of the public will tune out.

So, first, the journalistic forum should adhere to all the other journalistic principles, and, second, it should relate directly to Madison's recognition of the central role of compromise in democratic society. But if the primary role of the forum is to illuminate rather than agitate, how do journalists engage an audience? This is the next element of journalism.

ENGAGEMENT AND RELEVANCE

S arah Alvarez worried that the way journalists decided what to cover was leading them astray. It was also leaving too many people out.

A lawyer by training, she was struck by how random news judgment was. Reporters and editors, she thought, relied too heavily on an unspoken set of instinctive judgments and unexamined norms. Those judgments were too heavily influenced by journalists' limited personal, cultural, and professional experiences and constrained further by the fact journalists had only a vague sense of who their audience was or what they really needed. To make matters worse, she thought news organizations used crude metrics to see if the rough guesses their journalists made had been right.

This "feedback loop" seemed fraught with problems. The range of stories was too narrow, the criteria of judgment too subjective. Engagement was being tested on an existing audience that was also narrow, not to mention tending to be affluent, older, and shrinking—further leaving out often those most in need. Weren't there more systematic criteria for deciding what stories needed to be told, some way of including the audience in that discussion, and a better way of testing how audiences responded?

Alvarez, who was working in public radio at the time, wanted to report on people who had the greatest information needs. But she found she "wasn't reporting about low-income families *for* low-income families. . . . I was reporting about [low-income communities] for people who had money, and that was not the best way in my thinking to address the issue."[1]

On a fellowship at Stanford, she met scholars like economist James Hamilton and thought more about the structure of news. And that was when Alvarez landed on a radically simple idea: Why not develop a system for assessing where the information gaps already existed for most people and then fill those gaps on a technology platform nearly everyone already used, regardless of income? In other words, create a system, a process, with a clear set of criteria for deciding what news was important, and then testing whether you were right.

She created Outlier Media in Detroit.

Alvarez began by looking at civic data that might provide a signal about where gaps existed in city services and resources. Her team at Outlier started by examining call center data from the United Way's 211 service—a resource line for help with basic needs—as well as public complaints to the government and public health data. (They would later add 911 response times.) Where were city services not being distributed evenly? Where were there greater needs or resource gaps?

Outlier then used texting as its primary journalistic platform because it was a communications system nearly everyone used. On it, Alvarez set up a system in which people could easily look up data about housing, including ownership, foreclosure risk, and rental inspections. She also made it simple for people on the platform to ask Outlier additional questions. When they did, she and her team would find the answers and text back to the questioner. And when answers couldn't be found, the Outlier newsroom embarked on investigative reporting to find out why the information wasn't available and tried to address whatever systematic barrier was keeping the information secret or the need unaddressed.

Soon, she was answering questions every week from hundreds of people traditional media weren't usually reaching and providing them with actionable information about housing and utilities that they had specifically asked for.

This was journalism as service, the kind of two-way mix of citizen/

journalist/technology collaboration we have called journalism of collaborative intelligence. Alvarez calls it filling information gaps through a "direct service to news consumers" model.

In time, Alvarez's operation was getting and answering questions about more than housing, and she decided to strengthen that second level of enterprise investigative reporting. To do that, she also wanted to strengthen the data she used for choosing which stories to dig into. What kind of better feedback loop should she build for this higher-level reporting?

Once again, she tried to be systematic and interactive. In addition to the information gaps she was identifying from the civic data she was collecting, Outlier began surveying its readers in its texting community—but not by asking them what stories they wanted to see. Instead, they asked people about their lives, specifically what they were most worried about over the next few months. Outlier's editorial team then looked for patterns in the answers they were getting back from the texting service.

Finally, in choosing what stories to cover from this input, Outlier established three clear criteria of significance: (1) How widespread is the problem? (2) How significant is the harm it is causing? Is it, for instance, a life-and-death matter? (3) And how distinctive or local is the problem? Tax foreclosures, as an example, are much higher in Detroit than elsewhere.

This last idea was important. If something was happening in one place and not others, it was probably something that could be solved, precisely because it had been avoided elsewhere.

"Journalistic resources are so scarce, and there is a lot of judgment in deciding what is important. But there is a huge group of people we are ignoring while at the same time we are overburdening our elite audiences with a lot of repetitious information," Alvarez said.[2]

Using this system, Outlier's "accountability" work uncovered varied stories traditional media had missed. It found a pattern of disregard for the health and safety of prisoners within the Michigan Department of Corrections. It identified how an out-of-date algorithm in the state's unemployment insurance system was overidentifying fraud when there was none and was delaying or stopping needed benefits from getting to people. It uncovered the role of the city in Detroit neighborhood blight. It spotted language and access problems in Michigan regarding state and federal elections. It also began partnering with mainstream outlets so its work could reach even larger communities. It worked with local niche publications, such as the nonprofit education news site Chalkbeat, to leverage additional expertise that could answer users' questions. Journalists in places such as Milwaukee and Memphis sought them out to replicate the model. But the focus—"direct service to news consumers"—augmented by serious investigative reporting—remained.

"Serving people with the biggest information and accountability gaps, that's always our focus," Alvarez said. "The model is that when you can give people information that would allow them to watchdog these issues on their own, that should be our number one priority."

Alvarez's story is powerful because it is so simple and elegant. It also recalls the earliest days of journalism, when new forms were being invented to fill needs. It also translates into the seventh journalistic principle:

Journalism must make the significant interesting and relevant.

When people talk about making the news engaging and relevant, the discussion often becomes an unhelpful dichotomy—engaging versus relevant. Should we emphasize news that is fun and fascinating and plays on our sensations? Or should we stick to the news that is the most important? Should journalists give people what they need or what they want? The supposed dilemma may seem magnified a thousand-fold in the digital era—when the traffic to each story, as measured by page views, can be counted in real time and when the appeal of cat pictures, teenage pop stars, and amusing cultural memes seems to automatically overwhelm news with greater civic value.

This classic way of posing the question of engagement—as information versus storytelling, or what people need versus what people want—is a distortion. This is not how journalism is practiced. Nor is it, we believe, how people come to the news. The evidence suggests that most people want both: They read the sports and the business pages, *The New Yorker*'s long stories and its cartoons, the book review and the crossword puzzle. *The New York Times* supports some twenty-plus foreign bureaus and its Washington bureau, and it covers city council meetings, but it also has fashion, lifestyle, and food sections. BuzzFeed made a science out of predicting the viral potential of photos of basset hounds running, but it also has found that its appeal widens with political coverage, breaking exclusive stories, and even long-form content.

Storytelling and information are not contradictory. They are better understood as points on a continuum of communication. At one end, perhaps, is the bedtime story you make up to tell your children, which may have no point other than intimate and comforting time spent together. On the other might sit raw data—sports statistics, community bulletin boards, stock tables, or even databases—that contain no narrative at all. Most journalism, like most communication, exists somewhere in the middle.

Writing teachers Roy Peter Clark and Chip Scanlan say that effective writing about news can be found at the intersection of civic clarity, the information citizens need to function, and literary grace. By finding out what people want and tracking it down for them, Outlier has simplified the process of identifying the significant. By delivering that information on the medium people are already using, it has taken an enormous step in making it relevant.

Understood this way, the best work—that which rises above its subject matter—pushes a story further toward the middle of that continuum than the audience would expect. It does so through superior reporting, thinking, narrative, design, and presentation of data, in a way that helps readers make sense of what's going on in the world. Quality, in short, has less to do with the seriousness of the topic than with its treatment. It can be found in the Hollywood profile that says something deeper about filmmaking; the investigative exposé that also reveals the human condition; the treatment of demographic data that brings a neighborhood to life. The task of those engaged in journalism—whether they are professionals who make a living at it or community members who find themselves trying to explain what it was like to survive a disaster—is to find a way to make the significant parts of each story interesting, engaging, and meaningful. For those trying to offer a record of the day in the way newspapers or television news programs might, it also involves finding the right mix of the serious and the less serious that reflects what real life is like.

Perhaps it is best understood this way: Journalism is storytelling with a purpose. That purpose is to provide people with information they need to understand the world. The first challenge is finding the information that people need to live their lives. The second is to find a way to make it meaningful, relevant, and engaging.

Engagement should be seen as being part of journalism's commitment to the citizenry. As one reporter interviewed by our academic research partners put it years ago, "If you are the kind of person who, once you have found out something, find that you are not satisfied about knowing it until you figure out a way to tell somebody else, then you're a journalist."[3]

Part of journalism's responsibility, in other words, is not just providing information but also providing it in such a way that people will be inclined to both encounter it and consider it useful. And one of the extraordinary dimensions of digital presentation is that journalists are no longer limited to a conventional palette of news writing, or even traditional narrative.

This responsibility also implies, as it always has, choosing, selecting, deciding what is important and what is not, knowing what to highlight and what to leave out, and understanding which tools to place in the hands of citizens to help them discover the threads of a story on their own. Put another way, storytelling involves more than words. But whatever form of presentation it takes, its main purpose is distillation—critical analytical thinking that illuminates the matter under consideration.

"At one end of the spectrum it is what is most important—is there going to be war or peace, are taxes going up, are they going down?" said Howard Rheingold, an author, critic, teacher, and former executive editor of the online magazine *HotWired*. "The other end of the spectrum is just what's purely interesting. . . . And most stories are something of a mix of the two."[4]

So how does the question of making news engaging get so distorted, as if there were no way to balance engagement and significance of information? If people do not basically want their news one way or the other, why does the news so often fall short?

A multitude of problems stand in the way of news being delivered compellingly: habit, haste, ignorance, laziness, formula, bias, cultural blinders, a shallow grasp of the topic, lack of skill. It takes time to produce a story well if you're not using a ready-made template like the inverted pyramid style in print, the one-minute reported package in TV, or the static bar chart representation of data. It is, in the end, a strategic exercise that involves more than just plugging facts into short, declarative sentences, writing code, or pulling data from an Excel spreadsheet. And at a time when the public is more skeptical than ever of journalism and has ever more diverting alternatives to consuming news—from Instagram to Netflix to mobile games—cutbacks in traditional newsrooms have put more pressure on time and resources.

Another problem is that for years journalists didn't have to think all that hard about presentation. In the era of oligarchical media, questions about how to make news engaging were usually limited to better writing. Big-city newspapers and network newscasts in a four-channel media world largely decided which stories were well told on the basis of the subjective professional judgment of the top editors and producers. And trust in media was high enough that no one thought in terms of "fact-resistant" audiences or worried much about "confirmation bias" or how to present information so that skeptical audiences would believe it. Journalists operated by story techniques that were handed down through generations. The inverted pyramid in newspapers or the one-minute package in television (with a rigid structure—live intro, reporter narration, sound bite, narration, sound bite, standup close by reporter) were rigidly followed. And journalists assumed that, to a large degree, audiences understood and accepted what journalists reported. There wasn't much awareness of how people processed the news cognitively.

Today journalists must understand a new, deeper structural reality about when to even deliver the news and in what forms: In the old order, audiences had to adapt their behavior to fit the rhythms of the news media. They had to be home at 6:30 P.M. to see the newscast, or be sure to read the morning paper to be current with the news others had seen. Now the news media must adapt to fit the behavior and curiosity of the community that new technology has created. All of this demands that journalists research and understand, in a way they only guessed at before, the real needs and habits of the people they serve.

Rethinking is required in part because some of the conventional wisdom about shortened attention spans was misguided and has hurt, not helped, journalism. A multiyear study of local television news we designed at the Project for Excellence in Journalism, for instance, found that stations that ran more short stories—under forty-five seconds—tended to lose audiences. Stations that did more stories over two minutes, on the other hand, tended to gain viewership.[5]

Similarly, many early studies of the internet suggested that people would never read long-form material on digital screens. The average time people spent on Web pages tended toward about thirty seconds, according to eye-tracking studies by the Poynter Institute. The advent of the smartphone and then the tablet and the e-reader began to dispel this illusion. By 2012, studies were finding that people read at length on their devices, both books and long-form articles.[6] But the research was crude. The short attention span found on computer screens had less to do with anything inherent about the screens than it did with the fact that the people observed in earlier studies were using desktop computers, often in their offices at work.

The good news is that the same technology that devastated the economic foundation of commercial news in the beginning of the new century has also unleashed a profound new wave of creativity. The tools include new ways of using data, graphics, and technology, involving the community, and more. The level of experimentation is probably unprecedented in at least a century, and it offers the potential to make journalism more engaging, more relevant, and more empowering than in generations.

There are countless examples of innovators who defied conventional wisdom about what audiences want. Watch teens who have never read a newspaper talk about news because they are getting it through "flop accounts" on Instagram—joint accounts managed by friends—in effect creating small news collectives.[7] Or consider that 104 million Americans listen to podcasts monthly, and 16 million call themselves "avid" listeners to a medium that did not exist in meaningful form a decade ago. Many of these are the offspring, at least in concept, of the radio program *This American Life*, which broadcasts "stories that are like movies for radio," and whose average listener tunes in for forty-eight out of the sixty minutes of the show. *This American Life* reaches around 2.2 million people per week on the radio—but 3.1 million downloading a week by podcast—and usually runs three stories per episode, ranging from extended reports, to essays, to found audio material.[8] It is only one example that contradicts the conventional wisdom about the limited attention spans in an increasingly crowded media environment.

Many conventional news operations lack the will, resources, and strategic vision to embrace the storytelling potential that technology holds, and many of the technology companies that have the ability to employ these tools have little interest in producing journalism. Many of the pioneers who do care work outside conventional settings, have lacked scale or impact, and have seen slow adoption of their ideas. But as the rapid embrace of Outlier by new partners in the Midwest suggests, that may be beginning to change.

The sweet spot for innovation is the convergence point where technology is viewed as a way to fulfill the public interest mission that has always animated our best journalism.

THE LURE OF INFOTAINMENT AND SENSATIONALISM

In the first two decades of technological disruption, when cable television began to lure the audiences away from broadcast, and twenty-four-hour cable news took audiences away from traditional network evening and morning newscasts, one reaction was to make news more like entertainment. This was the age of infotainment, a late twentieth-century version of tabloid sensationalism. It reached its peak in the late 1990s, right before Americans and their media were jolted by the terrorist attacks of 2001. (It is finding a new form in the hyperpolarized "like" and "share" metrics by which social media platforms define engagement, discussed earlier.) Before the era of cheap-to-produce reality shows, the television schedule was punctuated by prime time journalism magazines devoted to celebrity and true crime. Stories like the murder of child beauty contestant JonBenét Ramsey dominated not just the front pages of tawdry supermarket tabloid newspapers but also the once hyperselective network evening newscasts. In the summer before the attacks of September 11, 2001, the biggest story in the nation's capital was not the growing unease in intelligence circles about a growing threat to America, or the implications of the weakening economy in the wake of the tech bubble bursting, but unfounded suspicions that a young Washington intern named Chandra Levy had been murdered by a congressman named Gary Condit with whom she had been having an affair. In fact, Levy had been killed in a random assault and robbery.

The journalism of the infotainment era shared some common characteristics.

Leo Braudy, the author of *The Frenzy of Renown*, has argued that a key feature of infotainment journalism was to "somehow present the story as a secret. You have to be the knowing reporter and to let the audience in on it. And unfortunately, more and more as time goes on, the secret is something scandalous or salacious." This, in turn, creates "an audience that likes to think of itself as being in the know"—that needs the next salacious fix.[9]

Other elements of news as a hidden secret included the titillation of forbidden or even violent sex, the lure of the innocent by an unscrupulous predator or a powerful manipulator, and the tragedy, downfall, or perhaps even redemption of a celebrity. The Condit story had many of the elements. So did the progenitor Washington scandal that had preceded it two years earlier, the Clinton-Lewinsky scandal. Such stories have hardly vanished. Infotainment, celebrity, and scandal will always provide easy ways to catch audiences' attention.

The tone of journalism always shifts with changes in culture, international crises, technology, and economics. The age of infotainment that dominated the end of the twentieth-century media culture faded with the attacks of September 11, wars in Afghanistan and Iraq, and the impact of the Web. The first wave of the Web was characterized by its own kind of digital tabloidization—a fascination with page views—then called "clickbait"—which were intended to help sell digital advertising. That led in some cases to more innovation. As some experimented with listicles, slideshows, and quizzes, for instance, others were innovating visual journalism and the use of data.

We have seen tabloid cycles come and go before with economic booms, cultural shifts, and political crises. As the immigrants of the 1890s moved into the middle class in the twentieth century, the sensationalism of yellow journalism gave way to the more sober approach of *The New York Times*. As the delirium of the Roaring Twenties gave way to the severity of the Depression, the celebrity age of the tabloids and gossip-mongers like radio and newspaper columnist Walter Winchell gave way to a new seriousness that lasted through the Cold War. The survivors of the great newspaper wars of the 1960s, which saw most cities become one-newspaper towns, were not the mass-circulation tabloids but the serious papers in each city—*The Washington Post, The New York Times,* the *Los Angeles Times, The Philadelphia Inquirer, The Boston Globe,* and countless others. It was true in television as well. In the age when the national nightly network newscasts commanded much of the national audience, the dominant television network news operation was generally the one with the largest number of bureaus and the greatest commitment to delivering serious news, whether it was the *Huntley-Brinkley Report* in the 1960s, the *CBS Evening News* with Walter Cronkite in the 1970s, *World News Tonight* with Peter Jennings from the mid-1980s to the mid-1990s, or NBC News's multiplatform approach in the late 1990s and into the new century.[10]

Some websites, such as TMZ, or even some of the more whimsical viral material on BuzzFeed—which also did significantly innovative work in journalism—are the digital reminder that infotainment is not far away. The Web poses its own potential for a new kind of infotainment or sensationalism. The age of disinformation is a kind of sensationalism of its own. And there is a temptation for editorial staffs to take Web metrics and follow the same mistakes that television made with ratings—assume that the path to the largest audience is to fill a publication with popular bits of diversion that people will want to share with friends. (We will discuss this in greater depth in the next chapter.) Investing in quality reporting, after all, is more expensive, and newsrooms are shrinking.

Yet history offers three reasons to believe that attracting audiences by being merely amusing is not a lasting business strategy for journalistic enterprises.

The first is that if you feed people only trivia and entertainment, you will wither the appetite and expectations of some people for anything else. This is especially true of those people who, because of a lack of inclination, time, or resources, are less likely to seek alternatives. This is the dilemma now faced by so much local television news. "Of those who do watch local news, more than half those surveyed no longer care which station they watch," INSITE Research, a leading television audience research firm in California, declared more than two decades ago.[11] The problem of local TV news losing audience would only intensify in the years to follow, as the infotainment on the air failed to translate into useful news online.

The second long-term problem with the strategy of infotainment is that it destroys the news organization's authority to deliver more serious news and drives away those audiences who want it. This, too, happened in local television news. Even in 2000, a survey by Indiana University researchers for the nonprofit research group NewsLab, for instance, found that five of the top seven reasons that people stopped watching local TV news were different ways of saying that it lacked substance (the other two top reasons were that people were not home or too busy).[12] This research is backed up not only by the intuition of many local newspeople but also by other survey research. "Avoidance of local news has doubled in the past ten years," say other data from INSITE Research. One reason given was: "More than half of those surveyed feel that most stations spend too much time covering the same stories over and over again."[13]

Finally, the infotainment strategy is faulty as a business plan because when you turn your news into entertainment, you are playing to the strengths of other media rather than your own. How can the news ever compete with entertainment on entertainment's terms? Why would it want to? The value and allure of news is that it is different. It is based on relevance. The strategy of infotainment, though it may attract an audience in the short run and may be cheap to produce, will build a shallow audience because it is built on form, not substance. Such an audience will switch to the next "most exciting" thing because that audience was built on the spongy ground of excitement.

These challenges, like a distracted public, do not make journalism impossible, only more difficult. They separate successful journalism from lazy, good from bad, the complete from the overly sensationalized.

Perhaps most important, winning back audience through better forms of storytelling is hard. It takes imagination. It requires experimentation. And above all it demands faith in and respect for the audience. There will almost certainly be haves and have-nots in the news industry. Innovative storytelling experiments are common now at places like *The New York Times*, from videos and podcasts to programming for streaming formats and cable, all of which are introducing the paper to new and younger readers. That kind of new product thinking, however, lags at most local operations.

When the Web began to take audience from print, those qualities were largely missing online. Many journalists working in legacy media tended to consider the Web an inferior platform and glorified the virtues of thumbing through the print paper, hoping audiences would share their nostalgia. When that began to change, the initial reaction was to use the internet as a place for posting the same material produced in print or on television rather than as a distinct platform with its own potential. This was the era in which leaders such as Arthur Sulzberger Jr., the publisher of *The New York Times*, would assert that they were "platform agnostic."[14] The problem with agnosticism is that it reflects ambivalence and uncertainty. The innovators of the digital age, however, weren't platform agnostic. They were "platform orthodox." They believed in, and wanted to exploit, the Web's unique potential to tell stories in new ways and engage the audience community in their news gathering.

By the second decade of the twenty-first century, the situation had begun to change. Organizations that believed in journalism, both in legacy media and online, began to emerge as Web innovators, from *The New York Times* to ProPublica to upstarts like Outlier Media. They eschewed the lure of digital sensationalism and began exploring the potential of new storytelling and engagement. With digital tools, this meant moving from seeing news as a static product—something an audience received—to instead seeing it as a service that could help people live their lives better. That service involved imagining new and better ways to perform the different functions of journalism outlined in chapter 1, from authentication and sense making to empowerment.

We cannot pretend to offer here an encyclopedia of methods for doing this. That is a different book. But we want to look at some more conceptual issues that may help citizens, citizen journalists, and professional journalists to begin to think differently.

This starts with understanding what so often was lacking in some traditional journalistic writing. Story forms such as the "inverted pyramid" were so formulaic that, although they were filled with facts and detail, journalists had no idea if they engaged readers. All they knew was that the formula was what their editors expected. So they delivered it. Much of this news writing did not come alive in the way that good storytelling can. Indeed, most news writing tends to share some common flaws:

- Character is missing—sources become templates, not real people.
- Time is frozen and lacks movement. Everything happened yesterday or this evening.
- Information is designed for a single audience, not multiple ones.
- The news is presented as a conversation among insiders.
- Stories don't illuminate a greater meaning.
- There is little attempt to globalize the local or localize the global.
- Storytelling is predictable and formulaic.
- The Web is used as a new platform, but the material remains in the legacy platform and fails to take advantage of technology with new possibilities.

MODELS OF INNOVATIVE STORYTELLING

If you seek out the industry's most talented writers, you find compelling new thinking about how to present news that addresses many of these failings. What follows are some of those concepts, some of which have to do with storytelling, but many of which apply to any kind of content—from curated content, to photos, graphics, and videos, to telling stories with data.

First, better storytelling doesn't begin after one sits down to edit a story or video, begins to write a script, or pulls up to an empty screen to draft a story. It begins earlier, before someone ever goes out to report, at the moment of story choice and conception. And it involves reporting differently, talking to different sources, and asking different questions.

ASK: WHO ARE THE AUDIENCES AND WHAT DO THEY NEED TO KNOW?

Often journalists begin a story by gathering what official or establishment voices have to say about it and then reporting the newest development. This incremental piling on of developments, however, can limit the story and can confuse people who may be most affected but are paying haphazard attention. It also gives news an insider taint.

Some of the most creative people in news advocate a different approach. When taking on a story, or thinking about engaging a topic, one should ask the following questions about the audience first:

1. What is this story really about? (What do the facts we know so far, or the data we have seen, suggest?)
2. Whom does this story or these facts affect, and how? What information do these people need to know to make up their own minds about the subject?
3. Who has the information, and who can put it in context?
4. What's the best way to tell this story? Is it even a narrative, or is it better told other ways?

These simple questions can make a big difference. They direct coverage toward the citizen first—the audience—and away from interest groups, insiders, and other direct participants. They also may lead journalism to a new set of sources not found in the previous coverage. These questions pull the coverage away from the old routines, which may already have limited the audience rather than expanded it.

Using this method, a story about a small proposed change in a bill in Congress or the state legislature, for instance, might turn into a story about how the bill has never really addressed the most important issues—and how the latest incremental compromise doesn't help.

ANSWER AUDIENCE QUESTIONS

A whole field of practice is forming around how newspeople can listen to and ask questions of audiences, and then try to answer them for the public. Companies Hearken and GroundSource both offer tools to help news organizations do that. Outlier is another example.

But one of the simplest and most effective practices we've encountered has come from the public radio station KPCC in Southern California. It has emphasized the idea that its news organization is a help desk, responding directly to users who pose a question through engagement tools like Hearken. As at Outlier Media, the audiences get an actual answer from the journalists and are pointed to coverage or information that can help them. The station meets people where they are rather than having them find the relevant information hidden in an inverted pyramid structure somewhere else. Between March and August of 2020, it received 4,000 questions from its audience about the pandemic, and it was able to answer 3,900 of them.[15]

THE STAKEHOLDER WHEEL

Pulitzer Prize–winning writer Jacqui Banaszynski takes this audience or public-centric approach to a level higher. She teaches people to make coverage of issues more engaging by thinking about "stakeholders"— the people who are most affected by or most invested in events (these two groups could be different).

To do this, she has people draw a circle on a piece of paper with the event or issue written inside. Then they draw "spokes" radiating from the hub, one for every group of people or in some cases every specific person with a stake in the issue. Such an individual could be someone involved in, interested in, affected by, or even just curious about the event or subject. Initially people performing the exercise make only a few spokes on the wheel. Then Banaszynski gets them to think harder.

Take a subject like education, or the first day of school. People usually name initially:

- Students
- Parents
- Teachers

Then Banaszynski tells people to think more broadly. As they do so they begin to add new stakeholders to the list: school bus drivers, crossing guards, cafeteria workers, school administrators, janitors, school nurses, guidance counselors, even truant officers.

Banaszynski then says think wider still. Soon the spokes point to more people affected by schools: siblings, grandparents, teachers' unions, legislators, school boards, commuters, daycare and aftercare operators, retailers that sell school supplies, companies that make and sell children's clothes, employers who have kids, universities, researchers, taxpayers who pay for schools, parents of kids with special needs, young people thinking of becoming teachers. Now you are thinking about more than how to organize a few facts for a few people. You are thinking about the ecosystem of education and how it affects the community deeply.

Not every story, or piece of content, connects to all of them. Yet each of the spokes poses a host of questions that might prompt a good story, or alters the way to tell a story or what content modules should be included. Suddenly, in other words, the storyteller, whatever his or her tools, has focused on the audience and the community. The next time a reporter thinks about an education story, he or she has a stakeholders' map to explore which stories affect whom, who should be interviewed, and how those stories should be written.

BRING SYSTEMS THINKING TO THINKING ABOUT STORIES

The Journalism + Design group at the New School has adapted classic "systems thinking" strategies to news coverage. Systems thinking is used by scientists, environmentalists, sociologists, and others who work on complex problems. "Most of us aren't very good at thinking about complexity," said Heather Chaplin, who leads the Journalism + Design group. "Yet the most important stories of our time—global warming, immigration, how governments work or don't work—are complex by nature. We pulled what was useful from systems thinking to build a set of tools to help journalists tell these tricky stories."

The tools include such ideas as "chaos mapping," which helps reporters see the connections between seemingly disparate problems: For example, after participating in a Journalism + Design workshop, one local paper decided to pair their education and crime reporters together to cover the school-to-prison pipeline. Another exercise, "Identifying Key Stakeholders," helps reporters visualize the power dynamics in a story and unearth diverse sources. Other tools include making feedback loops to better understand the patterns at play in a story and uncovering the "mental models" that drive the behavior of people in a story.

The idea, Chaplin said, is that by expanding the lens beyond individual events and outcomes, journalists can begin to reveal *why* problems or conditions exist. When reporters just focus on the symptoms of a complex problem, it can get repetitive and also make readers feel the problem is hopeless. "Systems journalism is about helping people see where change might happen," Chaplin said.

The work can be likened to the difference between a cop walking the beat (and reacting to the symptoms of the social conditions of the city) versus the public safety leadership of that city trying to understand what causes those conditions in the first place. If journalism stays at the level of the cop walking the beat, it can only go so far in helping the community.

A NEW DEFINITION OF WHO, WHAT, WHEN, WHERE, WHY, AND HOW

Journalists can rethink the basic elements of news—who, what, when, where, why, and how. Roy Peter Clark, writing professor at the Poynter Institute in St. Petersburg, Florida, has done just that. He took the five W's and an H and turned them into reminders of how to create a story through storytelling. Years ago, Clark was struck by the ideas of Seattle writer and editor Rick Zahler, who argued that news writing took dynamic events and froze them. Time sequences become simply yesterday.

Place becomes a dateline. Zahler wanted to "thaw out" the news and put things in motion. Building on his ideas, Clark began to teach how this could be done.

"Who becomes character. What becomes scene. Where becomes setting. When is chronology. Why becomes motivation or causation." Finally, "how becomes narrative," or the way all the elements fit together, Clark explains.[16] At the beginning of *Romeo and Juliet*, Shakespeare tells in the first eight lines of a sonnet all the facts of the story, including the ending, he points out. So what's left to tell? As Clark explains it, the next two hours of the play fill in all that missing detail. "We often give the news, but you still want to know how it happened. Narrative is the way we answer the question 'How did that happen?'" says Clark.

If we think of *who* as character, *when* as chronology, *where* as setting, and *how* as narrative, we can blend information and storytelling. Quotes become dialogue. News becomes not just information but also meaning. Doing this, not so incidentally, requires more reporting and more curiosity on the part of the reporter.

Jack Hart, a writing coach at *The Oregonian*, said fifteen to thirty inches is a reasonable length for a narrative that can be produced in a day. The idea is to follow a character through a complication and show how he or she resolves it. This can be done in a five-part narrative arc. First comes the exposition, in which the character and the complication are introduced. Then the rising action, which is the bulk of the piece, showing the obstacles on the way to solving the complication. What follows are the point of insight, or the moment when the character has a revelation, and the resolution, when the complication is resolved. The ending is the denouement, a chance to tie up loose ends.[17] Suddenly, narrative theory, dramatic theory, and notions of storytelling and story arc have become part of news.

TAKE RESPONSIBILITY FOR WHAT THE AUDIENCE UNDERSTANDS—NOT JUST WHAT IT SEES

When Melissa Bell, Matt Yglesias, and Ezra Klein started Vox, they were launching a site for a new kind of journalist. While some readers wonder whether Klein's work, for instance, crosses a line between that of a columnist and a reporter, Klein's intelligent analysis of economics and public policy is serious and substantive, and it resonates with readers. He is part policy analyst, part researcher, part blogger, part reporter, part explanatory journalist.

Some of what distinguishes Klein's work is how he communicates with his audience. Too much of traditional journalism, he says, was about making information available to the public—and too little was concerned with taking responsibility for creating understanding—worrying about what readers really knew and thought.[18] He strives, he said, to give the readers the "feeling of a key turning in a lock," to create the sense that new knowledge is being revealed.

To do this, Klein argues, first one must genuinely understand the substance of what one is trying to convey. This means, he says, sitting down to read the academic scholarship and research reports. Then he tries to take readers on the same journey that he took, while omitting the parts that didn't lead anywhere.

He also tries to eliminate "the cognitive anxiety of the reader," the sense that concepts or issues in the news are dull or hard to follow. (In other words, make the significant interesting.) One way to do this is to think about lifting the heavy cargo of data and putting in charts and graphs—merging data visualization and narrative. Another is to think often about relying on understandable forms of discourse, such as bullet lists and Q&A. Whatever it is, your first concern should be whether your method for conveying the story will lead the reader to a greater understanding of the issue at hand. Lauren Williams, the editor in chief of Vox who joined shortly after its founding, has called this "explanatory value."[19]

THE MULTIPLE PATHS TO A STORY

Jacqui Banaszynski, who developed the stakeholder wheel, also notes that any piece of news—whether an event, idea, issue, press release, calendar listing, trend, agenda item, dinner conversation, billboard, or church bulletin—has potential for new forms of engagement beyond what is obvious or traditional. That potential plays out in three dimensions:

What stories to pursue
How best to tell those stories
What platform to use

Banaszynski talks about seven concepts to think about when deciding how to convey a story. We have added four more:

1. *Issues or trends.* Ask if there is a larger picture to explore. Does the event tie to some larger context? How has it developed over time? Is it a window of opportunity to revisit a bigger issue the public needs to know about, or to reveal how that issue plays out in specific ways?

2. *Explanatory piece.* Does the news offer an opportunity to dig inside to explain why something happened or how something works? More than just identifying an issue or trend, this approach explains how it evolved, and in so doing sheds some refracted light on how the world works.

3. *Profile.* Is there a relatable character at the center of an event or issue, or affected by it? Is there a "tour guide" to help your audience see/understand an issue? Profiles need not be about people, nor do they have to be narrative. They could be about a place or even a building. But they must, Banaszynski says, be about character.

4. *Voices.* Are there people who can speak to the event or issue in a way that illuminates it and how it affects people? This may be the video of a subject of the story talking, or it may dictate the way a story is structured.

5. *Descriptive.* Give the story a vivid setting. Re-create what it feels like, what it looks like, what it smells like to be present at the event or issue.

6. *Investigative.* Look into wrongdoing, "follow the money," analyze power struggles, and make use of available documents.

7. *Narrative.* Can the story hold together, with a beginning, middle, and end? Does it follow a central character through plot, action and forward motion, tension, conflict, and resolution?

8. *Visual.* Is the story better told without much text, through photographs, graphics, illustrations?

9. *Data.* Is the essence of the story told with numbers? Data visualization and data journalism are still storytelling. And what is left out is as important as what is left in.

10. To this list we would add now *Audio,* something that wasn't on it in 2013.

11. We would also add *Platform.* How would the story be told? In a text message form, à la Outlier? Via a Facebook post? On Instagram?

Each of these concepts, and others you might fashion for yourself based on your own approach to writing, are tools that should be kept in mind as you gather information and as you begin to organize your information prior to deciding which form of storytelling will most effectively serve to engage and inform the ultimate consumer of the information. The critical point here is to keep in mind what form your story might take so that you gather the information needed to best shape the story that way. For example, can the profile you are preparing be best told visually? If so, what visuals will best serve to profile the person? Or can the person best be profiled by a specific event or action? In that case, you'll need meticulous detail so that the profile will emerge from the powerful detail of the event or action.

THE HOURGLASS

In the early 1990s, Roy Peter Clark noticed what he called the "hourglass" structure. "It isn't purely narrative. It isn't just the inverted pyramid. . . . It is a form in which you begin by telling the news, telling what happened, and then there is a break in the pyramid, and a line that begins a narrative, often chronologically, as in, 'The incident began when . . .'" At that point, the news is thawed out and put in more dramatic form to create an engagement with the information.

Q&A

New York University journalism professor Jay Rosen has long thought about how to orient news more toward the interests of citizens rather than the needs of journalists. Some methods are deceptively simple. Rosen considers the Q&A story form (reframed online as FAQ) to be a powerful but underused method. It forces the journalist to frame the material around things that citizens might ask. It also allows audiences to scan a story and enter it wherever they want, rather than having to read it from the top down.

BUTCH WARD'S DINING TABLE EXERCISE

Butch Ward, a former editor at *The Philadelphia Inquirer* and then an executive at the Poynter Institute, developed a way to make people producing journalism think like citizens as they conceive of, and then imagine conveying, stories. He tells people they are no longer journalists but a group of neighbors gathered for dinner on Saturday night. Put a subject on the table (healthcare, public safety, our children) and go around the table. Each "neighbor" must share a personal (true) story about a recent experience with that topic. When was your last encounter with the healthcare system? Or the government? What happened? Take twenty minutes in total to retell your personal stories. Then take ten minutes to make a list of these stories as journalism. Turning the journalists first into storytellers is what made the resulting list look so much different than it would have if Ward had given journalists thirty minutes to sit down and develop a list of stories.

FLY ON THE WALL, OR STORY AS EXPERIENCE

The late Michael Herr, whose book *Dispatches* is considered one of the best to come out of the Vietnam War, added a new dimension to war reporting by carrying the "fly on the wall" technique employed by legendary magazine writer Gay Talese a step further. Talese would embed himself with his subjects to the point that they stopped noticing him and would begin to act completely naturally. He was not interviewing them. He was trying as closely as he could to merely observe them. Herr went further. Not only did he gather the copious detail that kind of reporting entailed. He also let the soldiers speak for themselves, selecting his material not only to tell their story about what they said and did but also to capture their state of mind and their thoughts. As Alfred Kazin wrote in a review of the book in *Esquire,* "Herr caught better than anyone else the . . . desperate code in which the men in the field showed that they were well and truly shit."[20]

BEING ON THE NOSE

The late Doug Marlette, a Pulitzer Prize–winning editorial cartoonist, said that the reason so much of news is boring is that it's not surprising enough.

"When you're bored," Marlette said, "you stop learning and communication fails."[21] The principal reason is that "you're never surprised." In the theater, there is a term for this boredom. It's called "being on the nose," which "is when you tell people what they already know."

In news, it is "telling not showing; lecturing; didacticism," Marlette said. "It is the moment in TV news when the correspondent tells the audience what they are already seeing." It is the moment a newspaper story belabors a point rather than moving on.

If you accept Marlette's argument that news should be about showing, not telling or lecturing, the problem of being on the nose can become even more complicated when journalists feel compelled, as they increasingly have in the age of Trump, to go beyond the descriptive and call out things for "what they really are"—to call a lie a lie, to call a racist remark racist, to call a misogynistic statement misogyny, to get at the meaning and the motive behind things. How do we keep news truthful without it being so on the nose that it becomes preachy, didactic, and in the process unsurprising and boring?

In the early days of Trump's presidency, editors at *The New York Times* explained their reasoning. To call something a lie—rather than simply describe it as a falsehood—required knowledge of intent. In other words, these editors and their reporters had to know without any doubt that the speaker knew the information he or she was passing on was false and did it anyway, knowingly, with malicious purpose. That is a higher bar than simply knowing something is untrue. As the Trump presidency continued, and Trump doubled and quadrupled down on repeating statements that had been repeatedly shown to be false, baseless, and clearly refuted, press coverage became more assertive.

But in the future the challenge for journalists remains. News in the end tells people what to think about. It has agenda-setting influence. But it will not tell people what to think. They bring their own meaning to the news, based on their lives and experience.

The more news tries to lecture, tries to tell people what to think, rather than what happened, the more they will resist it.

PICTURES OF THE MIND

One way is to help people build their own pictures in their minds, rather than drawing the pictures for them. Annie Lang, who teaches telecommunications and runs the Institute for Communications Research at Indiana University, says academic research has clearly established the power of mental pictures, including metaphor. "There is nothing more scary than to say to someone, 'There is a snake behind you.' That is so much more powerful than to show them the snake."[22]

CONNECTING THE STORY TO DEEPER THEMES: THE REVEAL

John Larson was one of the more thoughtful network TV reporters of his generation. The former NBC News correspondent thinks surprise is key to storytelling. But, he adds, "Surprise them in a meaningful way. Not just shock them and stun them."[23] Some in television call this "the reveal." In Larson's mind, the best kind of reveal is when a story connects to some deeper unexpected themes. It's when stories "reach us on some elemental level. They talk about a mother's love for her children, a husband's pride in his country. Ambition. Avarice. Greed. There's something very important that's always going on in a very simple way in good stories."

These themes are not stated by the journalist but are shown, or revealed, in how the journalist treats the material—using the right quote, showing the right camera shot on TV, or describing the look two people give each other when they are not talking. "Good stories lead you to the truth; they don't tell you the truth," as Larson puts it. They are not, in other words, so on the nose. They show, rather than tell. They reveal, rather than preach.

Robert Caro, the National Book Award–winning biographer of President Lyndon Johnson and New York power broker Robert Moses, says this notion has guided his life's work. When writing about Moses, a little-known bureaucrat who transformed New York City, Caro wanted to do something more than an exposé. "I was a reporter and I was covering politics, and I felt that I wasn't really explaining what I had gone into the newspaper business to explain, which was how political power worked, and a lot of it led back to this man, Robert Moses, a lot of what I didn't understand. Now, here was a guy who was never elected to anything, and I was coming to realize that he had more power than anyone who was governor or mayor."[24]

CHARACTER AND DETAIL IN NEWS

Other journalists believe character is the key to pulling people into stories and to showing rather than telling. Good characterization often is found in the minor details that make someone human and real. When the father of the shipwrecked boy Elián González came to America in 2000 to retrieve his son and take him back to Cuba, KARE-TV correspondent Boyd Huppert was struck most of all that in his interview with immigration officials, "the father knew [the son's] shoe size." For Huppert, this "put a whole new light on the man," revealing something about the father's relationship with the child, his involvement, and his character.[25]

Too much journalism fails to develop character in this way. The people are cardboard; they are names and faces fit into a journalistic template—the investigating officer, the prolife protester, the Black Lives Matter organizer, the aggrieved mother. A major reason for this is that the journalist doesn't allow the interview subjects to speak the way people do in real life. Quotes are too often used as tools, instead of being cast as part of a deeper conversation between the subjects of a story and the audience.

The way interviews are shot on TV is another major factor in this lack of depth—this cardboard templating of people that TV news does. Often people do not even look like real people when shot against artifi-

cial backgrounds in perfect light, or standing in front of a building sur-
rounded by microphones. They exist in an artificial world—the world
of news—and seem more caricature than character.

To call someone "the investigating officer" is to describe a source.
But "Detective Lewis, a second-generation homicide cop, whose father
had a case like this twenty years earlier," is a character. The first makes
homicide investigator Lewis fit a fairly rigid template, one that is pass-
able for journalistic purposes but shallow, and that turns him into a stick
figure who is indistinguishable from any other investigating officer.

"The second-ranking Republican member of the House Ways
and Means Committee" is a template. "The thirty-year veteran of the
House, who has opposed nearly every tax cut except for mental health
after becoming the grandfather to a disabled child," is already more
engaging to the reader. Yet turning sources into people involves thinking ahead about character. It involves asking different questions of the
officer, looking more for images and mannerisms, and being curious
about him as a potential character rather than merely a source. It may
take more time, but not as much time as one might think. "Have you
ever had any cases like this? Do you have any special style or method
for investigating?" Most important, this process involves looking at the
officer as a person rather than merely looking for quotes or facts, and
never forgetting that there is no person from whom you cannot learn
something you never knew before.

In a television context, this deepening of character may also mean
thinking differently about the way stories and segments are filmed.
David Turecamo, a filmmaker who shoots, interviews, writes, and edits
his own pieces, always tries to photograph his subjects as they actually
live—shopkeepers while behind the counter, salesmen while driving
in their cars, businessmen while walking to meetings—usually in long
takes. His pieces are small character studies, and the audience members'
view of the issue is changed because they suddenly see real people, businesspeople, and no longer "advocates" or parts of a "lobby."

EXPOSE PEOPLE TO OTHER "TRIBES"

In the chapter on verification, we already discussed journalist Amanda
Ripley's work about complicating the narrative. Ripley suggests that

some old journalistic thinking—that it is better to simplify everything, and particularly arguments, so that audiences will understand them—has backfired. Much of this journalistic effort to simplify people and their arguments has the ironic effect of reducing people and their ideas to polarizing stereotypes.

Ripley's work has been taken further by the Solutions Journalism Network in the development of a list of twenty-two interview questions that journalists might consider when covering controversy, some of which we touched on earlier. Some we didn't mention touch on a concept that neuroscientists call "metaperceptions." Metaperceptions, as we noted in chapter 5 on independence, refer to what people in one group think another group believes about them. If you are a progressive, the metaperception might be that conservatives think you are a socialist who hates America. For some more conservative Americans, a different metaperception might be that liberals see your support for the Second Amendment as clinging to guns out of despair and resentment. (Barack Obama was guilty of promoting this metaperception during one of his campaigns when he was overheard making such a remark.)

Ripley says one powerful technique when interviewing people is to run at these metaperceptions, not run away from them. She offers a list of questions that journalists, when talking to people about politics and political factions, might consider asking. The questions can be uncomfortable. That is the point. They are designed to get people to open up.

- What do you think the other group thinks of you?
- What do you think the group wants?
- What do you already know and what do you want to understand about the other side?
- Help me make sense of this. Because a lot of other people are saying X.
- Is there anything about how the media portray you or people with your views that feels inaccurate?

FINDING THE METAPHOR OR HIDDEN STRUCTURE IN EACH STORY

Perhaps no American journalist in radio and television has been more involved in making important topics interesting than Robert Krulwich, who over the course of his career has covered economics for NPR, science for ABC, and other supposedly dry topics in ways that were anything but dry and dull. Krulwich has always tried to find in each story the hidden material that makes it memorable and genuine. This means avoiding formulas, treating each story as unique, and letting the material suggest its own structure. "I do a lot of abstract stories, so you have to find a metaphor that people will remember. It's like a hook in the sense of a hook where you hang your coat. If you have the hook, then, 'Well, that was the story about the chicken who sang, right? What was he talking about? Oh, yeah, currency devaluations.'"

Krulwich's metaphors were often quite unexpected. To reinforce the idea of the slowing Japanese economy, he slows down the video. To reinforce that people cannot spell the word *millennium,* he shows a stern schoolteacher slowly spelling the word. Something similar has occurred in the work of the podcast *The Secret History of the Future.* That podcast, by *The Economist*'s Tom Standage and Slate's Seth Stevenson, talks about current issues that are beginning to bubble up around a new or emerging technology by discussing a moment in the past when a similar new technology was emerging. To make a point about the limits of DNA evidence in criminal prosecution, the episode focused on similar limits that had emerged around the advent of fingerprinting. To talk about the societal challenges around driverless cars, the hosts discussed how people had also worried about horseless carriages.

UNLEASH THE POWER OF THE WEB

The Web has probably done more to inspire new methods of storytelling than years of teaching writing.

Print, television, and radio are largely based on narrative, each having different tendencies or strengths (television is more easily emotional, print informational, and radio a blend that is also more intimate). Yet the options of any one of those media are limited. A print treatment of an event, we've noticed, generally can involve just seven key elements—a narrative, a headline, a photo, an illustration, a table, a chart, and perhaps some design elements such as pull quotes. Online, the list of storytelling tools and elements explodes—from data to hyperlinks to interactive graphics.

We can identify more than sixty such elements that can be combined (albeit more easily for a single running story, such as climate change, than for unrelated event news). Still, the list grows every month. "It's time to rethink the unit of journalism," says Bill Adair, the creator of PolitiFact, who now runs the Reporters' Lab at Duke University. It no longer needs to be the narrative story. But on any given story, the form or element employed should be driven by the goal of creating understanding, creating public insight, not just creating new forms for the sake of being new.

Here are a couple of conceptual approaches to doing so.

NEWS AS STRUCTURED DATA

The rich new wealth of data made possible by the Web can be rendered in ways that go beyond narratives about data (traditional "data reporting") or even the largely visual representations of numbers ("data visualizations"). One of these alternatives is to structure the journalism into new data points that tell the story. The data are organized and analyzed into points of meaning beyond raw data.

PolitiFact, the political "fact-checking" website that Adair created for the *Tampa Bay Times* and that is now housed at the Poynter Institute, is an example. Rather than write stories, the site rates the veracity of statements by political figures on a meter, from true to utterly false. Each rating, in effect, is a data point. These data points, in turn, can be combined to tell other stories over time, like charting the overall truthfulness of Donald Trump's statements and comparing his to other officials'. The essential unit of PolitiFact is not a story—it's the claim. Those claims are structured data. They can be searched and collated.

Since then, Adair and an engineer at Google named Justin Kosslyn adapted the notion of structured data so that any fact-checking content (though it could be used for any kind) could be turned into structured data, even traditional narrative stories. Using what Web developers call a "schema" design, someone can break down the content into "tags" or mini categories, effectively retrofitting anything into structured content, so that they can be identified later by a search. This makes news much easier to retrieve and sort than just doing it by story or headline.

Adair and Kosslyn created a schema called ClaimReview, which tagged fact-checks conducted by various outlets—not just PolitiFact—and entered them into an open database. Now anyone who wants to can search a politician or a statement and instantly find whether it has been fact-checked by anyone and see the result. Adair's team at Duke used it to build an experimental app called Squash that provides instant fact-checks during a speech or debate. Now they are building something called MediaReview, which will do the same thing for fake videos and images.

This notion of data points is akin to the way raw baseball statistics, such as hits and bases-on percentage, can be divided into new statistical units, such as On Base Plus Slugging Percentage (OPS) or the overall performance of a player versus others at his position (replacement value).

The Philadelphia Inquirer and the Lenfest Institute have explored the potential for tagging geo-location data in stories to identify patterns in the news by geography. A professor at the University of Southern California is collecting public data on traffic, weather, pollution indexes, and more to help consumers map how they should try to safely move around Southern California each day.

But the potential here is far greater than most news organizations realize, and more could be done with this kind of thinking than journalists are currently doing. When print publications went digital, every story was necessarily transformed from words on a page into a data record in a CMS database. Generally, however, few of these stories were treated as data that could be related to one another and analyzed programmatically. As an example, when newspapers posted to the Web real estate transactions that were printed in the paper, the different data points about location, price, and buyer could have been entered into different data fields, such as school districts, tax assessments, and access to public transportation. If they had been, the potential for understanding and analyzing the data would have grown exponentially. The publication would no longer just have stories archived. It would have knowledge about the community that could be used in different ways.

Turning news into data opens up profound new potential for creating a more deeply informed and engaged audience. Even news operations with fairly limited resources can analyze the data to do more insightful, efficient reporting. The data can be made sortable and interactive for users to manipulate. News organizations can build news apps and mobile apps that leverage the data, and news coded and treated as data can be leveraged into new revenue.

This notion of taking the information that news organizations gather and converting it into sortable data, rather than just narrative, is a mind shift. "A lot of what we do in journalism is counting. . . . Our devices can now do that for us," says Adair.[26] And, actually, our devices can do the simple counting better than we can.

BUILD TOOLS AND PRODUCTS OUT OF JOURNALISM

Some news organizations are using technology to help citizens answer questions for themselves. *The Washington Post*, for instance, created simple tools so users could estimate how Trump's then-proposed tax plan in 2017 would affect their taxes, situating the tool in the context of greater reporting and analysis by its team.[27] A nonprofit start-up news organization called The Markup built a tool called Blacklight to demonstrate the scale and presence of data collection on websites that people visit. Blacklight shows readers how much data any URL is collecting and where it might be sent, including what is being sold to generate revenue. This tool serves as an entry point for the overall reporting, done in a traditional long-form piece. In addition, The Markup published follow-up pieces, in a series called *Ask The Markup*, that continue to offer practical insights based on the reporting, such as how to limit some Web-based invasions of privacy.

TELL THE STORY WITH SOCIAL MEDIA'S NATIVE FEATURES

As a large number of Americans continue to spend time on social media, it's important for news organizations to make their journalism engaging on those platforms as well—to make their content platform orthodox, not platform agnostic.

For example, some stories may fit a tweet thread on Twitter or galleries on Instagram. *Philadelphia Inquirer* reporter Jonathan Lai regularly tweets about voting deadlines, for instance, information that is helpful in itself and is drawn from his deeper report. In 2020, he set up an automated tweet every morning to relay deadlines for registering to vote and to request absentee ballots—with information on how to do so. It is an example of a simple but powerful gesture that can be easily replicated with an automation tool for social platforms like Buffer or SocialOomph, which allows one to arrange tweets weeks or months ahead of time. The *Milwaukee Journal Sentinel* on Instagram also created shareable images with answers to questions people may have had about voting during the pandemic, which fit the platform and could act as entryways to other reporting.

NARRATIVE IN SERVICE OF TRUTH

Finally, a caution. At times, narrative news writing has come to be viewed by editors as "writing with attitude." This is writing in which the journalist interjects his or her own feelings or opinions like a stage whisper, as is evident in self-referential lines like "There was an audible groan from the reporters when the candidate began to speak."

In some cases, an attitude can evolve that plays itself out in story after story, reporter after reporter, and even across different publications—a kind of running metanarrative that journalists share. Politicians are in it only for power. Donald Trump is a sociopath. George W. Bush was a puppet of Vice President Dick Cheney, or a lost son motivated to go to war in Iraq out of a Freudian need to one-up his father. Al Gore was a serial exaggerationist. Barack Obama is a professorial wonk who, though elected twice to the presidency, doesn't really understand politics. Joe Biden is cognitively impaired. The metanarrative can become so powerful that it clouds the truth by oversimplifying it, although it lingers because it has strains of truth within it.

As we discuss technique, it is vital to take care to remember that form never determines substance. Technique should never alter the facts—the journalist's use of narrative forms must always be governed by the principles of accuracy and truthfulness, outlined earlier. Regardless of the form of presentation, the most engaging thing of all must be kept in mind: The story is true.

We have emphasized public affairs reporting in this discussion, but there is no subject for which the need for journalism that is engaging and relevant does not apply. In many ways, a story that helps the audience understand how the marketing strategy of Mark Zuckerberg affects their lives is as important as one that discusses a presidential candidate's position on internet policy. The celebrity profile that shows why Hollywood makes the films it does can be a major work illuminating American culture—or it can be press agent promotion. It depends on the treatment, not the subject matter. Thus citizens can use the principle of engagement and relevance to judge the value of any journalism they encounter.

The next principle puts engagement and relevance in a broader context: How do we decide which stories get covered in the first place?

9
MAKE THE NEWS COMPREHENSIVE AND PROPORTIONAL

When she ran a company called Research Communications Limited, in Florida, Valerie Crane liked to tell a story about how *not* to study audiences. It's about the head of market research at a major cable television network who was asked to include this question in a round of focus groups with young viewers: "What will be the next big trend for young people?"

The researcher felt that you could use tools such as survey research, psychographics, and focus groups to see how people react to things. You could even use them to learn more about how audiences live their lives and how they use the media. But they couldn't be used, or at least they shouldn't, to replace professional judgment.

The bosses wanted the question asked, however, so the researcher watched glumly as the focus group leader put the question to the teenagers gathered around a table on the other side of the one-way mirror: "What do you think the next trend will be?" To his delight the response came: "What do you mean, what will the next trend be? We rely on you to tell us what the next big trend will be."[1]

If the principle of engagement and relevance helps explain how journalists can more effectively approach their stories, the principle that follows informs what stories to cover.

What is news? Given the limits of space, time, and resources, what is important and what isn't, what is to be left in and what is to be left out? And in the age of internet infinity, who is to say? These questions inform the eighth principle citizens require from their press:

Journalism should make the news comprehensive and keep it in proportion.

But how? In the age of exploration, cartography was as much art as science. The men who sat over parchment and drafted the pictures of the expanding world were able to do a fairly accurate job of drawing Europe and even the neighboring seas. As they moved west to the New World, to the regions that were so inflaming people's imaginations, they mostly made guesses. What was there? Gold? Fountains of youth? The end of the earth? Demons? The size of distant continents they sketched would swell and shrink according to which audience they thought might be purchasing their charts. In the faraway Pacific, they painted sea monsters, dragons, or giant whales to fill in what they did not know. The more fanciful and frightening their monsters, the more exotic the gold mines and Indians they depicted, the more their maps might sell, and the greater their reputations as cartographers might grow. Sensation made for popular maps, even if they were poor guides for exploration or understanding.

Journalism is our modern cartography. It creates a map for citizens to navigate society. That is its utility and its economic reason for being. This concept of cartography helps clarify the question of what journalists should cover. As with any map, journalism's value depends on its completeness and proportionality. Journalists who devote more time and space to a sensational trial or celebrity scandal than they know it deserves—because they think it will sell—are like the cartographers who drew England or Spain the size of Greenland because doing so was popular. It may make short-term economic sense, but it misleads the traveler and eventually destroys the credibility of the mapmaker. The journalist who writes what he or she "just knows to be true," without really double-checking, is like the artist who drew sea monsters in the distant corners of the New World. A journalist who leaves out so much of the other news in the process is like the mapmaker who failed to tell the traveler of all the other roads along the way.

Thinking of journalism as mapmaking helps us see that proportion and comprehensiveness are key to accuracy. This goes beyond individual stories. A front page, a Web page, or a newscast that is fun and interesting but by no reasonable definition contains anything significant is a distortion. At the same time, an account of the day that contains only the earnest and momentous, without anything light or human, is equally out of balance. The metaphor works for niche outlets or those focused on a single subject as well. Within the parameters of any subject, the concepts of proportionality and comprehensiveness still apply.

Obviously the limits of time and resources mean no institutional newsroom—let alone a small community website—can cover everything. Small nonprofits that publish only a few stories a month, and lean toward large investigative pieces, will find this more difficult. But over time they can still look back and see if their work represents a fair and comprehensive portrayal of their topic. Not every exposé need be negative, even. A deep look at why some program works well when others do not is as valuable as—and maybe more accurate than—a portrayal of unrelenting failure.

One of the great challenges to commercial news production in the last decade has been shrinking resources. The notion of covering the waterfront has become harder and harder. Newsrooms with vision have had to decide which parts of the waterfront were most important and which parts could get by with only an occasional stroll by the watchman. The newspaper of record is a thing of the past. The newspaper of interest—which picks a few things to cover well—is closer to reality. Maybe it always was. But it means that comprehensiveness and proportion must be achieved over time. They are not an aspiration that is realistic every day.

Still, as citizens, we can ask these questions: Can I see the whole community represented in the coverage? Do I see myself? Does the report include a fair mix of what most people would consider either interesting or significant?

THE FALLACY OF TARGETED DEMOGRAPHICS

The mapmaker concept also helps us better understand the idea of diversity in news. If we think of journalism as social cartography, the map should include news from all our communities, not just those with demographics that are attractive to advertisers.

Unfortunately, journalism has fallen short. As we outlined in chapter 3, on loyalty to citizens, news organizations in the latter part of the twentieth century tended to focus on targeting—particularly on more affluent readers at newspapers and on women at television news—because it served the needs of advertisers. There were several reasons for the strategy, particularly at newspapers, which ironically were the only local media with large enough newsrooms to aspire to cover communities comprehensively. After twenty-five years of losing audience and advertisers to television and other media, newspapers decided that there were structural limits to how much circulation they could have in the video age. Newspapers, in effect, decided they were a niche medium for the better educated.

A second major reason had to do with costs. Newspapers sold each paper at a loss. The price of twenty-five cents, or even a dollar, covered only a fraction of what it cost to report, print, and deliver each copy. The rest—at one time roughly 75 percent—was made up in advertising revenue. Every copy of the paper sold to readers who didn't attract advertisers, in effect, cost money. The advertising business also decided to use newspapers mainly to reach the upper classes. Other media, especially television and radio, would be left to reach blue-collar audiences. (Local TV newscasts in effect replaced the blue-collar afternoon newspaper in America.) In time, newspaper business strategists rationalized that targeting circulation at the affluent was not only a necessity but also a virtue. Calculating cost per copy and revenue per subscriber could justify not appealing to the whole community, in the name of economic efficiency. Writing off certain neighborhoods also meant not having to invest heavily to cover them.

It became difficult to argue with the economics, or even—given the loss of readership to television—the idea that lower-income readers were not coming back. Bucking that trend would have meant believing in a long-term strategy that Wall Street and most conventional thinking disagreed with. The problem was that the path of narrowing ambitions for efficiency and profit made news outlets defensive, margin oriented, and woefully ill-equipped to innovate when the technology of the Web suddenly made audience growth not only a possibility but a business imperative. In other words, while abdicating journalistic responsibility looked attractive in the short term, it proved to be a bad business strategy in the long term.

Television in time also began to think about targeted demographics—caring more about younger viewers who had not yet developed brand loyalty and women who were considered the commercial decision-makers, particularly after more stations began to produce news coverage, shrinking everyone's share of the pie. The pressure was intensified by the fact that stations, and Wall Street, were accustomed to enormous operating profit margins from news at local television stations—usually more than 40 percent. To sustain the margins, stations kept fewer reporters on staff and required most to produce at least a story a day.[2] Covering the whole community was impossible. The news was aimed instead at the most desirable segment—younger women.

The collapse of the advertising model offers the chance to correct for these mistakes. Journalism's future will depend largely on a different equation than in the past. Instead of attracting the largest possible audience that will interest advertisers, the future of journalism now will depend primarily on creating content of such value that consumers will be willing to pay for it themselves. That changes the metrics of news. It also means that the demographics of the audience need to be wider and more inclusive. Many people can afford ten dollars a month. The data are clear that people pay this much for streaming services and many other services in their lives. A news organization needs to create content that is indispensable, unique, and of such quality and frequency that it makes its subscribers' lives better. But the bulletin board items that news once thrived on providing in the past are no longer sufficient. Deeper, more meaningful content—the kind the early days of the Web cast in doubt—now appears to be the most likely way journalism will survive. Put another way, to become sustainable, journalism must provide better content that is relevant to a wider range of people in their communities to survive—particularly people who are younger, people of color, and conservatives. And it can dispense with a lot of the high-volume, low-value content it once produced.

The passage of time makes it possible to see serious problems with the economic logic of targeting demographics that led in part to journalism's current economic ills. One is the willful neglect of Black audiences in cities, due to perceptions by advertisers that these audiences were not affluent enough to be worth targeting and to the ignorance of white-dominated newsroom managers about the lives of people in those communities. Another is that apart from the ethnic presses, the news industry largely ignored the rising immigrant communities that were changing America's cities—precisely the population that had served as the backbone of journalism's success one hundred years earlier. Pulitzer, Scripps, and the rest of the penny-press barons had made immigrants their core audience. Their prose was simple so immigrants could puzzle it out, and the editorial pages taught them how to be citizens. New Americans would gather after work to talk about what was in the papers or to read to one another and discuss the highlights of the day.

As the immigrants of the 1880s and 1890s became more Americanized and more middle-class, the papers changed with them, becoming more sober-minded and more literary. The New York *World* of 1910 was a far more serious paper than the *World* of twenty years before. Eighty years later, the journalism industry, now obsessed with economic efficiency, did not make that same investment in establishing a relationship with the newest Americans as it had done a century before. By the second decade of the twenty-first century, as the economic model of news shifted from advertising to consumer revenue—subscription or membership—this isolation from people of color could prove part of the industry's undoing.

So could another change. As journalism targeted itself to just the most profitable demographics, it did not make much investment in the youngest Americans. Stories were long and sophisticated and often required a college degree to follow. Critics such as Stephen Hess of the Brookings Institution began to talk about journalists writing for their sources.[3] On television, the emphasis on crime, and also titillation, transformed television news from something that families would gather to watch into something from which parents would shield children.[4] In the name of efficiency and profit margins, the news industry generally did little to help a new generation become interested in news.

There was for a time a theory that the digital generation was newsless because they didn't watch traditional news programs, subscribe to print magazines, or read print newspapers. The research, and the assumption behind it, was deeply flawed, an example of an industry clinging to old technology, not understanding its future audience.[5] These audiences were hardly newsless. They were simply getting their news from new platforms, initially on Facebook and now on other services (Instagram and YouTube being among the largest).

Could it have been otherwise? Could journalism have avoided this disconnect with the broader audience and reached out successfully to a more diverse audience and a younger one? This is difficult to answer definitively. But as journalism companies aimed at elite demographics and cost efficiency, as a general rule the industry did not try. By the time some publishers did, it was very late. The concept of the mapmaker makes the error clear. We created a map for certain neighborhoods and not others. And those who were unable to navigate where they lived gave it up.

The newscasts and newspapers that ignored whole communities also created problems for those they did serve. First, they left their audiences poorly informed because so much was left out. This left citizens vulnerable to making poor decisions about contemporary trends and about their needs. Ultimately, the strategy threatened the livelihood of the news organization, the institution with the greatest need for an interested citizenry. In the memorable phrase of Wall Street analyst John Morton, the nation's leading financial analyst of the news industry at the time, we had "eaten our seed corn."[6]

With whole communities left out, there was also the reverse problem of offering too much detail to the demographic group journalism was serving. Stories became longer and more copious, but aimed at a narrower segment of the population. The papers were sometimes more than a hundred pages a day and could take a full day to read. In television, targeting had a similar effect. The daily health segments on local TV today, for instance, which cover every new medical study no matter how preliminary, tend more to confuse citizens about health than inform them.

Is the mistake repairable? The Web makes possible new levels of engagement with audiences in ways inconceivable when news was limited to legacy platforms. Even with the disruption, the Web has made news audiences younger and increased the level of news people consume. Consider a few numbers. The average age of a print newspaper reader in 2017 was fifty-four. The average age of consumers of newspaper content on mobile devices was thirty-nine. And mobile is the platform—without question—if a news operation wants to get younger. Any effort that is not mobile first, second, and third is probably ill-conceived and a waste of time. Consider that 57 percent of people eighteen to twenty-four get their first news of the day on a mobile device; the same is true for just 29 percent of those over age thirty-five, according to data from the Reuters Institute.[7]

One challenge is the question of the public commons. Creating a viable public square, a place where solutions to problems facing communities can be arrived at, is not just part of journalism's responsibility; it also may be part of the path to financial viability. Thus those interested in journalism of community must act quickly to find ways to serve diverse populations—but to serve them as part of a whole community. We advised this in the first three editions of this book. Now, as we write the fourth, there is less time to waste. The rising awareness of racial and social injustice in the summer of 2020 reminded the news industry, yet again, of its failures in addressing what scholars and reformers often refer to as "underserved audiences." While that is a positive step, the industry has less time now to address this failing before its chances at financial sustainability are gone.

There is evidence the public agrees that the news should be more comprehensive—not just tailored by ideology or identity. For several years, the Project for Excellence in Journalism, which was founded and directed by one of the authors, studied what kind of local TV news builds ratings. A design team of local news professionals rated covering the whole community as the most important responsibility of a TV news station. The data found that viewers concurred. Stations that covered a wider range of topics were more likely to be building or holding on to their audience than those that did not.[8]

THE LIMITS OF METAPHOR

As with all metaphors, the mapmaking comparison has its limits. Cartography is scientific, but journalism is not. You can plot the exact location of a road and measure the size of a country, or even an ocean. The proportions of a news story are another matter. A big story for some is unimportant to others.

Proportion and comprehensiveness in news are subjective. Their elusiveness, however, does not mean they are any less important than the more objective road and river features of maps. To the contrary, striving for them is essential to journalism's popularity—and financial health. It is also possible—not just an abstract notion—to pursue proportion and comprehensiveness despite their being subjective. Honest people can disagree about a story's importance, but citizens and journalists alike know when a story is being hyped disproportionately. They may disagree on precisely when the line was crossed, but at a certain point they know it has happened. In an era of more competition for people's attention, it tends to happen more.

It is all the more important, then, that newsrooms be a place where those arguments can occur constructively. For that to happen, newsrooms need to become more diverse. They need to not just look like their communities but also think like them. This means they must reflect the differences in culture, class, ethnicity, race, and also ideology of their communities. These are difficult steps to make. But make them the news industry must, or the news, and the public, will continue to fragment and polarize.

As news has become atomized—as increasingly we get information from aggregators, RSS feeds, or delivery platforms such as Facebook or Twitter, in which we assemble our own news from disparate sources—the responsibility for proportionality and comprehensiveness also shifts by degrees from the news provider to the individual. To the extent that we now rely more on these self-styled systems and less on gatekeepers, we become both consumers and editors of our own news—and to an even greater degree, captains of our own civic awareness. The question is not "Is there anything I should know?" It is "Am I checking all the places I need to in order to inform myself?" We have become, in effect, the watchmen who must decide which parts of the waterfront to check.

Some assume that if there is anything worth knowing, someone will tell us. We will know it by osmosis. In reality, we won't. The platforms have changed their algorithms in ways that benefit them financially but increasingly make it unlikely we will see serendipitously everything we might want to know. We increasingly will be left behind. Civic awareness will slip away from us, like physical fitness, from disuse. Our worlds will narrow. Our definition of community will be distorted. Tribalism will intensify. We will forget how to disagree. We will resent pluralism. It has already begun.

The press did not create these problems. It did enable them.

THE PRESSURE TO HYPE

At moments when the news media culture is undergoing disruption, there is usually more pressure to hype and sensationalize. You might call it the principle of "the naked body and the guitar."

If you want to attract an audience, you could go down to a street corner, do a striptease, and get naked. You would probably attract a crowd in a hurry. The problem is, how do you keep people? Why should they stay once they have seen you naked? How do you avoid audience turnover? There is another approach. Suppose you went to the same street corner and played the guitar. A few people might listen on the first day. Perhaps a few more on the second. Depending on how good a guitar player you were, and how diverse and intriguing your repertoire was, the audience might grow each day. You would not, if you were good, have to keep churning the crowd by moving to new places, getting new people to replace those who grew tired of repetition. You would, to the contrary, benefit from staying on the same corner.

This is the choice, in effect, that the news media face at a time when new technology expands the number of outlets and each organization watches its audience shrink. When the future is uncertain, and it is unclear how long you can stay in business unless you generate audience fast, which approach should you pursue? To some extent, a news publisher has to operate according to a faith or philosophy, since empirical models of the past may not work in the future. Then add to this the new complexity of having real-time metrics that show how certain kinds of content can draw a quick crowd.

Some news organizations, even those with fairly serious legacies, have resorted to the path of the naked. Consider the websites of newspapers that display slideshows about celebrity starlets prominently on the home page. In part, this is driven by the idea that news has become a commodity that is in oversupply. As one Wall Street analyst, James M. Marsh Jr. of Prudential Securities, told us when we talked with him about television, "There is currently an overabundance of news programming, with supply easily outstripping demand."[9] In part, too, this path of the naked is driven by the fact that producing a lot of original reporting is expensive and requires a web of correspondents, camera crews, and bureaus in different parts of the world.

As noted earlier, in the chapter on engagement, television news employed a variety of techniques to try to lure audiences as cable disrupted its monopoly. Morning news programs put a heavy focus on celebrity, entertainment, lifestyle, and product cross-promotion.[10] Nightly newscasts for a time shifted to showing less coverage of civic institutions in order to offer more entertainment and the attraction of celebrities, although that changed measurably after the terrorist attacks of September 11, 2001.[11] More recently, the Trump years and the pandemic had a similar effect on the balance of coverage, but it remains to be seen how they manage in a post-Trumpian world.

Another technique is for TV newscasters to try to connect with audiences by telling people how they should feel about the news. They do this by lacing stories with emotional code words, words like *stunning, horrifying,* and *horrific* and phrases such as "a serious warning every parent needs to hear." On one randomly selected morning, for instance, the three network shows used such words thirty times in introducing the first five stories alone, often in the anchor introduction or the close, but sometimes by selecting sound bites in which sources used these words.[12]

Demonstrating emotion and even outrage can be a career booster for individual journalists, connecting them with audiences and demonstrating their humanity, in the vein of fictional anchorman Howard Beale of the Paddy Chayefsky film *Network,* who became more popular after he began declaring on the air, "I'm mad as hell, and I'm not going to take this anymore!" These bursts of emotion may be honest at first, but they can also be exploited. After he evinced a powerful sense of outrage over and empathy with the victims of Hurricane Katrina in 2005, CNN host Anderson Cooper was promoted to become the news channel's main prime time host, complete with an ad campaign showing him in moments of emotional reaction to the news. During the coronavirus pandemic, he was the principal host of the channel's frequent national town halls and host of political panels, where his emotionalism often came across as partisan.

Various observers have lauded signs of the newfound passion of the fourth estate. Others have questioned whether a hundred-year journalistic commitment to reporting the facts dispassionately is obsolete. It is another dynamic in the debate, or misunderstanding, over objectivity that we discussed in chapter 4.

President Trump's attacks on the press as the "enemy of the people," "fake news," and a failing industry during his presidency made the issue even more acute. How can journalists cover someone dispassionately who has described them as his enemy? It becomes an existential challenge. It also becomes a trap. Trump wants the press to hate him. It proves his case.

The issue cuts to the heart of what it means to be a journalist. In a profession that promises to suppress self-interest to assure credibility, when are emotionalism and outrage appropriate? It would be difficult to argue that emotions coming from journalists who are witnessing human suffering are always out of place. If emotionalism seems appropriate in some cases but not in others, where is the line?

The first question newspeople should ask is, What does the public need from journalistic inquiry? Is it anger? Is it dispassion? Does that change with the story? How do you know? Two analogies to keep in mind are doctors or police. If you walk into a hospital with a traumatic injury, what do you want from the doctor who is supposed to treat you? Emotionalism because your injury is so severe (or the threat to democracy so acute)? Or would you prefer the doctor to remain as professional and clinical as possible? Or imagine a police officer has stopped your car. Do you want that officer panicky and emotional? Or cool and collected?

Where is the line? One rule of thumb is that emotionalism should come at those moments when any other reaction would seem forced—when emotion is the only organic response. When anchorman Walter Cronkite wiped his eyes after John Kennedy's assassination in 1963, or showed the sense of awe he felt over the space shots a few years later, it struck Americans as appropriate—not fake.

The second rule of thumb is that the emotionalism should disappear between the moment of discovery of a problem and the subsequent search for information meant to put the event into a broader and deeper context. Once journalists have reacted in a human way to what they have seen, they must compose themselves to search for answers, and that requires professionalism, skepticism, and intellectual independence. Human emotion is at the heart of what makes something news. But once you try to manufacture it, or use it to bring attention to yourself, you have crossed the line into something there is already enough of—reality entertainment. At that point, emotionalism becomes a shtick to exploit the news, not a genuine and helpful reaction to it.

THE ANALYTICS OF METRICS

The Web introduces another dimension to all of this, one that is not as unprecedented as some in news believe. In theory, the Web allows publishers to know how many people read, watch, or listen to a particular piece of content, where they go on a page, and how long they stay on it.

But the first generation of Web analytics was replete with problems that kept publishers from using these data to accurately assess their work. For one, the metrics themselves were confused. What is the right thing to measure? Is it unique visitors—a proxy for the overall size of the audience—or the page views—a measure of how many eyeballs were laid on a specific piece of content? Is it "read time"—a difficult-to-get measure of how long people read a given story—or "active read time," the length of time people are actively engaged with a story? Or is engagement measured better by time spent on the site, or length of visit? Should you care about nonlocal visitors to your digital content if advertisers don't care and they won't subscribe? Should we care only about local and loyal visitors? All of these questions are confused by the fact that there is no standard way of measuring. Data from Comscore can vary widely from that supplied by Nielsen, Omniture (now part of Adobe), or Google Analytics. Emerging data also show that many page views may not actually be from people at all, but from bots, automated clicks designed to make traffic look higher. What are publishers to make, for instance, of the fact that one month Comscore gave *The Washington Post* seventeen million unique visitors while Nielsen counted ten million, or that the two firms' calculations of Yahoo's audience in a given month varied by thirty-four million uniques, a difference equivalent to the population of Canada?[13]

Page views, which are susceptible to manipulation, also tend to favor shallow engagement. The page view for a "listicle" headlined "You won't believe what these child stars look like now," which the user abandons in frustration and self-loathing after several clicks, is measured as equal to or more valuable (if it involves more pages) than a three-part series that the user shared on social media and emailed to friends and that contributed to his later decision to subscribe to the publication. Page views were designed in the early days of the Web to provide some measure against which to sell ads. As advertising becomes a smaller part of the journalism economic model, they become less relevant. Even putting aside their flaws and how easily they are manipulated by bots, page views hint at how many people (or machines) may have glanced at a page—even momentarily. They do nothing to measure the value of that page in the reader's mind.

We will talk in a moment about better measures for understanding how people engage with news and information on the Web. Before we do, it is worth noting the enormous cultural obstacles inside newsrooms involved with interpreting even good data. Many newspeople fear analytics. They worry that it will supplant their editorial judgment about what matters in society—a classic example of the machines replacing the moral and civic judgments of humans. Some of the best journalists have sensed the flaws with page views and unique visitors and have resisted following their dictates, even though they have done little to try to develop something better. Many newspeople have feared that bad managers were "weaponizing" analytics against them. As publications facing declining revenue cut staff, some of them looked at page views and fired people whose beats didn't get enough clicks.

If the experience of television, which has had real-time data for years, is a guide, there were reasons to be concerned that the news industry would struggle to make sense of it all. Using minute-to-minute ratings, a television news manager could tell at what point in certain stories people began to click away. So the medium began to tailor newscasts to ensure that every story had a wide viewership. But the strategy did little to forestall the declining audience—and it may have encouraged it.

"News organizations have been hoist on their own petard," explained John Carey, an audience researcher who worked with NBC and other media clients.[14] "Over time they have followed those ratings numbers, doing more and more of those stories that get high numbers, and they get stuck in those patterns." As a consequence, prime time newsmagazines were "stuck with an older audience, a more sentimental one and a more sensational one" while the bulk of viewers fled. "In a sense, the people at the network know it, but they don't know how to get out of it," Carey said at the height of the prime time magazine craze. He was right.[15]

In local TV news, meanwhile, managers tended to operate by a set of conventional ideas about what drove viewership, which imagined that the audience was fairly dumb and needed to be manipulated. Among those myths was the idea that stimulating visuals would hook viewers at the top of the broadcast and keep them watching. Another related idea was that crime and public safety stories that lent themselves to such visuals worked, and that stories about civic affairs, or information-dense stories about policy and government, would drive viewers away.

Managers often saw confirmation of these preconceptions in the way they interpreted their ratings data—and also in inexpensive market research designed by TV consultants that almost unwittingly reinforced conventional industry wisdom. But when more rigorous research was conducted, it repudiated much of this conventional thinking. Probably the most detailed effort was conducted over several years by the Project for Excellence in Journalism, in collaboration with scholars from the Shorenstein Center at Harvard and the University of Hawaii. Their effort involved several steps. Rather than simply identifying each story by its topic, their research deconstructed each story by the level and quality of the reporting. Rather than look at ratings minute by minute, the research looked at ratings over time to reveal deeper trends. And rather than look at how audiences reacted at one station, the research examined the relationship between content and long-term ratings across many stations, providing a more robust sample.

The analysis of 33,000 stories, from 2,419 newscasts on 150 stations over five years, found that how a story is gathered and reported—the number, balance, and expertise of sources, whether its relevancy to the audience and importance to the community are established, whether the story is more complete—is *twice* as important as the topic in determining audience ratings.[16] This finding is especially important in a digital age when increasingly the story—rather than the newscast—becomes the essential unit consumers will seek out.

The research revealed something basic but often overlooked. TV stations that found poor audience response to their civic affairs reporting were misunderstanding what they were hearing. People were not expressing a lack of interest in civic affairs. They were reacting to the fact that too much civic reporting wasn't very good. And it wasn't good because programmers thought viewers wouldn't be interested.

The research conducted, in turn, expected this and subtly reinforced it. We discovered that self-fulfilling prophecy when we worked with the Pew Research Center for the People & the Press to conduct an experiment that compared the wording in a survey from a popular TV market researcher with different question wording that Pew researchers considered more objective. The questions were probing the public appetite for news about government. The TV market research survey asked simply whether people wanted to see more stories about state and local government. Only 29 percent said they would be very interested in that kind of reporting. When Pew connected government to the problems it was focused on solving, the numbers changed dramatically. When people were asked whether they'd be interested in "news reports about what government can do to improve the performance of local schools," the percentage of "very interested" jumped to 59 percent. And when participants were asked whether they would be interested in reports on what government could do to ensure that public places were safe from terrorism, the percentage of "very interested" rose even further, to 67 percent.[17] Similar interest-level percentages were tallied for stories about reducing healthcare costs. All of these topics, from schools to healthcare to public safety, have everything to do with politics and government.

How can the Web avoid the problems television had with bad metrics? Steps are already under way. First, as journalism moves away from advertising toward consumer revenue (subscriptions, memberships, donations, and more), page views will become less important than other measures that signal deeper engagement with digital content. Any one metric or data point will have its weaknesses. At the American Press Institute, we innovated the concept that addressed that through "blended metrics," which is a way of taking several different indicators and blending them into indexes, just as economists use indexes to measure economic health. Blended metrics can signal in a more fully dimensional way how people engage with news content. An index can include a mix of how many people read a story (page views) with how long they read it (read time), whether they in turn shared it with others (sharing data), how often they came in a month (loyalty), and whether they looked like potential subscribers or were already paying customers. You can also add whether the story was read by someone who later did subscribe (in that session, week, or month) or whether it was something that a recent subscriber had read (correlation to subscription). API added other dimensions that were purely journalistic, such as how much enterprise went into producing the story in the first place, whether it was an opinion piece or a news story, what institutions and people were cited in the story, and what it was about at a deeper level.

By inventing better metrics, news publishers begin to create better information about digital behavior. They can create one way of measuring casual users who may show up only every couple months and are attracted by one kind of content. They can see that loyal readers are motivated by different content—longer stories, more civic-oriented news, major enterprise and opinion columns about local events. They can see what builds subscriptions and what communities they are failing to reach. Rather than the data being a force that encourages shallow click-bait, more sophisticated metrics, our data show, encourages newsrooms to produce higher-value content if they want to build subscriptions. It is a case where shifting business models and taking control of one's analytics, rather than merely accepting the frightening and flawed data that already exist, are reinforcing the journalistic mission, not threatening it.

A NEW MARKET RESEARCH FOR JOURNALISM

So what kind of audience research and metrics analysis would have more value and lead to a fuller approach to news in the digital age?

First, it should be designed to help journalists make judgments—not to eliminate their need to make them in the first place.

The late Andy Kohut, the president of Gallup and later president of the Pew Research Center, often said it was worthless to ask people questions they had not thought about before. You get meaningless answers. People will give you answers, but they are like bad guesses on a test for which the person hadn't studied. Rather than asking people to be surrogate editors or producers, a better research method would approach the person surveyed as a citizen and ask that person to talk about his or her life. How do you spend your time? Walk us through your day. How long is your commute? What are you worried about? What do you hope and fear for your kids? These kinds of questions are helpful because they probe broad trends of interest—the kinds of questions that will allow journalists to understand citizens better and then create a journalism that is comprehensive and proportional to their community and their needs.

At the American Press Institute, we studied one hundred thousand recent subscribers to a newspaper (meaning they had subscribed in the last ninety days) and found that there were nine different and distinct paths or factors that caused people to subscribe. Some had done so because of interest in specific areas of content—people subscribing because they were passionate about a particular issue and a publication was a good place to get it. Others were driven more by civic motivation. These included people who just felt that subscribing to a local publication was part of being a community. Others were people who had just gone through some life change, such as retiring or moving to the community. Some subscribed because they wanted to support journalism. Others subscribed because they wanted to get the coupons that would save them money. Some subscribed because everyone in their family and most of their friends did and the news helped connect them. A key point is that the marketing and content that each of these different kinds of readers saw should be different.[18]

Television researcher Valerie Crane at Research Communications Limited brought this kind of nuanced human-centered design approach to her research, which involved two broad approaches, neither of them strictly traditional. The first identified through in-depth interviews and then larger survey samples what basic needs in people's lives were met by the news they got—a quantitative way of going back to the function of news. "For some people it is about connecting to community," Crane said. "For some it is about making their life better [healthier, safer, more comfortable]. For others it's about making up their own mind. For others it is a way of winning social acceptance." Crane identified a range of needs that varied depending on the type of media, the way news categories were defined, and the kind of audience that was studied.[19] Instead of asking directly what kinds of topics people were interested in, Crane quantified for news companies the purposes for which people used news. "Too rarely do people [in news companies] think about what citizens' needs are," she said of her clients.

Second, Crane studied how people in a given community were living their lives, using a version of what some people call lifestyle and trends research. This type of research tends to group populations into clusters based not just on demographics but on attitudes and behavior. She studied fifteen different areas, from health to religion, work, consumerism, family relations, education, and more, and identified the top concerns and trends in a given place. Taken together, her research into why people used the news and her study of the deeper concerns and trends in their lives gave journalists insight into how to apply their own professional judgment. But the research, she said, should augment, not supplant, that judgment.

Al Tompkins, a former news director who teaches broadcasting at the Poynter Institute, believes Crane's research told journalists "how communities live, where their loyalties are, and not just what they are watching, but why are they watching."[20] Crane's work, Tompkins said, "guides the presentation of news but doesn't determine what stories you do." For instance, although a lot of research suggests people don't like politics, Tompkins said, "Crane's research shows us they do care about their community, but they don't trust the political institutions. . . . It wasn't the topic they were sick of, it was the approach to the topic."

Researcher John Carey conducted ethnographic research at Greystone Communication. Ethnography, which is an outgrowth of anthropology, works through direct on-site observation. Carey sat in people's houses and watched how they interacted with media and technology. He sat in people's houses through mealtimes, at breakfast, at dinner, early in the morning, and even late at night.

Carey's findings turned many of the conventional ideas about television on their head. For instance, although a good deal of social science research suggests what some academics have called "the supremacy of the visual"—the notion that pictures are more powerful than words in television—Carey's work found that "very often people are not watching but listening to television news. Many people are actually reading a newspaper while the news plays on their living room TV, and they tend to turn their attention to the television when they hear something that they think will have important pictures." Carey's research suggested that it would be a mistake to focus on the visuals of a TV news program at the expense of having engaging verbal content.

Carey's research also suggested that the concept of teasers, or tempting people to stay tuned a little longer for an important upcoming report, may be ineffective. "A big mistake is thinking that people are watching over a length of time. Teasers are a huge mistake. People don't wait." Those items that say, "Will it rain tomorrow? Well, tonight will be cold, and Jim will be back in seven minutes with the complete forecast"—those tend to drive people away. Carey's observations show that any time there is a commercial, most viewers immediately switch channels.[21] A better alternative, Carey believed, would be to provide key information like weather constantly, to pack information all over your newscast, even to scroll it during commercials. "You would grab people by the constancy of your information."

The late Carole Kneeland, a news director in Austin, Texas, in the late 1990s who was also known for defying conventional wisdom, followed the approach. She repeated the weather forecast throughout the newscast on the assumption that people wouldn't stay for the whole half hour but that if you could inform more people quickly, over time you would command the most loyal and the largest audience. "I think in the future we will have to break away from thirty-minute and sixty-minute content," Carey suggested. "You could have programming that is five minutes long in cycles," with longer pieces at certain times, much like radio programs with news and weather repeating every eight or twelve minutes, or NPR's broadcasts, in which repeating headlines are intermixed with longer stories.

Carey's ideas are even more powerful now, when citizens have so much control over their own news consumption, and better options are only a click away. His ideas adapt journalism to the needs of the citizen—rather than seeing the citizen as someone whose attention should be manipulated on behalf of an advertiser. Ultimately, this will make the journalism more valuable and more popular. It turns us toward a journalism that fulfills the promise of a digital age, one that is a service on behalf of the public—something that helps people improve their lives, rather than a static product designed for another era. That mind shift, from product to service, is one of the underlying ideas of this book.

At the American Press Institute, we developed this kind of research for the Web. Instead of asking consumers what kinds of stories they want a local publication or program to produce (asking them to play a role of journalist they have not thought much about), we ask them about their lives. What do they like about where they live? What do they not like? How do they spend their time? What are they most worried about in their lives? What are they most passionate about? And where do they go to find different kinds of information? We ask these questions in different ways, sometimes in multiple-choice questions, sometimes in open-ended questions. We want to hear about their fears and passions in their own words.

The result is that we end up with a lot of knowledge about how people feel about their communities and their lives. We can then match that with what we know from our analytics app about what content from a given outlet they are engaging with or not. Where there are gaps, there are opportunities. If people in the community are concerned in large numbers with a particular issue and the publication's content isn't getting a lot of traction, we know that the problem is likely that the content isn't produced well. If the publication is failing to produce much news and information that addresses what the data show is a major concern for a lot of people, there is an opportunity for new coverage. And if certain kinds of stories are connecting (say major enterprise) but others are not (briefs and a lot of midlength stories), we can tell that the publication is creating too much low-value content on a beat that actually does matter.

One publication, in Erie, Pennsylvania, discovered that crime was overwhelmingly the biggest concern in people's lives. The publication did an enormous number of spot crime stories. But the coverage was shallow. It noted new crimes, but it did little to get at the causes of rising crime or what could be done about it. With the research, and the better analytics, they changed their approach. They decided that if a crime was written about, it would be seen through to conviction or dismissal. And a good many spot crime stories would be replaced by more in-depth stories looking at causes and solutions. The audience for their crime coverage grew 200 percent. Shares grew 250 percent.[22]

THE NEW NEWS CONSUMER

Even if journalists have conducted better research and have begun to employ better, more relevant metrics that will help create more valuable content, they must take a third and final step to serve audiences better in the digital age. Those who produce news must understand how the people consume news and information about their lives today.

This is slightly different from asking people in a given market how they live their lives. And it is different from harnessing online metrics. Understanding the new news consumer involves research that discovers how people behave in acquiring news, now that they no longer have to adapt their behavior to the delivery cycles of the news media. This involves understanding how time of day influences the way people interact with news and how that, in turn, influences device choice. It involves understanding how setting—office versus home versus commuting, or weekends versus workday—influences news behavior. It also involves beginning to discover what we call the personal news cycle, or the path to learning about news. People no longer rely primarily on one medium for news. They tend to hear stories initially via word of mouth, social media, and television and then tend to go to a second source, and often a different platform, to learn more. They also choose different media for different kinds of stories and questions they want to answer. Now that publishers are no longer limited by format, device, or style of content, knowledge of these differences is critical to making journalism that serves the citizen.

Some of this work can be done through what is called human-centered design research, market research that is closer in style to ethnography than survey writing or focus groups. Human-centered design is an approach that involves listening to real people talk about their lives, in long open-ended interviews, and creating personas of such people and their needs as you set out to design products. Innovated at Stanford University, it is a way for companies to develop new products in uncertain environments, or to reinvent old ones that are failing to serve the needs of audiences. It involves meeting people where they are, creating profiles of different kinds of people, and walking people through their days and the ways they interact and employ information about different topics.

Human-centered design can also involve more detailed ways of looking at data outputs. *The New York Times* has done some of the most rigorous and early work of this sort, using data to understand its audience, as it led the way in charging for online content, against the doubts of many critics. By 2013, the company had a team of two hundred people working on its subscription system, twenty-five of whom were engaged in audience research and testing of content, pricing, and market strategies. The company relied heavily on involving readers in giving feedback on new designs, content, and marketing. Nearly every idea, from new content to sales approaches, went through A-B testing, the system of trying two different approaches to innovations and measuring the audience response.

This relentlessly empirical approach helped the paper succeed in introducing a paywall when virtually no consumers were used to paying for online content and there was no previously successful model to follow. Mistakes would have been easy to make, and almost all outsiders expected *The New York Times* to fail at this. Indeed, after the paper succeeded, many dismissed that success as evidence that the *Times,* as a national paper aimed at elites, was unique. In reality, what was unique was that the paper had studied the audience and listened to them while creating its new pricing model.

Product thinking is another term popular among people who are trying to reinvent journalism (and other fields) that has been disrupted or who are working in uncertain environments. All of these approaches, and others, share what might be called an "audience-centered focus." It involves listening in a deeper way to potential consumers to design products—rather than doing traditional market research, which is aimed at figuring out how to sell products or which version of the same product is more likely to sell better than another.

As with taking command of metrics, the field here is just emerging. But it will be critical going forward.

An embrace of data on behalf of better journalism is a significant shift for those who aspire to produce news in the public interest. The traditional resistance to research in newsrooms was often based on an urge to protect journalistic independence or, more specifically, to avoid allowing advertising and sales to make news decisions. Research tended to be controlled by the marketing and sales departments. For the most part, it was designed, particularly at print organizations, to inform advertisers.

"It's what I call the myth of the golden gut," Crane told us. That view was always self-defeating, even if it was an understandable response to bad data. It made newspeople seem like incurious know-nothings resistant to learning or to change. That view now is even more suicidal. It will likely be the difference between success and failure. Those who fail to study and understand the new news audience will almost certainly lose out to those who do. Ironically, journalists have more of the skills needed to do the kind of observational research about people's lives that might be best suited for journalism. Journalists, however, have not developed any tradition of doing it. Now they are trying.

If journalism lost its way, the reason in large part is that it lost meaning in people's lives, not only with its traditional audience but with the next generation as well. We have shown, we hope, that a major reason for this is that journalists no longer have the self-confidence to try to make the news comprehensive and proportional. Like the ancient maps that left much of the world terra incognita, journalism confronts contemporary audiences with similar blank spaces in place of uninteresting demographic groups or topics too difficult to pursue.

If journalists are nimble and creative enough to use it, the interactive nature of the Web offers opportunities to take dramatic steps in overcoming the problems created by shortsighted use of market research and demographic data. Using these new tools can create a journalism that truly meets the needs of communities and can create the kind of understanding that would allow the public itself to continuously fill in some of the blanks in the coverage of their world and provide knowledge based on their own peculiar experiences that give them unique insights.

The answer is not to return to a day when journalists operated purely by instinct. We hope we have spotlighted a group of new cartographers who are developing tools to chart the way people live their lives today and the needs for news these lives create. They are providing one of the most important tools a news organization needs to design a more comprehensive and proportional news report that attracts rather than repels the audience. Now it is up to journalists to try.

With all this, there is still another element that ties all the others together. It relates to what goes on in the newsroom itself.

10

JOURNALISTS HAVE A
RESPONSIBILITY TO CONSCIENCE

For three weeks in October 2002, Washington, D.C., was paralyzed by fear. With cunning stealth and deadly efficiency, someone stalked thirteen men, women, and children in the city and its Maryland and Virginia suburbs, shooting to death nine and seriously wounding four. The victims included a twelve-year-old boy who was shot while walking to school.

A nationwide manhunt ensued, with city, county, state, and federal law enforcement officials taunted by notes left at the murder scenes, including one that warned, "Your children are not safe anywhere, anytime." The murders seemed frighteningly like the opening of a guerrilla phase in the shadowy ill-defined "war against terror" declared by President George W. Bush thirteen months after hijacked jetliners had become suicide bombs, killing thousands when they obliterated the World Trade Center buildings in New York City and destroyed a section of the Pentagon in Washington. Press coverage of the murders pushed other news—including that of American troops fighting in Afghanistan—off the front page as the world focused on the fear that gripped America's capital community.

For Howell Raines, then executive editor of *The New York Times*, the Washington story presented another opportunity to send a message to his staff. Under Raines, the paper's strategy was to "flood the zone" of a big story and dominate everybody else. Raines had been promoted to the top job in 2001, a few weeks before the 9/11 attacks, and he had mobilized the staff to cover that historic event so well that it won the paper a record five Pulitzer Prizes. The Washington story was his opportunity to take on *The Washington Post* in its hometown and try to erase the hurt many *Times* staffers still nursed over the way the *Post* had outreported them on the Watergate scandal thirty years earlier.

Although the *Times* had the largest bureau in Washington, with a cluster of a half dozen of the paper's best investigative reporters, Raines kept direction of the coverage in New York. Among the people he dispatched to Washington was Jayson Blair, a twenty-seven-year-old former intern who had been a reporter for only twenty-one months. Within days the addition of Blair seemed an inspired choice. The new reporter was producing front-page stories with tantalizing details that other Washington-area reporters were unable to match.

But soon, experienced reporters in Washington began raising questions about "this guy Blair," whose name kept appearing in the paper but whom none of them saw in the bureau or in the field. One of those reporters, Eric Lichtblau, who covered the Department of Justice for the *Times*, became concerned when stories by Blair were routinely questioned by officials he had come to trust in the Department of Justice. Other reporters were raising questions as well, and when one source in exasperation told Lichtblau he "didn't know who the anonymous sources this guy Blair is depending on was, but much of what he was writing is just not true," Lichtblau went to Rick Berke, the bureau's news editor. Berke reported his concerns to New York, where he said he was "brushed off" with suggestions that the complaints were prompted by jealousy. Raines, Berke was told, "had already decided Blair was a great shoe-leather reporter."[1]

What none of the people in the Washington bureau knew was that complaints about Blair's work had infected the newsroom in New York for months before Blair was sent to Washington. Somehow, as Blair was moved from one supervising editor to another, the doubts about the quality of his work didn't travel with him. It was as if the editors worked on different continents instead of a few yards or miles from one another.

Washington reporters were considering filing an organized complaint to New York when two suspects were arrested and charged in the sniper shootings case. Coverage was reduced, and the tension and doubts began to ease as Blair was reassigned to other stories. The dateline on his stories was no longer Washington; they began to appear from Maryland, West Virginia, Ohio, even Texas, where Robert Rivard, the editor of the *San Antonio Express-News,* saw something in a Blair story that troubled him. It concerned him enough to send an email message to Raines and *Times* managing editor Gerald Boyd, telling them he had found an article written by Blair to be "disturbingly similar" to one his newspaper had published eight days earlier.

This outside complaint from the editor of another newspaper couldn't be ignored, and Raines and Boyd confronted Blair with it. The young reporter tried to explain himself but quickly became caught up in a web of contradictions. After two days, it became clear that he had never visited the Texas home he wrote about and that his "eyewitness" detail had come from pictures in the *Times* photo archives. The rest of his information came from stories by other reporters. On May 1, 2003, Blair resigned. News of his resignation had the effect of blasting open closed lines of communication inside the *Times.* One after the other, staff members realized that they were not the only ones who had been suspicious of Blair's behavior and his work.

A full-scale investigation revealed what many on the staff had suspected: Blair was not an aggressive, dedicated reporter but a troubled young man relying on deceit, plagiarism, and fiction to further his career at the expense of everyone around him. Staffers started to air long-repressed feelings of resentment, even betrayal, about the paper, feelings they had thought they were alone in having. For the next two weeks Raines and Boyd met with individuals and groups in the newsroom and tried to reassure them that the paper's values hadn't changed. The people they heard in those meetings were reporters and junior editors who believed that such basic violations of standards and values threatened to destroy their own credibility, and that of the newspaper.

Instead of being placated, staff discontent only became more intense and pointed, and publisher Arthur Sulzberger Jr. announced that he and Raines and Boyd would meet with the newsroom in a "town hall" meeting to address questions and concerns. The meeting, which was closed to non-*Times* journalists, was held in a nearby theater. The depth of suspicion and anger that focused on senior management during the session would later be described as "unusually raw, emotional, and candid." Some of those who took part not only described the confrontation to reporters from other news organizations but also sent email messages to journalism watch sites, where they were posted for everybody to see. Their messages began to build a public bill of particulars against the leadership of Raines and Boyd.

The picture these messages painted was of a newsroom in which internal communications had become so dysfunctional that five years of warnings about the quality and reliability of Blair's work were ignored as he was assigned to more and more important stories until his byline appeared on stories of national—even international—interest. Before the Blair episode concluded, both Raines and Boyd were forced out,[2] and more than two dozen newsroom employees engaged in a long-term reorganization of the newsroom's standards, structure, and operations.

By June the internal investigation had documented Blair's "frequent acts of journalistic fraud . . . widespread fabrication and plagiarism [that] represent a profound betrayal of trust and a low point in the 152-year history of the newspaper." As more information surfaced, it became clear to the staff that it had taken an outside voice to break open the dysfunctional lines of internal communication.

Much of the impetus for the collapse of the top newsroom managers was credited to the internet, on which many of the *Times* employees posted the complaints that previously had been ignored. Staff members who used the open architecture of the new medium to become "the outside voice" provided a check on internal behavior. Along with others, they realized that the Web had assumed an important role in opening new channels through which values and standards could be questioned and judged by the larger community, which depends on the integrity of the press.

In the end, journalism is an act of character. Given that there are no laws, no regulations, no licensing, and no formal self-policing practices governing journalism's production—and because journalism by its nature can be exploitative—a heavy burden rests on the ethics and judgment of the individual news gatherer and the organization that publishes the work. And this is even truer in an age when publishing can be an individual act.

This would be a difficult challenge for any profession. But for journalism there is the added tension between its public service mission—the aspect of the work that justifies its intrusiveness—and the interests that finance the work. Today, in addition to more revenue coming directly from subscribers and members, more of the work of journalism occurs in or is underwritten by think tanks, issue advocacy groups, donors, political organizations, and other organizations for whom journalism is a new and ancillary activity.

At the same time, the rise of the Web and the democratization of content production have given voice to citizens who are monitoring politics, society, and the press, creating a new broad cohort of media pundits and critics. Some operate independently; others express their views at a host of more formal settings that have grown up to watch the press—places such as Media Matters on the left or NewsBusters on the right. Together, they represent an unprecedented network of media watchdogs. Today, if trouble is brewing inside a newsroom, it will almost certainly leak, or even be written about by journalists from within those organizations complaining in public or private, as was the case when *The New York Times* published a controversial column by Senator Tom Cotton of Arkansas defending the use of the military to stop protests over George Floyd's murder by police in 2020. Flaws in the editorial, breakdowns in the *Times*'s editing process, and objections to its content led to the resignation of the paper's editorial page editor. If the organization is skirting responsibilities, somebody will point it out. The tension and fear of having organizational issues discussed outside the newsroom have prompted some editors to stop sending memos or putting decisions down on paper.

Some of these new monitors have not only increased demands for transparency in newsrooms but, as was the case with Jayson Blair, also helped expose ethical lapses and flaws in the hierarchical structure of organizations like *The New York Times*. It's true that a good deal of the new expanded digital public discourse about media does not rise above ideological accusations that the media is being too conservative or too liberal. When it does, however, and when it brings up serious issues, the credibility of that journalistic product can be greatly affected. For all the vitriol, we believe the public discourse about media has made those who produce news more thoughtful, more reflective, more searching about their work. After a decade of turmoil, criticism and epochal financial disruption have forced journalists to become better at their jobs.

It's important to keep this consequence in mind because, whether or not we are conscious of its importance, when all is said and done, what we are choosing when we download an app, follow a columnist on social media, subscribe to an email newsletter, choose a TV news program, or read a newspaper or its website is the authority, honesty, and judgment of the journalists who produce it. And it's part of journalists' responsibility, in whatever setting they work, to encourage a transparent and open culture that won't lead critics to call the credibility of the product into question.

As a consequence, there is one more principle that those engaged in journalism have come to understand about their work, and that we as citizens should recognize when we make our media choices. It is the most elusive of the principles, yet it ties all the others together:

Journalists have an obligation to exercise their personal conscience.

Every journalist, from the occasional citizen sentinel or freelancer, to the newsroom, to the manager who visits the boardroom, must have a personal sense of ethics and responsibility—a moral compass. What's more, journalists have a responsibility to voice their personal conscience out loud and allow others around them to do so as well.

Especially for journalists in institutional settings, the exercise of this conscience requires that managers and owners create an open newsroom. Such an environment is essential to fulfilling the principles outlined in this book. The ongoing reckoning in newsrooms over race, racial justice, the largely white, male, and older default culture in newsrooms, and concepts like objectivity is a clear sign that newsrooms and news companies often fall short. As we have said earlier, every generation to some degree invents its own journalism. The largely pliant journalism of the 1940s and 1950s, which partnered with the establishment, gave way to a more questioning and skeptical journalism in the 1960s, one that helped overturn the power of the Klan and Jim Crow in the South, identified the "credibility gap" with government, and questioned the Vietnam War. That helped lead to toppling a president in the 1970s. The journalism of the 1980s and 1990s was more explanatory and interpretive. The *Los Angeles Times*, then at its peak, described itself as a daily magazine. In 2020, journalism is going through another reckoning, led in part by the conscience of journalists of color.

Innumerable hurdles make it difficult to produce news that is accurate, fair, balanced, citizen focused, independent minded, and courageous. But the effort is smothered in its crib without an open atmosphere that allows people to challenge one another's assumptions, perceptions, and prejudices. We need our journalists to feel free, even encouraged, to speak out and say, "This story idea strikes me as racist," or "You're making the wrong decision," or "I want to raise a concern about something on the site." Only in a setting in which all can constructively bring their diverse viewpoints to bear can the news have any chance of accurately anticipating and reflecting the increasingly diverse perspectives and needs of American culture.

Simply put, those engaged in news must recognize a personal obligation to differ with or challenge editors, owners, donors, advertisers, and even citizens and established authority if fairness and accuracy require they do so. That engagement must be constructive in order to be effective, not self-serving, egoistic, or designed to create pyrotechnics.

In turn, those who run news organizations, whether large institutions or small Web experiments, must encourage and allow staff to exercise this personal obligation. It would be naive to assume that journalists' individual commitment is enough, in an age of uncertainty about the future of the press. Many journalists are so worried that they might be swept away by the next wave of layoffs that challenging authority and a flawed organizational culture is the last thing on their minds. Others feel fearful about pushing back against leadership because they don't want to get caught up in generational or political battles. So news publishers need to build a culture that nurtures individual responsibility. And then managers have to be willing to listen, not simply manage problems and concerns away.

There is no separate section in this book on ethics. That is because this moral dimension, this quality of judgment, tone, taste, and character, is implicit in why we choose one magazine, newscast, or website over another. Ethics are woven into every element of journalism and every critical decision that journalists make. As citizens engaging with media, we sense this often more acutely than do journalists themselves, who sometimes cordon off ethics as an isolated topic.

As Chicago newscaster Carol Marin told us some twenty years ago, "I think a journalist is someone who believes in something that they would be willing to quit over."[3]

In 1993, as NBC's *Dateline* was preparing a segment called "Waiting to Explode?" alleging that the gas tanks in General Motors trucks had a tendency to rupture and ignite in crashes, the reporter of the piece voiced concern. Although correspondent Michele Gillen had collected footage of actual accidents in which drivers wound up trapped inside burning cars, she knew that crash tests NBC had conducted had not produced the same results. A small fire had broken out, but it had lasted only fifteen seconds before burning itself out. So when she learned that the network was setting up additional crash tests rigged to be more dramatic, Gillen called her boss, Jeff Diamond, and expressed her concerns. She wanted the new tests stopped. Diamond assured her that her concerns would be noted in the final broadcast and that the tests would be labeled as "unscientific." In the end Gillen agreed to narrate the piece anyway, against her instincts, telling herself, "At some point, you have to have faith in your executive producer."[4] Gillen was wrong, and the embarrassment of the rigged explosions was a low point in the history of NBC News.

The incident shows how delicate the question of moral compass can be. Conscience is not something to be gotten past, as it was in the *Dateline* case. It is something to be revered. The burden of protecting conscience cannot be laid entirely on the individual, nor can it be suffocated, as Gillen's objections were. Had Gillen's objections been heeded,

NBC News would have avoided the embarrassment that eventually led to the resignation of Michael Gartner as president of the news division.

The Web hardly eliminates errors or arguments in journalism. It does make many of the internal debates that occur about them more public. In the wake of the death of retired basketball star Kobe Bryant in 2019, *Washington Post* staff writer Felicia Sonmez thought the wave of adoring coverage of Bryant's life was neglecting that he had been arrested for sexually assaulting a young woman at a resort in Colorado. She posted a story about it in social media. *Post* editor Marty Baron felt she was trying to make a political statement, not just add context, and asked her to take the post down and not do more. The internal debate inside the *Post* became a public one around the country. Sonmez was subsequently suspended for not listening to her editors. Baron later had to admit they had mishandled the matter internally. It is one of scores of cases where the exercise of conscience in newsrooms today is likely to quickly become public. That changes the dynamics. But it does not only add pressure on managers to make good decisions. It makes the whole decision process more pressured. The public discussion of private debates rarely captures the context of those debates particularly well.

It also means that the decision of one organization may easily be contradicted by a decision at another. In 2016, most news organizations in Washington had a copy of the famous Russian "dossier" of raw intelligence accusations about then-candidate Donald J. Trump, collected by a former MI5 British intelligence agent, that spoke to Trump's moral fitness. Some of the accusations may have been true. Some probably were false. It was raw intelligence of the sort that MI5 or any other intelligence agency would work to corroborate before acting on any of it. All the news organizations that had the dossier spent weeks trying to substantiate the claims it contained and could not. But one news outlet, BuzzFeed, decided it didn't need to corroborate anything. It published the dossier anyway. As Ben Smith, then the editor of BuzzFeed, glibly wrote afterward: "We trust you to reckon with a messy, sometimes uncertain reality."[5]

Smith's defense was self-serving and facile, but it was also damaging to journalism and to BuzzFeed. It stretches credulity to imagine that ordinary people, without their own sources in Russia, could "decide for themselves" about the veracity of raw intelligence and the reliability of unnamed intelligence assets of a retired British spy in a faraway country. Instead, BuzzFeed turned information into a simple and meaningless journalistic Rorschach test: If you hated Trump you wanted to believe it, or at least some of it. If you liked Trump, you hated the press all the more.

But the exercise of journalistic conscience in this case was no longer an exercise. It was an argument after the fact because one outlet decided to abandon trying to corroborate or verify anything.

EXERCISING CONSCIENCE IS NOT EASY

Introducing the need for conscience into the journalistic process creates another tension. By necessity, newsrooms are not democracies—and that is even more the case in the age of layoffs, buyouts, and expanded use of low-paid or free contributors. The staffs who produce news have less leverage in that environment than before. By necessity, news operations also tend to be pluralistic dictatorships. Newsrooms are full of people who chafe under authority, which is part of what led them to journalism. But in their newsroom, someone atop the chain of command has to make the ultimate decision—whether to publish, to stand by a piece of content, to leave in the damning quote or take it out, to pull down the controversial story or leave it up. Even in a setting where content is posted without much initial supervision, there are ultimately commands and controls.

And when revenue is scarce, and the business side is increasingly experimenting with ideas such as sponsored content (in effect, advertising that looks more like editorial content) or grants from foundations that want to change the world, what formerly seemed firm ethical ground has become softer sand. Such factors are a significant issue facing journalism's future, and that issue must be carefully managed and thought through. As Bob Woodward, who when he was a young reporter covering Watergate had many higher pressures against pursuing the story, has said: "The best journalism is often done in defiance of management."[6]

History suggests this is culturally an uneven playing field. People of color in newsrooms, women, members of an LGBTQ community, and members of any other group that is not well represented at the top have a harder time exercising conscience in any organization. Unless a newsroom is genuinely open, it is harder for those who feel like outsiders to challenge decisions from which they feel excluded. It is the responsibility of management to create an atmosphere where debate is encouraged and where people who are different from each other all feel they belong. If it does not, three things almost certainly will happen. Many of those people brought into the newsroom, in part, to broaden the thinking of the organization will leave, and these efforts to diversify and open the consciousness of the newsroom will fail—again. Those who remain will not be honest with management because they know they will not be heard. Whatever default culture exists in the newsroom, usually a combination of the culture and personality of the people at the top, will harden and become more blind to itself.

In a time when the existential crisis facing journalism is financial, technological, generational, racial, and philosophical, it is important to recognize that journalistic conscience is at risk. Allowing individuals to voice their concerns makes running any news operation more difficult. But it makes the quality of the news better. And that, in the end, is the real existential crisis. The rest is tactics.

This notion of moral conscience is something many, if not most, of those engaged in news believe in deeply. "Each individual reporter has to set his own rules, his own standards, and model his career for himself," longtime television journalist Bill Kurtis told us more than a decade ago.[7] This is even truer now, when everyone who imagines him- or herself a journalist is more likely to be the entrepreneur of his or her own career and work through many different venues.

When he began doing media criticism, writer Jon Katz sensed this about being a journalist and even more so about being a critic of journalists. Katz felt compelled to sit down and write his own personal code of ethics. "I think you have to have a moral context in the work you do for it really to have any meaning," he told our research partners. "Whatever you do, I think you have to do it in a way that is morally satisfying to you."[8]

Most journalists are far less formal about it than Katz. They simply sense that journalism is a moral act and know that all of their background and values direct the choices they make when producing it. "My own instincts, and the way I was raised . . . and I suppose my own emotional and intellectual development, have led me to some pretty strong beliefs over the years, and I pay attention to them around here," Tom Brokaw told our research partners.[9]

Many engaged in journalism are drawn to it because of some of its basic elements—calling attention to inequities in the system, connecting people, creating community. In our survey of journalists with the Pew Research Center for the People & the Press, these factors outstripped all others by nearly two to one as distinguishing features of journalism.[10] In short, for those who practice it, the craft has a moral aspect.

One reason journalists feel strongly about the moral dimension of what they are doing is that without it they have so little to help them navigate the gray spaces of ethical decisions. As Carol Marin told us, since "there are no laws of news . . . it ends up being sort of your own guiding compass that will determine what you do and don't do."[11]

As audiences, we are guided by what stories seem interesting and well reported. But we are guided, too, by a more subtle combination of factors, and this moral sense of journalism is part of it. We are looking for information, but we are also looking for authority, for honesty, and for a sense that the journalists have our interests at heart, a sense, in effect, of shared morality.

Consider the experience Marin encountered in Chicago. Early in 1997, she was the anchor at WMAQ, the NBC-owned and -operated station in the city. The man in charge of the news at the station, Joel Cheatwood, had an idea to sweeten the ratings of the struggling 6 P.M. newscast. Cheatwood, who had made a name for himself in Miami by turning a Fox affiliate into the number one station by going to "All Crime All the Time," planned on upping the ante in Chicago. He hired Jerry Springer, the disgraced Cincinnati mayor turned talk show host, to do commentaries at the end of the news. Springer was local. He taped his syndicated TV show about bizarre love triangles and violent confrontations right from WMAQ's studios.

When Cheatwood's plan was announced, WMAQ staff were despondent. Were they in the shock-show business? They had thought they were doing something important, something that was a public service. Marin shared these concerns and decided, eventually, that enough was enough. She thought WMAQ was degenerating into sleaze. Management already had put her on probation once because she had refused to narrate health segments that had been a collaboration between the station and a local hospital, which was given airtime in exchange for buying ads on the station. Now came Springer. Marin had no illusions about herself. She was no saint. But journalists live and die by their reputation as people with ethics. It's all they have. She decided she would resign.

Marin's colleagues burst into loud applause when she announced her decision on camera. You could see them, right on the air. Many wept. It meant something that a public person would take such an ethical stand about her own job. Marin left for another station, and in the wake of her departure, WMAQ's viewers fled as well.

Afterward, Marin was "awestruck" by the response, especially the "quantity and the quality of the letters and emails. . . . People wrote long tracts, and they did three things in many of the letters. They explained their relationship to the news. . . . They described themselves in demographic terms. . . . They explained an ethical dilemma that had happened to them. . . . A lawyer that I know in Chicago wrote me and said, every one of us in our lives will face a so-called Springer decision. I talked to butchers who won't short-weigh meat, and one who got fired. A real estate banker who wouldn't pad assessments in Lake Forest and lost two critical accounts with Chicago banks."[12]

Such cases are isolated, but they are not unique. In 2020, when a young producer named Ariana Pekary resigned from the cable news channel MSNBC, she wrote an online letter about how corrosive she thought cable news had become to the political culture of the United States. The network, which airs talk interviews for most of the day and evening, books guests largely for how they "rate" or their effect on ratings—a model that Pekary said "blocks diversity of thought and content because the networks have incentive to amplify fringe voices and events, at the expense of others, all because it pumps up the ratings."

She quoted an unnamed colleague saying, "We are a cancer and there is no cure. . . . But if you could find a cure, it would change the world."[13]

Pekary went on to say, "This cancer risks human lives, even in the middle of a pandemic. The primary focus quickly became what Donald Trump was doing (poorly) to address the crisis, rather than the science itself. As new details have become available about antibodies, a vaccine, or how COVID actually spread, producers still want to focus on the politics. Important facts or studies get buried. . . . Trump smothers out all other coverage. Also important is to ensure citizens can vote by mail this year, but I've watched that topic get ignored or 'killed' numerous times. Context and factual data are often considered too cumbersome for the audience."

Pekary then quoted James Baldwin: "Not everything that is faced can be changed, but nothing can be changed until it is faced."

A CULTURE OF HONESTY

"The ability of journalists to exercise conscience is much more important than anything they believe or any beliefs they bring to their job," Linda Foley, then the president of the Newspaper Guild, told us as we went around the country and talked to those engaged in news about what set the practice apart. "It's credibility, more than objectivity, that's important for us in our industry. . . . There has to be a culture in newsrooms that allows a journalist to have a free and open discussion."[14]

Some years ago, Donald Shriver, the president emeritus of Union Theological Seminary in New York City, reviewed four books on journalism ethics and offered this about the handbook on the subject prepared by the Poynter Institute in Florida: "The most useful piece of the Poynter schematic for journalistic ethics is its illustration of the transition from 'gut reaction' ethics to observation of rules to the maturity of reflection and reasoning. At the top of this hierarchy is their assertion that 'collaboration is essential.' That is, check the story with your colleagues. Given the rush to deadline and competition among reporters in most newsrooms, this is rare advice. Yet, if journalism is a medium of dialogue among citizens, it seems right for the dialogue to begin in the newsroom."[15]

Interestingly, some of the best and most difficult decisions in journalism history have been made through just the kind of elusive collaboration Shriver is talking about. When publisher Katharine Graham made the decision to publish the Pentagon Papers in 1971, the process was extraordinarily open. Graham had to decide whether *The Washington Post* should risk legal sanction by publishing secret Pentagon documents after the Justice Department had already gone to court to block *The New York Times* from making them public. Here is how Graham herself described the decision-making process in her autobiography:

> Ben [Bradlee] was beginning to feel squeezed between the editors and the reporters, who were solidly lined up for publishing and supporting the *Times* on the issue of freedom of the press, and the lawyers, who at one point suggested a compromise whereby the *Post* would not publish the Papers on Friday but would notify the attorney general of its intention to publish on Sunday. Howard Simons, who was one hundred percent for publishing, summoned the reporters to talk directly with the lawyers.
>
> [Don] Oberdorfer said the compromise was "the shittiest idea I've ever heard." [Chalmers] Roberts said the *Post* would be "crawling on its belly" to the attorney general; if the *Post* didn't publish, he would move his retirement up two weeks, make it a resignation, and publicly accuse the *Post* of cowardice. Murrey Marder recalled saying, "If the *Post* doesn't publish, it will be in much worse shape as an institution than if it does," since the paper's "credibility would be destroyed journalistically for being gutless." [Ben] Bagdikian reminded the lawyers of the commitment to [Daniel] Ellsberg to publish the Papers and declared, "The only way to assert the right to publish is to publish." . . . Gene Patterson . . . gave me the first warning of what was to come, saying that he believed the decision on whether to print was going to be checked with me and that he "knew I fully recognized that the soul of the newspaper was at stake."
>
> "God, do you think it's coming to that?" I asked. Yes, Gene said, he did. . . .
>
> Frightened and tense, I took a big gulp and said, "Go ahead, go ahead, go ahead. Let's go. Let's publish."[16]

As Anthony Lewis, then an editorial columnist for *The New York Times*, noted seventeen years later:

> Examining that episode afterward, a law review article by Professors Harold Edgar and Benno Schmidt Jr. of the Columbia University Law School said it marked the "passing of an era" for the American press. It was an era, they said, in which there was a "symbiotic relationship between politicians and the press." But now, by printing the secret history of the Vietnam War over strenuous objections, establishment newspapers had "demonstrated that much of the press was no longer willing to be merely an occasionally critical associate [of the Government], devoted to common aims, but intended to become an adversary."[17]

A year after the Pentagon Papers, *The Washington Post* began looking into Watergate.

INTELLECTUAL DIVERSITY IS THE REAL GOAL

This notion of open dialogue in the newsroom is what a growing number of people who think about news consider the key element in the question of diversity and in the pursuit of a journalism of proportion.

"Is there a culture of the newsroom?" television journalist Charles Gibson asked during a forum we held in the late 1990s. "Are you challenging each other, are you talking to each other, are you pushing each other?"[18]

"I'll tell you how it plays out for Christians in my newsroom," answered David Ashenfelter, a Pulitzer Prize winner at the *Detroit Free Press*, who is also a Christian and a member of a large weekly Bible study group in suburban Detroit. "They don't talk. They're afraid of being ridiculed. They're there. I know who a bunch of them are. We sort of have this little underground, and we talk to each other and we talk among ourselves. One thing we've been asking ourselves lately is, why are we just talking among ourselves?"[19]

Traditionally, the concept of newsroom diversity was defined largely in terms of numerical targets that related to ethnicity, race, and gender. The news industry belatedly recognized that its newsrooms should more closely resemble the culture at large.

The diversity hiring goals the industry sets are critical. Without diverse newsrooms, there can be no real meaningful debate in newsrooms about coverage. The chance of a default culture, by age, race, gender, class, and generation, becomes much higher. Without diversity, journalism will be less accurate and more likely to fail as a business and in its constitutional responsibility to be something that serves all citizens.[20]

Seen in the broader context of personal conscience, however, newsroom hiring goals alone are insufficient. Creating more diverse newsrooms by itself does not achieve diversity, equity, and inclusion, or what colleagues at the Maynard Institute now call belonging. It does not guarantee that an institution has become a place where people can exercise conscience. Hiring more women and people of color in the newsroom is an essential step, but it will accomplish nothing if the newsroom culture then requires that these people from different backgrounds all adhere to a single mentality. The local newspaper or TV station may "look like America," as President Bill Clinton was fond of saying, but it won't think like the community and it won't understand it or be able to cover it. Diversity is a first step. Equity and belonging are additional steps. None of them work unless you create a culture of openness in which intellectual diversity is seen as the ultimate goal. For only thinking differently—not just hiring differently—will change a newsroom's journalism.

For this final step to occur, newsrooms must create an open culture where they can achieve what we call intellectual diversity, which encompasses and gives meaning to all the other kinds.

Intellectual diversity means not just assembling a roomful of people who think differently and come from different experiences and backgrounds. It means creating a culture in which people are then allowed to let those experiences and backgrounds inform the production of the news. It means creating an open newsroom where debates over stories are encouraged, where uncomfortable conversations are embraced as a professional necessity, where despite differences trust and a common goal in the work are mutually aspired to. Diversity begins with hiring.

Equity involves giving the people who've been hired some agency. Belonging or inclusion means having people who are different from one another authentically involved in making decisions.

Intellectual diversity works in practice only if it is understood that those debates are about making the journalism better. The arguments, in other words, aren't personal. They are about the work. It is a hard balance to strike. In some newsrooms these conversations have sometimes taken on some of the worst qualities of social media, shaming and campaigns to cancel people. That is not what we have in mind. The fact that these discussions can be difficult is why so many newsrooms tend to slide into avoidance and fail.

"We have defined . . . diversity too often in gender and genetic terms as people who look a little different but basically sound the same," Mercedes de Uriarte, who taught journalism at the University of Texas, told us. "We extend that too often to sources, who echo the thing that we're comfortable in hearing on both sides of a very narrow spectrum of debate." But, said de Uriarte, "it is intellectual diversity that we still have difficulty including in the news. Intellectual diversity is, according to scholars of American culture, among the most difficult for Americans to accept."[21]

In our minds, as we noted in the chapter on independence, true intellectual diversity also must include another dimension that many newsroom managers struggle with as much as or more than they do with racial diversity—and that is ideological and cultural. Yet most editors we work with chafe at the idea of ideological hiring diversity. "I will never ask anyone I am considering for a job who they voted for," one of the most celebrated editors in America told us. But no one is asking anyone to do that. Good managers learn much from looking at the background and experience of people's résumés. Diversity in hiring goes more than skin deep; it also goes deeper than asking people who they voted for, a question that would be inappropriate. And while we are not trying to measure which gap is greater—race, class, gender, or ideology—intellectual diversity that ignores ideology also doesn't face the reality of how the news is created.

In 1992, author Rosenstiel was given "fly-on-the-wall" access for a year inside ABC News as it tried to cover the race for president for a book he was writing, *Strange Bedfellows*. The book explored how the news media, and particularly television, shaped presidential campaigning. The White House correspondent for ABC News was Brit Hume, a conservative who also freelanced for the conservative *American Spectator*. The anchor was Peter Jennings, a Canadian-born journalist who was quite liberal. Each night before the broadcast, Jennings, his executive producer Paul Friedman, and each correspondent would line-edit the correspondent's script. This line editing was done over an open phone line on which only Jennings, Friedman, and the correspondent could speak. But the editors on the senior editing desk, called The Rim, could listen in. So could Rosenstiel. Jennings and Hume would squabble over words in Hume's scripts and in Jennings's lead-ins each night, in respectful but sometimes stiff exchanges. And each would make changes. They respected each other and made each other's work better. Clinton won that election, and in the years that followed, Clinton's own West Wing staff would vote Hume the best of the three network news correspondents covering the White House, even knowing his conservative leanings. By our reckoning, Hume's work was not as strong, as enlightening, or as fair when he moved to Fox News. And Jennings, too, who died in 2005, was not the better for Hume's departure. Their ideological friction made them both better, fairer, smarter journalists—even if they didn't always enjoy it.

THE PRESSURES AGAINST INDIVIDUAL CONSCIENCE

Various factors pull toward making a newsroom setting homogeneous—even in the networked era of the Web. One is simply human nature. "Editors have a tendency to create people in their own image. If the editor doesn't like you for some reason, you don't rise. So there's a self-selection process that goes on within the profession," Juan González, a columnist at the New York *Daily News*, noted.[22]

"We have hiring systems in this country that make it very difficult to take risks on people. The people who are outside the mainstream as we would define it . . . are precisely the people who don't get a chance," Tom Bray, then a conservative columnist for *The Detroit News*, told us.[23]

Another problem is a kind of bureaucratic inertia that sets in at any organization—even new media start-ups that have only been around for a short time. Inertia causes people to take the easy route of doing in any circumstance whatever is normally done. Routines become safe havens. Even online collaborative virtual communities, such as Twitter or Reddit, begin to adopt their own nomenclature and norms of behavior.

Some journalists have always worked at the edge of such routines, even in the era of more institutional journalism. Guided only by their commitment to the truth, these individuals pursue stories with single-minded, sometimes idiosyncratic purpose and regularly reveal unpopular truths others have ignored, avoided, or simply not seen—people like Thomas Paine, George Seldes, I. F. Stone, or, more recently, David Burnham and Charles Lewis.

In an age when it is easier than ever before to publish first and check later, to retweet a startling post or statistic without first verifying it, to pass on what one has not read carefully, or to phrase one's comment provocatively, the new norms tend toward action rather than contemplation, and overstatement rather than understatement. In this kind of environment, skepticism and deliberation—sometimes even civility—may be a form of personal conscience.

BUILDING A CULTURE WHERE CONSCIENCE AND DIVERSITY CAN THRIVE

Perhaps the biggest challenge for the people who produce the news is recognizing that their long-term health depends on the quality of the culture they create, and the degree to which it allows people to be different—whether in a physical workplace or a virtual community of users. As difficult as the obstacles are, the history of journalism is filled with cases where collaboration and confrontation occurred and were even nurtured. Some engaged in news naturally gravitate to a culture where people feel free and encouraged to operate according to conscience. But when an industry is under pressure, particularly financially, that may become far less true.

One model is to have this culture flow down in clear demonstrations from the top, in public, where managers set a tone for others to see. One of the most famous examples is the story that the late journalist David Halberstam told of his first meeting with Orville Dryfoos, who had only recently been made publisher of *The New York Times:*

> It was in early 1962, maybe February. I had been in the Congo only since the previous July and had been called back to New York to receive an award. A man walked up to the desk where I was sitting and introduced himself as Orville Dryfoos. "I heard you were here," he said, "and I wanted to let you know how much I admire what you do, how much we are all aware of the risks you take. It is what makes this paper what it is." As much as anything else it was that attitude and the ease with which that conversation could occur between the publisher and a reporter that set that newsroom apart from any other.[24]

The next year, Halberstam, one of the bravest journalists of his generation, would take on President Kennedy's policies in Vietnam, against enormous pressure, and win a Pulitzer Prize for establishing, years before most other reporters, that the war was becoming a quagmire America could not win.

In the end, most journalists should feel that communicating to fellow citizens is a mission that transcends the institution where they work—that it is a calling—and that everyone who works in a newsroom is a steward of that mission. For their part, managers need to help their journalists fulfill that mission to their best potential. Gregory Favre, former editor of *The Sacramento Bee,* vice president of news for the McClatchy chain, and later a faculty member at the Poynter Institute, often talked to journalists about this larger sense of mission—years before the political divides in the United States and elsewhere seemed so steep.

> You help people whether it's a time of calm or whether it is a time of crisis. You help them speak to each other, allowing many voices to be heard, and providing them with information necessary to function as productive citizens. You help them build a bridge across their gulf of differences. And you have an obligation to question yourselves, just as you question others. An obligation to live and work by the same set

of values that you ask of those you cover. An obligation to help bring about a change in the culture throughout our business, a culture that has a sense of caring, that demands diversity in our ranks, that has a human touch, internally and externally, a culture that is wrapped in a moral fabric that won't be ripped apart in the moments of tough times.[25]

Indeed, Favre told people this mission is so significant that journalists have an obligation to preserve it and strengthen it, for both those journalists and citizens who came before and those who will come after.

THE ROLE OF CITIZENS

The final component in the equation is how the members of the community, the citizens, become part of the process. What responsibilities do they have?

One frequent response of journalists is that if the press is failing—if it is overly sensational or biased toward infotainment—then these are ultimately failures of the citizenry. If people wanted better journalism, they say, the market would provide it. The problem with this rationalization, as we have seen, is that journalism is not shaped by a perfect market. The kind of local news we get in television, for instance, owes a great deal to the level of profitability required by Wall Street. The nature of a newspaper, we have learned from news executives, is heavily influenced by the values of the ownership. The quality of the decisions journalists make from day to day is heavily influenced by editors and the culture of the newsroom. Newspapers once were monopolies, but even that was not always so. Those monopoly papers of the millennium were the winners of the newspaper wars of the 1960s and 1970s. Their sense of responsibility—and their arrogance—were born of that history, and so in turn was their slowness to understand and respond to the Web. TV stations, which are licensed on the public airways, are largely oligarchies but in a highly competitive business. At this point, the internet is still too young to predict what market reality it will come to represent, but twenty years into its history, it appears to have become more monopolistic than the oligarchical and much more civically oriented media system it replaced. And for all its best intentions, the primary reason for that seemed to be anticompetitive greed.

The market does not, as it is so often said, provide citizens simply with the news they want. They also get the news that Wall Street, ownership, journalism training, the cultural norms of each medium, and the conventions of news dictate be made available to them. If this is to change and if the principle that the journalist's primary allegiance is to the citizens is to have meaning, a new relationship between the journalist and the citizen must evolve.

There is a mythical dimension to the idea of a free and open internet. For a public that desires quality content, however, the new system brings with it new transaction costs. Advertising will finance a smaller share of the news that informs civic engagement. In its place, the highly engaged, through meters and subscription fees, will pay a growing proportion of the cost. In effect, the few increasingly will be subsidizing the whole to create informed publics. With this shift toward audience comes another, more invisible transaction cost in the form of responsibility. The people formerly known as the audience will need to be more attentive and critical consumers of information than they were before. The public will also need to contribute to journalism itself, not by performing all of its functions but by supporting and engaging in more aspects of them. What those aspects are, and what growing responsibilities they convey, constitute the final element of journalism, one that has always been at play but that in the new century is becoming more palpable, and more vital. It is the role of the citizen.[26]

11
THE RIGHTS AND RESPONSIBILITIES OF CITIZENS

On the morning of July 7, 2005, three bombs exploded in the London subway, followed shortly by an explosion on a double-decker bus. The suicide bombings killed fifty-two people in an attack evocative of the 2004 train explosions in Madrid.

The British Broadcasting Corporation, or BBC, understood that this was an important story and threw its staff at it, trying to get information first and, as Richard Sambrook, then director of the news division, wrote, "get things right."[1] On that day, the BBC received unprecedented help from London residents. Six hours after the attack, the organization counted more than one thousand photographs, twenty video clips, four thousand text messages, and twenty thousand emails—all of which had been sent in by citizens.

The BBC had always encouraged citizen involvement in the news, but this level of participation was new. "The quantity and quality of the public's contributions moved them beyond novelty, tokenism or the exceptional and raises major implications that we are still working through," recalled Sambrook.

The concept of "crowdsourcing," or using the public to help gather the news, was only beginning to form in 2005. The notion that reporters should monitor the public conversation on their beats every day, with a product like TweetDeck open on their screens, was not yet widely accepted. Twitter did not yet exist. Facebook was limited to a few college campuses. But in the wake of the 2005 London bombings, the managers at the BBC made good use of the material, even going so far as to open a newscast with video footage received from citizens. Sambrook called the reporting of the London story a partnership and noted that his organization had learned that "when major events occur, the public can offer us as much new information as we are able to broadcast to them."

In less than two decades, it sometimes seems as if more has changed than remains the same. In truth, the changes are in one sense bringing us back to the coffeehouse, to the news as a continuing conversation.

Sambrook, who went on to teach and direct the Centre for Journalism at Cardiff University, was an early advocate of the new relationship between journalists and citizens. By 2001, the BBC had started the Digital Storytelling Project, which involved local workshops where BBC professionals taught ten people at a time to craft scripts, record audio, and edit stills and video. With the media corporation's help, local authorities off the coast of Scotland had created a participatory media project called Island Blogging, in which islanders were issued a personal computer and a narrowband Web connection, which they put to use posting pictures and stories and sparking debate on numerous community issues. The BBC Action Network had attempted to reconnect citizens with the political process by offering them a forum to discuss issues relevant to them.

"As someone who supports this new direction, I don't suggest the BBC staff abdicate their responsibility for accuracy, fairness or objectivity," Sambrook wrote back then. "As we open up to contributions from the public, we must do so in a way that is consistent with our editorial values. However, I believe that truth, accuracy, impartiality and diversity of opinion are strengthened by being open to a wider range of opinion and perspective, brought to us through the knowledge and understanding of our audience."[2]

THE FUTURE OF NEWS AS COLLABORATIVE INTELLIGENCE

Entering the fourth decade of the Web, journalism is still exploring ways in which it can better involve the public and turn journalism into collaborative intelligence. The process of finding how the public and the press combine to make this new journalism will take time and likely on occasion frustrate both the public and the journalists. As we noted in an even more detailed discussion of the tensions in chapter 1, some advocates of the new have imagined that professional journalism is now, if not largely obsolete, an artifact of an industrial age, and plays a much-diminished role. Others tend to doubt that citizens operating as occasional watchmen have the skills and organization to monitor events in a meaningful way. A community watch program may be helpful, but it cannot fully supplant a professional police force. On the other hand, as we were reminded in 2020, police are not the best response for every problem.

Our view, reflected throughout this book, is that the two sides, citizen and professional journalist, are not in competition. They must work in combination. The new citizen sentinel will not replicate the work of the professional journalist, or even displace it, but rather inform, interact with, and elevate it.

At the same time, the utopian fantasy about technology—that it would bring people together and lead to a more peaceful world with more momentum to solve difficult political problems—has faded in the wake of manipulated elections and rising global despotism and anti-democracy governments. Consumers and governments and even some inside the platform companies have come to the recognition that these monopolies need to exercise more editorial rectitude and responsibility than they have up to now. In part they were forced to when the president of the United States, still arguably the most powerful political figure in the world, became a serial abuser of the platforms' rules, continually using social media to tell lies, pass on disproven conspiracy theories, and finally and perhaps most corrosively discredit the system that brought him to power in the first place after it also cast him out. Governments globally began to take steps to offer regulatory guardrails for the technology giants that now controlled so much of our information environment. By the beginning of the third decade of the twenty-first century, it was clear that the technology companies, which were now the common carriers of information life, did not themselves grasp the political and social implications of the system they had built, or have the knowledge or will to fix it.

Added to that, trust between the public and whatever the press will become in this new environment is damaged. As of 2020, just 40 percent of Americans expressed a "great deal" or a "fair amount" of trust in the press. But that number was only 10 percent among Republicans (versus 40 percent among independents and 73 percent among Democrats).[3]

Time is still sorting out the new relationship between the public and the press in the digital age. But we know it is already leading to a new journalism that we call collaborative intelligence. And the result, if embraced with a practiced attitude rather than merely a tribal one, will be better than what came before.

It took some two hundred years for the diffusion of knowledge that began with the discovery of mechanical printing to engender the structural transformation of Western society. This transformation was powered by the spread of knowledge via the printed word, and it enabled the people to become a public sufficiently empowered with knowledge to form a public opinion and take part in its own social, economic, and political systems. Much of this information came to be distributed to the broad mass of the people by what came to be known as journalism. It was that information that helped them become informed citizens, and it would be in this climate that public opinion was formed. Public opinion, in turn, made possible the rise of self-government. That experiment of democracy is still young in human history and, as the last two decades have shown, still fragile.

In this sense, journalism and democracy were born together. In the first phase of development, the role of the press was simply to provide the people with information about the activities and institutions of power that controlled their lives. Today, when the world is awash in information, the role of the press is different. When information is abundant and available, all the time and everywhere, the underlying values of journalism, which are dictated by what the public requires of the press, do not change. People still need the news to be accurate and transparent; and it is even more important than ever that it be independent. But how journalists live up to the elements of journalism today must change drastically. Where journalism's role once was to simply provide information as a tool of self-governance, it now becomes a role of providing citizens with the tools they need to extract knowledge for themselves from the undifferentiated flood of rumor, propaganda, gossip, fact, assertion, and allegation that the communications system now produces. Thus the journalist must not only make sense of the world but also help people make sense of the flood of information about it.

To do this, newspeople must first invite the community into the process by which news is produced. That notion of the new journalism as a product of collaborative intelligence is an ongoing theme in this volume. Into this collaboration, each player brings special strengths. The community brings diversity of viewpoints, subject expertise, and real-life experience to the news that journalists alone cannot match. They can be many places at once as eyewitnesses. They have vast networks journalists do not. Journalists, on the other hand, have other skills citizens lack. They have access to officials and people in power to ask tough questions; they have storytelling skills, including with visualizations, graphics, and more; they have the ability to collate and curate the collective information and access to wire services and enhanced abilities to compare; they have access to experts to help them make sense of the intelligence that has been collected. Machines, the third key element in the journalism of collaborative intelligence, bring the ability to count and synthesize large amounts of data, to make the intelligence more empirical.

In our chapter on verification (chapter 4), we called on journalists to make a major shift toward transparency, arguing that this concept came closer to the real meaning of objectivity than the more muddled notions associated with neutrality that some journalists have used. Instead of using the often-misunderstood term *objectivity*, as we noted in that same chapter, journalists should think of their ethos, or professional calling, as open-minded independent rigorous inquiry. For that inquiry to be as free of bias as possible, it must be transparent. Transparency is the first step in the beginning of a new connection between the journalist and the citizen. It allows the public a chance to judge the principles by which the journalists do their work. They are equipped with information that invites them to compare these principles with other choices available. Most important, transparency gives the public a basis on which to judge whether a particular kind of journalism is the kind they wish to encourage and trust.

The next step involves seeking out members of the community who can help journalists identify and gather the news in ways that are more sophisticated than we imagine. This involves more than creating places for citizens to post and publish. It means approaching them as a new group of sources, organizing their intelligence, and vetting and synthesizing that intelligence into a whole. Minnesota Public Radio was a pioneer of this approach when in the 1990s it surveyed their listeners for details on their background and expertise and organized them into groups to help suggest and vet stories in their particular areas of knowledge. On the heels of Minnesota Public Radio's "Public Insight Network" came many more efforts to tap the public's intelligence and curiosity in this way. Those include the open journalism of *The Guardian,* start-ups like Outlier, and technologies such as Hearken and GroundSource, which are platforms that make it easier for journalists to ask the public what questions they want answered. All of these efforts elevate the public beyond the template of the person on the street, or the source of a "user-generated" photo or a video.

The third step involves listening when the public reacts to the news and facilitating dialogue to help the public work through it. It means structuring the public forums for citizens to have a conversation among themselves. Online, that includes smart use of comments, social media groups, and video-based discussions. More broadly, in our polarized landscape accelerated by digital platforms, it means finding the frames that make civic discourse possible. Journalists can help citizens envision what kind of community, removed from partisan frames, they want to be in the future, much as the *Erie Times-News* did in its initiative "Erie Next." Journalists can likewise help communities in which citizens are at complete odds with one another uncover their commonalities and even common priorities, as the Bowling Green *Daily News* has with "civic assembly" combining local polling and virtual town halls. And journalists can go further, helping communities have the actual conversations across political and other social divides, such as the work

Spaceship Media has done to help liberals and conservatives talk to one another. All these and other efforts help people discuss what's in the news, inform further journalism, and invite citizens into closer relationship with the press, helping both in their common mission.

The more active citizens become in the news, in turn, the more responsibility they begin to bear for it. Consider it the tenth element of journalism, one growing with the advent of new empowering technology:

Citizens, who shape news production by the choices they make, have rights when it comes to news, but they also have responsibilities—even more so as they become producers and editors themselves.

Citizens must set aside prejudice and judge the work of journalists on the basis of whether it contributes to their ability to take an informed part in shaping their society. But the way journalists design their work to engage the public must provide not only the needed content but also an understanding of the principles by which their work is done. In this way, the journalists will determine whether the public can become a force for good journalism.

Market demand is clearly a powerful force shaping society today, but so are the platform companies themselves, their algorithms, their corporate values, their monopolistic tendencies, and the business models they have built. It would seem obvious that it is in the interest of journalists to do what they can to create a market for the kind of journalism this book attempts to describe: a journalism that recognizes and applies principles that assist in assuring reliable, timely, proportional, comprehensive news to help citizens make sense of the world and their place in it. A critical step in that direction has to be developing a means of letting those who make up that market finally see how the sausage is made—how we do our work and what informs our decisions. Another critical step is developing journalists' skills to listen to and understand the public they serve, to make their interactions with the public less transactional (getting quotes) and more empathetic (seeking genuine understanding).

If the relationship between journalists and the public is to become more meaningfully interactive and less transactional, what does this mean for the public? More precisely, what should we as citizens expect from the news? What should we do if we believe we are not getting it? And what skills are required to be literate citizens, to know how to participate in the news? These questions are important. The elements of journalism belong to citizens as much as they do to journalists for the simple reason, as we said at the beginning of this book, that these principles grow out of the function news plays in people's lives, not out of some professional ethos.

In that sense, the elements of journalism are a citizens' bill of rights as much as they are a journalists' bill of responsibilities. And with rights naturally come responsibilities for citizens as well—responsibilities that in the twenty-first century are growing along with the increased ability of the citizen to interact with the news. Thus it is useful to enumerate how we as citizens can recognize whether the elements of journalism are evident in the news we receive.

A CITIZENS' BILL OF RIGHTS AND RESPONSIBILITIES

1 • ON TRUTHFULNESS

We have the right to expect that the evidence of the integrity of the reporting be explicit. This means that the process of verification—how newspeople made their decisions and why—should be transparent. There should be a clear indication of open-minded examination. There should be humility, a clear signal of what is not known or not understood. We should be able to judge the value and bias of the information for ourselves.

To live up to this responsibility, what elements would such a piece of reporting contain? As we detailed in another of our books, *Blur: How to Know What's True in the Age of Information Overload*, there are several keys the public should expect: (1) A story should make clear the sources of information and the evidence they offer, or the basis of their knowledge. (2) The story's relevance and implications should be obvious from the way it is presented. (3) Important unanswered questions should be noted. (4) The different sides represented should be given the opportunity to make their best case—even those whose position has less support. (5) If the story raises a point of controversy, we should expect follow-up. (6) Other stories should continue the public discussion over time so that the sorting-out process that leads to truthfulness can take place. News, in other words, should not only engage us but also challenge us and make us think. Not all of these qualities may be found in every piece of content, but they should be expected in the treatment overall.

To this we would add a seventh, related factor. Somewhere in the presentation (and we would advocate that it be billboarded in a way that is impossible to miss), a story should note and explain any choices that were made by journalists that would logically raise questions in the public's mind. For some stories, people might wonder why the story was done in the first place, whether its publication might be dangerous, why anonymous sources were used, what is really new, or what the most important takeaways are. With billboarding or highlighting of such questions, the public will see how seriously journalists are about leveling with them, and journalists, in turn, will take some responsibility for helping the public become more discerning or fluent news consumers. (We dislike the term *news literacy*.)

All of this, in turn, implies a two-way process. Citizens have an obligation to approach the news with an open mind and not just a desire that the news reinforce their existing opinion.

2 • ON LOYALTY TO CITIZENS

We should expect to see evidence that the material has been prepared for our use above all. This means stories should answer our needs as citizens and not just the interests of the players and the political or economic system. It also means that there is a demonstrated effort by journalists to understand the whole community.

Perhaps the best way to judge this is by noting how well the news over time avoids stereotypes. In news, stereotypes are characterizations that may be true in some cases but are not in the specific case being reported. A story about local crime that focuses on only one part of the community, when the facts show that crime is spread generally throughout the whole community, is an example. Usually, stereotyping is a failure of execution. Stereotypes of this kind can almost always be avoided by more reporting and more specific reporting, both of which should be recognizable in any story carefully done. Stereotypes are a sign of bias, default culture, and journalistic ignorance, as well as haste and superficiality.

We should also expect to see clear cases in which the news provider—whether it is a commercial entity, a political nonprofit, a think tank, or any other source—will at times put its own interests at risk in order to bring us important information through its news, artistic and commercial reviews, and consumer and retail coverage. Katharine Graham did this when she chose to print the Pentagon Papers, but countless others do it every day when they publish a critical review of a restaurant that is also an advertiser, or a tough-minded report on an important local industry. As special-interest groups increasingly move into the production of news, the information provided should still be held to the same expectation of integrity. Work that reflects only the point of view and interests of one source should be considered for what it is, a form of propaganda.

Loyalty to citizens also means disclosure of any synergy, connecting partnerships, or conflicts of interest as they relate to a particular story. This would include reporting on a journalist's or organization's own lobbying efforts, the organized pressure they put on government that is favorable to their own business interests. We have every reason to expect that our news providers be as transparent in their operations as we expect them to demand other institutions of power to be.

3 • ON INDEPENDENCE

We have a right to expect that commentators, columnists, and journalists of opinion present their material with supporting evidence that demonstrates they are viewing the subject to inspire open public debate, not to further the narrow interests of a faction or a move toward a predetermined outcome. This is no less true of a solitary writer with an email newsletter on Substack than it is of a professional columnist at a national newspaper. The voice that demonstrates intellectual independence, that is thinking for itself, is simply more interesting and adds more value to civic discourse.

Merely having an opinion or admitting a bias does not make something more accurate or honest. In a journalistic realm, evidence, rigor, skepticism, and open-minded inquiry do that.

This intellectual independence is not to be found in commentaries that are in lockstep with factions or vested interests. Independence implies that we can expect to see Republicans at times criticized by conservative commentators and Democrats at times by liberals. Recalling that the journalist's primary allegiance is to the citizen's needs also implies that while those engaged in journalism need not be neutral, we can expect them *not* to have divided loyalties. We can expect that they are not writing speeches or secretly counseling those they cover or opine about. Because we look to opinion writers to help us sort through the complex and competing issues confronting citizens, we should expect to see evidence in the body of their writing or reporting that they have examined the ideas of others on the subject.

4 • ON MONITORING POWER

We have a right to expect that journalists monitor and hold to account the most important and difficult-to-challenge centers of power. While this includes government, there are other institutions and individuals in society that wield economic, coercive, social, moral, and persuasive powers equal to or exceeding those of government.

Since this investigatory role vests considerable power in the press itself, we can expect to see great care and discretion in its use. This means that the news organizations have a responsibility to lead—to uncover things that are important and new and that change community paradigms. We have a right to expect that the watchdog role will demonstrate the news organization's public interest obligation. This implies that we can expect that that power will not be frittered away on minor or pseudoscandals such as safe levels of bacteria in frozen yogurt or harmless amounts of dirt in hotel bedding. Instead, news organizations should focus their time and resources on major issues, unexpected scoundrels, and new perils. To matter, those who lay claim to the mantle of a free press should also focus on questions that matter.

5 • ON CREATING A PUBLIC FORUM

We should expect our news providers to create several channels through which the public can have constructive civic conversation, both among citizens themselves and with journalists. This means people should expect to be able to interact with journalists directly: answering email and the phone, answering questions online, and, despite trends to the contrary, assigning someone inside an institution to act as an ombudsman in some way. But it should also include spaces in person and online where people can talk to each other, informed by journalism, to discuss priorities and values, understand commonalities across differences, and otherwise engage with people different from ourselves for the sake of the civic good.

As technology continues to influence our lives in new ways, we as citizens should expect news organizations not to let public discourse be subsumed only inside the platforms and controlled by the values of those companies. We should expect to be invited to participate in the production of news, through our photos and our eyewitness testimony, and to be sought out for our experience and expertise to inform the gathering of news. Importantly, if news, as James Carey once wrote, is ultimately conversation among citizens, informed by accurate information provided by journalists, then citizens and journalists together must seize back this conversation so that it serves a civic purpose, so that it is civil and constructive. For now it has become commoditized and in many ways destructive.

And over time we should expect to see our views and values reflected in the news coverage and not just those of the most polarized positions on important issues. If the democratic ideal of compromise is to be reached, we should expect the media's public forum to build toward community understanding from which that compromise can be realized.

At the same time, we as citizens have an obligation to approach the news with open minds, willing to accept new facts and examine new points of view as they are presented. We also have a responsibility to show up at these public forums and to behave in a way that encourages respect and civility that make the ultimate goal of journalism—community—actually possible.

6 • ON PROPORTIONALITY AND ENGAGEMENT

We have a right to expect journalists to be aware of our basic dilemma as a public: that we have a need for timely and deep knowledge of important issues and trends at a time when the proliferation of information and outlets has become increasingly unmanageable.

Being aware of this, we have a right to expect journalists to use their unique access to events and information to put the material they gather into a context that will engage our attention and, over time, will help us to see these trends and events in proportion to their true significance in our lives. We should not find matters of transitory importance overplayed and distorted for commercial returns.

So that we as citizens may make sound and well-informed decisions about the many issues that touch our lives, we have a right to news reports that reflect the true nature of threats to our community, such as crime, as well as those aspects of community life that are functioning well. Our successes should be as apparent as our failures.

For all this, as the wellspring of information grows, we have a responsibility as citizens not to narrow our focus. We must not simply indulge ourselves in subjects that entertain us or affirm our views. We also must seek out the critical, challenging information that citizens require. The responsibility to focus on what matters, in other words, is ours as well as the journalist's. The challenge of our age—that we not amuse ourselves to death, as Neil Postman warned—is increasingly in our hands.

A close reader will notice two elements of journalism discussed in this book—verification and conscience—missing from this list of citizens' rights. This is because, when restated from the standpoint of how a citizen should recognize these rights, some elements are best understood as part of others. In this context, the journalist's process of verification becomes a hallmark of adherence to a truthful account of the news and is covered under the heading of truthfulness. By the same token, conscience becomes part of the interaction that occurs between citizens and news providers in the public forum function of a news organization and is covered under the public forum heading.

What do we do as citizens if these rights are not met? What action, for instance, can and should we take if a newspaper reports on a case of business or political fraud but doesn't follow up on the controversial issues that it raises, if a television broadcast manipulates us with pseudoinvestigative reporting, or if a website that pretends to be independent is really a political front for some faction and passing along propagandistic talking points? First, of course, we should reach out, either publicly or privately, to that outlet. But such contact works best if it comes constructively, as advice and information rather than condemnation. If it is ignored, it should be offered again, perhaps through more than one means. If, for example, an email is not acknowledged, send it again, and then pick up the phone or post something in a public platform. But if the complaint or inquiry is authentic and you want it heard—as opposed to your wanting to simply vent your condemnation for your own satisfaction—it should come in the spirit of sincere and constructive inquiry or criticism. If the news organization is sincere in its journalistic aspirations, you will be surprised how well you will be heard. If that genuine inquiry is ignored, that is a telling sign about the news organization.

What can we do if as citizens we offer this feedback and our contributions, ideas, or criticisms are still ignored? Rights mean something only if they are viewed as non-negotiable. At the point when these rights of yours are ignored, withhold your business. Stop visiting. Drop the subscription. Withdraw from participating on that platform. Delete the app. Stop watching. Most important, write a clear explanation of why you have done so and send it to the management, to media critics, or on social platforms, or post it on your own site. The marketplace fails if we as citizens are passive, willing to put up with a diminishing product. It used to be that there was no alternative, but today traditional news organizations don't hold a monopoly on some of the content. They will probably listen and engage in dialogue if we act with a voice and a reason. And if they don't, they have failed their purpose.

But this inquiry must be genuine. If as citizens we begin to condemn first, accusing without genuinely seeking answers, we become part of the polarization that threatens the democratic process. If we resort first to calls to boycott, condemnation, or shaming, we become part of the problem we imagine we are trying to fix. The citizen, too, in other words, has an obligation to maintain an attitude of open-minded inquiry.

In the end it may be that, as TV journalist Carol Marin once put it, "there are no laws of news." But our research and our conversations with journalists and citizens have told us that certain enduring ideas about the flow of news and the role of journalism can be identified. These ideas have ebbed and flowed, and have been misunderstood and abused—usually by those working in their name. Still, they are not artificial creations. The elements of journalism stem from the function that news plays in people's lives, and they have been forged and tempered by three hundred years of experience and testing in the marketplace of competing forms of information. Those who produce journalism must use these elements to steer an ethical course in their work. Time suggests we vary from them at our peril.

The elements of journalism we have outlined here form the basis of the journalism of the new century, a journalism of sense making based on synthesis, verification, and fierce independence, a journalism that is a collaborative organized intelligence combining the network, the community, and the unique skills of trained journalists. These elements also hold the only protection against the force that threatens to destroy journalism and thus weaken democratic society—the threat that the press will be subsumed inside the world of commercialized speech, manipulated propaganda, disinformation posing as journalism, or the undifferentiated world of broad communication. The only way to avoid this threat is for those who are committed to journalism to have a clearer and more rigorous understanding of the elements that make journalism a thing of value, a transparent enterprise that creates its own demand by inviting citizens into the process, reconnecting journalists and citizens in a conversation and not a lecture, and that turns journalism into a service that improves people's lives. This shift is not only something citizens and journalists have in their own control; it is something for which both bear responsibility.

Civilization has produced one idea more powerful than any other: the notion that people can govern themselves. And it has created a largely unarticulated theory of information to sustain that idea, called journalism. The two rise and fall together. This book is an attempt to articulate that theory. Our best hope is not a future that returns to the past, which was never as sweet as people remember it. Our freedom in a digital century depends on not forgetting that past, or the theory of news it produced, in a time when technological and corporate influence is surging and politics has moved dangerously toward populist authoritarianism in response. We fought two conventional world wars and a largely covert Cold War in the last century against such technological utopianism and the tyranny it ultimately inspires. We may not survive another.

ACKNOWLEDGMENTS

This book is not ours alone. It is the fruit of the years of work by the Committee of Concerned Journalists and the twelve hundred journalists who gave their names, their time, and their care to its creation. It is also informed by the more than three hundred people who came to our forums to give us their thoughts, by the hundreds who answered our surveys, and by the roughly one hundred more who sat for hours for interviews by our academic partners. In the years since the first edition, it has been the product of the scores of journalists who have tried to innovate amid the economic disruption of the news and the polarization and fragmentation of our social and economic culture. Our goal with this book was not to offer an argument of what journalism should be but to outline the common ground on which journalists already stood and will find firm footing in the future. Since journalists are so independent, they have always resisted putting these ideas in one place, or even working through them consciously. But in a time of confusion and doubt about the differences between journalism and all the other forms by which information is communicated, we believe clarity of purpose and professional theory are more crucial than ever. Innovation requires some fundamentals on which to build. Purpose and theory are also important for journalists who doubt themselves. Knowing the purpose and theory of journalism is essential to help a generation new to the newsroom. And knowing the aspirations of journalism, its fundamentals, matters to members of the public, who express a longing for news they can trust. This was our intention. If we have succeeded in some measure, it is because of the journalists whose work we have described. If we have failed, it is because we have let them down.

We owe a special debt to some in particular. That list begins for this new edition with Kevin Loker, researcher, our critic, partner, and counsel. He is the fourth wonderful partner to have played this role, each of them different and superb. For the first edition it was Dante Chinni. For the second, paperback edition, it was Cristian Lupsa. For the third it was Jesse Holcomb. New colleagues Millie Tran, and Jeff Sonderman, Amy Kovac-Ashley, Liz Worthington, and others at the American Press Institute, and Joy Mayer at Trusting News are teachers as much as colleagues. We are grateful for their valuable ideas about new tools and new promise. Journalists such as Bill Adair, Mark Stencel, Neil Brown, and Mónica Guzmán, and scholars James Hamilton and Heather Chaplin added important insights to this new edition.

We should not forget those who were there in the early days when this book came out of the work of the Committee of Concerned Journalists, an effort we led in the late 1990s, during a time of sensationalism and early disruption in media, to identify core journalistic values of conviction. Amy Mitchell was the staff person responsible for managing the committee, organizing the forums, and helping us supervise the survey research, and this book bears her stamp. Tom Avila took over for Amy in shepherding the committee in its next phase and caring for it as if it were his own creation. Carrie Brown-Smith, Wally Dean, Brett Mueller, and a strong cohort of superb journalists served as trainers in newsrooms for the committee's traveling curriculum; their work informed many of the new insights in this edition. In addition, we want to thank Howard Gardner, Mihaly Csikszentmihalyi, and William Damon for sharing their research with us. Damon also became our partner in training journalists and a great friend. A few key friends played a vital role in encouraging, counseling, and guiding this book. A special bow to two of them. One is the late and incomparable James Carey, who never failed to elevate our thinking and excite our imagination. Jim was our Yoda—a philosopher-scholar and a Jedi warrior for journalism. A fond remembrance for our great friend Andy Kohut, who studied the public and its interaction with news along with us for many years. Our thanks, too, to Roy Peter Clark, Tom Goldstein, Richard Harwood, John Kovach, Geneva Overholser, Sandra Rowe, Matthew Storin, Mark Trahant, the late Jim Naughton, and the late David Halberstam.

The staff of the Project for Excellence in Journalism over many years was critical in the first two editions of this book: Nancy Anderson, Jennifer Fimbres, Stacy Forster, Chris Galdieri, Carl Gottlieb, Kenny Olmstead, Mark Jurkowitz, Cheryl Elzey, Dana Page, Monica Anderson, Nancy Vogt, Laura Santhanam, Steve Adams, Hong Ji, Sovini Tan, Heather Brown, Tricia Sartor, Katrina Matsa, Emily Guskin, and Paul Hitlin. We will always owe a debt to the wisdom, humor, and friendship of the late John Mashek. Important help, too, was provided for the original edition by Julie Dempster at the Nieman Fellowship program at Harvard. The steering committee of the CCJ played a pivotal role in guiding us along the way. We owe great thanks to the universities, newspapers, and individuals who cohosted, organized, and in several cases financed our forums, including the Park Foundation. The many hours of conversation with journalists in newsrooms around the country that informed this revision of the book were made possible by a generous grant from the John S. and James L. Knight Foundation, a foundation committed to improving journalism worldwide. We thank our agent, David Black, for his confidence and his passion, and Sarah Smith and our editors at Crown, first Bob Mecoy, then Annik Lafarge, Lindsey Moore, and now twice Derek Reed, for their belief in this project.

The research for this book in its early editions would not have been possible without the initial support of the Pew Charitable Trusts and also Eric Newton and Hodding Carter at Knight.

Finally, we owe a debt to those journalists who came before us, who helped create the First Amendment and then gave it its meaning. Their legacy imposes on us the obligation to accept the responsibility of a free and independent press and realize its promise to a self-governing people.

NOTES

INTRODUCTION

1. Mitchell Stephens, *A History of News* (Fort Worth, TX: Harcourt Brace College Publishers, 1996), 27. See also Michael Schudson, "Theorizing Journalism in Time Fourteen or Fifteen Generations: News as a Cultural Form and Journalism as a Historical Formation," *American Journalism* 30, no. 1 (2013): 29–35. Schudson differs somewhat with Stephens about the strict constancy of news values. We sit in the middle, seeing a consistency among them over time and across cultures, but acknowledge that context, economics, and national mood all influence what is in favor and out of favor in news over time. *The Economist's* Tom Standage traces the circulation of news through letters and other documents at least as far back as Cicero. See Tom Standage, *Writing on the Wall: Social Media—The First 2,000 Years* (New York: Bloomsbury, 2014).

2. Harvey Molotch and Marilyn Lester, "News as Purposive Behavior: On the Strategic Use of Routine Events, Accidents and Scandal," *American Sociological Review* 39 (February 1974): 101–12.

3. Stephens, *History of News*, 12.

4. Ibid.

5. John McCain, *Faith of My Fathers*, with Mark Salter (New York: Random House, 1999), 221.

6. "Deprived of Media, College Students Describe Ordeal," Poynter, November 14, 2012, https://www.poynter.org/reporting-editing/2012/deprived-of-media-college-students-describe-ordeal/.

7. Thomas Cahill, *The Gift of the Jews: How a Tribe of Desert Nomads Changed the Way Everyone Thinks and Feels* (New York: Nan A. Talese/Anchor Books, 1998), 17.

8. Committee of Concerned Journalists (CCJ) and Pew Research Center for the People & the Press, "Striking the Balance: Audience Interests, Business Pressures and Journalists' Values," Pew Research Center, March 30, 1999, 79, https://www.pewresearch.org/politics/1999/03/30/striking-the-balance-audience -interests-business-pressures-and-journalists-values/.

9. Pew Research Center for the People & the Press, "American Trends Panel: Wave 62, February-March Survey Final Topline," August 2020, https://www .journalism.org/wp-content/uploads/sites/8/2020/08/ATP-W62-Topline.pdf.

10. Pew Research Center for the People & the Press, "In Changing News Landscape, Even Television Is Vulnerable," September 27, 2012, https://www .pewresearch.org/politics/2012/09/27/in-changing-news-landscape-even -television-is-vulnerable/.

11. Knight Foundation and Gallup Organization, "American Views: Trust, Media and Democracy, a Deepening Divide," August 4, 2020, https://knight foundation.org/reports/american-views-2020-trust-media-and-democracy.

12. C. W. Anderson, Emily Bell, and Clay Shirky, *Post-industrial Journalism: Adapting to the Present* (New York: Columbia Journalism School Centennial, 2012).

CHAPTER 1: WHAT IS JOURNALISM FOR?

1. Anna Semborska, interview by Dante Chinni, January 2000.

2. Thomas Rosenstiel, "TV, VCR's, Fan Fire of Revolution: Technology Served the Cause of Liberation in East Europe," *Los Angeles Times,* January 18, 1990, A1.

3. Maxwell King, at founding meeting of Committee of Concerned Journalists (CCJ), Chicago, June 21, 1997.

4. Tom Brokaw, unpublished interview by Howard Gardner, Mihaly Csikszentmihalyi, and William Damon for their book *Good Work: When Excellence and Ethics Meet* (New York: Basic Books, 2001).

5. Yuen-Ying Chan, unpublished interview by Gardner, Csikszentmihalyi, and Damon for their book *Good Work.*

6. James Carey, *A Critical Reader,* ed. Eve Stryker Munson and Catherine A. Warren (Minneapolis: University of Minnesota Press, 1997), 235.

7. Jack Fuller at CCJ Forum, Chicago, November 6, 1997.

8. Omar Wasow at CCJ Forum, Ann Arbor, MI, February 2, 1998.

9. David Karas, "Justin Auciello Turns Facebook into Journalism with Jersey Shore Hurricane News," *Christian Science Monitor,* October 17, 2013, https:// www.csmonitor.com/World/Making-a-difference/Change-Agent/2013/1017 /Justin-Auciello-turns-Facebook-into-journalism-with-Jersey-Shore -Hurricane-New.

10. Chris Satullo, "Jersey Shore Hurricane News Experiments in Listening to Get to 'Deeper' Community Issues," Democracy Fund's Local News Lab,

March 9, 2017, https://localnewslab.org/2017/03/09/jersey-shore-hurricane
-news-experiments-in-listening-to-get-to-deeper-community-issues/.

11. Author Rosenstiel at the time ran a nonprofit also funded by Pew; for seven years after that, he ran the media research at the Pew Research Center.

12. CCJ and Pew Research Center for the People & the Press, "Striking the Balance: Audience Interests, Business Pressures and Journalists' Values," Pew Research Center, March 30, 1999, 79, https://www.pewresearch.org/politics/1999/03/30 /striking-the-balance-audience-interests-business-pressures-and-journalists -values/.

13. William Damon and Howard Gardner, "Reporting the News in an Age of Accelerating Power and Pressure: The Private Quest to Preserve the Public Trust," unpublished paper, November 6, 1997, 10.

14. In total, all twelve of the ethics codes on file with the American Society of Newspaper Editors that mention purpose describe this as journalism's primary mission. Four of the twenty-four that don't mention purpose include it inside the texts of their ethics codes.

15. ProPublica, "About Us: The Mission," n.d., accessed January 25, 2021, https:// www.propublica.org/about/.

16. "Welcome to San Antonio Report: Our Story," *San Antonio Report,* n.d., accessed January 25, 2021, https://sanantonioreport.org/about-us-2/.

17. Pope Francis, "Message of His Holiness Pope Francis for World Communications Day: Fake News and Journalism for Peace," Vatican, January 24, 2018, https://static1.squarespace.com/static/57f66ded59cc68cbbd3e6f81/t/5aeca63 8575d1ffa84f4862b/1525458488807/World+Day+of+Communications+Mess age.pdf.

18. Mitchell Stephens, *A History of News* (Fort Worth, TX: Harcourt Brace College Publishers, 1996), 27.

19. John Hohenberg, *Free Press, Free People: The Best Cause* (New York: Free Press, 1973), 2.

20. Stephens, *History of News,* 53–59. The creation of this government-sponsored daily newspaper was the first formal act of Julius Caesar on becoming consul of Rome in 60 B.C.

21. Hohenberg, *Free Press,* 38. The writers were John Trenchard and William Gordon.

22. Thomas Jefferson to George Washington, September 9, 1792, Founders Online, https://founders.archives.gov/documents/Jefferson/01-24-02-0330.

23. "The Virginia Declaration of Rights," adopted by the Virginia Constitutional Convention, June 12, 1776, https://www.archives.gov/founding-docs/virginia-declaration-of-rights. The relevant portion is Section 12.

24. New York Times Co. v. United States, 439 U.S. 713 (1971).

25. Lee Bollinger at CCJ Forum, Ann Arbor, MI, February 2, 1998.

26. John Seely Brown to author Rosenstiel at a meeting to discuss the future of journalism curriculum, sponsored by Columbia University Graduate School of Journalism, Menlo Park, CA, June 15–16, 2000.

27. Paul Saffo to author Rosenstiel, same meeting.

28. Jonathan Stray, "Objectivity and the Decades-Long Shift from 'Just the Facts' to 'What Does It Mean?,'" Nieman Journalism Lab, May 22, 2013, https://www.niemanlab.org/2013/05/objectivity-and-the-decades-long-shift-from-just-the-facts-to-what-does-it-mean/.

29. C. W. Anderson, Emily Bell, and Clay Shirky, *Post-industrial Journalism: Adapting to the Present* (New York: Columbia Journalism School Centennial, 2012), 22.

30. Stephen Brook, "News Reporting Faces Web Challenge, Writes New York Times Editor," *The Guardian*, November 29, 2007.

31. CBS News/New York Times poll (October 1994), "Do you happen to know the name of the representative in Congress from your district? (If yes, ask:) What is your representative's name?" Data provided by the Roper Center for Public Opinion Research. Data for 2019 are from the Annenberg Public Policy Center of the University of Pennsylvania, "Americans' Civics Knowledge Increases but Still Has a Long Way to Go," September 9, 2019, https://www.annenberg publicpolicycenter.org/americans-civics-knowledge-increases-2019-survey/.

32. For United States Elections Project data, still in estimates for 2020 at time of writing, see http://www.electproject.org/home/voter-turnout/voter-turnout -data.

33. Pew Research Center, "For Local News, Americans Embrace Digital but Still Want Strong Community Connection," March 26, 2019, https://www .journalism.org/2019/03/26/for-local-news-americans-embrace-digital-but -still-want-strong-community-connection/.

34. Walter Lippmann, *The Essential Lippmann,* ed. Clinton Rossiter and James Lare (New York: Random House, 1963), 108.

35. Carey, *Critical Reader,* 22.

36. John Dewey, review of *Public Opinion,* by Walter Lippmann, *New Republic,* May 1922, 286.

37. Two authors have notably made this argument: Carey in *Critical Reader,* and Christopher Lasch in *The Revolt of the Elites and the Betrayal of Democracy* (New York: W. W. Norton, 1995).

38. Lou Urenick, "Newspapers Arrive at Economic Crossroads," *Nieman Reports,* special issue, Summer 1999, 3–20, https://niemanreports.org/articles /newspapers-arrive-at-economic-crossroads/.

39. Several researchers have found this tendency in political coverage over the years.

Some examples include Joseph N. Cappella and Kathleen Hall Jamieson in *Spiral of Cynicism: The Press and the Public Good* (New York: Oxford University Press, 1997), Thomas E. Patterson in *Out of Order: How the Decline of the Political Parties and the Growing Power of the News Media Undermine the American Way of Electing Presidents* (New York: A. Knopf, 1993), and the Project for Excellence in Journalism in "In the Public Interest: A Content Study of Early Press Coverage of the 2000 Presidential Campaign," February 2, 2000; https://www.journalism.org /2000/02/03/in-the-public-interest/.

40. Carey, *Critical Reader*, 247.

41. David Burgin was Rosenstiel's editor in 1980 and 1982 at the *Peninsula Times Tribune* in Palo Alto, CA, where he taught the author this theory of laying out newspaper pages.

42. C. W. Anderson, *Rebuilding the News: Metropolitan Journalism in the Digital Age* (Philadelphia: Temple University Press, 2013), 164–65.

43. Alexandra Jaffe, "Kellyanne Conway: WH Spokesman Gave 'Alternative Facts' on Inauguration Crowd, NBC News.com, January 22, 2017, https://www.nbc news.com/storyline/meet-the-press-70-years/wh-spokesman-gave-alternative -facts-inauguration-crowd-n710466.

44. Will Fischer, "How the Neighborhood Media Foundation Provides a Collaborative Blueprint for Local Journalism in Ohio," Center for Cooperative Media, Medium, November 5, 2020, https://medium.com/centerforcooperativemedia /how-the-neighborhood-media-foundation-provides-a-collaborative -blueprint-for-local-journalism-b8aca5048689.

45. Adam Hughes and Stefan Wojcik, "10 Facts about Americans and Twitter," Pew Research Center, August 2, 2019, https://www.pewresearch.org/fact-tank /2019/08/02/10-facts-about-americans-and-twitter/.

46. Joanna Brenner and Aaron Smith, "72% of Online Adults Are Social Networking Site Users," Pew Internet and American Life Project, August 5, 2013, https://www.pewresearch.org/internet/2013/08/05/72-of-online-adults-are- social-networking-site-users/.

47. Daniel Liberto, "Facebook, Google Digital Ad Market Share Drops as Amazon Climbs," Investopedia, June 25, 2019, https://www.investopedia.com/news /facebook-google-digital-ad-market-share-drops-amazon-climbs/.

48. Dan Gillmor, "Google, Please Be a Benevolent Internet Overlord," *The Guardian*, May 16, 2013, http://www.guardian.co.uk/commentisfree/2013/may/16 /google-io-conference-internet-dominance.

49. Rebecca MacKinnon, *Consent of the Networked: The Worldwide Struggle for Internet Freedom* (New York: Basic Books, 2013).

50. Carey made this remark at a CCJ steering committee meeting in Washington, DC, June 19, 2000.

CHAPTER 2: TRUTH: THE FIRST AND MOST CONFUSING PRINCIPLE

1. Hedrick Smith, "U.S. Drops Plans for 1965 Recall of Vietnam Force," *The New York Times,* December 21, 1963.

2. Benjamin C. Bradlee, "A Free Press in a Free Society," *Nieman Reports,* special issue, Winter 1990.

3. David Halberstam, "Crucial Point in Vietnam," *The New York Times,* December 23, 1963.

4. Bradlee, "Free Press."

5. Committee of Concerned Journalists (CCJ) and Pew Research Center for the People & the Press, "Striking the Balance: Audience Interests, Business Pressures and Journalists' Values," Pew Research Center, March 30, 1999, 79, https://www.pewresearch.org/politics/1999/03/30/striking-the-balance-audience-interests-business-pressures-and-journalists-values/.

6. American Press Institute and Associated Press National Opinion Research Center, "Americans and the News Media: What They Do and Don't Understand about Each Other," June 11, 2018, https://www.americanpressinstitute.org/wp-content/uploads/2018/06/Americans_and_News_Media_Topline_journalists.pdf.

7. A number of journalists, unpublished interviews by Howard Gardner, Mihaly Csikszentmihalyi, and William Damon for their book *Good Work: When Excellence and Ethics Meet* (New York: Basic Books, 2001).

8. Patty Calhoun at CCJ Forum, Chicago, November 6, 1997.

9. Peter Levine, *Living Without Philosophy: On Narrative, Rhetoric, and Morality* (Albany: State University of New York Press, 1998), 169.

10. This concept of image taking precedence over reality is most dramatically portrayed in Joe McGinniss, *The Selling of the President 1968* (New York: Trident Press, 1969).

11. Ron Suskind, "Without a Doubt," *The New York Times Magazine,* October 17, 2004.

12. Claudette Artwick, "Reporters on Twitter: Product or Service?" *Digital Journalism* 1, no. 2 (2013): 212–28.

13. Alexandra Jaffe, "Kellyanne Conway: WH Spokesman Gave 'Alternative Facts' on Inauguration Crowd," NBC News.com, January 22, 2017, https://www.nbcnews.com/storyline/meet-the-press-70-years/wh-spokesman-gave-alternative-facts-inauguration-crowd-n710466.

14. Susan Benkelman, "Fact Checkers Adapt to Heightened Combat, Facing Politicians Who Are Repeating Lies and Pushing Back," American Press Institute, January 30, 2019, https://www.americanpressinstitute.org/fact-checking-project/fact-checkers-adapt-to-heightened-combat-facing-politicians-who-are-repeating-lies-and-pushing-back/.

15.   Hannah Arendt, "Lying in Politics," in *Crisis of the Republic* (New York: Harcourt Brace, 1972), 7.

16.   John Hohenberg, *Free Press, Free People: The Best Cause* (New York: Free Press, 1973), 17.

17.   Joseph Ellis, *American Sphinx: The Character of Thomas Jefferson* (New York: Alfred A. Knopf, 1997), 303.

18.   Edwin Emery, *The Press in America*, 2nd ed. (Englewood Cliffs, NJ: Prentice-Hall, 1962), 374.

19.   Cassandra Tate, "What Do Ombudsmen Do," *Columbia Journalism Review*, May/June 1984, 37–41.

20.   Ibid.

21.   David T. Z. Mindich, *Just the Facts: How "Objectivity" Came to Define American Journalism* (New York: New York University Press, 1998), 115. Mindich says the first textbook to question objectivity was Curtis MacDougall's *Interpretative Reporting* (New York: Macmillan, 1938).

22.   Gordon Wood, "Novel History," *The New York Review of Books*, June 27, 1991, 16.

23.   Clay Shirky, "Truth Without Scarcity, Ethics Without Force," in *The New Ethics of Journalism: Principles for the 21st Century*, ed. Kelly McBride and Tom Rosenstiel (Thousand Oaks, CA: CQ Press, 2013), 10.

24.   Richard Harwood at CCJ Forum, New York City, December 4, 1997.

25.   Everette E. Dennis, "Whatever Happened to Marse Robert's Dream? The Dilemma of American Journalism Education," *Gannett Center Journal* 2 (Spring 1988): 2–22.

26.   Mindich, *Just the Facts*, 6–7. All three of these examples come from this book, but they are representative of statements we have heard from many journalists through the years.

27.   Mindich makes this point as well in *Just the Facts*, 141.

28.   Bill Keller at CCJ Forum, New York City, December 4, 1997.

29.   Robert D. Leigh, ed., *A Free and Responsible Press* (Chicago: University of Chicago Press, 1947), 23.

30.   Jack Fuller, *News Values: Ideas for an Information Age* (Chicago: University of Chicago Press, 1996), 194.

31.   Carl Bernstein has made this point on several occasions in speeches, interviews, and conversation with the authors.

32.   Eugene Meyer, "The *Post*'s Principles," in *The Washington Post Deskbook on Style*, 2nd ed., ed. and comp. Thomas W. Lippman (New York: McGraw-Hill, 1989), 7.

33.   Wood, "Novel History," 16.

34.   Hodding Carter, interview by author Kovach, April 1998.

35. Michael Golebiewski and danah boyd, "Data Voids: Where Missing Data Can Be Easily Exploited," Data and Society, October 29, 2019, https://datasociety .net/library/data-voids/.

36. Robby Soave, "A Year Ago the Media Mangled the Covington Catholic Story. What Happened Next Was Even Worse," *Reason,* January 21, 2020, https:// reason.com/2020/01/21/covington-catholic-media-nick-sandmann-lincoln -memorial/; Sarah Mervosh and Emily S. Rueb, "Fuller Picture Emerges of Viral Video of Native American Man and Catholic Students," *The New York Times,* January 20, 2019, https://www.nytimes.com/2019/01/20/us/nathan -phillips-covington.html; Cleve R. Wootson Jr., Antonio Olivo, and Joe Heim, "'It Was Getting Ugly': Native American Drummer Speaks on His Encounter with MAGA-Hat-Wearing Teens," *The Washington Post,* January 22, 2019, https://www.washingtonpost.com/nation/2019/01/20/it-was -getting-ugly-native-american-drummer-speaks-maga-hat-wearing-teens -who-surrounded-him/.

37. M. J. Crockett, "Moral Outrage in the Digital Age," *Nature Human Behaviour,* September 18, 2017, https://www.nature.com/articles/s41562-017-0213-3.

38. Reeves Wiedman, "Times Change: In the Trump Years, the New York Times Became Less Dispassionate and More Crusading, Sparking a Raw Debate over the Paper's Future," *New York,* November 9, 2020, https://nymag.com /intelligencer/2020/11/inside-the-new-york-times-heated-reckoning-with -itself.html.

39. More about the International Fact Checking Network can be found at Poynter, "The International Fact Checking Network," n.d., accessed January 25, 2021, https://www.poynter.org/ifcn/.

40. Paul Lewis, "Disproving the Police Account of Tomlinson's Death (How Citizen Journalism Aided Two Major Guardian Scoops)," in *Investigative Journalism: Dead or Alive?,* ed. John Mair and Richard Lance Keeble (Suffolk, UK: Abramis, 2011).

41. Fahrenthold has told this story on several occasions. One was on the NPR program *Fresh Air.* David Fahrenthold, "Journalist Says Trump Foundation May Have Engaged in 'Self-Dealing,'" interview by Terry Gross, *Fresh Air,* September 28, 2016, NPR, https://www.npr.org/2016/09/28/495782978/journalist-says-trump-foundation-may-have-engaged-in-self-dealing. Some details here, including the quotation, are also from an account he gave at the Google News Lab Summit in Mountain View, CA, on December 7, 2016, and a private discussion with him by the author afterward.

42. This story is included in Jack Nelson's posthumous memoir, *Scoop: The Evolution of a Southern Reporter,* edited by his widow, Barbara Matusow (Jackson:

University Press of Mississippi, 2012), 122–23. The detail about Nelson's use of the double notebooks, not admitted to in the book, came from Gene Roberts, recounting the story at a book event for Scoop at the Washington, DC, bookstore Politics & Prose in February 2013.

43.   Tom Reiss, "The First Conservative: How Peter Viereck Inspired—and Lost—a Movement," *New Yorker,* October 23, 2005, 42.

44.   Nassim Nicholas Taleb, *The Black Swan: The Impact of the Highly Improbable,* 2nd ed. (New York: Random House, 2010), 144.

45.   Variations on this quote have been used by many politicians, writers, and journalists. Mark Twain is often quoted as having said, "A lie can travel halfway around the world while the truth is putting on its shoes."

46.   Peter Dizikes, "On Twitter: False News Travels Faster Than True Stories," MIT News, March 8, 2018, https://news.mit.edu/2018/study-twitter-false-news-travels-faster-true-stories-0308.

CHAPTER 3: WHO JOURNALISTS WORK FOR

1.   Geneva Overholser, "Editor Inc.," *American Journalism Review* 20, no. 10 (December 1998): 58.

2.   Ibid., 57. "A Project on the State of the American Newspaper," a survey of seventy-seven senior newspaper editors, found that 14 percent reported spending more than half their time on business matters, while another 35 percent spent between one-third and one-half of their time on business matters.

3.   Committee of Concerned Journalists (CCJ) and Pew Research Center for the People & the Press, "Striking the Balance: Audience Interests, Business Pressures and Journalists' Values," Pew Research Center, March 30, 1999, 79, https://www.pewresearch.org/politics/1999/03/30/striking-the-balance-audience-interests-business-pressures-and-journalists-values/.

4.   Research findings by our academic partners, Howard Gardner, Mihaly Csikszentmihalyi, and William Damon, unpublished interviews for their book *Good Work: When Excellence and Ethics Meet* (New York: Basic Books, 2001).

5.   Nick Clooney, unpublished interview by Gardner, Csikszentmihalyi, and Damon for their book *Good Work*.

6.   Brian Steinberg and Matthew Rose, "Top *New York Times* Editors Resign Over Blair Scandal," *Wall Street Journal,* June 5, 2003, https://www.wsj.com/articles/SB105484743079127100.

7.   Statement made to author Rosenstiel at a gathering at the Foreign Press Center in Washington, DC, in July 2013.

8.   Rachel Martin, Ashley Westerman, and Simone Popperl, "Philippine Journalist Maria Ressa: 'Journalism Is Activism,'" interview on NPR's *Morn-*

ing Edition, August 6, 2020, excerpted on NPR.org, https://www.npr.org/2020/08/06/898852112/philippine-journalist-maria-ressa-journalism-is-activism.

9.   Pew Research Center for the People & the Press, "In Changing News Landscape, Even Television Is Vulnerable," September 27, 2012, https://www.pewresearch.org/politics/2012/09/27/in-changing-news-landscape-even-television-is-vulnerable/.

10. Elisa Shearer and Elizabeth Grieco, "Americans Are Wary of the Role Social Media Sites Play in Delivering the News," October 2, 2019, https://www.journalism.org/2019/10/02/americans-are-wary-of-the-role-social-media-sites-play-in-delivering-the-news/.

11. Cary Funk, Brian Kennedy, and Courtney Johnson, "Trust in Medical Scientists Has Grown in U.S., but Mainly Among Democrats," Pew Research Center, May 21, 2020, https://www.pewresearch.org/science/2020/05/21/trust-in-medical-scientists-has-grown-in-u-s-but-mainly-among-democrats/.

12. Alex Jones and Susan Tifft, *The Trust: The Private and Powerful Family Behind The New York Times* (Boston: Little, Brown, 1999), 43.

13. Thomas W. Lippman, ed. and comp., *The Washington Post Deskbook on Style,* 2nd ed. (New York: McGraw Hill, 1989).

14. Tom Goldstein, "Wanted: More Outspoken Views," *Columbia Journalism Review,* November/December 2001, 144–45.

15. Paul Alfred Pratte, *Gods Within the Machine: A History of the American Society of Newspaper Editors, 1923–1993* (Westport, CT: Praeger, 1995), 2.

16. "Dow Jones Code of Conduct," Dow Jones, 2000, https://www.dowjones.com/code-conduct/?LS=Retargeting.

17. "Project for Excellence in Journalism, Local TV Project," focus groups, January 26, 1999, in Atlanta, and January 28, 1999, in Tucson.

18. American Society of Newspaper Editors (now the News Leaders Association), "The Newspaper Journalists of the '90s," a study, 1997.

19. Ibid. In 1988, 41 percent said they were less involved than others. In 1996, that number had risen to 55 percent.

20. Tom Rosenstiel, "The Beat Goes On: Clinton's First Year with the Media," Twentieth-Century Fund essay, 30. By 1993, a two-month examination of the front pages of *The New York Times,* the *Los Angeles Times,* and *The Washington Post* showed that only slightly more than half of the stories could be classified as straight news, while nearly 40 percent were analytical or interpretative treatments of news events or trends.

21. Daniel Hallin, "Sound Bite News: Television Coverage of Elections, 1968–1988," *Journal of Communications* 42 (Spring 1992): 6.

22. Ibid., 11.

23. Joseph N. Cappella and Kathleen Hall Jamieson, *Spiral of Cynicism: The Press and the Public Good* (New York: Oxford University Press, 1997), 31.

24. Rosenstiel, "Beat Goes On," 30.

25. Philip J. Trounstine at CCJ Forum, Washington, DC, March 27, 1998.

26. Lou Urenick, "Newspapers Arrive at Economic Crossroads," *Nieman Reports,* special issue, Summer 1999, 3–20, https://niemanreports.org/articles/newspapers-arrive-at-economic-crossroads/.

27. Ibid., 6.

28. Ibid., 5. According to figures from the Inland Press Association, these percentages are for the five years ending 1992 and the five years ending 1997. Smaller newspapers were defined as papers of around fifty thousand circulation. Larger were defined as papers of roughly five hundred thousand circulation. Newspaper payroll was cut 8 percent and 15 percent, respectively. Production costs were trimmed 21 percent and 12 percent, respectively. Rather than investing more in product, the newspaper industry invested more in marketing and marketing technology, number of sales staff, and advertising presentations.

29. From interviews with television news executives, we believe the practice is equally common for broadcast.

30. Overholser, "Editor Inc.," 54.

31. Thomas Leonard, "The Wall: A Long History," *Columbia Journalism Review,* January 2000, 28.

32. These calculations on revenue are derived by the Poynter Institute's Rick Edmonds, using data from former newspaper analyst Lauren Rich Fine and data from the Newspaper Association of America (now News Media Alliance).

33. Sara Guaglione, "Newspapers Record Strong Readership, Print or Digital," MediaPost, December 27, 2016, https://www.mediapost.com/publications/article/291865/newspapers-record-strong-readership-print-or-digi.html.

34. Ken Doctor, "What Was Once Unthinkable Is Quickly Becoming Reality in the Destruction of Local News," Nieman Journalism Lab, March 27, 2020, https://www.niemanlab.org/2020/03/newsonomics-what-was-once-unthinkable-is-quickly-becoming-reality-in-the-destruction-of-local-news/. Doctor in his analysis also cites Pew Research Center, "Newspapers Fact Sheet," n.d., accessed July 29, 2019, https://www.journalism.org/fact-sheet/newspapers/.

35. Ibid.

36. Alexandre Tanzi and Shelly Hagan, "Public Relations Jobs Boom as Buffett Sees Newspapers Dying," Bloomberg, April 27, 2019, https://www.bloomberg.com/news/articles/2019-04-27/public-relations-jobs-boom-as-buffett-sees-newspapers-dying.

37. Peter Goldmark, "Setting the Testbed for Journalistic Values," paper presented

at the Fourth Annual Aspen Institute Conference on Journalism and Society, August 23, 2000, in *Old Values, New World: Harnessing the Legacy of Independent Journalism for the Future*, ed. Peter C. Goldmark Jr. and David Bollier (Washington, DC: Aspen Institute, Communications and Society Program, 2001).

38. An eyewitness to this meeting recounted this moment to the authors. The executive, who still works at the network, has requested anonymity for fear of losing his or her job, and we have granted it.

39. Joseph N. DiStefano, "Former Knight Ridder Journalists Plan to Nominate Board Candidates," *The Philadelphia Inquirer,* November 18, 2005.

40. Ken Auletta, "The Inheritance," *New Yorker,* December 19, 2005, 76.

41. Mark Thompson on The New York Times Company's third-quarter 2014 earnings conference call, a week before the *Times* launched NYTimes.com In-School Access, "a new digital subscription offering for K-12 institutions." For script for earnings call, see "The New York Times Company Third-Quarter 2014 Earnings Conference Call October 30, 2014," https://s23.q4cdn .com/152113917/files/events/3Q14-earnings-script-FINAL-for-nytco-v2 .pdf. See also "The New York Times Launches In-School Digital Subscription Program for K-12," The New York Times Company, November 6, 2014, https:// investors.nytco.com/news-and-events/press-releases/news-details/2014/The -New-York-Times-Launches-In-School-Digital-Subscription-Program-for -K-12/default.aspx.

42. Zacks Equity Research, "NY Times (NYT) Q3 Earnings Top, Digital-Only Subscription Up," Nasdaq, November 6, 2020, https://www.nasdaq.com /articles/ny-times-nyt-q3-earnings-top-digital-only-subscription-up-2020- 11-06.

43. Marc Tracy, "The New York Times Tops 6 Million Subscribers as Ad Revenue Plummets," *New York Times,* May 6, 2020, https://www.nytimes .com/2020/05/06/business/media/new-york-times-earnings-subscriptions -coronavirus.html.

44. Alex Williams, "Paying for Digital News: The Rapid Adoption and Current Landscape of Digital Subscriptions at U.S. Newspapers," American Press Institute, February 29, 2016, https://www.americanpressinstitute.org/publications /reports/digital-subscriptions/.

45. Felix Simon and Lucas Graves, "Factsheet: Pay Models for Online News in the US and Europe: 2019 Update," Reuters Institute for the Study of Journalism, Oxford University, May 2019, https://www.digitalnewsreport.org/publications /2019/pay-models-2019-update/.

46. Tom Johnson, "Excellence in the News: Who Really Decides," speech delivered at Paul White Award Dinner, October 2, 1999.

47. Joe Pompeo, "The Hedge Fund That Bleeds Newspapers Dry Now Has the

Chicago Tribune by the Throat," *Vanity Fair,* February 5, 2020, https://www
.vanityfair.com/news/2020/02/hedge-fund-vampire-alden-global-capital-that
-bleeds-newspapers-dry-has-chicago-tribune-by-the-throat.

48. Joe Strupp, "Where There's a Wall There's a Way," *Editor & Publisher,* December 11, 1999, 23.

49. Rick Edmonds, "At The Salt Lake Tribune, an Editor Resigns, and Huntsman Family Ownership Faces Fresh Challenges," Poynter, September 8, 2020, https://www.poynter.org/locally/2020/at-the-salt-lake-tribune-an-editor
-resigns-and-huntsman-family-ownership-faces-fresh-challenges/.

50. Edward Seaton, at the convention of the American Society of Newspaper Editors (now called the News Leaders Association), April 13–16, 1999.

51. Kevin Eck, "Louisville Station Stops Using 'Breaking News,'" TVSpy, June 4, 2013.

CHAPTER 4: JOURNALISM OF VERIFICATION

1. Thucydides, *History of the Peloponnesian War,* bks. 1 and 2, trans. C. F. Smith (Cambridge, MA: Harvard University Press, 1991), 35–39.

2. Walter Lippmann, *Liberty and the News* (New Brunswick, NJ: Transaction, 1995), 58.

3. Ira Glass, "Retracting 'Mr. Daisey and the Apple Factory,'" *This American Life,* March 16, 2012, https://www.thisamericanlife.org/extras/retracting-mr
-daisey-and-the-apple-factory.

4. Mike Daisey, untitled statement on website, March 16, 2012, http://mike
daisey.blogspot.com/2012/03/statement-on-tal.html.

5. Claudia Puig, "Getting Inside the Truth, Filmmakers Accused of Fiddling with Facts Cite Dramatic Accuracy," *USA Today,* November 3, 1999.

6. Dan Gillmor, "The End of Objectivity," *Bayosphere,* January 20, 2005.

7. Michael Schudson, *Discovering the News* (New York: Basic Books, 1978), 6. Schudson's book has a particularly useful analysis of the move away from the naive empiricism of the nineteenth century to the initially more sophisticated idea of objectivity.

8. Walter Lippmann and Charles Merz, "A Test of the News," *The New Republic,* August 4, 1920, republished in *Killing the Messenger: 100 Years of Media Criticism,* ed. Tom Goldstein (New York: Columbia University Press, 1989), 91.

9. Walter Lippmann, "The Press and Public Opinion," *Political Science Quarterly* 46 (June 1931): 170. The fact that Lippmann wrote this last passage in 1931, twelve years after his study of the Russian Revolution, is a sign of how the problem continued to dog him.

10. Lippmann, *Liberty and the News,* 74.

11. Ibid., 60.

12. Ibid., 74.

13. Schudson, *Discovering the News,* 155–56.

14. Here are two pieces by Jay Rosen in which he has talked about his use of the term *the view from nowhere.* "The View from Nowhere: Questions and Answers," *PressThink,* November 10, 2010, https://pressthink.org/2010/11/the-view-from-nowhere-questions-and-answers/, and "Why Trump Is Winning and the Press Is Losing," *The New York Review of Books,* April 25, 2018, https://www.nybooks.com/daily/2018/04/25/why-trump-is-winning-and-the-press-is-losing/.

15. Thomas Nagel, *The View from Nowhere* (New York: Oxford University Press, 1986), 70.

16. Ibid.

17. From the "About" page of *The Dispatch,* n.d., accessed February 13, 2021, https://thedispatch.com/about.

18. Wesley Lowery, "A Reckoning over Objectivity, Led by Black Journalists," *The New York Times,* June 23, 2020, https://www.nytimes.com/2020/06/23/opinion/objectivity-black-journalists-coronavirus.html.

19. David H. Weaver, Lars Willnat, and G. Cleveland Wilhoit, "The American Journalist in the Digital Age: Another Look at U.S. News People," *Journalism and Mass Communication Quarterly* 96, no. 1 (July 4, 2018): 101–30, https://journals.sagepub.com/doi/10.1177/1077699018778242.

20. William Damon to Committee of Concerned Journalists (CCJ) steering committee, February 12, 1999, private meeting.

21. Geneva Overholser at CCJ Forum, Minneapolis, MN, October 22, 1998.

22. Paul Farhi, "Media Too Quick to Fill in Gaps in Story of School Shooting in Newtown, Conn.," *The Washington Post,* December 18, 2012.

23. Robert Parry, "He's No Pinocchio," *Washington Monthly,* April 2000, https://www.washingtonmonthly.com/2000/04/01/hes-no-pinocchio/.

24. Ibid.

25. Phil Meyer at CCJ Forum, St. Petersburg, FL, February 26, 1998.

26. Tom Goldstein, ed., *Killing the Messenger: 100 Years of Media Criticism,* essay "The Legend on the License," by John Hersey (New York: Columbia University Press, 1989), 247.

27. Author Rosenstiel was a member with Bradlee of the panel "Why Don't We Trust the News Media? How Can the News Media Recover Public Trust?" Oswego, NY, October 27, 2005.

28. CCJ and Pew Research Center for the People & the Press, "Striking the Balance: Audience Interests, Business Pressures and Journalists' Values," Pew Research Center, March 30, 1999, https://www.pewresearch.org/politics/1999/03/30

/striking-the-balance-audience-interests-business-pressures-and-journalists
-values/; Amy Mitchell and Tom Rosenstiel, "Don't Touch That Quote," *Columbia Journalism Review*, January 2000, 34–36.

29. Bill Kovach and Tom Rosenstiel, *Blur: How to Know What's True in the Age of Information Overload* (New York: Bloomsbury USA, 2010).

30. The information is taken from Ron Ostrow's "Case Study: Richard Jewell and the Olympic Bombing."

31. Walter Lippmann, *Public Opinion* (New York: Free Press, 1965), 226.

32. Jay Mathews, interview by Dante Chinni, September 12, 2000.

33. What the Scripps TV station WCPO did to be more transparent and develop trust was explained in a case study by Trusting News: Lynn Walsh, "Today's Trust Tip: Explain Why a Story Is Being Done and Encourage Audience Participation," Trusting News, n.d., accessed January 25, 2021, https://mailchi .mp/a4cdc96ebbb2/trust-tips-explain-why-a-story-is-being-done-encourage -audience-participation?e=106dd8197c; Gina M. Masullo and Ori Tennenboim, "Gaining Trust in TV News," Center for Media Engagement, June 2020, https://mediaengagement.org/research/trust-in-tv-news/; Mike Canan, "Why WCPO Is Reporting So Much on Coronavirus, or COVID-19," WCPO Cincinnati, March 12, 2020, https://www.wcpo.com/about-us/trust/why-wcpo-is -reporting-so-much-on-coronavirus-or-covid-19.

34. Michael Oreskes at CCJ Forum, Washington, DC, October 20, 1998.

35. Jack Fuller, *News Values: Ideas from an Information Age* (Chicago: University of Chicago Press, 1996), 350.

36. Michael Yoemans, Julia Minson, Hanne Collins, Frances Chen, and Francesca Gino, "Conversational Receptiveness: Improving Engagement with Opposing Views," *Organizational Behavior and Human Decision Processes* 160 (September 2020): 131–48.

37. Laurie Goodstein at CCJ Forum, Detroit, MI, February 2, 1998.

38. Cho explained the *Post*'s reasoning at an event hosted by the author's organization, the American Press Institute, and probed more deeply in this subsequent exploration on handling misinformation. See Susan Benkelman, "The Sound of Silence: Strategic Amplification," December 11, 2019, https://www.american pressinstitute.org/publications/reports/strategy-studies/the-sound-of-silence -strategic-amplification/.

39. "Facebook's, Twitter's Clampdowns on Controversial NY Post Story Cause Backlash," CBS News.com, October 16, 2020, https://www.cbsnews.com /news/facebook-twitter-change-policies-to-limit-spread-of-ny-post-story-on -biden/; Todd Spangler, "Twitter CEO Admits Blocking NY Post Story Was Wrong, Changes Hacked-Content Policy," Variety, October 16, 2020, https://

variety.com/2020/digital/news/twitter-ceo-nypost-block-wrong-hacked
-materials-policy-1234807399/.

40. Andrew Duehren and James T. Areddy, "Hunter Biden's Ex-Business Partner
Alleges Father Knew About Venture, Former Vice President Says He Had
No Involvement; Corporate Records Review by the Wall Street Journal Show
No Role for Joe Biden," *The New York Times,* October 23, 2020, https://www
.nytimes.com/2020/10/25/business/media/hunter-biden-wall-street-journal
-trump.html.

41. MacCluggage, in an address to regional editors, argued, "Edit more skeptically.
If skeptics aren't built into the process right from the start, stories will slide
onto page one without the proper scrutiny." "APME President Urges Editors to
Challenge Stories for Accuracy," Associated Press, October 15, 1998.

42. Amanda Bennett, interview by author Rosenstiel, April 13, 2000.

43. Sandra Rowe, interview by author Rosenstiel, April 13, 2000.

44. Bennett, interview by author Rosenstiel, April 13, 2000.

45. Amanda Ripley, "Complicating the Narratives," Solutions Journalism, updated
January 11, 2019, https://thewholestory.solutionsjournalism.org/complicating
-the-narratives-b91ea06ddf63.

46. "22 Questions That Complicate the Narrative," Solutions Journalism, February 11, 2019, https://thewholestory.solutionsjournalism.org/22-questions-that
-complicate-the-narrative-47f2649efa0e.

47. Pew Research Center for People & the Press, "Most Americans See a Place
for Anonymous Sources in News Stories but Not All the Time," September 9,
2020, https://www.pewresearch.org/fact-tank/2020/10/09/most-americans-see
-a-place-for-anonymous-sources-in-news-stories-but-not-all-the-time/.

48. Carol Marin at CCJ Forum, Chicago, IL, November 6, 1997.

CHAPTER 5: INDEPENDENCE FROM FACTION

1. William Safire, note to author Kovach, April 18, 2006. Subsequent quotes attributed to Safire are from the same note.

2. Safire died in 2009 after thirty-six years working with *The New York Times,*
where he also wrote a wildly popular column on language. He retired from his
formal political column role in 2005; "On Language" ran until the month of his
death.

3. Anthony Lewis, note to the authors, October 10, 1999.

4. John Martin, quoted in William L. Rivers, *Writing Opinion: Review* (Ames:
Iowa State University Press, 1988), 118.

5. James Carey, *A Critical Reader,* ed. Eve Stryker Munson and Catherine A. Warren (Minneapolis: University of Minnesota Press, 1997), 233.

6. Davey Alba and Jack Nicas, "As Local News Dies, a Pay-for-Play Network Rises in Its Place," *The New York Times,* October 18, 2020, https://www.ny times.com/2020/10/18/technology/timpone-local-news-metric-media.html.

7. Knight Foundation and Gallup Organization, "American Views 2020: Trust, Media and Democracy, a Deepening Divide," August 4, 2020; https://knight foundation.org/reports/american-views-2020-trust-media-and-democracy.

8. Ibid.

9. Carol Emert, "Abortion Rights Dilemma: Why I Didn't March—A Reporter's Struggle with Job and Conscience," *The Washington Post,* April 12, 1992.

10. Jacques Steinberg and Geraldine Fabrikant, "Friendship and Business Blur in the World of a Media Baron," *The New York Times,* December 22, 2003.

11. Mary McGrory, "Casualty: George Will Finds Being a 'Stablemate to Statesmen' Can Cost," *The Washington Post,* July 12, 1983.

12. Erik Wemple, "MSNBC's Jon Meacham Problem," *The Washington Post,* November 11, 2020, https://www.washingtonpost.com/opinions/2020/11/11/msnbcs-jon-meacham-problem/.

13. Howard Kurtz, "Journalists Say Their White House Advice Crossed No Line," *The Washington Post,* January 29, 2005.

14. Elliot Diringer, unpublished interview by Howard Gardner, Mihaly Csikszentmihalyi, and William Damon for their book *Good Work: When Excellence and Ethics Meet* (New York: Basic Books, 2001).

15. In a Twitter exchange with author Rosenstiel, and on panels where the two were on together, Lowery was clear he was not endorsing subjectivity in place of rigorous inquiry. He simply felt the term *objectivity* had been hopelessly conflated with *neutrality.* Original Twitter thread on Rosenstiel's feed at https://twitter.com/TomRosenstiel/status/1275773988053102592.

16. Erin Blakemore, "How the Willie Horton Ad Played on Racism and Fear," History Channel, November 2, 2018, https://www.history.com/news/george-bush-willie-horton-racist-ad; Max Grinnell, "Five Presidential Campaign Ads from Elections Past," *Boston Magazine,* November 6, 2012, https://www.bostonmagazine.com/news/2012/11/06/five-past-presidential-campaign-ads/.

17. Aila Slisco, "Right-Wing News Site Warns Readers Not to Get Hypothetical Coronavirus Vaccine Because Vaccines Are a 'Scam,'" *Newsweek,* March 10, 2020, https://www.newsweek.com/right-wing-news-site-warns-readers-not-get-hypothetical-coronavirus-vaccine-because-vaccines-are-1491579.

18. Juan González at Community of Concerned Journalists (CCJ) Forum, New York City, December 4, 1997.

19. Richard Harwood at CCJ Forum, New York City, December 4, 1997.

20.   Tom Minnery at CCJ Forum, Ann Arbor, MI, February 2, 1998.

21.   Adam Hughes, "A Small Group of Prolific Users Account for a Majority of Political Tweets Sent by U.S. Adults," Pew Research Center, October 23, 2019, https://www.pewresearch.org/fact-tank/2019/10/23/a-small-group-of-prolific -users-account-for-a-majority-of-political-tweets-sent-by-u-s-adults/.

22.   American Press Institute and the Associated Press-NORC Center for Public Affairs Research, "'My' Media Versus 'the' Media: Trust in News Depends on Which News Media You Mean," May 24, 2017, https://www.americanpress institute.org/publications/reports/survey-research/my-media-vs-the-media/.

23.   Joshua P. Darr, Matthew P. Hitt, and Johanna L. Dunaway, "Newspaper Closures Polarize Voting Behavior," *Journal of Communication* 68, no. 6 (December 2018): 1007–28, https://doi.org/10.1093/joc/jqy051.

24.   González at CCJ Forum, New York City, December 4, 1997.

25.   David H. Weaver, Lars Willnat, and G. Cleveland Wilhoit, "The American Journalist in the Digital Age: Another Look at U.S. News People," *Journalism and Mass Communication Quarterly* 96, no. 1 (July 4, 2018): 101–30, https://doi .org/10.1177/1077699018778242.

26.   Ibid.

27.   Peter Bell at CCJ Forum, Ann Arbor, MI, February 2, 1998.

28.   Nikole Hannah-Jones, "On Using Narrative to Make Us See the Invisible," speech delivered at the Power of Storytelling Conference in Bucharest, Romania, 2017, quoted in Karl Howard, "Nikole Hannah-Jones on Reporting About Racial Inequality: 'What Drives Me Is Rage,'" Nieman News, October 26, 2017, www.nieman.harvard.edu/stories/nikole-hannah-jones-on -reporting-about-racial-inequality-what-drives-me-is-rage.

29.   Clarence Page at CCJ Forum, Ann Arbor, MI, February 2, 1998.

30.   Mónica Guzmán, *The New Ethics of Journalism: Principles for the 21st Century,* ed. Kelly McBride and Tom Rosenstiel (Thousand Oaks, CA: CQ Press, 2013), 206.

31.   Ariel Zirulnick, "How KPCC Answered 4,000+ Community Questions About Coronavirus," The Membership Guide, September 16, 2020; https://member shipguide.org/case-study/how-kpcc-answered-4000-community-questions -about-coronavirus.

32.   Kim Bui, "The Empathetic Newsroom: How Journalists Can Better Cover Neglected Communities," American Press Institute, April 26, 2018, https://www .americanpressinstitute.org/publications/reports/strategy-studies/empathetic -newsroom/.

CHAPTER 6: MONITOR POWER AND ADD VOICE TO THE LESS POWERFUL

1. A "Local Reporting" category was added again to the Pulitzer Prizes in 2007.

2. John C. Sommerville, *The News Revolution in England: Cultural Dynamics of Daily Information* (New York: Oxford University Press, 1996), 65.

3. Mitchell Stephens, *A History of News* (Fort Worth, TX: Harcourt Brace College Publishers, 1996), 226–27.

4. *Near v. Minnesota,* 283 US 697 (1931).

5. *New York Times Co. v. United States,* 403 US 713 (1971).

6. For a detailed account of Henry Mayhew's work, see Anne Humphreys, *Travels into the Poor Man's Country: The Work of Henry Mayhew* (Athens: University of Georgia Press, 1977).

7. Committee of Concerned Journalists (CCJ) and Pew Research Center for the People & the Press, "Striking the Balance: Audience Interests, Business Pressures and Journalists' Values," Pew Research Center, March 30, 1999, 79, https://www.pewresearch.org/politics/1999/03/30/striking-the-balance-audience-interests-business-pressures-and-journalists-values/.

8. Knight Foundation/Gallup, "American Views: Trust, Media and Democracy Wave Two—Topline," August 2020, https://knightfoundation.org/wp-content/uploads/2020/08/2019-2020-Knight-Foundation-Gallup-ABS-topline-FINAL.pdf; American Press Institute, "Americans and the News Media: What They Do—and Don't—Understand About Each Other," General Population Survey conducted by the Media Insight Project, June 2018, https://www.americanpressinstitute.org/wp-content/uploads/2018/06/Americans_and_News_Media_Topline_genpop.pdf; Pew Research Center's Project for Excellence in Journalism, "News Leaders and the Future," April 8, 2010, https://www.journalism.org/2010/04/08/news-leaders-and-future/.

9. James Hamilton, "Subsidizing the Watchdog: What Would It Cost to Support Investigative Journalism at a Large Metropolitan Daily Newspaper?," speech presented at the Duke Conference on Nonprofit Media, May 4–5, 2009.

10. James T. Hamilton, *Democracy's Detectives: The Economics of Investigative Journalism* (Cambridge, MA: Harvard University Press, 2016), 131.

11. Ibid., 10.

12. Katherine Fink and Michael Schudson, "The Rise of Contextual Journalism," *Journalism* 15 (2014): 13.

13. Tom Rosenstiel, Marion Just, Todd Belt, Atiba Pertilla, Walter Dean, and Dante Chinni, *We Interrupt This Newscast: How to Improve Local News and Win Ratings, Too* (New York: Cambridge University Press, 2007).

14. Finley Peter Dunne, in *Bartlett's Familiar Quotations.* Dunne actually put the quote into the mouth of a fictional wag of his creation named Mr. Dooley. The full quote shows Dunne's satirical tone: "The newspaper does everything for

us. It runs the police force and the banks, commands the militia, controls the legislature, baptizes the young, marries the foolish, comforts the afflicted and afflicts the comfortable, buries the dead, and roasts them afterward."

15. Emilio Garcia-Ruiz, sports editor of the St. Paul *Pioneer Press*, quoting his executive editor, Walker Lundy, at the annual Premack Journalism Award presentation, Minneapolis, MN, April 10, 2000.

16. American Press Institute, "How the Press and the Public Can Find Common Purpose," December 18, 2019, https://www.americanpressinstitute.org /publications/reports/survey-research/holding-power-accountable-the-press -and-the-public/.

17. Signed in 1798, the Act for the Punishment of Certain Crimes, as the Sedition Act was known, made it illegal to "write, print, utter or publish . . . any false, scandalous, and malicious writing or writings against the government of the United States, or the President of the United States." The law was basically a partisan measure aimed at silencing the opposition to the Federalist Party in the 1800 elections—it had a built-in sunset of 1801. In total there were twenty-five arrests, twelve trials, and eleven convictions under the act.

18. Ida B. Wells Society, "Our Namesake," n.d., accessed January 26, 2021, https:// idabwellssociety.org/about/our-namesake/; Dasha Matthews, "Ida B. Wells: Suffragist, Feminist, and Leader," February 21, 2018, https://info.umkc.edu /womenc/2018/02/21/ida-b-wells-suffragist-feminist-and-leader/.

19. "Nellie Bly Biography (1864–1922)," Biography, updated November 12, 2020, https://www.biography.com/activist/nellie-bly.

20. The story that began the Union-Tribune/Copley News Service investigation, "Cunningham Defends Deal with Defense Firm's Owner," ran June 12, 2005. It was written by Marcus Stern.

21. Though the series included several pieces, the first main story was bylined by Russ Buettner, Suzanne Craig, and Mike McIntire, "The President's Taxes: Long-Concealed Records Show Trump's Chronic Losses and Years of Tax Avoidance," *The New York Times*, September 27, 2020.

22. Robert Samuelson, "Confederacy of Dunces," *Newsweek*, September 23, 1996. Jack Fuller makes a virtually identical argument against "America: What Went Wrong" in *News Values: Ideas for an Information Age* (Chicago: University of Chicago Press, 1996).

23. Arlene Morgan, interview by author Rosenstiel, March 2000.

24. Matthew C. Nisbet, "Nature's Prophet: Bill McKibben as Journalist, Public Intellectual and Activist," Shorenstein Center Discussion Paper D-78, March 2013, https://shorensteincenter.org/wp-content/uploads/2013/03/D -78-Nisbet1.pdf.

25. Hamilton, *Democracy's Detectives*, 46.

26. Seymour Hersh, "The Intelligence Gap," *The New Yorker*, December 6, 1999, 76.

27. Kirsten Lundberg, *The Anatomy of an Investigation: The Difficult Case(s) of Wen Ho Lee*, with Philip Heymann and Jessica Stern, case 1641.0 (Boston: Harvard University, Kennedy School of Government, 2001).

28. Thomas Patterson at CCJ Forum, Washington, DC, March 27, 1998.

29. Maynard Institute for Journalism Education, "Best Practices Webinar: Maintaining Momentum for Newsroom Diversity," May 6, 2020, https://www.you tube.com/watch?v=B2fUfiSVWY4&feature=youtu.be.

30. Mark J. Rochester, "Investigative Journalism, Long Criticized for a Lack of Diversity, Has Made Significant Developments Since March," Poynter, May 13, 2020, https://www.poynter.org/business-work/2020/investigative-journalism -long-criticized-for-a-lack-of-diversity-has-made-significant-developments -since-march/.

31. Project for Excellence in Journalism, "Changing Definitions of News: A Look at the Mainstream Press over 20 Years," March 6, 1998, 3, https://www .journalism.org /1998/03/06/changing-definitions-of-news/.

32. Marc Gunther, "The Transformation of Network News: How Profitability Has Moved Networks Out of Hard News," *Nieman Reports*, special issue, Summer 1999, 27.

33. Patty Calhoun at CCJ Forum, Chicago, November 6, 1997.

34. Michael Stahl, "TVN's Newsroom Innovators: Gray Builds InvestigateTV Into an OTT Brand," TV News Check, September 16, 2020, https://tvnewscheck .com/article/253521/gray-builds-investigatetv-into-an-ott-brand/ https://www .investigatetv.com/team/.

35. Report for America, "Molly Duerig Spectrum News 13: Reporter Profile," n.d., accessed January 26, 2021, https://www.reportforamerica.org/members/molly -duerig/.

36. Katerina Eva Matsa, "Fewer Americans Rely on TV News; What Type They Watch Varies by Who They Are," Pew Research Center, January 5, 2018, https://www.pewresearch.org/fact-tank/2018/01/05/fewer-americans-rely-on -tv-news-what-type-they-watch-varies-by-who-they-are/.

37. Pew Research Center for the People & the Press, "Fewer Favor Media Scrutiny of Political Leaders: Press 'Unfair, Inaccurate and Pushy,'" March 21, 1997, https://www.pewresearch.org/politics/1997/03/21/fewer-favor-media -scrutiny-of-political-leaders/.

38. Pew Research Center for the People & the Press, "Public More Critical of Press, but Goodwill Persists," June 26, 2005, https://www.pewresearch.org /politics/2005/06/26/public-more-critical-of-press-but-goodwill-persists/.

39. Media Insight Project, "Partisanship and the Media," American Press Institute, July 13, 2017, https://www.americanpressinstitute.org/publications/reports/survey-research/partisanship-attitudes-about-news/.

40. "Watchdog Conference: Reporters Wrestle with How to Use Sources," *Nieman Reports,* Fall 1999, 7.

41. Ibid., 8.

42. Rifka Rosenwein, "Why Media Mergers Matter," *Brill's Content,* December 1999–January 2000, 93.

CHAPTER 7: JOURNALISM AS A PUBLIC FORUM

1. Jeff Orlowski, dir., *The Social Dilemma* (Exposure Labs, 2020).

2. Ibid.

3. Robert D. Leigh, *A Free and Responsible Press* (Chicago: University of Chicago Press, 1947), 23.

4. Peter Dizikes, "Study: On Twitter, False News Travels Faster Than True Stories," MIT News, March 8, 2018, https://news.mit.edu/2018/study-twitter-false-news-travels-faster-true-stories-0308.

5. *Social Dilemma.*

6. *Hardball with Chris Matthews,* CNBC News, transcript, May 11, 1999.

7. Gene Lyons, "Long-Running Farce Plays On," *Arkansas Democrat-Gazette,* May 26, 1999, B9, available in LexisNexis.

8. Cody Shearer, interview by Dante Chinni, June 2000.

9. Warren G. Bovée, *Discovering Journalism* (Westport, CT: Greenwood Press, 1999), 154–55.

10. Tom Leonard, *News for All* (New York: Oxford University Press, 1995), 152.

11. Sasha von Oldershausen, "Marfa's Answer to the Collapse of Local News: Coffee and Cocktails," *The New York Times,* February 20, 2020, https://www.nytimes.com/2020/02/20/style/marfa-newspaper-big-bend-sentinel.html.

12. These estimates are based on television in Washington, DC, July 10, 2000. The percentage of chat was based on the fact that, on broadcast TV, there were 39.5 hours of news, 27 hours of talk, 3 hours of pseudonews (Access Hollywood, Inside Edition), plus 108 hours of cable news, which was a mix of both talk and news.

13. Michael Crichton, "Mediasaurus," speech delivered to National Press Club, Washington, DC, April 7, 1993.

14. Robert Berdahl, speech delivered to American Society of Newspaper Editors Credibility Think Tank, San Francisco, October 8, 1998.

15. In 1994, for example, fully half of Americans (49 percent) held views that were a mix of liberal and conservative positions. By 2017, that number had fallen to 32 percent, a drop of about a third. Jocelyn Kiley, "In Polarized Era, Fewer

Americans Hold a Mix of Conservative and Liberal Views," Pew Research Center, October 22, 2017, https://www.pewresearch.org/fact-tank/2017/10/23/in-polarized-era-fewer-americans-hold-a-mix-of-conservative-and-liberal-views.

16. *Crossfire,* CNN, transcript, October 15, 2004.

17. In June 2013, CNN's new president, Jeff Zucker, announced that *Crossfire* would return to the air later that year.

18. Jonathan Haidt and Tobias Rose-Stockwell, "The Dark Psychology of Social Networks," *The Atlantic,* December 2019, https://www.theatlantic.com/magazine/archive/2019/12/social-media-democracy/600763/.

19. Mark Zuckerberg, speech at Georgetown University, October 17, 2019, transcript posted by Facebook, https://about.fb.com/news/2019/10/mark-zuckerberg-stands-for-voice-and-free-expression/.

20. Jack Fuller at Committee of Concerned Journalists (CCJ) Forum, Chicago, November 6, 1997.

21. David Haynes, "Why the Milwaukee Journal Sentinel Replaced Opinion Content with Solutions Journalism," American Press Institute, October 30, 2019, https://www.americanpressinstitute.org/publications/reports/strategy-studies/why-the-milwaukee-journal-sentinel-replaced-opinion-content-with-solutions-journalism/.

22. David Plazas, "How The Tennessean's Opinion Section Is Working to Combat Polarization," American Press Institute, October 30, 2019, https://www.americanpressinstitute.org/publications/reports/strategy-studies/how-the-tennesseans-opinion-section-is-working-to-combat-polarization/.

23. *Erie Times-News* staff, "Erie Times-News' Erie Next Initiative Receives National Recognition," *Erie Times-News,* March 1, 2018, https://www.goerie.com/news/20180301/erie-times-news-erie-next-initiative-receives-national-recognition.

24. Bowling Green Civic Assembly efforts are archived in part on the Bowling Green *Daily News* website, https://www.bgdailynews.com/civicassembly/. A report is available from the American Assembly at Columbia University, "The Bowling Green Civic Assembly Report," June 30, 2018, https://americanassembly.org/publications-blog/the-bowling-green-civic-assembly-report.

CHAPTER 8: ENGAGEMENT AND RELEVANCE

1. Sarah Alvarez, interview by author Rosenstiel.

2. Ibid.

3. Ray Suarez, unpublished interview by Howard Gardner, Mihaly Csikszentmihalyi, and William Damon for their book *Good Work: When Excellence and Ethics Meet* (New York: Basic Books, 2001).

4. Howard Rheingold, unpublished interview by Gardner, Csikszentmihalyi, and Damon for their book *Good Work*.

5. Tom Rosenstiel, Carl Gottlieb, and Lee Ann Brady, "Local TV News: What Works, What Flops, and Why," *Columbia Journalism Review* 37 (January 1999): 53–56, "Quality Brings Higher Ratings, but Enterprise Is Disappearing," *Columbia Journalism Review* 38, no. 4 (November 1999): 80–89, and "Time of Peril for TV News," *Columbia Journalism Review* 39, no. 4 (November 2000): 84–92.

6. Pew Research Center, "Future of Mobile News," October 1, 2012, https://www.pewresearch.org/wp-content/uploads/sites/8/legacy/Futureofmobilenews final1.pdf.

7. Taylor Lorenz, "Teens Are Debating the News on Instagram," *The Atlantic*, July 26, 2018, https://www.theatlantic.com/technology/archive/2018/07/the-instagram-forums-where-teens-go-to-debate-big-issues/566153/.

8. Andy Smith, "A Touch of Glass," *Providence Journal*, April 14, 2005.

9. Leo Braudy at Committee of Concerned Journalists (CCJ) Forum, Los Angeles, March 4, 1998.

10. Tom Rosenstiel, Walter Dean, Marion Just, Dante Chinni, and Todd Belt, *We Interrupt This Newscast: How to Improve Local News and Win Ratings, Too* (New York: Cambridge University Press, 2007).

11. INSITE Research, Television Audience Survey, October 1999, available from INSITE Research, 2156 Rambla Vista, Malibu, CA 90265.

12. NewsLab Survey, "Bringing Viewers Back to Local TV News: What Could Reverse Ratings Slide?," NewsLab, September 14, 2000, https://www.newslab.org/bringing-viewers-back-to-local-tv-news/. People in the survey specifically answered that they got "local news elsewhere," there was "too much crime," "local news is always the same stuff," "too many fluff feature stories instead of real news," and "TV news seldom presents positive things that occur in your community."

13. INSITE Research, Television Audience Survey, October 1999, available from INSITE Research, 2156 Rambla Vista, Malibu, CA 90265.

14. Mark Bowden, "The Inheritance," *Vanity Fair*, May 2009, https://archive.vanity fair.com/article/2009/5/the-inheritance.

15. Ariel Zirulnick, "Case Study: How KPCC Answered 4,000+ Community Questions About Coronavirus," The Membership Guide, September 16, 2020, https://membershipguide.org/case-study/how-kpcc-answered-4000-community-questions-about-coronavirus/. Also see Caitlin Hernandez, "How KPCC Embraced Its Role as a Help Desk and What We've Learned Along the Way," Medium, May 28, 2020, https://medium.com/engagement-at-kpcc/how-kpcc-embraced-its-role-as-las-help-desk-and-what-we-ve-learned-along

-the-way-10b548ea23ca; Ashley Alvarado, "How KPCC-LAist's COVID-19 Help Desk Is Driving Newsletter Subscriptions—and Memberships," July 2020, https://betternews.org/kpcc-laist-covid-19-help-desk-driving-newsletter -subscriptions-table-stakes-knight-lenfest-newsroom-initiative/.

16.   Roy Peter Clark, interview by author Rosenstiel, June 2000.

17.   Jack Hart described this narrative arc in detail in an October 2004 article in *Above the Fold,* a newsletter on writing and editing published for the employees of the Minneapolis *Star Tribune.*

18.   Roy Peter Clark, "Writing and Reporting Advice from 4 of the Washington Post's Best," Poynter, May 20, 2013, https://www.poynter.org/reporting-editing/2013 /writing-and-reporting-advice-from-4-of-the-washington-posts-best/.

19.   In November 2020, Klein and Williams both announced they were leaving *Vox,* Klein for *The New York Times,* Williams to create a new start-up.

20.   Alfred Kazin, "Vietnam: It Was Us vs. Us: Michael Herr's *Dispatches*: More Than Just the Best Vietnam Book," *Esquire,* March 1, 1978, 120.

21.   Doug Marlette at NewsLab retreat on storytelling, Washington, DC, April 12 and 14, 2000.

22.   Annie Lang at NewsLab retreat on storytelling, Washington, DC, April 12 and 14, 2000.

23.   John Larson at NewsLab retreat on storytelling, Washington, DC, April 12 and 14, 2000.

24.   *Booknotes,* C-Span, April 29, 1990.

25.   Boyd Huppert at NewsLab retreat on storytelling, Washington, DC, April 12 and 14, 2000.

26.   Bill Adair, interview by author Rosenstiel.

27.   Philp Bump, "How Much Trump's Tax Plan Would Save—or Cost—You (and Your Wealthiest Neighbors)," *The Washington Post,* October 5, 2017, https:// www.washingtonpost.com/news/politics/wp/2017/10/05/how-the-trump-tax -plan-could-affect-someone-in-your-state-with-your-income/.

CHAPTER 9: MAKE THE NEWS COMPREHENSIVE AND PROPORTIONAL

1.   Valerie Crane, interview by author Rosenstiel, June 2000.

2.   Tom Rosenstiel, Carl Gottlieb, and Lee Ann Brady, "Quality Brings Higher Ratings, but Enterprise Is Disappearing," *Columbia Journalism Review* 38, no. 4 (November 1999): 80–89, https://www.pewresearch.org/wp-content/uploads /sites/8/legacy/report.pdf.

3.   Several people have noted this phenomenon. Stephen Hess was one of the first, in *The Washington Reporters* (Washington, DC: Brookings Institution, 1981).

4.   Various people have made this point, including the authors themselves, local newscasters, and viewers in focus groups and meetings with local broadcasters.

5. Carnegie Corporation of New York, "Use of Sources for News," May 1, 2005. A slide show of the report is available online on the Carnegie Corporation website, www.carnegie.org/pdf/AbandoningTheNews.ppt.

6. John Morton, "When Newspapers Eat Their Seed Corn," *American Journalism Review,* November 1995, 52, https://ajrarchive.org/Article.asp?id=76&id=76.

7. Antonis Kalogeropoulos, "How Younger Generations Consume News Differently," Reuters Institute, 2019, https://www.digitalnewsreport.org/survey/2019/how-younger-generations-consume-news-differently/.

8. Project for Excellence in Journalism Local TV Project, "Quality Brings Higher Ratings."

9. "Transformation of Network News: How Profitability Has Moved Networks Out of Hard News," *Nieman Reports,* special issue, Summer 1999.

10. The trend has been reflected in data compiled by the Project for Excellence in Journalism in its annual State of the News Media reports beginning in 2004, available at https://www.pewresearch.org.

11. Tom Rosenstiel, "Coverage of Economy, International News Jump in Year of Big Breaking Stories," Pew Research Center, March 19, 2012, https://www.pewresearch.org/2012/03/19/state-of-the-news-media-2012/.

12. Project for Excellence in Journalism, "State of the News Media 2006," March 2006, https://assets.pewresearch.org/wp-content/uploads/sites/13/2016/06/30143308/state-of-the-news-media-report-2016-final.pdf.

13. Lucas Graves and John Kelly, "Confusion Online: Faulty Metrics and the Future of Digital Journalism," with Marissa Gluck, Tow Center for Digital Journalism, Columbia University Graduate School of Journalism, September 2010, https://www.academia.edu/1307635/Confusion_Online_Faulty_Metrics_and_the_Future_of_Digital_Journalism.

14. John Carey, interview by author Rosenstiel, June 2000.

15. Ibid.

16. Tom Rosenstiel, Walter Dean, Marion Just, Dante Chinni, and Todd Belt, *We Interrupt This Newscast: How to Improve Local News and Win Ratings, Too* (New York: Cambridge University Press, 2007).

17. Tom Rosenstiel and Dave Iverson, "Politics and TV Can Mix," *Los Angeles Times,* October 15, 2002.

18. Media Insight Project, "Paths to Subscription: Why Recent Subscribers Chose to Pay for News," American Press Institute, February 27, 2018, https://www.americanpressinstitute.org/publications/reports/survey-research/paths-to-subscription/.

19. Crane, interview by author Rosenstiel, June 2000.

20. Al Tompkins, interview by author Rosenstiel, June 2000.

21. Carey, interview by author Rosenstiel, June 2000.

22.   Rosenstiel and his team at the American Press Institute worked with the Erie newspaper and had access to their internal data.

CHAPTER 10: JOURNALISTS HAVE A RESPONSIBILITY TO CONSCIENCE

1.   This account comes from interviews with Lichtblau and Berke conducted by author Kovach, March 2006.

2.   "Top New York Times Editors Quit," CNN, March 1, 2004, www.cnn.com /2003/US/Northeast/06/05/NYTimes/resigns/.

3.   Carol Marin at Committee of Concerned Journalists (CCJ) Forum, Chicago, November 6, 1997.

4.   Benjamin Weiser, "Does TV News Go Too Far? A Look Behind the Scenes at NBC's Truck Crash Test," *The Washington Post,* February 28, 1993.

5.   Ben Smith, "Why BuzzFeed News Published the Dossier," *The New York Times,* January 23, 2017, https://www.nytimes.com/2017/01/23/opinion/why -buzzfeed-news-published-the-dossier.html.

6.   Bob Woodward at Nieman Fellows seminar, Harvard University, Fall 1998.

7.   Bill Kurtis, unpublished interview by Howard Gardner, Mihaly Csikszentmih- alyi, and William Damon for their book *Good Work: When Excellence and Ethics Meet* (New York: Basic Books, 2001).

8.   Jon Katz, unpublished interview by Gardner, Csikszentmihalyi, and Damon for their book *Good Work.*

9.   Tom Brokaw, unpublished interview by Gardner, Csikszentmihalyi, and Damon for their book *Good Work.*

10.   CCJ and Pew Research Center for the People & the Press, "Striking the Balance: Audience Interests, Business Pressures and Journalists' Values," Pew Research Center, March 30, 1999, 6, https://www.pewresearch.org/politics/1999/03/30 /striking-the-balance-audience-interests-business-pressures-and-journalists -values/.

11.   Marin at CCJ Forum, Chicago, November 6, 1997.

12.   Ibid.

13.   Ariana Pekary, "Why I Quit MSNBC," on her website, August 3, 2020, https:// www.arianapekary.net/post/personal-news-why-i-m-now-leaving-msnbc.

14.   Linda Foley at CCJ Forum, Ann Arbor, MI, February 2, 1998.

15.   Donald W. Shriver Jr., "Meaning from the Muddle," *Media Studies Journal* 12, nos. 2–3 (Spring/Summer 1998): 138.

16.   Katharine Graham, *Personal History* (New York: Alfred A. Knopf, 1997), 449.

17.   Anthony Lewis, Eleventh Annual Frank E. Gannett Lecture, Capitol Hilton Hotel, Washington, DC, November 28, 1988.

18.   Charles Gibson at CCJ Forum, Ann Arbor, MI, February 2, 1998.

19.   David Ashenfelder at CCJ Forum, Ann Arbor, MI, February 2, 1998.

20. American Society of Newspaper Editors, *1999 Newsroom Census: Minority Employment Inches Up at Daily Newspapers* (Reston, VA: American Society of Newspaper Editors, 1999).

21. Mercedes de Uriarte at CCJ Forum, St. Petersburg, FL, February 26, 1998.

22. Juan González at CCJ Forum, New York City, December 4, 1997.

23. Tom Bray at CCJ Forum, Ann Arbor, MI, February 2, 1998.

24. David Halberstam, interview by author Kovach, June 10, 2000.

25. Favre delivered a version of this speech at the Portland *Oregonian*'s annual Fred Stickel Award ceremony in April 2006.

26. Again, as throughout this book, we use *citizen* here not in a legal sense but in a civic one, to suggest that anyone consuming news is not just a member of an audience but a member of the public acting in a civic sphere, regardless of his or her citizenship status.

CHAPTER 11: THE RIGHTS AND RESPONSIBILITIES OF CITIZENS

1. Richard Sambrook, "Citizen Journalism and the BBC," *Nieman Reports,* Winter 2005, 13–16, https://niemanreports.org/articles/citizen-journalism-and-the-bbc/.

2. Ibid.

3. Megan Brenan, "Americans Remain Distrustful of Mass Media," Gallup Poll, September 20, 2020, https://news.gallup.com/poll/321116/americans-remain-distrustful-mass-media.aspx.

INDEX

ABOUT THE AUTHORS

BILL KOVACH is the former Washington bureau chief of *The New York Times*, editor of *The Atlanta Journal-Constitution*, and curator of the Nieman Fellowships at Harvard. He was the founding chairman of the Committee of Concerned Journalists, as well as the senior counselor to the Project for Excellence in Journalism. He has won the Elijah Parish Lovejoy Award and the Richard M. Clurman Award for Mentoring. His writing has appeared in *The New York Times Magazine*, *The Washington Post*, *The New Republic*, and many other newspapers and magazines in the United States and abroad.

TOM ROSENSTIEL is executive director of the American Press Institute in Arlington, Virginia, and previously was the founder and director of the Project for Excellence in Journalism and the vice-chairman of the Committee of Concerned Journalists. A former media critic for the *Los Angeles Times* and chief congressional correspondent for *Newsweek*, he is the coeditor of *The New Ethics of Journalism: Principles for the 21st Century*, with Kelly McBride, and *Thinking Clearly: Cases in Journalistic Decision Making* with Amy Mitchell, and author of *Strange Bedfellows: How Television and the Presidential Candidates Changed American Politics* and *We Interrupt This Newscast: How to Improve TV News and Win Ratings, Too*. His writing has appeared in such publications as *Esquire*, *The New Republic*, *The New York Times*, the *Columbia Journalism*

Review, and the *Washington Monthly.* A former media critic for MS-NBC's *The News with Brian Williams,* he is a frequent commentator on radio and television and in print.

TOGETHER, BILL and Tom are also the authors of *Warp Speed: America in the Age of Mixed Media* and *Blur: How to Know What's True in the Age of Information Overload.* Both live in Washington, D.C.